Understanding Prison St

Understanding Prison Staff

Edited by

Jamie Bennett, Ben Crewe and Azrini Wahidin

Routledge
Taylor & Francis Group
LONDON AND NEW YORK

PRISON SERVICE
JOURNAL

First published by Willan Publishing 2008
This edition published by Routledge 2012
2 Park Square, Milton Park, Abingdon, Oxon OX14 4RN
711 Third Avenue, New York, NY 10017

Routledge is an imprint of the Taylor & Francis Group, an informa business

ISBN   978-1-84392-274-2 paperback
       978-1-84392-275-9 hardback

British Library Cataloguing-in-Publication Data

A catalogue record for this book is available from the British Library

Published in association with the Prison Service Journal

Project managed by Deer Park Productions, Tavistock, Devon
Typeset by GCS, Leighton Buzzard, Bedfordshire

Contents

PART 3   PRISON MANAGERS

PART 6   CONCLUSION

List of abbreviations

ACAS	Advisory, Conciliation and Arbitration Service
AEEWU	Amalgamated Engineering and Electrical Workers Union
ALI	Adult Learning Inspectorate
APPG	All-Party Parliamentary Group on Further Education and Lifelong Learning
AUDIT	Alcohol Use Disorders Identification Test
BMA	British Medical Association
BME	black and minority ethnic
BPS	British Psychological Society
CAPS	Certificate in Advanced Professional Studies
C&R	control and restraint
CARATs	Counselling, Assessment, Referral, Advice and Throughcare services
CBI	Confederation of British Industry
CCSA	Canadian Centre on Substance Abuse
CIPD	Chartered Institute of Personnel and Development
CPD	continuing professional development
CPT	(European) Committee for the Prevention of Torture
CRE	Commission for Racial Equality
CSC	Close Supervision Centre
DANOS	Drugs and Alcohol National Occupational Standards
DCLP	Division of Criminological and Legal Psychology
DDU	Drug Dependency Unit
DfES	Department for Education and Skills
DFP	Division of Forensic Psychology

DIP	Drug Interventions Programme
DoH	Department of Health
ESOL	English as a second or other language
ETS	Enhanced Thinking Skills
FDAP	Federation of Drug and Alcohol Professionals
FE	further education
HIPP	Health in Prisons Project
HMCIP	HM Chief Inspector of Prisons
HMIP	HM Inspectorate of Prisons
HO	Home Office
HoC	House of Commons
HoLS	Head of Learning and Skills
HR	human resources
HRM	human resource management
IBCF	Integrated Behavioural Competency Framework
ICPS	International Centre for Prison Studies
ICT	information and communications technology
IDS	Intensive Development Scheme
IEP	Incentives and Earned Privileges
IR	industrial relations
JIRPA	Joint Industrial Relations Procedural Agreement
JOSHED	Justice and Offender Services Health Education and Development Group
JSAC	job simulation assessment centre
KPI	key performance indicator
KPT	key performance target
LEA	local education authority
LMU	Lifer Management Unit
LSC	Learning and Skills Council
LSDA	Learning Skills and Development Agency
MQPL	Measuring the Quality of Prison Life
MUFTI	Minimum Use of Force Tactical Intervention
NACRO	National Association for the Care and Rehabilitation of Offenders
NAOPV	National Association of Prison Visitors
NAPO	National Association of Probation Officers
NATFHE	National Association of Teachers in Further and Higher Education
NDPDU	National Drug Programme Delivery Unit
NEC	National Executive Committee
NFER	National Foundation for Educational Research
NIACE	National Institute of Adult Continuing Education

NIDA	National Institute on Drug Abuse (US)
NOMS	National Offender Management Service
NOS	National Occupational Standards
NPD	National Probation Directorate
NPM	New Public Management
NTA	National Treatment Agency
NVQ	National Vocational Qualification
OASys	Offender Assessment System
OD	Organisational Development
OLASS	Offender Learning and Skills Service
OLSU	Offenders' Learning and Skills Unit
PBA	Probation Boards' Association
PCT	Primary Care Trust
PDF	Professional Development Framework
PDW	prison drug worker
PGCE	Post-Graduate Certificate in Education
PLSU	Prisoners' Learning and Skills Unit
POA	Prison Officers' Association
POELT	Prison Officer Entry Level Training
POINT	Prison Officer Initial Training
PORB	Prison Officers' Representative Board
POST	Prison Officer Selection Test
PPAG	Professional Psychology Advisory Group
PSSCWS	Prison Service Care and Welfare Service
PSA	Public Service Agreement
PSC	Prison Service College
PSR	pre-sentence report
PSU	Prison Service Union
PRB	Pay Review Body
PSI	Prison Service Instruction
PSO	Prison Service Order
QCA	Qualifications and Curriculum Authority
RESPECT	Prison Service Minority Ethnic Staff Support Network
RESPOND	Racial Equality for Staff and Prisoners
SDS	Severity of Dependency Scale
SEU	Social Exclusion Unit
SHA	Strategic Health Authority
SMT	senior management team
SPO	senior probation officer
SO	senior officer
SOTP	Sex Offender Treatment Programme

SPC	Succession Planning Committee
SPDR	Staff Performance and Development Record
SU	Special Unit
TDG	Training and Development Group
TES	Training Evaluation System
TSO	The Stationery Office
UKCCNHV	UK Central Committee for Nursing and Health Visiting
YJB	Youth Justice Board
YOI	Young Offenders Institution

Notes on contributors

Helen Arnold is a PhD student at the Institute of Criminology, University of Cambridge, and has been working and conducting research in prisons for the past ten years. She has worked with Alison Liebling on several projects including 'An Exploration of Decision-Making in Discretionary Lifer Panels' and 'Measuring the Quality of Prison Life' before beginning her doctorate titled 'Identifying the High Performing Prison Officer', and has produced a number of single and co-authored publications including 'The Effects of Prison Work' (in *The Effects of Imprisonment*, eds Alison Liebling and Shadd Maruna, Willan, 2005) and 'Prison Officers and Prison Culture' (with Alison Liebling and Sarah Tait in *Handbook on Prisons*, ed. Yvonne Jewkes, Willan, 2007).

Keith Baxter is a chartered psychologist who began his career as an occupational psychologist with the army, he moved to HM Prison Service where he has worked since 1977. He worked for Training Services for eleven years as an occupational psychologist, then worked in a number of prisons before becoming the area psychologist for the North West Area. Over the past ten years he has been responsible for the design and development of job sample selection processes for the selection and promotion of prison staff. He co-authored (with Kirstin Davis, Eliot Franks and Sonia Kitchen) the chapter *The contribution of job simulation assessment centres to organizational development in HM Prison Service* in *Applying Psychology to Forensic Practice* (eds Adrian Needs and Graham Towl, BPS Blackwell, 2003).

Phil Bayliss is a Lecturer in Continuous Professional Development in the Faculty of Education at the University of Plymouth. His research interests are associated with the benefits of education in prisons. A current research project concerns the mentoring of offenders from custody to the community. He is a patron of UNLOCK the national association for reformed offenders.

Jamie Bennett is a prison manager who has worked for HM Prison Service since 1996. He has held posts including Deputy Governor of HMP Gartree, a prison specialising in managing life-sentence prisoners, and HMP Whitemoor, a high-security prison. He has written extensively on prison issues and is editor of the *Prison Service Journal*. He is co-editor (with Yvonne Jewkes) of the *Dictionary of Prisons and Punishment* (Willan, 2007).

Maggie Bolger is Head of Curriculum Development for the Prison Service. She is an educationalist, and has worked in a variety of educational settings before joining the Prison Service in 2003.

Sue Brookes is Head of Leadership and Management Development within HMPS. She joined the Prison Service in 2002, initially working across 28 establishments and across two prison areas. Prior to joining the Prison Service she worked in education, which involved consultancy work in a range of organisations in both the private and public sector.

Shane Bryans is Assistant Director of the Government Office for the West Midlands, with responsibility for Community Safety. He is a former prison governor and vice president of the Prison Governors' Association. From 2004 to 2006 he was the Council of Europe's resident Expert Advisor to the Ministry of Justice of Turkey on their Judicial Modernisation and Penal Reform programme. He has written a number of books and articles on prison management, most recently *Prison Governors: Managing Prisons in a Time of Change* (Willan, 2007).

Leonidas K. Cheliotis is a Lecturer at the School of Law, Queen Mary, University of London, having previously studied at the University of Athens, the American College of Greece-Deree College and the University of Cambridge. Among other outlets, his research work has appeared in such journals as *Punishment and Society*, the *British Journal of Criminology, Criminology and Criminal Justice* and the *International Journal of Law and Psychiatry*. He is also the editor of *The*

Banality of Good: Roots, Rites and Sites of Resistance (forthcoming, 2008). He is presently engaged in authoring a monograph on professional resistance to penal managerialism, editing a collection of essays on the implementation and effectiveness of arts-based programmes in prisons, and co-editing a collection of essays on crime and punishment in contemporary Greece.

Andrew Coyle CMG is Professor of Prison Studies at King's College, University of London. Between 1997 and February 2005 he was Director of the International Centre for Prison Studies. Before that he had worked for 25 years at a senior level in the prison services of the United Kingdom, during which time he was governor of several major prisons, the last of which was Brixton prison in London. He is a prisons adviser to the UN, the Council of Europe, including its Committee for the Prevention of Torture, the Organisation for Security and Cooperation in Europe and several national governments. He is a member of the UK Foreign Secretary's Expert Committee against Torture. He has a PhD in criminology from the Faculty of Law at the University of Edinburgh and is a Fellow of King's College London. His latest book *Understanding Prisons* was published by the Open University Press in 2005.

Elaine Crawley teaches undergraduate and postgraduate Criminology at the University of Salford. She has researched and published extensively in the field of imprisonment, particularly with regard to the working and personal lives of prison officers and the prison lives of elderly men. Her publications include *Doing Prison Work* (Willan, 2004).

Peter Crawley teaches undergraduate sociology and postgraduate criminology with the Open University. A sociologist and anthropologist by training, his research interests include the sociology of place, ideas of 'community' and community safety and the occupational cultures of criminal justice practitioners. His publications (with Elaine Crawley) include 'Culture, Performance and Disorder and the Communicative Quality of Prison Violence', in Byrne and Faye Taxman (eds), *Prison Violence and Prison Culture* (Allyn & Bacon, 2007).

Ben Crewe is a Senior Research Associate at the Institute of Criminology, University of Cambridge. From 2001 to 2005, he was a Nuffield Foundation New Career Development Fellow in the Social Sciences, during which time he carried out a semi-ethnographic study of a medium-security prison, which is being written up as a research monograph entitled *Wellingborough: Power, Adaptation and the Everyday Social World of an English Prison*. He has published widely on aspects of prison social life and culture, including the 'inmate code', drug culture and drug dealing, relationships between male prisoners and female officers, and power and resistance in the context of contemporary imprisonment. He is currently working with Alison Liebling on an ESRC-funded study of 'Values, Practices and Outcomes in Public and Private Corrections'.

David Crighton is currently the Deputy Chief Psychologist with the Ministry of Justice and is visiting Professor in Forensic Psychology at London Metropolitan University. He has previously worked as Deputy Head of Psychology for the Home Office and Department of Health Directorate of Health and Offender Partnerships, as Deputy Head of Psychology for the Prison and Probation Services and as a Consultant Psychologist in the NHS. He is a previous Secretary of the Division of Forensic Psychology of the British Psychological Society (BPS) and is Chief Examiner for the Board of Examiners in Forensic Psychology. He has published widely in the area of forensic mental health with particular interest in the areas of suicide and self-injury, sexual offending and risk assessment.

Deborah H. Drake is a Lecturer in Criminology at the Open University and holds a research associate post in the Prisons Research Centre at the Institute of Criminology, University of Cambridge. She received her BA (2001) and MA (2003) in Sociology at the University of Saskatchewan, Canada. Her PhD research compared two English, maximum-security prisons and focused on the history, culture, practices, orderliness and quality of life. Her main research interests include prisons-as-organisations, high-security prisons and the experience of long-term prison conditions for both staff and prisoners.

Paul Fallon has had a career in local government, social services and in health. Most recently, he was head of primary care at a Department of Health Regional Office until 2003 and Head of Prison Health Development for NHS Yorkshire & the Humber until March 2007. Currently a Fellow at the Centre for Public Innovation, where he is implementing a programme for the introduction of telehealth in order to provide fast access by prisoners to quality NHS care.

Julia Fossi earned her BSc in Psychology and her PhD at Nottingham University. She currently works as a Senior Research Officer for HM Inspectorate of Prisons.

Jim Heavens joined the Prison Service in 1984 as an assistant governor and has worked in a variety of operational and headquarters' roles. In the mid 1990s he was staff officer to the Director General before becoming Governor of Hindley Young Offender Institution and Wandsworth Prison. He is currently the Head of Resourcing within the Service's newly reformed Directorate of Human Resources.

Shirley Hughes has a long involvement in Adult Education. A Senior Lecturer in Post-complulsory Education with the University of Plymouth she currently teaches the Certificate and Postgraduate Certificate in Education in a range of different settings including prisons. Her research work at present is about the transformatory nature of teaching in prisons.

Roy D. King is Emeritus Professor of Criminology and Criminal Justice at the University of Wales, Bangor and since 2004 has been Senior Research Fellow at the Institute of Criminology at Cambridge. He is the author of several books and numerous articles, mostly on prisons and imprisonment in England and Wales, Russia and the United States, and particularly on high-security custody and so called super-max facilities. He has recently (2007) edited the second edition of *Doing Research on Crime and Justice* with Emma Wincup (Oxford University Press).

Alison Liebling is Professor of Criminology and Criminal Justice at the University of Cambridge and Director of the Institute of Criminology's Prisons Research Centre. She has published several books, including *Suicides in Prison* (Routledge, 1992), *Prisons and Their Moral Performance: A Study of Values, Quality and Prison Life* (with Helen Arnold, Oxford University Press, 2004) and *The Effects of Imprisonment* (with Shadd Maruna, Willan, 2005).

Morag MacDonald is the Professor and Director of the Centre for Research into Quality at the University of Central England, and is on partial secondment to the Centre for Criminal Justice Policy and Research Centre, Faculty of Law and Social Sciences, UCE. Her main fields of expertise are prisons, drugs and related health issues, and social research methodology. Her research and consultancy expertise include working as a consultant for HEUNI (the regional office of the United Nations for Central and Eastern Europe) and the European Union. She is also the joint editor of the *International Journal of Prisoner Health*.

Martin McHugh is a Chartered Forensic Psychologist who has worked in a variety of roles within HM Prison Service in high-security prisons and at headquarters. As Head of Suicide Prevention Policy he wrote a number of articles and co-edited (with Graham Towl and Louise Snow) *Suicide in Prisons* (Blackwell, 2002). Between 2000 and 2006 he has worked in HR on graduate and management recruitment and development. Having recently retired from the Prison Service he devotes an increasing amount of time to the baritone saxophone and bass trombone.

Clare McLean is a PhD student at the Institute of Criminology, University of Cambridge, working on a doctorate entitled 'Well-being and Quality of Life in Public and Private Sector Prisons'. Previously, she was a research assistant at the Institute of Criminology working on the Safer Locals project, an evaluation of an initiative aimed at reducing suicide and self-harm in local prisons in England and Wales, and providing support to the Prison Service Standard Audit Unit.

David Scott is Course Leader of the MA in Criminology and Criminal Justice at the University of Central Lancashire. He is co-editor (with Alana Barton, Karen Corteen and Dave Whyte) of *Expanding the Criminological Imagination* (Willan, 2006), co-author (with Helen Codd) of *Controversial Issues in Prison* (Open University Press, forthcoming) and author of the *Sage Course Companion: Penology* (Sage, 2007).

Joe Sim is Professor of Criminology at Liverpool John Moores University. He is the author of a number of texts on prisons including *British Prisons* (with Mike Fitzgerald, (Blackwell, 1982)), *Medical Power in Prisons* (Open University Press, 1990) and *Prisons Under Protest* (with Phil Scraton and Paula Skidmore, (Open University Press, 1991)). His new book, *The Carceral State: Power and Punishment in a Hard Land* is to be published by Sage.

Hindpal Singh Bhui is a Team Leader in HM Inspectorate of Prisons and a Senior Lecturer in Criminal Justice at the University of Hertfordshire. He specialises in inspection of the immigration detention estate and foreign national prisoners. He has been the editor of *Probation Journal: The Journal of Community and Criminal Justice* since 1997 and is a co-editor of the 'Issues in Community and Criminal Justice' Monograph Series, established in 2001.

Karen Smith has 25 years of experience within the criminal justice sector working mainly in the fields of training, learning and development. She has worked for the Prison Service for the past five years as an adviser on management development and leadership, managing national and local projects, primarily focused within London prisons. She is a fellow of the Chartered Institute of Personnel and Development.

Sarah Tait is a PhD student at the Institute of Criminology, Cambridge University. Her thesis is entitled 'Prison Officer Culture and Care for Prisoners in One Male and One Female Prison'. Before starting her PhD in 2004, she was a research assistant on an evaluation of suicide prevention initiatives in local prisons, and co-authored the Home Office report: *An Evaluation of the Safer Locals Programme* (with Alison Liebling, Linda Durie, Annich Stiles and Joel Harvey, 2005).

Graham Towl has worked in psychiatric hospitals and prisons. He is an Honorary Professor in Forensic Psychology at the University of Birmingham. Previously he was the professional head of psychological services nationally for the Prison and Probation Services in England and Wales. Currently he is the Chief Psychologist with the Ministry of Justice. He is a previous chair of the Division of Forensic Psychology of the British Psychological Society (BPS) and recipient of the BPS award for distinguished contributions to professional psychology. He was the first chair of the Board of Examiners in Forensic Psychology. He has published widely including six books and numerous book chapters and journal papers.

Azrini Wahidin is a Reader in the School of Sociology, Social Policy and Social Work at Queen's University, Belfast. She has written widely on the subject of older offenders, prison staff experiences of managing the needs of older offenders, crime in later life, women in prison and the prison estate. Some of her publications include: *Older Women in the Criminal Justice System: Running Out of Time* (Jessica Kingsley, 2004); *Foucault and Ageing* (with Jason Powell, Nova, 2006); *Criminology* (edited with Chris Hale, Keith Hayward and Emma Wincup, Oxford University Press, 2005); *Ageing, Crime and Society* (with M. Cain, Willan Publishing, 2006). She is a trustee for the

Howard League for Penal Reform and on the executive of the British Society of Criminology.

Jason Warr was seventeen years old when he was incarcerated and was nearly thirty by the time he was released. He studied in a haphazard fashion throughout his imprisonment until being inspired by Alan Smith, a teacher at HMP Wellingborough, to take his work more seriously and embark on an Open University degree in the Humanities. In April 2004, at a conference in Cambridge, he met, among others John Irwin, Shadd Maruna, Alison Leibling, Ben Crewe and Pat Carlen who all inspired him to higher academic ambitions than he had ever dared to plan. Since his release, he has undertaken a Philosophy degree at one of the top Russell Group universities and will graduate in 2007. He plans to continue his studies at Masters and PhD levels in the areas of criminology and penology.

Michael Wheatley is a senior manager leading the reducing reoffending unit for the Directorate of High Security, HM Prison Service. His career spans twenty years in the drug and alcohol profession working mainly within criminal justice organisations. He is a Director of the Federation of Drug and Alcohol Professionals and editorial board member of the *Prison Service Journal*. His publications include 'Drugs in Prison' (in *Handbook on Prisons*, ed. Yvonne Jewkes, Willan, 2007), 'Drugs' (in the *Dictionary of Prisons and Punishment*, eds Yvonne Jewkes and Jamie Bennett, Willan, 2007) and 'An Evaluation of Auricular Acupuncture with High Security Male Substance Misusers' (in *Auricular Acupuncture and Substance Misuse*, eds Sue Cox and Kim Wager, Elsevier, forthcoming).

Brian Williams died suddenly and tragically on 17 March 2007, and this biography was written posthumously. He was Professor of Community Justice and Victimology at Leicester De Montfort University. He has written several key books in the area of victimology and criminal justice including *Victims of Crime and Community Justice: Justice Rebalanced?* (Jessica Kingsley, 2005) and *Working with Victims of Crime: Policies, Politics and Practice* (Jessica Kingsley, 1999). He was an active member of the British Society of Criminology.

Chapter I

Introduction

Ben Crewe, Jamie Bennett and
Azrini Wahidin

Why study prison staff?

Anyone embarking on a study of prison staff needs to ask themselves why they are doing it, as there are obvious risks in pursuing this course. First, particularly for prison staff researching themselves, there is a danger of partiality or even indulgence. Historically, prison staff have seen themselves as neglected and unappreciated (Thomas 1972; Crawley 2004), and as a result sympathetic students of prison staff may be drawn into taking sides, or becoming partial. Second, the study of prison staff may be considered marginal or a distraction. It could be argued that the primary focus of prison research should be prisoners, since they are the people who are most significantly affected by the prison experience. Third, it could be argued that the study of prison staff acts to reinforce existing power structures either by promoting their interests above those of prisoners, or, when research is critical of prison staff, legitimising the increased centralisation of power and undermining attempts to allow and develop professional judgment and discretion. However, these concerns bring to mind three main reasons why the study of prison staff is both important and legitimate. The first is the impact of prison staff upon those in their custody. To understand the prison experience – the difference between a regime that is decent and one that is unsurvivable, or one that aids reform or one that incubates social hatred – we need a refined analysis of staff cultures, practices and ideologies and the outcomes they produce. In other words, we need to understand the *effects of* prison staff. The second is that prison

I

staff, like postal workers or journalists, should be seen as a distinct occupational group (or set of groups), a topic worthy of study in their own right. Although we might argue that prison staff matter primarily because of their effects on others, it should not be forgotten that they also matter in themselves, as workers and members of the public. We know from recent research that prison officers experience exceptionally high levels of occupational stress (Arnold *et al.* 2007), that their work often spills over into their family lives (Crawley 2004), and that many are profoundly affected by their everyday experiences on the front-line of criminal justice. These consequences, the *effects on* prison staff, are of intrinsic concern. A third reason is that the study of prison staff can tell us about conceptual issues beyond the realm of criminal justice, such as the nature of power, punishment, order, inequality, care, discretion and resistance. Prison officials are representatives of the state and, as international and comparative studies illustrate (Piacentini 2004), they reveal a great deal about its power, means, resources and ambitions.

Until relatively recently, prison research tended to focus on prisoners and the effects of imprisonment, with staff variables either being invisible or subsumed within broader concerns. This is not to say that the classic studies of prison life paid no attention to the roles and functions of prison officers (though it was officers rather than other staff who were generally highlighted). Sykes (1958) emphasised the compromised nature of officer authority, contrasting the official tasks of custodial work with the realities of maintaining everyday order and relationships. Mathiesen (1965) noted the difficulties of discharging power in a bureaucratic institution, where decisions were always vulnerable to criticism for being either too rule-bound or too inconsistent. Jacobs (1977) demonstrated how officer ideologies and the relationships between managers and the uniformed workforce were critical determinants of institutional climate. Few analyses of prison life have ignored staff altogether. In places, however (for example, Cohen and Taylor 1981; Morris *et al.* 1963), staff have been depicted as ghoulish figures, facelessly patrolling the landings, obstructing researchers or enforcing their power in monolithically authoritarian ways.

Such studies were not directly concerned with prison staff and it would be unreasonable to criticise them for focusing elsewhere. And while portrayals of prison staff as hostile and indifferent are almost certainly partial, they should not be dismissed simply because the picture is invariably more complex. Staff brutality must not be glossed over, nor should we forget the ease with which terrible things can occur in penal contexts. Two of the most famous and frequently cited experiments in social psychology (Haney *et al.* 1973; Milgram 1974), let alone in penology, suggest that power has a tendency towards abuse and that personal ethics are easily obliterated in certain structural situations of which the prison is emblematic. As Roy King notes in this volume, we should not forget that these were experiments, and their real lesson is not that power *inevitably* corrupts but that, without accountability or regulation, its misuse is far more likely. Recent events in Abu Graib, not to mention Wormwood Scrubs, are testament to such tendencies and their enduring possibility even in countries where penal practices are relatively enlightened.

What remains unclear and critical are the conditions under which malign subcultures, or benign ones, are likely to emerge. We have little sense of exactly how or why cultures differ between establishments, or the dynamics by which they are sustained. A good deal of the early literature on prison officer culture was conducted in the US (e.g. Crouch 1980; Kauffman 1988; Fleisher 1989), whose exceptionalism in penal matters limits the generalisability of findings. Nonetheless, as this book demonstrates, considerable progress has been made in the UK in recent years in terms of understanding the roots and characteristics of prison officer culture (e.g. Crawley 2004), the nature, experience and effects of officer work and training (e.g. Liebling and Price 2001; Arnold 2005), the dispositions of staff towards prisoners (Scott 2006) and vice versa (Crewe 2005 and forthcoming), and some of the connections between staff perceptions and behaviour and prisoner well-being (Liebling and Arnold 2004; Sparks *et al.* 1996).

Certainly, past complaints that prison officers were the 'invisible ghosts of penality' (Liebling 2000: 337) and that prison sociology relied on a 'depiction of the guards as merely shadowy figures, peripheral to the main action, who are just *there* as an inertial and conservative influence' (Sparks *et al.* 1996: 60) can no longer be maintained. Research on uniformed staff now assumes from the start that the work, identity and culture of officers is complex and differentiated, that it is deeply inscribed by discourses of masculinity and femininity (for example, Sim 1994; Zimmer 1986; Britton 2003; Tait, this volume), and that there are huge differences between practices and attitudes in different establishments. In some prisons, particularly in the women's estate, it is little exaggeration to say that uniformed staff spend much of their time directly preventing death; in others, they participate fully in therapeutic interventions (see Genders and Player 1995), or remain primarily engaged in the traditional 'core tasks' of order and security. As Liebling and Arnold (2004) notes, all establishments have histories and traditions that give rise to particular conceptions of 'the prisoner', and particular cultures of care and control.

The literature on non-uniformed staff is much more limited. Prison governors have provided some autobiographical accounts of their work (e.g. Coyle 1994), but relatively little systematic research has been conducted to supplement what are insightful but often unusual accounts of management practices and ideologies (though see Adler and Longhurst 1994; Bryans and Wilson 2000; Rutherford 1993; Jacobs 1977). The absence of literature in this area is particularly striking given the increasing centralisation of power within the prison system. This shift, and the increasing influence of risk assessment and actuarial management, has promoted considerable theoretical attention – and has highlighted the expanding power of psychological expertise within the penal domain – but much less empirical scrutiny. Equally notable is the relative dearth of academic research on specialist prison workers. The prison system has become a major provider of state welfare, healthcare and educational services; indeed, some have argued, in other jurisdictions, that this is its main functional role as the welfare state withers and the penal state flourishes in its place (Wacquant 2000). However theorised, it is clear that educational staff, health workers, chaplains and imams, drug specialists, probation officers, workshop instructors, voluntary workers and a raft of other civilian staff contribute in increasingly significant ways to the prison's mission. Indeed, it seems likely that, while treatment and relationships on the landings are the primary determinants of the quality of the prison experience, the kinds of transformations in self-image that promote desistance (Maruna 2001) are encouraged by relationships and opportunities outside the prison wings (see Williams, this volume).

Prison staff today

At the end of 2005, HM Prison Service in England and Wales employed 48,425 staff. Of these staff, 25,971 were in the unified grades (prison officers and managers including prison governors), who usually work directly in prisoner contact roles. The breakdown of staff employed by group is set out in Table 1.1.

Although some progress has been made in making the staff group more diverse, prison work continues to be largely a white, male occupation. In total, 34 per cent of staff are female, although this is

Table 1.1 Breakdown of prison staff employed by group

Officers (including senior and principal officers)	50.7%
Operational support grades (who carry out support work such as staffing the prison gate and perimeter security cameras and escorting vehicles)	15.2%
Administration	15.3%
Healthcare	2.2%
Chaplaincy	0.6%
Psychology	1.9%
Industrials (i.e. workshop instructors)	7%
Other	4%
Operational managers (i.e governor grades)	2.8%

Source: HM Prison Service (2006).

more concentrated in non-operational posts such as administration, healthcare and psychology. Of the officer grades, 21 per cent are women. Less than 6 per cent of staff are black or from minority ethnic backgrounds, although there are continuing efforts to increase this in order to reflect the local communities in which prisons are situated.

The prison staff group is largely stable. In total, there is a 6 per cent turnover rate for all staff, although this is lower within the unified staff group at 3.5 per cent. There are approximately 5–6,000 new recruits to the Prison Service annually, with around 1,500 of those being new prison officers. The pay and benefits are competitive, particularly the pension arrangements. Pay for operational staff is set annually by an independent Pay Review Body, established in 2001.

Over the last 15 years, the development of the practice of New Public Management (NPM) has had an important impact of all prison staff. NPM emerged in the 1980s as part of a new right ideology that emphasised the pre-eminence of the deregulated market. This movement proposed that public services could be made more efficient and effective through the importation of private sector practices (Hood 1991; Pollitt 1993; Ferlie *et al*. 1996). In particular, this approach married two ideas: the introduction of choice and competition, and the use of business-style management practices in the public sector (Hood 1991). Within the Prison Service in England and Wales, these changes have been incorporated through techniques such as the introduction of quantitative performance measures, known as key performance targets and indicators (KPTs and KPIs), the development of audit procedures, the delegation of financial and personnel responsibility to prisons, the establishment of efficiency targets, greater controls on union activity and the introduction of private sector competition. These changes have also had an impact on the approach taken towards staff in the public sector (Farnham and Horton 1996). This change can be summarised as a move from 'personnel management' to 'human resource management'. Traditional personnel management has been described as administrative, process-based and employee-centred, a welfare-orientated approach emphasising the needs of individual employees (Legge 1995). This contrasts with human resource management (HRM), which is resource-centred and directed at management. HRM emphasises the alignment of HR issues with organisational strategy and making HR an integral part of the organisation and the practice of individual managers. The differences have been summarised as entailing a more dynamic approach focused on the needs of the organisation. This transformation was an integral part of NPM, with a move from 'a predominantly "soft" welfare-centred, paternalist approach to personnel management to a "harder", market-orientated, rationalist one' (Farnham and Giles 1996: 112).

Some of the trends that have emerged as a result of these developments include specialisation, professionalisation, decentralisation and individualisation. Specialisation describes the focus on the core role of each post. The most significant example is the growth of the operational support grade, which carries out tasks formerly conducted by prison officers – such as gate work and prisoner escorts – without requiring the full range of prison officer skills leaving prison officers to focus on direct work with prisoners. Another example is the national review of works departments which resulted in staff who were previously required to have both officer and trade skills now being expected either to be trade specialists or to revert to mainstream officer duties. A similar change has occurred in prison catering. These changes have enabled the Prison Service to recruit staff at lower cost, while ensuring that prison officers focus on their specialist roles working with prisoners and other roles (trades, catering) focus on their own specialisations.

Professionalisation can be seen both in the increase in the number of professional staff, such as psychologists, but also in the changing requirements placed on staff. An example of this is that heads of finance are now required to gain accountancy qualifications, and heads of human resources to gain qualifications in personnel management.

However, this is in contrast to prison officers who do not require any qualifications. For a period, it was an entry requirement that officers had five GCSEs, but this led to significant shortfalls in recruitment and was rescinded. Instead, for prison officers there has been a move to base professionalisation on more practical competences. Competency criteria are widely used to inform recruitment, selection and appraisal. In addition, a national vocational qualification in custodial care has been developed and supported, and this will be mandatory for new prison officers from 2007.

Decentralisation refers to the increasing move both to delegate finance and human resource management to each establishment and to contract prison work to private or other public sector providers. The primary examples of this are in education and health care. The provision of teaching is subject to competitive tendering, with teachers being employed by the contractor rather than directly by the prison. Health care services have transferred to local primary care trusts and as a result many staff have transferred to those organisations. This accounts for the reduction in directly employed health staff in recent years. There are also many other examples of this; for example, prison shops have been contracted out, and probation staff are employed by their probation services rather than the prison.

Individualisation describes the move to break down the collective representation of occupational groups, in particular prison officers, while recognising individual employee rights. This has been achieved partly by restricting the power of trade unions in prisons, but also by attempting to create an employee-relations culture where employees are directly consulted and managed, rather than industrial relations where these tasks are conducted through the medium of trade unions.

Organisation of the book

When this book was initially envisioned, it was as an update to an earlier Prison Service Journal related title – *The Prison Officer*, by Alison Liebling and David Price (2001). Very quickly, we realised what a partial account of prison staff this would provide, and that a text which sought to be an introduction to the world of prison staff required a much broader remit. We have also tried to vary the tone and orientation of our contributors, who include research students, established academics, practitioners and one former prisoner. Several authors span more than one of these categories. Some come from more

7

radical political positions than others and some expressed, from the start, a desire to write descriptive rather than analytical chapters. We hope that the volume achieves a good balance between these various approaches, and that it will be a valuable resource for practitioners keen to reflect on their world, and for students and academics who are interested in understanding more about the complexities of prison work. With this in mind, each chapter is accompanied by review questions that can be used to structure discussions and suggestions for further reading.

This book is arranged in four sections. The first is Prisons and Staff Issues, which introduces the reader to key issues relating to the role, composition and practices of prison staff. Jason Warr's, 'Personal Reflections on Prison Staff', provides a first-hand account of the nature of staff–prisoner relationships and the differences that these relationships can make to the views, pains and self-perceptions of the prisoner. Roy King's 'Prison Staff: An International Perspective' uses research from three continents to illustrate the huge differences between the responsibilities and behaviour of prison officers within regimes with very different goals and standards. Hindpal Singh Bhui and Julia Fossi's chapter, 'The Experiences of Black and Minority Ethnic Prison Staff', describes the experience of these groups in relation both to prisoners and other staff, and provides a critical analysis of the way that the challenges faced by these staff are being addressed within the wider race relations context in the Prison Service. Sarah Tait's chapter, 'Prison Officers and Gender', uses survey data to examine the similarities and differences between the attitudes and perceptions of male and female officers. Based on qualitative research on the experiences of male and female officers in one men's and one women's establishment, it also explores the complex relationship between culture and gender in prison officer work. Clare McLean and Alison Liebling's 'Prison Staff in the Public and Private Sector' compares the views, experiences, demographic composition and conditions in four public and four private sector establishments, offering an early analysis of ongoing research in an area that is likely to be of increasing significance within a world of private sector involvement in penal delivery.

The second section, Prison Officers, focuses more specifically on basic-grade, uniformed staff. Jamie Bennett and Azrini Wahidin's chapter, 'Industrial Relations in Prisons', describes the inception and development of the Prison Officers' Association, and the historical tensions between the POA and the Prison Service, and explains how there has emerged a period of constructive, if uneasy, cooperation.

Elaine and Peter Crawley's 'Understanding Prison Officers: Culture, Cohesion and Conflict' gives a sociological account of the occupational norms of prison officers, suggesting that many elements of officer culture represent functional responses to the conditions of front-line work and that this culture is difficult for many officers to manage or resist. Deborah Drake's 'Staff and Order in Prisons' highlights the changed role played by prison officers in accomplishing everyday order. Drawing on research findings from two maximum-security prisons in England, she illustrates the shift over recent years from a culture which emphasised the role of good relationships and legitimacy in achieving order to one which relies increasingly on the implementation of formal power, systems, policies and routines.

Both David Scott and Joe Sim offer more critical portrayals of officer culture. Scott outlines the various techniques by which the majority of officers in his study denied the suffering of those in their care, and draws attention to the ways that the penal environment can promote moral indifference. Joe Sim's '"An Inconvenient Criminological Truth": Pain, Punishment and Prison Officers' reflects on some similar themes, asserting the need to acknowledge more fully the brutality, fear and routine violence that continue to characterise imprisonment and that are deeply embedded in occupational and gendered norms. Sim argues, that these norms have a corrosive impact both on prisoners and on those officers with more humane professional orientations, and suggests a number of measures in relation to training, accountability and wider cultural values that could progressively transform prison officer culture.

The third section addresses the work of managers in prisons. 'Prison Governors: New Public Managers?' by Shane Bryans, a former prison governor, uses the results of interviews with almost 50 prison governors in order to describe the impact of New Public Management on the role of prison governors. He argues that the proliferation of procedural prescription, performance measurement and private sector competition has eroded the professional independence of governors and created a more compliant occupational group. However, he also argues that the unique nature of prison work means that the governor will always retain a role in shaping the culture and moral atmosphere of the organisation. In 'Change Management in Prisons', Professor Andrew Coyle, also a former prison governor with extensive experience of international prison systems, describes the role of governors in managing change. Coyle notes that prisons operate within a political, cultural and economic context, which can have implications both for the operational demands placed upon prisons, such as the size of the prison population, and for the way in which those prisons are expected to operate. Coyle describes how prisons are in a constant state of flux where the only certainty is that things will change, and goes on to describe the crucial role of the governor in giving moral coherence to an organisation by paying attention to its human dynamics and providing visible leadership. Leo Cheliotis's contribution, 'Resisting the Scourge of Managerialism: On the Uses of Discretion in Late-Modern Prisons', argues that, despite rather bleak portrayals of managerialism and related developments within criminal justice, we should not assume that managers and officials are merely passive conduits who implement policy without sometimes resisting ideologies and altering outcomes. Sue Brookes, Karen Smith and Jamie Bennett's 'The Role of Middle and First-Line Managers' is a more descriptive chapter, which breaks new ground by documenting the experiences and work practices of middle and first-line prison managers. This group has largely been overlooked in the study of prison staff, and this chapter provides a crucial glimpse into their working lives.

The next section focuses on the range of non-uniformed staff who work in prisons. Brian Williams's chapter, 'The Changing Face of Probation in Prisons', documents the historical development and role of probation work in prisons, and addresses the impact of the objectives and ideologies of managerialism and modernisation on this area of practice. Phil Bayliss and Shirley Hughes, in 'Teachers and Instructors in Prisons', examine the role and effects of education in prison and the motivations and experiences of both uniformed and civilian staff involved in prisoner education. In 'Psychologists in Prisons', Graham Towl and David Crighton describe recent developments in the recruitment, professional development and organisational role of psychological services in prisons, and highlight future strategic concerns relating to the introduction of the National Offender Management Service (NOMS). 'The Prison Drug Workers', by Mike Wheatley, looks at the services provided by prison drug specialists, the context in which their role has developed and the key attributes required for the job. Morag MacDonald and Paul Fallon's chapter, 'Health Professionals in Prisons', concludes the section.

The penultimate section, Developing the Human Resources of Prisons, introduces readers to the dynamics of recruitment, retention and training of prison staff and explores the relationship between policies in these areas and the actual experiences of staff. In 'Recruitment and Assessment of Prison Staff', Martin McHugh, Jim Heavens and Keith Baxter give a descriptive overview of recruitment and promotion assessment practices in the Prison Service and the methods involved in selecting and assessing key groups of staff. Maggie Bolger and Jamie Bennett's 'Training and Developing Prison Staff' outlines the logistical complexity of designing and delivering training to almost 50,000 staff in the Prison Service, and highlights the transformations in training and personnel functions that have seen them becoming increasingly aligned with the strategic goals of the organisation. In the final chapter of this section, 'The Experience of Prison Officer Training', Helen Arnold draws on her research as a participant observer, alongside interviews and surveys with her training cohort, to detail the realities of the Prison Officer Entry Level Training course, its impact on trainees and some of the consequences and limitations of its content.

The book concludes with 'Concluding Comments on the Social World of Prison Staff', Ben Crewe's summary of some key themes and suggestions for further research. This book is intended as a starting point for researchers interested in prison staff, and we make no claims that it is comprehensive or conclusive. Rather, our main hope is that it will go some way towards remedying the widespread perception among prison staff that their labour is invisible and undervalued and that the public is wilfully ignorant about the conditions under which it is undertaken.

The production of this book has itself been a complex task. We would like thank all the contributors for their enthusiasm and good grace in the face of our editorial diktats! Likewise we would like to thank our editor Brian Willan for having confidence in the project from the start.

References

Adler, M. and Longhurst, B. (1994) *Discourse, Power and Justice: Towards a New Sociology of Imprisonment.* London: Routledge.

Arnold, H. (2005) 'The Effects of Prison Work', in A. Liebling and S. Maruna (eds), *The Effects of Imprisonment.* Cullompton: Willan, pp. 391–420.

Arnold, H., Liebling, A. and Tait, S. (2007) 'Prison Officers and Prison Culture', in Y. Jewkes (ed.), *The Handbook on Prisons.* Cullompton: Willan.

Britton, D. (2003) *At Work in the Iron Cage: The Prison as Gendered Organisation.* New York: New York University Press.

Bryans, S. and Wilson, D. (2000) *The Prison Governor: Theory and Practice.* Leyhill: Prison Service Journal.

Cohen, S. and Taylor, L. (1981) *Psychological Survival.* Harmondsworth: Penguin.

Coyle, A. (1994) *The Prisons We Deserve*. London: Harper Collins.

Crawley, E. (2004) *Doing Prison Work: The Public and Private Lives of Prison Officers*, Cullompton: Willan.

Crewe, B. (2005a) 'Codes and Conventions: The Terms and Conditions of Contemporary Inmate Values', in A. Liebling and S. Maruna (eds), *The Effects of Imprisonment*. Cullompton: Willan, pp. 177–208.

Crewe, B. (forthcoming) *Wellingborough: Power, Adaptation and the Everyday Social World of an English Prison*.

Crouch, B. (1980) *Keepers: Prison Guards and Contemporary Corrections*. Springfield, IL: Thomas.

Farnham, D. and Giles, L. (1996) 'People Management and Employment Relations', in D. Farnham and S. Horton (ed.), *Managing the New Public Services*, 2nd edn. Basingstoke: Macmillan, pp. 112–37.

Farnham, D. and Horton, S. with contributions by Corby, S., Giles, L., Hutchinson, B. and White, G. (1996) *Managing People in the Public Services*. London: Macmillan.

Ferlie, E., Pettigrew, A., Ashburner, L. and Fitzgerald, L. (1996) *The New Public Management in Action*. Oxford: Oxford University Press.

Fleisher, M. (1989) *Warehousing Violence*. Newbury Park, CA: Sage.

Genders, E. and Player, E. (1995) *Grendon*. Oxford: Oxford University Press

Haney, C., Banks, W.C. and Zimbardo, P.G. (1973) 'Interpersonal dynamics in a simulated prison', *International Journal of Criminology and Penology*, 1: 69–97.

HM Prison Service (2006) *HR Planning Staff Profiles and Projections Review – January 2006*. London: HMPS.

Hood, C. (1991) 'A Public Management for All Seasons', *Public Administration*, 69: 3–19.

Jacobs, J. (1977) *Stateville: The Penitentiary in Mass Society*. Chicago: University of Chicago Press.

Kauffman, K. (1988) *Prison Officers and Their World*. Cambridge, MA: Harvard University Press.

Legge, K. (1995) *Human Resource Management: Rhetorics and Realities*. Basingstoke: Macmillan.

Liebling, A. (2000) 'Prison Officers, Policing, and the Use of Discretion', *Theoretical Criminology*, 3 (2): 173–87.

Liebling, A. and Arnold, H. (2004) *Prisons and Their Moral Performance: A Study of Values, Quality and Prison Life*. New York: Oxford University Press.

Liebling, A. and Price, D. (2001) *The Prison Officer*. Leyhill: Waterside Press.

Lombardo, L.X. (1981) *Guards Imprisoned: Correctional Officers at Work*. New York: Elsevier.

Maruna, S. (2001) *Making Good: How Ex-convicts Reform and Rebuild Their Lives*. Washington, DC: American Psychological Association.

Mathiesen, T. (1965) *The Defences of the Weak: A Sociological Study of a Norwegian Correctional Institution*. London: Tavistock.

Milgram, S. (1974) *Obedience to Authority*. London: Tavistock.

Morris, T.P., Morris, P. and Barer, B. (1963) *Pentonville: A Sociological Study of an English Prison*. London: Routledge & Kegan Paul.

Piacentini, L. (2004) *Surviving Russian Prisons: Punishment, Economy and Politics in Transition*. Cullompton: Willan.

Pollitt, C. (1993) *Managerialism and the Public Services: Cuts or Cultural Change in the 1990s?* Oxford: Blackwell.

Rutherford, A. (1993) *Criminal Justice and the Pursuit of Decency*. Winchester: Waterside Press.

Scott, D. (2006) 'Ghosts Beyond Our Realm: A Neo-Abolitionist Analysis of Prisoner Human Rights and Prison Officer Occupational Culture'. Unpublished PhD thesis, University of Central Lancashire.

Sim, J. (1994) 'Tougher than the Rest?', in T. Newburn and E. Stanko (eds), *Just Boys Doing Business?* London: Routledge, pp. 100–17.

Sparks, R., Bottoms, A. and Hay, W. (1996) *Prisons and the Problem of Order*. Oxford: Clarendon.

Sykes, G. (1958) *The Society of Captives: A Study of a Maximum-Security Prison*. Princeton, NJ: Princeton University Press.

Thomas, J. *(1972) The English Prison Officer Since 1850: A Study in Conflict*. London: Routledge & Kegan Paul.

Wacquant, L. (2000) 'The New "Peculiar Institution": On the Prison as Surrogate Ghetto', *Theoretical Criminology*, 4 (3): 377–89.

Zimmer, L. (1986) *Women Guarding Men*. Chicago: University of Chicago Press.

Part 1

Prisons and Staff Issues

Chapter 2

Personal reflections on prison staff

Jason Warr

My intention in this chapter is to talk on four central themes. The first concerns the impact that members of staff can have on inmates, both positive and negative. The second regards the brutalising effects of imprisonment and how these can affect everyone who steps behind the prison walls. The third describes the imbalance of power between staff and inmates, and the impact this has on the relationships that can develop between them. The fourth theme is how this power relationship, and its manifestations, can be affected by the nature of the establishment and what impact this has for staff/inmate relations.

What authority do I have to speak in this regard? I was incarcerated for a period of just over twelve years, from when I was 17 until I was 29. During that period, I became acquainted with almost every type of establishment in the penal estate – including Young Offender Institutions, Category B Locals, high security Main Lifer Centres and Category C and D establishments. I had extended stays in nine establishments and shorter stays in a further four. During that period I experienced staff of all ilks, some more congenial than others, in many differing and varied circumstances.

When reflecting upon prison staff it would be all too easy to resort to certain clichés: that all screws are bastards, 'failed coppers', people who were bullied at school and are seeking revenge. Some officers do fall into this stereotype. Given that the staff of the prison estate are as representative of the wider community as those that inhabit the cells, it would be surprising if some did not. However, the majority of prison staff are, unsurprisingly, ordinary people going about their business – paying their mortgages and putting food on the table.

The prison is an enclosed environment; a result of this is that the impact of the individuals who wield authority within that environment can be stunningly profound, positively or negatively. Those who wield that power can, however, be quite unaware of this. In 1994, as a prisoner in a long-term Young Offenders establishment, I experienced this obliviousness at first hand. One particular officer, whom I shall refer to as Officer X, made no secret of the fact that he perceived his role was to punish young offenders for their infractions against society. He was, at a certain point, assigned as my personal officer, and was therefore asked to write a report on me for my first F75 board. Those reports were, like all F75 reports, to be submitted to the Lifer Management Unit (LMU). At that time, I was in the midst of an appeal against my sentence and my case was being investigated by a TV production company interested in miscarriages of justice. After two formal interviews, lasting about an hour in total, Officer X wrote his report, the thrust of which was that he considered me to be a habitual liar (due to my denial of offence), a seditious influence on others on the wing and a considerable danger to the public. His conclusion, which happened to be shared by the Lifer governor who chaired the board, proposed that, for as long as I continued my stance of denial, I should never be released from prison. I was less than 21 years old and was told that I would never be released from prison.

It is impossible to put into words the torrent of emotions that this pronouncement evoked in me. On returning to the wing, I immediately phoned my solicitor to inform him of what had happened and to get him to contact the LMU to check if that pronouncement was a certain prediction of my future. By the time I had put the phone down (with my solicitor's warnings not to do anything stupid ringing in my ears) Officer X was waiting for me. 'That was exciting!' he said. 'That was my first ever F75 board.' He continued to talk, but I walked away. His excitement was about the role he had played in the process that meant I would never be released, and not only did he have no idea of how this might make me feel, but he castigated me for walking away from him. He was not, I believe, a malicious individual, nor someone with malign intentions, but his behaviour was, to say the least, thoughtless. He demonstrated, in this instance, no comprehension of, or empathy for, the effects that his power and pronouncements could have on a 20-year-old person. He had forgotten, it seemed, that he was talking to someone with feelings, someone rendered vulnerable by his environment and loss of freedom.

That was perhaps the most negative impact that any officer had on me – far more profound than any of the physical violence that I endured early in my incarceration, which only had the consequence of making me resentful and determined (I shall return to this issue later). In the case of Officer X, I had no way of venting the rage that had been engendered in me without causing more problems for me and my family. I had to bottle up those emotions for many years before I was able to deal with them in ways that were not destructive. Doing so also had negative consequences: I was considered, for many years, cold and unemotional, a lay profile that kept me in high security establishments for some time.

Other officers had equally profound effects on my life but in more positive ways. One such, Officer Y, was my personal officer for the five years I was held in a Main Lifer Centre. This officer stood out because of the frequency and manner with which he would stick up for those inmates who he felt were being unfairly treated by the regime or the Home Office. He was honest and reliable, and was prepared to bypass the prison bureaucracy if it meant getting justified results – in my case, directly phoning my caseworker at the LMU to sort out a significant factual error on my file, which if left unchecked, could have caused all manner of problems and which would normally have required a lengthy bureaucratic intervention.

Officer Y made another important intervention for me on another F75 board. On this occasion, a probation officer made a number of assertions about me that were not only outside his remit, but were also completely unjustified. Based on two interviews, and despite having no psychological expertise, he 'diagnosed' me as having a severe and dangerous personality disorder, an assessment which would have meant me being held in custody indefinitely. His diagnosis, which he presented with confidence, contradicted the findings of a psychologist with whom I had been in consultation for over a year. I could not believe what I had heard. The psychologist looked embarrassed, but did not challenge his assessment. With the chair of the board on the verge of concluding matters, it was Officer Y who asked permission to respond to what had been said. Turning to the probation officer, he asked him what authority he had to make his claims and on what basis they had been made. After some heated debate, during which I was asked to leave the room, it was decided that the probation officer's report should be struck from the record. Officer Y was aware of the effect that this unjustified diagnosis could potentially have on my future, and it was thanks to his courage that I was never forced to endure the deprivations of an indefinite stay within some Special Secure Unit. He stood up for what was right, and would not give in to institutional or peer pressure. On another occasion, he challenged an officer who was being racist to an Asian prisoner, despite this officer being the prison's union representative. Put under pressure to drop his complaint, he continued to pursue it because he was unwilling to stand by and let things that were wrong occur. Officer Y gained the respect of the prisoners in a way that no other officers in that establishment did at that time.

The profundity of an officer's impact does not necessarily have anything to do with the system itself, or their attempts at rehabilitive methods, or, even, any abusive actions. It is the nature of the officer, in and of themselves, and whether or not their nature remains unaffected by the cynicising effects of the environment that matters. The officer who becomes so cynical that he reifies all inmates into the stereotypical recalcitrant will impact on inmates in a negative way, whereas the officer who maintains an individuated idea of those whom he deals with, and treats them humanely, can have an amazingly positive impact.

This is not only true for prison officers but for other staff as well. A prime example of this is educational staff. Many of the staff that you meet within prison educational departments are well-intentioned individuals who struggle to deliver educational opportunities to those who may well never have had such opportunities in often difficult circumstances. Like officers, education staff can have a profound impact on inmates, but this impact is somewhat different to that of officers. The reason for this is that the primary role of educational staff is not concerned with security issues nor with control but with imparting certain forms of knowledge. As a result, a different kind of relationship can develop between the inmate and the 'teacher': the very nature of the teacher's role dictates that they take a personal interest in you as an individual. This is something that is incredibly rare within any penal establishment. If a teacher seems to genuinely take an interest in those whom s/he encounters then this imparts a sense of care that is otherwise absent from the prisoner's life.

An example of this is a teacher whom I shall refer to as Teacher S. I met him while being held in a Category C establishment, where he ran a number of unorthodox classes. However, that was not what attracted inmates to his classes; instead, it was that he cared about the inmates that he taught. He would spend time with them, listen to them and help them. The impact of this is especially profound for those who have been incarcerated for lengthy periods. Much of what you experience as an inmate is negative and that affects your self-image; the longer the exposure to that negativity, the more your self-image is affected. You start to feel as if you are a person of very little worth. Teacher S had the ability to make you feel as if you were a person of worth again. In his classes you never felt like a 'con' because that was not the way that he treated you or saw you.

Teacher S firmly believed in the power of education to effect real changes in the lives of those who passed through his class and because he cared that message was received. However, it is my experience that although many teachers may feel as Teacher S does, the manner in which they deliver their message is rather disillusioned and fatigued. Many within the penal education system have fallen foul of the cynicism that is endemic to their environment. This cynicism means that their supposedly hopeful message – of education being a way out, a means of change – is, in effect, only given lip service. When education staff fall foul of the negativity of the environment, when all they are concerned with is meeting 'targets', when they no longer take an interest in the individual, they impart no sense of care and their role is therefore seen as specious and a waste of time.

The prison environment is, as I have hinted at above, brutalising for all who have cause to abide within it. Just as prisoners suffer from the pains of imprisonment and from institutionalisation, it seems obvious that officers, and other members of staff, must also have their 'pains', derived from internalising the norms and mores of the environment. What aspects of their emotional states do staff, like inmates, have to 'manage' in order to reconcile their emotional selves with their role in the prison?

The most obvious way in which the brutalising effect of the prison is manifested is in the graduated cynicism that steals over those who are subject to its environment. Once removed from the setting, it is striking to see just how profoundly this cynicism infects everyone in a prison (to differing degrees). Some people, including some education staff, retain balance and optimism. By and large though, the majority fall prey to the psychological brutality that is particular to prisons. Recently, I met a probation officer who, years after returning from a secondment to a high security establishment, had reason to review some of the reports that she had written at that time. She was disgusted by the cynical tone and attitudes she had adopted and expressed at that time, and was shocked that she would have been unaware of them had she not seen those reports years later.

I also saw officers change at first hand. When I met Officer Z, at the start of my sentence, he was a young, idealistic and decent man. He had taken the job because it offered secure employment at a time when he had recently become a father. As an officer, he was open-minded and gave everyone the benefit of the doubt. He could not be pushed around, but he was fair and, considering the environment, gentle. Ten years later, I came across Officer Z in a different establishment. I barely recognised him. His face was hardened and bitter. His gentle manner had been replaced by a facade of cynicism and sarcasm. He was brutal, underhand and petty in his methods, quick to give out nickings and verbal abuse. He was despised by inmates, whose complaints against him were received by other officers with a complete lack of surprise. The change in him was shocking, and he was completely unaware that it had occurred. When I asked what was up with him, his response was 'Same old, same old; you know me.'

I now realise that I had gone through similar changes, equally unaware of them until I entered open conditions. Here, I realised that I had absorbed the brutal traits of the previous environs when my father walked straight past me in a visiting room. He had become so used to seeing me hard-faced and tense that when he saw me in circumstances where a tough exterior was unnecessary, he failed at first to recognise me. Institutionalisation is insidious because you can be powerless to prevent it from happening, even when, like me, you are aware of its dangers. It is only once a degree of separation is realised that you are able to recognise what has happened to you. For officers, as well as inmates, while subject to the prison environment, that degree of separation and self-awareness cannot be obtained.

For years, I held to the 'Four I's Theory' to explain the behaviour and attitudes of staff: I was convinced that all actions undertaken by officers were determined by Ignorance, Indifference, Idleness and Incompetence. This 'theory' shapes the attitude of many inmates towards the staff around them. It helps them, by categorising all staff in the same manner, maintain an identity within what is a hostile environment. You also hear officers make similar proclamations, perhaps for the same reasons, about managers, and managers lay the same accusations at the people who operate at regional level and at prison headquarters. Only now that I have gained a degree of separation do I realise that this is too cynical a view of the system, and that, although policy may be indifferent to the individual, the majority of staff are not, nor are they largely idle in the performance of their duties. I know this to be true, but still there is some remnant of the cynicism that makes me search out validation of the theory, not only in relation to prisons but bureaucratic institutions in general.

The imbalance of power in prison, and the monopoly of power held by the establishment, deeply affects the relationships between staff and inmates. Even the most peripheral of staff wield a disproportionate amount of authority over you as an inmate. One consequence is that, as an inmate, you cannot trust members of staff. This is not because of the individual members of staff or their personal level of trustworthiness. It is a reflection of the power that they wield, and the impossibility of trusting someone who holds dominion over you. You are always aware that, at any minute, that power could be brought to bear upon you, with potentially damaging consequences.

This is particularly relevant with regard to prison psychologists, who, over the years I spent in prison, became increasingly powerful. The reason for that is the expansion of their particular remit. No longer would the assessments of a psychologist be for mainly rehabilitative purposes; increasingly those assessments would focus on security/control concerns. To explain how their power is a barrier to trust, let me contrast the prison with the world outside. I have a friend who, due to issues from his childhood that he has never learned to cope with, has anger management issues. He is not violent in any way, has never committed a crime and is considered an upstanding member of his community. However, he does have anger issues and recently decided to see a psychologist to help overcome them. One issue that arose in his sessions was the aggression he felt towards his boss, whom he felt persecuted and ridiculed by. He revealed that, at one point, his feelings had been so intense that he had plotted various ways of killing his boss and disposing of the body. Of course, these thoughts were merely cathartic and he had no real intention of acting upon them. Telling them to the psychologist was a way of expressing the intensity of his emotions.

Imagine a similar situation in prison: an inmate who is having a personality clash with an officer on his wing and who is frustrated and angry at his powerlessness. For him to vent his feelings to a psychologist in the above manner would have profound consequences. It would not be seen as catharsis but as a threat against a member of staff that would have to be reported. At best, he would be ghosted from the prison. At worst, if the prisoner were a lifer, years could be added to his sentence as a result of his admission. Inmates know that these exclamations have such consequences and therefore they never admit to such feelings. This is in itself counter-productive. If an inmate truly wants to change their behaviour, they should have opportunities to be completely honest and open about their emotional states. But the power of those psychologists to whom inmates have access is a barrier to such admissions.

To give another example of how the power wielded by a psychologist can have a negative impact and act as a barrier to trust, when I was in a YOI, I was assigned Officer W as a personal officer. Over the period that he was my personal officer we established a good relationship, or perhaps a working 'understanding'. Though he never stated, to me at least, that he accepted my stance of innocence he did allow that there was the possibility that the jury could have got it wrong. At that time, I was also assigned a psychologist, Miss P, whose job it was to assess me and construct the foundations of a sentence plan. During our first meeting the question of my conviction and my stance of denial was raised. Miss P was unwilling to accept that there was any possibility of a wrongful conviction and explained to me that it was her role to get to the truth behind my motive in having committed the offence for which I had been convicted. At some point during that meeting I mentioned that even Officer W, who, being a remnant of the Borstal system, was not an officer who was seen as overly sympathetic towards the plight of an inmate, accepted the possibility that I was telling the truth. Within a day of that meeting, Officer W was no longer my personal officer – and was replaced by Officer X (see above). I later found out from the wing SO (senior officer) that the reason for the reassignment was a report lodged with the lifer governor by Miss P, suggesting that the relationship between Officer W and me was unhealthy because he encouraged my delusions of innocence.

I felt that Miss P had wilfully removed from my existence the one member of staff who, among the prison authorities, was the closest person I had to an ally at that time. I felt that I was in a hopeless position, a position that was intensely hostile, where I was rendered vulnerable, frustrated and disbelieved. I felt besieged by the prison and every member of staff within it. When I confronted her about this, I was accused of being excessively aggressive, having a problem with women in authoritative roles and of having formed a dependency on Officer W. All I had asked was for her to justify to me why she felt that his accepting the possibility of my innocence was 'unhealthy'. From that moment on, and for the next five years, I rarely engaged with any psychologist. I felt unable to trust them in any way, because to be open would have negative consequences. I felt that they were not there to help me but to aid and abet the prison in controlling me. These feelings got worse over the years as the power that was accorded to psychologists grew within the prison environment.

From personal experience, this increasing power of psychologists, and the manner in which they can affect the future of any particular inmate in such a devastating way, acts as a barrier to trust. This experience is pervasive to many, especially long-term, prisoners, many of whom have suffered some kind of consequence by being open and unguarded in their responses to a psychologist. This also has negative consequences for the penal estate, because it creates a situation where the very power that a psychologist wields renders them untrustworthy and therefore makes it impossible for them to make accurate assessments. If this is the case, then not only is their role impotent but the power/authority that they wield is unjustified.

During my time in confinement, just as the power of psychologists changed, so did the power dynamic in prisons more generally. When I was first imprisoned, the manner in which the power of an establishment was manifested was very immediate: it was with the officers on the wing. You were confronted with that power on a daily basis and at every turn. The brutality of the environment was physical and confrontational. This was a bad thing, but it provided certain satisfactions. Physical brutality was destructive and harmful, but you could engage with it. Beatings strengthened your resolve. They did not have the lingering effects that more insidious, psychological forms of power have. They were over quickly, and, unless they were repeated or sustained abuse, they caused less long-term psychological damage.

Over the years that I was incarcerated, as various policies were implemented and different penal ideologies came to the fore, the power within the establishments began to change. It was as if the power began to retreat or bleed away from individual officers, away from the wing itself. The wing staff were still there, but it was as if they, as a unified entity, had been enervated. Instead of being the focal expression of the establishment's power they now seemed more like a buffer between the inmate and the directors of that power. A consequence of this was that the domination of the establishment changed from being simply physical to a more pervasive psychological domination. This was the beginning, and the consolidation, of the managerialisation of the prison estate.

One of the many frustrations, for inmate and officer alike, in this era of managerialism was attempting to engage with those who made decisions that affected your life. At one time, if a decision was made about some aspect of wing life that you, as an inmate, did not agree with, you could easily voice your complaints to the staff that had made such decisions because they would be those present on the wing. Managerialism made this impossible, because those who were directing the power of the establishment were no longer those that you encountered in your day-to-day life. For instance, in 1999/2000 when I was in the Main Lifer Centre there was an attempt to homogenise all aspects of the various wings. This homogenisation, and the ever increasing personal regulation and restrictions that came with it, were part of the ideology behind the IEP (Incentives and Earned Privileges) system. At one point, Governor R was issuing at least four to five diktats a week. Many seemed ill thought out and impractical. Nevertheless the staff were expected to enforce them and that created friction between the wing staff and the inmates.

The inmates were frustrated because they were being regulated and constrained over activities that had not previously been subject to such attention. The wing staff were frustrated because they were having to enforce regulations that they saw as being unnecessary, troublesome and petty. The problem was that inmates could not voice their concerns to Governor R directly as they had no access to him, other than through the Request/Complaints procedure which was by and large a futile enterprise. Therefore, the only 'target' for those frustrations and complaints were the officers that worked on the landings, but who were powerless to effect any change. A further problem was that because the POA had also been largely emasculated, the complaints made by the staff about these diktats and the expectations that went with them were also ignored. This had two consequences: the first of these was a perception held, and openly expressed, by many officers that there now existed a division between themselves and the objectives of the management; the second was that their reduced autonomy was increasingly being made evident not only by their exclusion from the decision-making process but also by the ever increasing level of scrutiny being levelled at them. Both of these things seemed to lead to mounting frustrations among the staff.

Unfortunately, for the inmate at least, many of the frustrations of the officers ended in petty reprisals, using the new powers of regulation (the IEP system in particular) against inmates. Perhaps that was one of the more aggravating issues in this period; not only were the restrictions that were being imposed more intrusive and constraining, but they were being imposed in such a petty manner. An example of this, from a later period, was Officer Z's actions towards four inmates who were playing snooker. In that particular establishment, if you were on a specific IEP band, then it would take two strikes before you could be demoted to a lower band. With about 15 minutes to go before the end of association Officer Z instructed the four inmates who were playing snooker to start packing up. He returned after no more than a couple of minutes and told them again to pack up. With only a few colours left, the inmates argued that they would be done soon and would pack up before the end of association. Officer Z walked off to the office, and gave two 'strikes' to each of the four inmates for twice having failed to adhere to his instructions. This meant that in one hit all four inmates would be dropped one whole IEP band, depriving them of privileges such as private cash access, visiting orders, association, work positions, their own clothing and gym access. The behaviour of Officer Z in this instance was not only unnecessary but seemingly spiteful as well.

This kind of pettiness was rife in this period. I suspect that it is still the case that many officers, due to the frustrations that are caused by their own position, use regulations in the way that I have described. It almost seems as if these petty displays of control are the only manner in which certain wing staff can regain some sense of the power that has ebbed from them. This pettiness has become symptomatic of the power shift within the penal estate.

A further aspect of the penal system that affects not only the relationships between inmates and staff but also the manner in which power relations are played out is the classification of the particular establishment that you happen to be in at any given time. I always found the staff in adult, high-security, long-term establishments to be far more relaxed, easy going and fair than officers in short-term, low-security prisons. I also found officers in Young Offenders Institutions to be more callous and physical than those in the adult system. In my experience, the officers that displayed the most pettiness tended to be located in large, short-term/remand establishments where there is a high and rapid turnover of the inmate population.

These particular behaviours may well have more to do with the establishment itself, and the relationships that can develop within them, than the individual officers. I was held in my main lifer centre for a period of five years and, at one point, the population on my wing remained static for two years. There are two consequences for staff/inmate relationships when the inmate population remains that stable. The first of these is that there is very little internal strife among the inmates, which means the level of 'policing' that the staff need to undertake is minimal. This allows them to be more relaxed with the inmates, an attitude that is often reciprocated. The second consequence is that it creates a situation where the relationships that develop between inmates and staff can be more personable. The reason for that is the length of time that you actually spend in each other's space. It is difficult to maintain an attitude of overt hostility when you are with the same individuals, day in, day out, for years on end. Of course that hostility can be reignited at a moment's notice, and can be particularly serious in lifer centres, but their occurrences in such contexts tend to be quite rare.

My experience of Young Offender Institutions in the early 1990s was that officers perceived their role to be one of correction as opposed to containment or rehabilitation. This attitude pervaded the Young Offender system and dictated the actions of many officers within that system. This created a situation where it was more difficult for the inmate to interact with officers in any positive way, and where rebellion seemed like the best way to maintain some kind of identity. Because of these attitudes, the attitude of the staff towards 'policing' the inmates was more strict, and this made the relationships between inmates and officers more tense, combative and distrustful.

In establishments that act as remand centres, the Category B locals that have large, transitory populations, the staff–inmate relationship is often more hostile than elsewhere, including Young Offender Institutes (though a large YOI remand centre has double the problems). Traditionally, such establishments were the most brutal, petty and depriving of places, with strong POA influence and control. Officer Z is more typical of this kind of establishment than any other. The reason for this is that, where there is no opportunity or desire for any type of personal relationship to develop, a situation is created where there is no trust, understanding or empathy. It is the norm for officers to act in a brutal and petty manner, and for inmates to repond in kind, exacerbating the culture of hostility. My experiences of staff in open conditions were limited and apparently unusual. In my Category D establishment officers were largely absent from the day-to-day life of the inmate. I have been informed by inmates who spent time in other open prisons that officers were constantly trying to 'trip-up' inmates or 'catch them out'.

Although I have tried to provide a certain degree of generalisable analysis, much of what is outlined in this chapter reflects my subjective experiences and will not necessarily reflect the feelings of all other prisoners. What should be clear though, and what I have sought to highlight, is that although the nature of an establishment affects inmate–staff relations, it is the *character* and disposition of the member of staff that often has the most profound impact upon the inmate, and it is the monopoly of power held by staff that deeply affects the manner in which trust can develop and relations can be formed.

Seminar questions

1 In their current incarnation, how could prisons be made less psychologically damaging?
2 Are the roles of psychologists in assessing inmate risks and seeking to aid their rehabilitation mutually compatible?
3 Are there 'pains of imprisoning' and what are their consequences?
4 How does the prison environment generate cynicism and undermine trust, and what could be done to change these tendencies?

Recommended reading

Personal reflections on prison staff are most easily found within prisoner autobiographies. Erwin James's (2003) *A Life Inside: A Prisoner's Notebook*, a compilation of articles written for *The Guardian*, provides a humane portrayal of a variety of staff figures and interactions. Ruth Wyner's (2003) *From the Inside: Dispatches from a Women's Prison* presents a view of incarceration from the perspective of a female prisoner. Tom Shannon's (1996) *The Invisible Crying Tree* (letters between a life sentence prisoner and his civilian penfriend) gives considerable insight into the general experience of life imprisonment. Razor Smith's (2005) *A Few Kind Words and A Loaded Gun* offers a more damning and jaded account of prison staff, particularly in relation to the behaviour of officers in an earlier era of imprisonment.

References

James, E. (2003) *A Life Inside: A Prisoner's Notebook*. London: Atlantic Notebooks.
Shannon, T. and Morgan, C. (1996) *The Invisible Crying Tree*. Sussex: Pinehurst.
Smith, N. (2005) *A Few Kind Words and A Loaded Gun*. London: Penguin.
Wyner, R. (2003) *From the Inside: Dispatches from a Women's Prison*. London: Aurum Press.

Chapter 3

Prison staff: an international perspective

Roy D. King

Preamble

In accepting a commission to write a short chapter on prison staff from an international perspective I was aware of a major dilemma. Prison staff have rarely been the central focus of my research, though they have always formed part of the context. On the one hand any attempt to offer a representative, still less a global, view would require exhaustive new research but would still be likely to fall foul of a lack of comparable data and end up patchy and superficial. On the other hand, to limit it to just the jurisdictions I know, at least to some degree, either from first-hand research or from study visits, or from investigations on behalf of various international bodies concerned with human rights, would inevitably be incomplete and tend towards the anecdotal.

There being no way out of this dilemma, and in the knowledge that time for new research was limited, I have opted for the latter. Indeed, for considerations of space, I have had to be severely restrictive in my approach. In particular I have had to leave out any consideration of European systems, whether from Western, Central or Eastern European countries. What follows is based primarily on research I have carried out in the United States and on investigations and an attempted change project in Brazil.[1] Although the situation in England and Wales represents a touchstone for comparative purposes, perhaps the most important lessons are to beware of cultural imperialism when judging what happens elsewhere, but always to be thankful for small mercies.

Images of prison staff

Prison staff rarely get a good press. At best they may be taken for granted and ignored, at worst they are stereotyped as brutal, even sadistic, and sometimes corrupt disciplinarians. This has not been helped by the much quoted so-called Stanford prison experiment by Haney *et al.* (1973), which divided university students into two groups. One, 'the prisoners', were dressed in demeaning garb and locked up in a basement under the supervision of the other, 'the guards', who were given riot sticks and mirrored sunglasses, but no training, and allowed to make up their own rules. The 'experiment' had to be ended early because of the oppressive behaviour of the guards and the depressive behaviour of the inmates. Although the study was intended to dispel the idea that the brutality of prison stems from the dispositions of guards – like Stanley Milgram (1974) they wanted to show that good people did evil things when placed in situations which seemingly condoned that behaviour – the *fact* of brutality remained, even though it was now attributed to the 'deep structure' of the institution with its inevitable imbalance of power. When I first came across the experiment my experience of prisons was limited to those I was researching in England, and their 'simulated' prison was hard to square with that experience. What I saw in British prisons of the late 1960s and early 1970s was mainly lofty aspirations interspersed with routine incivilities. However, there was also a gung-ho canteen culture which at times and in some prisons tipped over into institutionalised oppression, particularly in segregation units and, heaven forbid, some hospital wings. But most prisons, most of the time, seemed to find ways in which prisoners and staff managed to live together. It might not have been comfortable or just but it was a long way short of widespread, entrenched and violent abuse.

Shortly afterwards, when I was teaching a college class at Yale I dismissed the experiment as unethical – a position I still maintain – and unrealistic. Giving students power over others, unlimited by training, rules or systems of accountability, I argued, told us little about the real world of prisons, although it did say something about human nature, albeit less eloquently than William Golding (1954) did in *Lord of the Flies* (see also the critique in Jones and Fowles 1984). My colleague, Kelsey Kauffman, and I arranged for ourselves and our students to be voluntarily incarcerated in Haddam – a former prison then part of the academy for prison staff in Connecticut. Real prison officers subjected us to a 'real' incarceration experience, bounded by pre-existing rules and standardised procedures – exactly the same kind of experience which all new recruits to the Department of Corrections had to undergo in those days. The experience included the many 'wind-ups' and indignities which form so much of prison life but the point of this was to show future prison officers what prison was like from a prisoner's point of view. The intention behind this part of their training was to promote a more considerate and responsible exercise of authority. Our students, not to mention Kelsey and me, got to see not only some of the pains of imprisonment which prisoners experience but also gained some insight into the way in which prison officers carried out their role.

One area where both the Stanford experiment and our Yale incarceration experience were unrealistic concerns the past of the 'prisoners'. In real prisons, prisoners have real criminal histories, many will have lived a substantial part of their lives on the street, and will have experienced violence at home, as members of gangs, or in the course of their criminal activity. They may have known other prisoners outside and have scores to settle, or may compete for 'reputation' and 'respect' once they are inside. Others may be altogether less experienced as criminals and more fragile in their capacity to survive. Prison scandals are as likely to occur from the failure of staff to intervene to prevent incidents between rival or incompatible prisoners and the solitary desperate acts of self-harm as they are from the deliberate brutality of guards on prisoners. While I will be documenting some examples from other systems later, I am painfully aware that in England and Wales our record on suicides is far from good (Liebling *et al.* 2005) and that, as with the killing of Zahid Mubarek in Feltham, we are not always successful in preventing prisoner-on-prisoner violence.

Until comparatively recently prison staff have fared little better in the empirical research literature than they have done in the press. In the first major sociological study of a British prison (Morris 1967: 148) the investigators regarded the staff as mere facilitators whose cooperation had to be gained if the research were to be successful and, admittedly at a time when ex-military personnel were the preferred recruits, described many of them as 'martinets who have merely exchanged a khaki uniform for a blue one' (Morris *et al.* 1963: 77). Incidentally, as we shall see, actual military ranks are still used to describe supervisory grades in the United States, though sometimes without the military discipline. And while most former Soviet territories have used both military ranks and military discipline, under the influence of the Council of Europe they have been encouraged to demilitarise in an effort to bring about more humane systems (see

Walmsley 2003). I have argued elsewhere, however, that if one is interested in changing systems then a willingness to follow orders from above may be no bad thing (King 1996).

Both the Morrises and Sykes (1958), in the classic American study which did so much to stimulate prison research, reported on the cultural affinities between staff and prisoners, the former pointing out that both groups came from similar backgrounds, read the same newspapers and magazines, and so on. While the official report on the Attica prison riot (New York State Special Commission 1972) demonstrated that a largely white guard force from rural upstate New York had little in common with the black inmates from the metropolis, it also did little to dispel an image of staff as uncouth 'rednecks'. It was not until the 1970s in a series of papers, following his work on *Stateville*, that Jim Jacobs began to unpick the stereotype, though he was more concerned with issues of unionisation and the impact of introducing more women and ethnic minorities into what had hitherto been a white male preserve than to explore the differentiated ways in which staff carry out their roles. He even speculated about what would be the effect on public understanding of prisons if a system of national service required young men and women to work for a year as prison staff (see Jacobs 1983, for a collection of those papers).

In 1978, King and Elliott, in their study of Albany, showed that staff 'adapted' (in the jargon of prison literature at that time) to prison in ways that were as varied as those through which prisoners adapted and indeed in some ways mirrored them. They argued that those adaptations to the particularities of doing time in, or working in, Albany depended in part on past biographical experience, including doing time, or working, in other prisons. Back in the United States, Kauffman (1981, 1988) noted that the privately expressed attitudes of prison officers often differed markedly from the values which, in a state of pluralistic ignorance, they assumed that other officers shared and which they themselves publicly acknowledged. This rather resembled David Matza's (1964) suggestion that young delinquents egged each other on because of their belief that the others were more committed to the delinquent enterprise than in fact they were. On the basis of their attitudes to fellow officers and towards prisoners Kauffman developed an interesting typology of prison officers in an American maximum security facility which, in part at least, was congruent with the adaptations observed by King and Elliott.

Although most prison systems, including our own, have paid repeated lipservice in countless official publications to the importance of prison staff as their most valued asset, it has often been hard to find much evidence that uniformed prison officers have in fact been valued either by their senior managers in the field or by Home Office mandarins. Some time after the Report of the May Committee (Home Office 1979), which had failed to resolve the industrial relations problems of the 1970s, leaving Prison Service managers still locked in conflict with the Prison Officers' Association, I gave an address to the Howard League (King 1982) in which I pointed out that the prison service got the staff it deserved. In 1963 the POA had sought a new role for the prison officer which would involve uniformed staff playing a much greater part in the welfare and rehabilitation of prisoners, in order to replace the 'military martinet' image which had been berated by the Morrises, but they had received little response. With the apparent rejection both of a role based on military discipline and a role based on professional responsibility, small wonder that prison officers saw themselves as mere wage labourers keen to maximise their overtime and take-home pay by whatever means. There followed an even more acrimonious period in which members of the Prison Board described their uniformed staff as indulging in 'Spanish practices' in the run up to Fresh Start (King and McDermott 1991). Although Fresh Start created a salaried service in which a more professional stance could take root, it was not until the threat of privatisation and the legislative removal of the right to take industrial action in 1994 that the power of the POA was effectively curbed.[2]

Since then there has been increasing interest on the part of the Prison Service to explore both what makes a good prison officer and what constitutes right relationships between prison officers and prisoners. The stream of publications by Liebling and colleagues (Liebling 2000; Liebling and Price 1999, 2001; Liebling et al. 1999; Liebling and Arnold 2004) has explored these issues and provided a welcome rebalancing of the literature which has hitherto dwelt on what Liebling and Price (2001: 108) called the 'dark side' of prison officer work. Today prison officers in England and Wales have many more opportunities than hitherto to play positive roles as personal officers or in running programmes of various kinds. This burgeoning of research on prison officers (see also Crawley 2004, for a study of prison officers at work and at home) does not seem to have been matched in other countries, although there have been occasional studies which have explored the changing roles of correctional staff, both conducted in house (for example, Camp et al. 1996) and by academics (for example, Josi and Sechrest 1998). However, McMahon (1999) has examined the problems experienced by women officers in Canada, and Britton (2003) found little support for the stereotype of the brutal and sadistic guard in her study of Texas prisons as gendered organisations, reporting that correctional officers were more likely to have problems with co-workers and supervisors than they were with prisoners.

Thirty-three years on from teaching that class in Yale, and having experienced prison systems in many other parts of the world including the United States in the interim, I may need to revise my judgment on the Stanford experiment, at least somewhat. I still regard it as unethical and I still regard it as mostly unrealistic. But while I have no direct experience of prison systems so well staffed that they enjoy an effective staff:prisoner ratio of 1:3 at any one time (there are none), or where they work *completely* in the absence of rules, training or accountability, there are certainly systems where the rules are incomplete, unclear or manifestly unfair and even perverse, where training is sparse and remote from reality, and where systems of accountability are virtually non-existent and even more rarely enforced. In short, there are clearly some circumstances where prison officers can, and do, act with near impunity. It is important also to note that, as I write, there are allegations of corruption among prison staff in England and Wales. It also has to be said that while successive Chief Inspectors of Prisons have drawn attention to incidents of abuse and have recorded fears harboured by prisoners about the possibility of assaults by staff, the record of bringing recalcitrant prison officers to book is not particularly impressive.

The danger here is one of making sweeping generalisations on the basis of preconceived positions. It is not so much that Foucauldian notions of the power relationships in prisons do not have an appropriate place in our understanding of prisons but rather that such notions have to be tempered by the empirical realities. The question is not whether prisons offer opportunities for abuse – of course they do. Rather the question is to what extent, and in what circumstances, those opportunities are realised in real situations, and what can be done to minimise them.

In what follows I offer some examples of violence, negligence and abuse in various jurisdictions and consider how they might be avoided by improvements in the staff:prisoner ratio and the way in which staff are trained, organised and deployed, as well as changes to the rules themselves and more effective forms of supervision and accountability. However, I end on a more positive note about two prisons where staff were considered highly professional – albeit by different audiences.

Brazil

My first example is taken from the Prison Improvement Project
– a change project in the Brazilian state of São Paulo, which was
undertaken by the Centre for Comparative Criminology and Criminal
Justice in collaboration with the International Centre for Prison
Studies. The project was consequent upon proposals I submitted to
the Brazilian Ministry of Justice for rewriting policies and procedures,
creating stronger internal structures to support them and external
bodies to inspect and monitor them, which were based upon my
participation in a wide ranging enquiry into prison conditions by
Amnesty International (1999). After some years of negotiation with
successive Ministers of Justice, rioting in São Paulo prisons and the
appointment of an enlightened judge, Dr Nagashi Furokawa, as the
Director of the prison system created the conditions in which the
project could take off. By that time it was linked to a programme
for training of prison staff proposed by the International Centre for
Prison Studies. One year into the programme, a white-collar criminal,
in prison for the first time, who had injudiciously offered to help
a fellow prisoner was held hostage for several months within his
pavilion in the prison where I was acting as facilitator for change. He
was repeatedly beaten, raped and tortured by fellow prisoners until
he signed over all his realisable assets on the outside – about $20,000
– to criminal associates of his captors. He was unable to attract the
attention of staff, and although some of the beatings took place in
the courtyard, if they were seen by staff they were ignored. He was
placed under duress to give the names, addresses and telephone
numbers of relatives who could similarly be intimidated, and for his
wife to give sexual favours to other inmates when she visited.[3] He
tried to resist but, in fear for his life, he managed, when he had to
be produced by his tormentors for a legal visit, to get transferred to
protective custody where I interviewed him.

How could such a situation occur over such a protracted
period? Well clearly only with substantial collusion from staff. The
accommodation for prisoners in this prison comprised some eight
pavilions, four on each side of a wide central corridor. Each pavilion
comprised eight cells, again four on either side of an open yard. Each
cell had 12 concrete bunks providing 96 bed spaces per pavilion. The
cells were routinely overcrowded by about 50 per cent so that the 768
spaces were in fact occupied by 1,180 prisoners. No staff of any kind
were directly assigned to work inside the pavilions. A small number
of social workers operated from a central location, and occasionally

prisoners would be escorted to them for interviews. Uniformed security staff were allocated to the central corridor, although there were never more than a handful on duty at any one time, and also to other locations around the prison – the gate, reception, visits, punishment, etc. Where it really mattered, the effective staff:prisoner ratio was probably of the order of 1 to 140 prisoners. Staff supervision of the pavilions was limited to periodically looking through the window from the corridor. There were occasional searches to look for signs of escape tunnels, on which occasions several members of staff would enter the pavilion armed with iron bars.

With so few members of staff on duty at any one time responsibility for maintaining order within the pavilions was effectively transferred to *faxinas* – ostensibly trusted orderlies and cleaners, who were once presumably handpicked by the security staff rather in the way that cell leaders (or more popularly cell bosses) were chosen in similarly poorly staffed Russian prisons and corrective labour colonies. But over the last 15 years or so the *faxinas* had been infiltrated by members of the PCC (the First Command of the Capital), originally a prisoner group campaigning for better conditions following a massacre at Carandiru prison in 1992 but which had evolved into a criminal gang that controlled drugs and rackets in the city. Inside the prison the *faxinas* operated under the control of a *piloto*, the most senior ranking member of the PCC, who happened to be in that prison at the time. To some degree the *faxinas* did provide a social service for other prisoners – rather as paramilitaries did in Northern Ireland in the absence of a trusted body to uphold law and order. They ensured, or so they claimed, that from the many parcels of food and clothing sent in by relatives those prisoners who had no one on the outside were given a basic minimum, and the 'brothers' offered everyone protection from other prisoners in return for taxes. But it was a power easily abused, as my example shows, and I could have cited many others.[4] Such a system could not operate without the full knowledge and approval of the supervisory grades of security staff and indeed of the prison Director, who was unable to imagine how it would be possible to run a prison without the help of the *faxinas*. As far as uniformed staff were concerned it was simply part of the system within which they became acculturated. The *faxinas* effectively controlled all access to the pavilion so that staff had to negotiate entry when necessary, and they filtered applications from prisoners to see the doctor or social worker as well as all requests to staff.[5]

It is not difficult to recognise that massive increases in the staff: prisoner ratio would be required to turn this situation around.

However, this was not just a question of staff numbers. In Brazilian public services, among which prisons came close to the bottom of the heap, there is an aphorism which runs as follows: 'You pretend to work and we'll pretend to pay you.' Since no one could live and raise a family on the wages of a prison officer, a shift system had been devised whereby security staff worked 24 hours on and 48 or 72 hours off – a scheme which enabled them to have second, and even third jobs, often as security guards. Such a scheme did not attract high-quality staff and inevitably led to divided loyalties, not to mention a tired workforce and the near impossibility of developing roles (for example as personal officers) which required a degree of continuity of contact. One prison officer told me of his first day working in the nearby and notorious Carandiru prison. On arrival he was simply told to go and supervise one of the landings. When he got there he found he was the only member of staff supervising about a hundred prisoners. He spent the entire day sitting on his chair, too frightened to move and hoping that no one would notice him, until his tour of duty was over. Assuming that staff pay and working conditions could be changed sufficiently to make being a prison officer a career capable of attracting better educated recruits there would still be a massive task of training. As things stood, the local penitentiary training school provided a short initial training for new recruits which was largely theoretical and classroom based, as well as periodic refresher courses. Training was not a priority of prison directors in the field, and there was little to support the work of the training school. Its Director told me during my Amnesty visits of the uphill task he faced and of how, when staff left the school, they were simply 'retrained' by officers already in post and 'resocialised' into the old prison routines.

The director of the training school became a member of the team trying to implement changes, but it was clear that if training were to have any relevance it had to come out of the classroom and address issues in the workplace. One of the issues in the workplace was that there were no very clear rules governing relations between staff and prisoners – presumably because there were hardly any occasions that staff and prisoners came into regular contact. For example, there appeared to be no clear rules or procedures which related to the use of force, i.e. when, and in what circumstances, force was permissible and what levels of force could be used. Likewise, there were no clear rules governing the way in which searches of cells, of prisoners or of visitors should be conducted – despite the fact that conjugal visits were often held in the cells themselves. In the absence of such rules it is hard to see how classroom training, for example on human rights, could begin to break down the existing culture and historical traditions. In Brazilian police stations, where suspects may be legally held for up to a week, prisoners are often held for months and even years both before trial and after conviction. In some police stations police officers have often been found to use iron bars, which are ostensibly for testing 'locks, bolts and bars', to beat and intimidate prisoners as a way of maintaining order. Although such happenings are less common in the prisons, we have seen that order may sometimes be maintained no less brutally by prisoners and, indeed, mass escapes, rebellions and the taking of visitors as hostages occur quite frequently. On such occasions the shock troops of the military police, who traditionally have been responsible for external security, may be called in by the prison director to restore order. Sometimes they decide to enter the prison regardless of the views of the prison director. When they do come in they may use firearms in an indiscriminate show of force. On 2 October 1992 the Carandiru House of Detention – then South America's largest prison – became the scene of a bloody massacre when, after fighting broke out in one of the cell blocks, shock troops 'restored order' by shooting dead 111 prisoners, many in the back of the head after they had surrendered.

In addressing the need to develop rules, policies and procedures with their Brazilian partners, members of the project team (mistakenly in my view but under obvious pressures of time and resources) used too many Prison Service Orders from England and Wales as models which, when wrenched out of context, failed to navigate around the issues of prison culture, existing role models, established patterns of staffing organisation and even the legal requirements under the Brazilian constitution. If reform efforts are to be successful, it is far better to identify the problems and then encourage solutions which are more consistent with existing cultures and traditions. It remains to be seen how far the project will transcend the departure of Dr Nagashi, who resigned in 2006 amid the political struggles following further prison riots. Among the many achievements of his time in office was the symbolic demolition of Carandiru.

Colorado and California

My second and third examples come from the American west – respectively Colorado and California. In Colorado, on average, the

39

ratio of prison officers to prisoners is reported to be 1:6.6 and in California, despite the powerful California Correctional Peace Officers Union, the ratio is 1:7.8, in both cases worse than the national average of 1:5.5 (Camp 2003: 164). There were no extraordinary features to the shift systems, such as we saw in Brazil, but to allow for 24-hour coverage of the prisons, and to take account of sickness, holidays and absenteeism, these ratios probably need to be multiplied by 2.5 to 3 times to produce effective staff ratios. Even so, sufficiency of staff in these instances was not the main issue, but rather the nature of the rules, policies and procedures in Colorado and the poorly defined use of force policy, inadequate training of officers, lack of supervision by line managers and an attitude of indifference on the part of the Department of Corrections in California.

At the Colorado State Penitentiary, a supermaximum-security facility, an incident occurred whereby one prisoner was killed by others in the full sight of prison officers who were powerless to intervene. The incident took place in a so-called 'step-down' unit, in which prisoners who had previously been held in complete lock-down and only allowed out of cells in isolation from other prisoners, were now permitted limited periods of association with other prisoners preparatory to release back to normal location or to the community. Such units had been introduced following understandable concerns that some prisoners were released straight from long periods of solitary confinement to the streets. Since prisoners were normally locked down, prison officers only entered the living units to escort prisoners one at a time to the shower or the telephone or to escort prisoners to the doctor or to be interviewed by me. It was enshrined in policy documents at the penitentiary that whenever a prisoner was out of his cell he was handcuffed, belly-chained and sometimes spit-masked, and accompanied by three officers. In the step-down unit prisoners were allowed to mix a few at a time, observed by staff from outside the unit in the security bubble. When the fight commenced there were simply insufficient officers in the establishment to allow them to enter the living unit to intervene and still maintain the requisite ratio of at least three staff to every prisoner. Those who were on duty could only stand and watch.[6] Subsequently the rules were changed to ensure that fewer prisoners were allowed out of their cells at a time in order to make certain that such a situation could not be repeated.

There is no suggestion here that the prisoners were set up to fight one another, or that staff were unconcerned or negligent. If one can accept the extraordinary terms of reference that apply to supermax facilities, Colorado State Penitentiary was generally run in a professional manner, according to the rules, and its managers have played a leading role in trying to set appropriate standards (Atherton 2002; Neal 2002). This was certainly not the case in California, the state where the Stanford 'experiment' was born. At Corcoran Prison officers stood accused of 'stacking the tiers' so that known members of different gangs would share yard time and get involved in fights.

Corcoran, like other Californian prisons, had its share of prison gangs – the Aryan Brotherhood, Nuestra Familia, Mexican Mafia, Black Guerilla Family and so on – as well as street gangs, many members of which might pursue vendettas in prison. In the special housing units at Corcoran an integrated yard policy required that about twenty prisoners who were allowed to use the yard at the same time had to be 'balanced' according to racial and ethnic criteria, and were required to sign waivers that indicated they had no known enemies on the tier. The tiers were supposedly 'staggered' so that adjacent cells, and cells above and below one another, did not contain 'enemies', and correctional officers were expected to release prisoners to the yard one cell at a time. However, the policy was poorly drafted, and lawyers described it as more of a 'practice' than a 'policy' which could be manipulated by staff. Moreover, California had a use of force policy which embraced lethal force. Staff could progress from 37 mm gas guns which fired five wooden or rubber bullets, to the Mini-14 rifle, later replaced by a 9 mm rifle. Corcoran opened in December 1988 and in the first year there were more than a thousand fights on the yard. No fewer than 24 prisoners were shot and killed in Californian prisons between 1989 and 1994, seven of them in Corcoran, mostly for failing to obey an order to cease their assaults on other prisoners.

On 2 April 1994, Preston Tate, a convicted rapist, was shot by staff inadvertently. They were aiming at his assailants in the yard. Tate, who was not known to be a violent prisoner, had only gone to the yard to support his cell mate who had been expecting trouble. Not surprisingly, accounts of the incident varied. It was alleged that such cases formed part of a pattern of so called 'gladiatorial combat' in which prisoners were set up to fight one another, and staff – according to some accounts including secretarial staff – were invited to watch and place bets on the outcome. Certainly there were several people in the control booth that day including a sergeant, a relief lieutenant with little experience of special housing units and two correctional officers in addition to the gunner. A warning shot from the 37 mm gas gun was usually sufficient to stop the fights, but in this instance the officer followed this up four seconds later with the lethal rifle shot. A shooting review board held that the killing was accidental. Indeed, review boards had similarly justified all 24 fatal shootings as well as more than 50 non-fatal woundings. The Tate case was eventually settled out of court with substantial damages to his surviving family whose lawyers made it plain, perhaps in the interest of getting a settlement, that they did not regard the issue as one of rogue officers acting out of personal malice but rather the failure to supervise and monitor an inherently flawed policy and to provide staff with appropriate training. Indeed, some staff at Corcoran had long protested against the integrated yard policy and the lack of clarity and training about the use of lethal force.

My own view of the situation at Corcoran and some other Californian prisons, having read many of the documents in the Tate case, and having attempted to reconstruct things on the basis of subsequent visits where I was able to talk to staff and prisoners there in 1996, was that there had been signal failures of monitoring and supervision at all levels. The Department of Corrections had been content to leave matters to local wardens rather than to impose or review policies from the centre; local wardens took a laissez-faire approach to what went on in parts of the institution which they rarely visited; captains made routine but perfunctory visits to residential areas; and lieutenants were not based in the residential units themselves but supervised from administrative quarters via regular and easily anticipated tours of the units for which they were responsible. It was clear that the ethos of the Department required each level to support the decisions of subordinates for whom they were nominally responsible – to the point where at its worst it amounted to an impenetrable 'code of silence'. It is intriguing, for example, that the Department of Corrections' shooting review board in the Tate case could not find a reason why a lieutenant should have been in the control booth at the material time, but did not appear to question why, given that he was there, he did not exercise control over the situation.

In the even more notorious supermax prison at Pelican Bay in northern California, to which many 'difficult' prisoners from Corcoran were transferred, the Madrid Court in *Madrid versus Gomez* (1995) found that the complaisant defendants – the Department of Corrections – 'have permitted and condoned a pattern of using excessive force, all in conscious disregard of the serious harm that these practices inflict'. Space precludes detailed consideration of the Madrid Court, the evidence placed before it and the findings which it reached. But when I was conducting research at Pelican Bay in 1996, the prison was operating under the watchful eye of the Madrid Compliance Unit. I was privileged to view the video recordings of cell extractions – most of which appeared to be carried out according to the book. A serious problem, however, was the nature of the book itself. Thus staff had no qualms about conducting a pod (living unit) extraction of a prisoner who, having been released electronically from his cell to have access to the 'dog-run' exercise yard, refused to return to his cell while I watched the whole proceedings. The prisoner was the only prisoner out of his cell and sooner or later would have returned to it of his own volition. Nevertheless, he was deemed to be 'holding the pod to hostage'. A warning was given that if he did not comply he would be forcibly extracted. A supervising lieutenant was called who repeated the warning. The prisoner did not comply. The gunner fired the 37 mm gas gun three times, each time discharging five rubber bullets. The third volley brought the prisoner to his knees. The five-man extraction team faced the video camera, identified themselves, stated their role (one for each limb and one for the head) and declared that they would use no more force than was necessary. They then entered the pod, pepper sprayed the fallen prisoner, removed him, tied him to a gurney and took him to the infirmary where he was cleaned up and eventually returned to his cell. I was relieved that no one felt it necessary to use the Mini-14 rifle, but I was painfully aware that I had been asked to wear a flak-jacket throughout my time in the prison, and that the bare walls carried a message that there would be no warning shots.

State Senate hearings in 1998, at about the time of the Tate settlement, spawned legislation that increased correctional officer training from six to 16 weeks and expanded a fledgling prison ombudsman programme. However, the local press and websites continue to carry stories that give great cause for concern.

Minnesota and England

I promised to end on a more positive, if still slightly puzzling note. Nearly twenty years ago, when I conducted a comparative study of Gartree – then still a dispersal prison – and Oak Park Heights in Minnesota – a forerunner of supermax facilities but run on very different lines – there were some remarkable differences. Oak Park Heights scored better in almost all respects: it was very much safer for both staff and prisoners, more secure and less trouble prone, and it operated much fuller and more highly rated programmes of treatment, industry and education, and had much better contact with the outside world. The only item on which Gartree was rated more highly by its prisoners was physical education.

Both prisons were well staffed compared with the other examples considered here. England and Wales has, on average, better staff: prisoner ratios at about one prison officer for 3.4 prisoners, and staff are better paid than in most other jurisdictions, including virtually all of those in the United States (Liebling and Price 2001; Camp 2003). Minnesota, with one correctional officer for every four prisoners, is one of the six best staffed prison systems in the United States (Camp 2003). Staff ratios vary widely from prison to prison according to security level and historical factors, but as the highest security establishments in their respective systems, both Gartree and Oak Park Heights were among the best staffed. A typical wing in Gartree was staffed by one principal officer, one senior officer and five or six prison officers for 72 prisoners – a ratio of about 1:10. Each living unit in Oak Park Heights was staffed by two officers on the floor and one in the security bubble, with a lieutenant having oversight of two adjacent units and spending half the time in each. With 50 prisoners to a unit this produced an effective ratio of about 1:15.

It should be noted that the design of the units was very different: in Gartree it was difficult to persuade staff to visit the upper landings where they were out of sight of their colleagues. In Oak Park Heights it was possible to see the whole of the living unit, including the staff members inside, from the security bubble. This meant that not only could additional support be quickly summoned if needed, but that any inappropriate behaviour by staff was immediately observed by their colleagues.

Oak Park Heights staff were on the whole better qualified, with one-third of correctional officers having college degrees. Moreover, the charismatic warden and his captain enjoyed the luxury of interviewing and handpicking every member of staff, who were imbued with, and for the most part faithfully followed, the enlightened policies and procedures which were based on the principle that staff should treat prisoners as they would like their sons, brothers, fathers to be treated if they were prisoners. To the outsider, and to this researcher who spent several months in the living units observing and interviewing staff and prisoners, staff were unfailingly smartly turned out, they respectfully addressed prisoners as Mr so and so, and were able to articulate clearly both the policies and the reasoning behind them. Of course, Gartree at that time, having recovered from some traumatic incidents, was a well led institution, albeit in a very different style, by a future Director General of the prison system. But he certainly was not in the position of picking and choosing his staff, and then, as now, the idea of referring to prisoners by a title was anathema to most prison officers. And yet it was Gartree staff who were the more highly regarded by the prisoners in their custody. Gartree prisoners rated the officers as more helpful, more likely to be fair, more consistent in applying the rules and more likely to be non-racist – than did their counterparts in Oak Park Heights (although the overall rating for professionalism was only marginally better in Gartree). It seemed to me then that part of the explanation might lie in the prior experiences of prisoners as they compared current staff with those they had known in other prisons. Certainly all Gartree prisoners would have passed through local prisons, and Gartree staff might well have benefited from that comparison. But many Oak Park Heights prisoners had prior experience of Stillwater which had such a troubled past that the Minnesota Department of Corrections embarked on the building of Oak Park Heights in the first place. More recently I have wondered whether part of the explanation was that in Oak Park Heights the warden was seen as the driving force with officers merely carrying out policies in a closely observed way, whereas in Gartree staff were seen as having greater discretion and exercising it in a responsible, or perhaps just more liberal, way. But now, as then, I am left with the question: given that Gartree was well led in the field and its staff were seen as more professional than those in Oak Park Heights, why did it deliver much the poorer regime?

Seminar questions

1 What ethical considerations are raised by experiments involving volunteers placed in simulated prison environments?
2 How appropriate is it to compare staff working in different cultures, and to what extent might good practice in one jurisdiction be transferred to another?
3 Assess the relative importance of staff numbers, staff training, policies and procedure, and leadership in the provision of effective and humane staff–prisoner relations.
4 How should prison officers address prisoners?
5 Under what conditions might prisoners usurp the proper role of staff?

Recommended reading

There are precious few sources for internationally comparative data on prison staff, or indeed for many individual jurisdictions. For the United States I have already referred to a number of sources in the text, and full citations are contained in the references: the various editions of *The Corrections Yearbook* edited by Camille and George Camp provide useful outline statistical information. I know of nothing in English on staffing in Brazil although the various reports by Amnesty International and Human Rights Watch contain useful material and can be accessed via their websites. Drauzio Varella's account of his time as a volunteer doctor working in Carandiru, *Estaçio Carandiru*, is available only in Portuguese but it has been turned into a must-see film, *Carandiru.*

Notes

1 The work in the United States was conducted in Arizona, California, Colorado, Illinois, Minnesota, New York, Pennsylvania, Texas and Virginia, and was carried out at different times under two ESRC research grants. In Brazil I acted as adviser to two Amnesty International missions, following which I submitted proposals to the Brazilian Ministry of Justice for a programme of action research which, after protracted negotiations, was eventually funded by the British Embassy.
2 Full trade union rights were eventually restored in 2005 in exchange for a voluntary agreement not to strike.
3 In Brazil conjugal visits are the norm and these frequently take place inside the main prison and actually in the prisoner's cells. While the majority of prisoners appear to behave with great respect in these situations there are obvious opportunities for abuse.
4 In this case the *faxinas* had gone beyond the code of the PCC and initially were taken to task by the *piloto.* But when that pilot moved on his successor took a different view and the abuse continued this time with death threats.
5 In this prison, the Director who claimed a good relationship with prisoners (but probably actually with *faxinas*) did sometimes visit the pavilions. Another prison director in the programme never visited his pavilions for fear of being taken hostage.
6 A somewhat similar incident occurred in the Nieuw-Vosseveld supermax style prison in the Netherlands, although there the staff could not intervene to prevent the death of a prisoner not so much because of the lack of staff but because of the number of physical and electronic barriers through which they had to pass.

References

Amnesty International (1999) *No-one Here Sleeps Safely: Human Rights Violations Against Detainees*, AMR 19/09/1999.

Atherton, E.E. (2002) 'Use of Force in the Supermax Prisons: Setting the Example', in D. Neal (ed.), *Supermax Prisons: Beyond the Rock*. Lanham, MD: American Correctional Association.

Britton, D.M. (2003) *At Work in the Iron Cage: The Prison as a Gendered Organization*. New York: New York University Press.

Camp, C.G. (ed.) (2003) *The Corrections Yearbook: Adult Corrections 2002*. Middletown, CT: Criminal Justice Institute.

Camp, G.M., Camp, C.G. and Fair, M.V. (1996) *Managing Staff: Corrections' Most Valuable Resource*. Washington, DC: National Institute of Corrections.

Crawley, E. (2004) *Doing Prison Work: The Public and Private Lives of Prison Officers*. Cullompton: Willan.

Golding, W. (1954) *Lord of the Flies*. London: Faber & Faber.

Haney, C., Banks, W.C. and Zimbardo, P.G. (1973) 'Interpersonal dynamics in a simulated prison', *International Journal of Criminology and Penology*, 1: 69–97.

Jacobs, J.B. (1983) *New Perspectives on Prisons and Imprisonment*. Ithaca, NY: Cornell University Press.

Jones, K. and Fowles, A.J. (1984) *Ideas on Institutions: Analysing the Literature on Long-Term Care and Custody*. London: Routledge & Kegan Paul.

Josi, D.A. and Sechrest, D.K. (1998) *The Changing Career of the Correctional Officer: Policy Implications for the 21st Century*. Boston: Butterworth-Heinemann.

Home Office (1979) *Report of the Committee of Inquiry into the UK Prison Service* (Report of the May Committee), Cmnd 7673. London: HMSO.

Kauffman, K. (1981) 'Prison officers' attitudes and perceptions of attitudes: a case of pluralistic ignorance', *Journal of Research in Crime and Delinquency*, July: 272–94.

Kauffman, K. (1988) *Prison Officers and Their World*. Cambridge, MA: Harvard University Press.

King, R.D. (1982) 'Industrial relations in the Prison Service', *Howard Journal*, XXI: 71–5.

King, R.D. (1996) 'Prisons in Eastern Europe: some reflections on prison reform in Romania', *Howard Journal*, 35 (3): 215–31.

King, R.D. and Elliott, K.W. (1978) *Albany: Birth of a Prison – End of an Era*. London: Routledge & Kegan Paul.

King, R.D. and McDermott, K. (1991) 'A Fresh Start: Managing the Prison Service', in R. Reiner and M. Cross (eds), *Beyond Law and Order: Criminal Justice Policy and Politics into the 1990s*. London: Macmillan.

Liebling, A. (2000) 'Prison officers, policing, and the use of discretion', *Theoretical Criminology*, 3 (2): 173–87.

Liebling, A. and Arnold, H. (2004) *Prisons and Their Moral Performance: A Study of Values, Quality and Prison Life*. New York: Oxford University Press.

Liebling, A. and Price, D. (1999) *An Exploration of Staff–Prisoner Relationships at HMP Whitemoor*, Prison Service Research Report No. 6. London: Prison Service.

Liebling, A. and Price, D. (2001) *The Prison Officer*. Leyhill: Prison Service Journal.

Liebling, A., Price, D. and Elliott, C. (1999) 'Appreciative Inquiry and Relationships in Prison', *Punishment and Society*, 1 (1): 71–98.

Liebling, A., Durie, L., Stiles, A. and Tait, S. (2005) 'Revisiting prison suicide: the role of fairness and distress', in A. Liebling and S. Maruna (eds), *The Effects of Imprisonment*. Cullompton: Willan.

McMahon, M. (1999) *Women on Guard: Discrimination and Harassment in Corrections*. Toronto: University of Toronto Press.

Madrid versus Gomez (1995) No. C90-3094-THE, Class action: findings of fact, conclusions of law, and order, US District Court for the Northern District of California.

Matza, D. (1964) *Delinquency and Drift*. New York: John Wiley & Sons.

Milgram, S. (1974) *Obedience to Authority*. London: Tavistock.

Morris, T.P. (1967) 'Research on the prison community', in *Collected Studies in Criminological Research*, Vol. 1. Strasbourg: Council of Europe, European Committee on Crime Problems.

Morris, T.P., Morris, P. and Barer, B. (1963) *Pentonville: A Sociological Study of an English Prison*. London: Routledge & Kegan Paul.

Neal, D. (2002) 'Technology and the Supermax Prison', in D. Neal (ed.), *Supermax Prisons: Beyond the Rock*. Lanham, MD: American Correctional Association.

New York State Special Commission (1972) *Attica: The Official Report of the New York State Special Commission on Attica*. New York: Bantam Books.

Sykes, G.M. (1958) *The Society of Captives: A Study of a Maximum Security Prison*. Princeton, NJ: Princeton University Press.

Walmsley, R. (2003) *Further Developments in the Prison Systems of central and Eastern Europe: Achievements, Problems and Objectives*. Helsinki: European Institute for Crime Prevention and Control (HEUNI).

Chapter 4

The experiences of black and minority ethnic prison staff

Hindpal Singh Bhui and Julia Fossi

Introduction

In recent years there has been an increasing focus on prisoners' experiences of racism. The murder of Zahid Mubarek in Feltham Young Offenders Institution and the subsequent Commission for Racial Equality (CRE 2003a, 2003b) and public inquiries (Keith 2006) have highlighted the severity and impact of racism within prison. While both inquiries were extremely critical of some prison staff for racism, collusion or incompetence, it was not part of their specific remits to examine the experiences of black and minority ethnic (BME) staff. In fact, remarkably little attention has been devoted to the experiences of prison staff of any background in the wider prison literature, although this is slowly increasing (e.g. Liebling and Price 2001; Crawley 2004).

This gap has been addressed to a limited extent. A now dated study by Alfred (1992) explored the recruitment of BME officers into the Prison Service and their experiences within the prison system. More recently, Edgar and Martin (2004) considered how perceptions of racism influenced relationships between officers and minority ethnic prisoners. They interviewed members of staff and prisoners who had recently been involved in a conflict situation, and uncovered how 'informal partiality', or discretion on behalf of prison officers, could be construed as disadvantaging certain racial groups. Meanwhile, Edgar and Roberts (2005) looked at the views of prison staff who had joined the Prison Service's RESPECT programme (Racial Equality for Staff), aiming to find out why staff had decided to engage with

RESPECT and the extent to which they felt it was an effective organisation.

However, the most extensive examination of the perspectives of BME staff was undertaken by HM Inspectorate of Prisons (HMIP 2005a) during its thematic review of race relations in prisons. The review garnered the views and experiences of hundreds of BME[1] and white staff and sought to identify barriers to the delivery of race equality in prisons. It focused mainly on front-line prison officers rather than governors or the large numbers of statutory and voluntary sector staff currently working in most prisons. Nevertheless, it enabled important insights into the question of how BME staff were experiencing an organisation considered by the CRE (2003a, 2003b) to be guilty of racial discrimination. Consequently, this chapter reports the main results of that review, drawing on original source material, some of which was not published in the report. It also considers the evidence from other studies and inquiries, and places the experiences of prison staff into the wider context of a troubled history of race relations in the Prison Service. This latter issue will be addressed first.

The race relations challenge in prisons

Any examination of the experience of BME staff requires some understanding of the context in which they work. The history of race relations and the response to racism in the Prison Service shows that while management structures to enable anti-racist practice have been in place, the next step towards implementation has often not been taken. For example, the Prison Inspectorate Annual Report for 2003–4 (HMIP 2004) described a continued prevalence of:

> at best insensitive and at worst racist remarks … In most cases, they [i.e. black prisoners] attributed this to a lack of understanding, rather than deliberate and overt racism; and to a minority of officers. But in some prisons, there were clearly endemic problems … (p. 23)

This is not dissimilar to the messages from earlier Home Office funded research studies by Genders and Player (1989) and Burnett and Farrall (1994). These studies have for some time been the most extensive academic examinations of race in prisons, although there have been a number of more limited studies and reviews (e.g. NACRO 2000;

Ellis *et al*. 2004; Edgar and Martin 2004; Wilson 2004; Cheliotis and Liebling 2006). All the published work has tended to come up with remarkably similar evidence of both direct and indirect, obvious and subtle racism, mainly by staff against prisoners (discussed further below).

The cumulative messages of the academic research and Inspectorate findings were reinforced by the CRE's investigations into Brixton, Parc and Feltham prisons (CRE 2003a, 2003b), which considered racism between prisoners as well as staff racism towards prisoners. The CRE's findings showed not only how basic human decency can sometimes be lost in the closed world of prisons, but also demonstrated the complexity of understanding, assessing and responding to racism in a pressured prison environment. The CRE report on Feltham Young Offenders Institution (2003a) explicitly stated that the prevalence of racism in the prison had desensitised staff to such an extent that signs of racism by Robert Stewart, the young man who murdered Zahid Mubarek, were not registered. Of the 10 per cent of staff interviewed at Feltham for the inquiry, half were from a BME background and some said they too were subject to racist comments or jibes. Although the inquiry highlighted examples of overtly racist behaviour towards prisoners from some members of staff, it was not within the remit of the investigation to examine the difficulties faced by BME staff detailed to work alongside individuals who displayed such behaviour. The pressures on BME staff in an environment where racism was prevalent are likely to have been considerable. How would they have managed professionally and personally if they had witnessed racism or potential racism from other staff, where the options included challenge and confrontation (and possible isolation), further investigation and collusion? The consequences of racist behaviours can impact on all members of the targeted group, regardless of their status or grade in an organisation.

However, there has been undoubted progress with regard to race relations in the Prison Service over the last 25 years. The major aim of anti-racist prison policy in the 1980s and 1990s was to tackle extreme and overt racism. Prison officers were stopped from wearing National Front and similar badges, and openly racist staff were dismissed.[2] From this starting point, more stringent management, lines of accountability, reduced discretion and use of disciplinary procedures have been successful to a degree. There are now established structures for dealing with racism in prisons – for example, race relations committees, race relations officers, sophisticated range-setting ethnic monitoring,[3] regular audits and racial complaints procedures, all of which should exist in all public prisons.[4] Many prison staff have also worked hard to support the principles of anti-racism and promote diversity, and this is obvious from the pockets of good practice that the prison Inspectorate finds across the country (e.g. HMIP 2004, 2005a).

In recent years, there is no doubt that at a strategic level the Prison Service has also had a genuine commitment to tackling racism. When he was Director General, Martin Narey gave a clear message that he believed the Prison Service was institutionally racist and launched the 'decency agenda', part of whose focus was on tackling institutional racism. This was also supported by his successor Phil Wheatley, who signed up to the CRE/Prison Service five-year joint action plan to tackle race equality.[5] Narey's appointment of a race adviser and the launch of RESPOND (Racial Equality for Staff and Prisoners) and RESPECT (Racial Equality for Staff) were also significant and progressive steps. More recently, two new key performance targets (KPTs) have been piloted, which use a basket of measures, including prisoner and staff perceptions of racism, to measure progress.[6]

However, even with this strategic activity, the evidence still indicates that the major shift in prison race relations has been from overt to more 'covert' racism against and between prisoners (HMIP 2005a; Edgar and Roberts 2005). The *culture* in individual prisons has been less supportive of the efforts of individual staff who want to challenge racism, good policies have not been properly implemented and, consequently, the Prison Service as an institution has found it difficult to provide an effective foundation for the development of anti-racist practice. There is therefore a need for strong organisational commitment to change at all levels. This is highlighted by Hogan *et al.*'s (2006) study, which concluded that such commitment was important in positively affecting correctional staff behaviours and improving levels of job performance. Organisational stressors such as role ambiguity and role conflict were inversely correlated with organisational commitment. This study concluded that correctional workers wanted clearly defined roles, directions, expectations and guidance for their jobs, something that comes from prison governors as much as from central policy units. In order for staff to achieve 'commitment' there must be commitment from managers as well as the central organisation, which is driven through training, resources and the allocation of sufficient time to do race relations work in each establishment. Interestingly, the HMIP (2005b) review found that about a quarter of governors were negative about the CRE findings and were unsure about how to make progress on race equality in their own prisons. At the same time, staff, particularly BME staff, said they were looking to them for evidence of commitment in this area.

It is important to recognise the inherent difficulties of achieving race relations progress in prisons. The Prison Service task does not stress the uniqueness of the individual, but rather the importance of security and the effective management of prisoners. It encourages suspicion and defensiveness. However, anti-racist practice is, to a degree, tied up with recognition of individuality, of the diversity of people, something actively discouraged in institutions designed to maintain order. Carlen (2002) touches on this when she argues that attempts at reform and change in women's prisons are compromised by 'carceral clawback', the tendency of the prison system to confound genuine attempts at reform by reverting back to its most basic purpose of containment and the perceived requirements of control and security. Similarly, Houchin (2003) argues that prison policy focused on incapacitation 'emphasises the "otherness" of the offender' and 'sits uncomfortably with the positive promotion of the fundamental rights of prisoners and with policies based on rehabilitation' (p. 145).

Alongside these intrinsic characteristics of the prison environment, there are other factors discouraging the development of anti-racist practices. This includes a prison estate dangerously close to its absolute capacity,[7] and the tendency this encourages to focus on security above all else; performance management structures that, until the new KPTs were launched, had not come close to effectively incorporating anti-racism; the continued stress on the 'otherness' of the offender, which discourages positive engagement between staff and prisoners; and relatively superficial staff training and selection procedures. None of these encourages prison cultures where one can consistently expect to see respect for individual rights or promotion of race equality. Tools and strategies are needed to challenge and develop individual and cultural attitudes, the most obvious being to reduce overcrowding which stifles the capacity for professional development, improved training and selection, and robust managerial structures in which diversity is an integral part.

With regard to training, the eight-week prison officer course is insufficient to enable prison staff to do complex interpersonal work in highly stressful environments, while also being pressurised from outside bodies like the CRE and the prisons Inspectorate. They are not given enough time to reflect on and develop their own views and values, despite the fact that reflective time is critical to the development of anti-racist attitudes and practice. Such practice aims ultimately to achieve the considerable feat of bridging the gap between instincts which can lead to racial stereotyping and the individual and professional maturity which only comes with knowledge. It cannot be learned by rote and does not allow for complacency or unthinking, uncritical implementation, and it certainly cannot be picked up during a few weeks of training (see Thompson 2001, who convincingly outlines what is required for genuine anti-discriminatory practice, which requires change on the personal, cultural and structural levels). In-service training is currently limited to half-day diversity sessions which are often delivered less than annually, and both diversity training and the now non-mandatory race relations training which preceded it have often been delivered by staff who have an imperfect understanding of the issues themselves and a lack of the skills necessary to challenge stereotypes (Alfred 1992; HMIP 2004). The Prison Service acknowledged the need to rethink training on race and diversity in the action plan agreed with the CRE (CRE/Prison Service 2003). There are in any event some promising types of training available which could be further investigated; for example, the RESPECT study (Edgar and Roberts 2005) found that members were extremely positive about the cross-cultural communication training delivered to them.

Given this complex and challenging context, it would be a considerable surprise if inevitable tensions between and among staff and prisoners were not affected to some degree by ethnic and cultural differences.

Findings from the HMIP thematic review of race relations

The thematic review included interviews with 178 prison staff, mainly officers in prisoner contact roles, of whom 58 (34 per cent) identified themselves as BME.[8] Analysis of the comments made by staff showed a gulf between the general perceptions of BME and white staff about a range of prison race relations issues. The difference in views was so great that the report was eventually entitled 'Parallel Worlds'. For example, when staff were asked 'How does racism show itself in this prison', white staff were much more likely to say that BME prisoners 'play the race card' compared to BME officers (23 staff compared to 2). White staff were also more likely to identify prisoner-on-prisoner racism (39 staff compared to 2). BME staff were more likely to say that the needs of BME prisoners were not being met (see Table 4.1). Interestingly, the perceptions of whether needs were met were lower

Table 4.1 Staff perceptions of whether the needs of BME prisoners were met

	Needs met	Needs partly met	Needs not met
White officers	79%	21%	
BME officers	54%	29%	17%
White managers/governors	50%	50%	
BME managers/governors	46%	36%	18%

for more senior staff than for officers, and this occurred for both white and BME staff. Table 4.1 illustrates the gulf in perceptions between white and BME staff.

In relation to staff experiences, the review identified a significant problem of racism from other staff and a lesser but still considerable problem of prisoner-on-staff racism. Staff who identified as black were especially likely to have experienced some form of racism in their work. Overall, 20 out of 28 BME staff (71 per cent) who identified themselves as black reported such experiences compared to 8 out of 14 Asian staff (57 per cent) and 7 out of 11 mixed race staff (64 per cent).

Racism from other staff

More than two-thirds of the BME staff interviewed (n = 38: 66 per cent) said they had experienced racism in their establishments and almost half (n = 24: 41 per cent) said they had experienced racism from colleagues.[9] Nine staff (16 per cent) said that other staff were obviously racist, sometimes towards them. This might manifest itself in 'banter' or offensive statements or insinuations:

> Jokes and banter from colleagues which is very wearing. There is a long way to go, [the] anti-racist message [is] burying the racist mindset not changing it.

> Two white male officers said in the presence of prisoners 'you know where she's going', implying I was having an affair with a particular black prisoner. I found this deeply upsetting because it was tainting my professional name and standing amongst the prisoners.

> ... some officers would blatantly describe prisoners as silver backs, niggers and jigaboos.

Thirteen (22 per cent) staff said they had experienced more 'indirect' racism from colleagues, whereby racist attitudes were apparent from things that staff said or the way they acted.

> When I was receiving training, a colleague was talking about black people, forgot himself and said 'the Niggers ...' He apologised and said he had black friends so he was not racist.

> The use of stereotypes by colleagues at meetings is not challenged by managers, e.g. Jamaicans are Yardies.

> There is a general 'feeling' from some colleagues, but it is hard to put your finger on what it is that they are doing – and certainly nothing that could be backed up with evidence.

> The job of senior officer was advertised ... I got the post and it was reported to me that other officers were saying that I only got the job because I'm black – 'They've got a woman, now they need a black'. They thought I got the job because of my colour and not my ability. It made me so angry, I challenged them about it but they denied saying it.

While sometimes the action taken against staff behaving in an identifiably racist manner was robust, BME staff often suggested that the 'underlying' problems of racism were not being addressed. What effective action against such undercurrents of racism might look like was, however, difficult for staff to identify. If they were referring to the general culture or 'feel' of their workplace, as seems likely, this lack of specificity and clarity is unsurprising. This is a question which might usefully be further explored in future research on the views of BME prison staff.

Sixty-two per cent of BME staff said they dealt differently with black and Asian prisoners, usually citing the fact that BME prisoners were more likely to approach them because they felt they could better empathise with them than with a white member of staff. Although this was seen as a strength in some establishments, it was perceived as something that could increase the vulnerability of BME staff to suspicion and malicious allegations. Some expressed concern over possibly alienating white colleagues whose support they needed to progress professionally. A number of BME prisoners also suggested that BME staff took an exaggeratedly firm approach towards them for this reason, and some BME staff did suggest that they were under pressure to distance themselves from BME prisoners. One BME officer commented that 'staff see me talking to black inmates and they see it as a problem'. In one prison, a number of BME staff said they were not motivated towards promotion because of the possible consequences of suspicions of collusion. One commented:

> BME officers don't want promotion because they feel they will be targeted on trumped up charges and get dismissed because there seems to be a history of this.

For those who did want to be promoted, there was a perception of problems in getting the experience, training and encouragement necessary to achieve progress:

> If you're not in the clique, you don't hear about these things. In terms of promotion – no black staff have ever been promoted into a managerial position here.

> I've not been encouraged to go for promotion, my contemporaries who joined the civil service at the same time have much more senior positions because they've gone elsewhere and had promotion.

There was a general lack of understanding or insight on the part of some white staff into the perspective of staff and prisoners from minority ethnic groups, consistent with the paradigm of 'parallel worlds'. It was notable that many white staff described feelings of defensiveness and of being victimised by a race relations agenda which they perceived as casting them in the role of 'bad guys'. This is clearly something that needs recognition in training courses as it will ultimately undermine progress towards race equality. For BME staff, the impact of racism from colleagues was considerable and appeared to exceed the distress that was felt as a result of prisoner racism. One officer mentioned the fact that colleagues would ignore him and were 'very careful around you ... scared of saying the wrong thing so [they] don't say anything'. An officer who had experienced direct racist abuse from a colleague had been deeply affected:

> I often think about leaving the Prison Service, my home life is affected, I don't know what to do. My aim was to keep a low profile and to blend in but I can't handle what I am now encountering.

Racism from prisoners

Twenty-one (36 per cent) BME staff said they had experienced racism from prisoners and all but one reported direct verbal abuse or name calling. Only one interviewee said that racism from prisoners was 'indirect', manifesting itself when 'prisoners ... go to colleagues and ask for things, [but] won't ask me'. BME staff were also vulnerable to behaviour from BME prisoners with a similar heritage, which seemed designed to undermine their professionalism and to unsettle and rile them:

> If I am smoking, I get yelled at by some Asian prisoners saying: 'What's your family going to say?' I also feel that my personal life is constantly being drawn into discussions with the prisoners asking about my cultural background.

The emotional energy and maturity required to deal with such goading is clearly considerable. The challenge is not only to professional status, but also to personal identity. It is not something that can easily be prepared for, and requires ongoing support for staff who have to face it, a role filled to some extent by RESPECT (see below). There was an unusually strong sense of professional understanding from some staff about the stress that prisoners were under. In some cases perhaps too much effort was made to excuse or deny the reality of racist abuse. BME staff often referred to 'silly comments from prisoners'. One stated:

> I have been called racist names by some prisoners in the past but it doesn't hurt me. If they would hit me then that wouldn't be OK. You need broad shoulders. It is human nature to start name calling if people get angry enough.

Tackling racism

All racist incidents should be recorded on a racial incident reporting form, but less than a third of BME staff in the HMIP study (n = 12: 31.5 per cent) who had encountered racism said they had completed racist incident reporting forms about their experiences. Only three staff said they had submitted forms complaining about the behaviour of colleagues. Six (27 per cent) officers stated that they had no confidence in the complaints system, with one commenting that 'I would not fill one in as I have no confidence that it would be looked at objectively and I feel that it would backfire on me if I did'.

More BME staff in prisons can increase the legitimacy of prison among BME prisoners and is desirable for that reason alone. Available statistics on current promotion and retention shows a worrying if slightly improving picture. According to the analysis done by Peart and Le-Faye (2005), there is a significant association between attrition rates of prison staff and ethnicity. The leaving rate of BME staff (excluding healthcare and headquarter staff) over the period April 2004–March 2005 was 9.1 per cent, compared to 6.2 per cent among white staff, a differential of 2.9 percentage points. BME staff left the service at higher rates within every grade group analysed. With regard to new recruits, 19 per cent of BME staff left within the first year of service, compared to 15 per cent of white recruits.

Meanwhile, the milestone key performance indicator target for BME staff representation in 2005–6 was not met (6 per cent); on 31 March 2006 it was 5.73 per cent, a shortfall of 133 staff. At a senior level, the dearth of BME governing governors is well known. However, the promotion rate of BME staff into principal officer and senior operational manager D grades is higher than for white staff, although at the stage of promotion into manager F jobs the rate is higher for white staff (Prison Service Annual Staff Ethnicity Review 2005/6).

In any event, a more diverse prison staff does not in itself guarantee a positive environment or equate to progress on race relations issues. Indeed, the push to achieve diversity targets may encourage abuses: one white member of staff interviewed for the HMIP research, who was identified as BME on the prison's personnel list, claimed that a governor at his previous establishment had cynically asked him to: 'change ethnic code from White British as it would be better for promotion and protect against racist complaints'.

Even in prisons with substantial numbers of BME staff, there was considerable discontent among prisoners about treatment by staff and no room for complacent assumptions about equality. The HMIP report highlighted how BME staff were disillusioned with the support and direction delivered by management and were experiencing subtle forms of racism from both colleagues and management. Managers need to break free of the 'colour blind' approach to staff management as there is obviously a difference in the way that BME staff view their roles and the prison environment. There needs to be a move towards an approach that strives for genuinely equal treatment achieved through recognition of difference and a multidimensional approach to understanding the prison environment from the stance of minorities.

To this end, the future shape of training is important. The case for a more professionalised Prison Service with a code of ethics which describes professional values for prison staff was made at a recent international conference on 'New Models for Training Prison Staff', which was organised jointly by the Council of Europe, the Hungarian Prison Administration and the International Centre for Prison Studies at King's College, University of London. The conference also noted the importance of training delivered at academic and practical levels, which leads to a recognised qualification (see: http://www.kcl.ac.uk/depsta/rel/icps/files/newmodel.rtf).

Edgar and Roberts's (2005) study on RESPECT – the black and minority ethnic prison staff support network – broadly supported the findings of the HMIP study. They found that members of RESPECT felt that 'direct and blatant forms of racism have become less frequent, and that covert and structural forms are the main concern' (p. iv). A prominent form of perceived 'structural' discrimination was in relation to promotion and job prospects, and the first four recommendations made by the authors were about promotion. They included the Prison Service making public ethnic monitoring data on career progression, and RESPECT providing a mentoring scheme for full members.[10]

Over 60 per cent of full members (i.e. BME staff) interviewed said they had experienced some form of racism. They were more likely to report racism or discrimination from colleagues than associate members, and were less likely than associate members (i.e. BME staff) to identify prisoners as a source of racism. However, only 40 per cent of those who said they had experienced racial discrimination reported it. Edgar and Roberts concluded the following from this:

> This suggests that the HMPS working environment does not enable people to be open about their perceptions of racism. If in addition to this low reporting rate there is evidence of a lack of trust in how complaints are handled, then it would be important for RESPECT (and HMPS) to develop ways of encouraging more staff to report incidents. (p. 60)

Conclusions

There is an emerging sense from the limited research of the multifaceted role that BME staff must perform in the prison environment. In the HMIP review, they described pressure from some BME prisoners to give them more favourable treatment and pressure from other staff to demonstrate that they were not colluding. They were forced to balance their identities as BME people with cultural similarities and sympathies with BME prisoners, with their identities as prison officers who need to establish and maintain clear professional boundaries and who can progress in their careers. While all prison staff have to fulfil a range of complex roles, an added dimension is therefore apparent for BME staff.

Taking the analysis a step further, ethnic identities are bound up with other sources of identity such as gender, age, class, religion and sexuality, and each creates pressures on BME staff that should be acknowledged. Phillips and Bowling (2003) have argued that race and ethnicity cannot be removed from a historical context; society has constructed categories to define individuals based on 'race', predominantly placing Aryan and whites at the top of the hierarchy over time in order to justify colonialism and slavery. The result of these practices has led to the exclusion of minority groups socially, economically and politically. While there has been much progress, it would be remiss to exclude the historical context within which individuals reside in society today (Phillips and Bowling 2005).

This chapter has highlighted the complex role performed by BME prison officers and the particular challenges they face in the prison system. The HMIP research has to some extent uncovered the *feelings* of BME staff, something that has not been significantly addressed in previous literature. It has highlighted that the main source of racism and its associated stresses is not prisoners but colleagues, a disturbing fact given that BME staff are being recruited in greater numbers as part of the Prison Service action plan agreed with the CRE to promote racial equality. The emotional stresses on BME staff, including conflicts of loyalty and identity, are complex and the need to put greater investment into supporting them is clear. This is not least because, as the figures given above suggest, unless BME staff believe they are part of a service that values them, they will not stay.

Seminar questions

1 Is the experience of working in prisons significantly better for BME staff now than it was 20 years ago, and if so, why?
2 How does the function and history of prisons affect the working experience of BME prison staff?

3 How can BME prison staff address racism by prisoners?
4 How can BME staff address racism by staff?
5 What role can or should prison management and staff organisations play in promoting positive change? What help do they need from policy-makers to ensure progress?

Recommended reading

Mr Justice Keith's (2006) *Report of the Zahib Mubarek Inquiry* into the racist murder at HMYOI Feltham in 2000 has been compared by some to the Stephen Lawrence Inquiry for the Metropolitan Police. It is an essential starting point for anyone considering the issues of race in prisons. The most recent research was completed for the HM Inspectorate of Prisons Thematic Review (2005) *Parallel Worlds*, which provides research, analysis and recommendations regarding the experience of black and minority ethnic staff and prisoners.

Notes

1 In the HM Inspectorate of Prisons report, as the aim was to identify people likely to experience racism or racial discrimination in prison because of their skin colour, the term 'visible minority' was used. However, this chapter will use the more encompassing term 'black and minority ethnic' (BME).
2 Personal communication with official responsible for developing that policy.
3 Ethnic monitoring in prison uses a range-setting formula to interpret, with 95 per cent confidence, whether prisoners from black and minority ethnic groups are fairly represented within the activity in question. This is interpreted by calculating whether the proportions of minority ethnic prisoners in any activity are within the range expected for the size of activity and the size of the BME population in the prison.
4 Private sector prisons are lagging behind in the implementation of protective race relations structures. See, for example, HMIP (2005a: 24).
5 It is notable that in December 2005 the CRE declined to sign up to a further action plan as a result of poor progress on race equality in a number of establishments.
6 One of the key performance targets is an operational indicator that incorporates the results of the race relations audits, ethnic monitoring, prisoner and staff surveys, and the management of racial complaints. The other looks at a staff race equality audit, staff complaints, the percentage of BME staff and the percentage in contact roles on the prison landings.

7 The prison population exceeded 80,000 in early 2007 and pressure on spaces meant that contingency plans were activated to make use of both police and court cells. In June 2007, an early release scheme was introduced to try to manage the prison population crisis.

8 See HMIP (2005b) for a more detailed discussion of methodology.

9 The RESPECT study (Edgar and Roberts 2005) showed that 153 out of 220 (70 per cent) staff had experienced racial discrimination at work, 76 (35 per cent) of whom were BME.

10 'Full' members are BME staff and 'associate' members are white staff who support the aims of RESPECT.

References

Alfred, R. (1992) *Black Workers in the Prison Service*. London: Prison Reform Trust.

Burnett, R. and Farrell, G. (1994) *Reported and Unreported Racial Incidents in Prisons*, Occasional Paper No. 14. Oxford: University of Oxford Centre for Criminological Research.

Carlen, P. (2002) 'Women's Imprisonment: Models of Reform and Change', *Probation Journal*, 49 (2): 76-87.

Cheliotis, L.K. and Liebling, A. (2006) 'Race matters in British Prisons', *British Journal of Criminology*, 46 (2): 286–317.

Commission for Racial Equality (CRE) (2003a) *The Murder of Zahid Mubarek: A Formal Investigation by the Commission for Racial Equality into HM Prison Service of England and Wales. Part 1*. London: CRE.

Commission for Racial Equality (2003b) *A Formal Investigation by the Commission for Racial Equality into HM Prison Service of England and Wales. Part 2: Race Equality in Prisons*. London: CRE.

Commission for Racial Equality and HM Prison Service (2003) *Implementing Race Equality in Prisons: A Shared Agenda for Change*. London: CRE.

Crawley, E.M. (2004) 'Emotion and Performance. Prison officers and the presentation of self in prisons', *Punishment and Society*, 6 (4): 411–27.

Edgar, K. and Martin, C. (2004) *Perceptions of Race and Conflict: Perspectives of Minority Ethnic Prisoners and of Prison Officers*, Home Office On-line Report 11/04.

Edgar, K. and Roberts, L. (2005) *RESPECT Five Years On. A Prison Reform Trust Study of the Effectiveness of RESPECT: The Prison Service Minority Ethnic Staff Support Network*. London: Prison Reform Trust

Ellis, T., Tedstone, C. and Curry, D. (2004) *Improving Race Relations in Prisons: What Works?*, Home Office Online Report 12/04. London: Home Office.

Genders, E. and Player, E. (1989) *Race in Prisons*. Oxford: Clarendon Press.

HM Inspectorate of Prisons (2004) *Annual Report*. London: Home Office.

HM Inspectorate of Prisons (2005a) *Annual Report*. London: Home Office.

HM Inspectorate of Prisons (2005b) *Parallel Worlds. A Thematic Review of Race Issues in the Prison Service*. London: Home Office.

HM Prison Service (2006) *Annual Staff Ethnicity Review 2005–2006*. London: Home Office.

Hogan, N.L., Lambert, E.G., Jenkins, M. and Wambold, S. (2006) 'The Impact of Occupational Stressors on Correctional Staff Organisational Commitment: A Preliminary Study', *Journal of Contemporary Criminal Justice*, 22 (1): 44–62.

Houchin, R. (2003) 'Significant change is likely in our prisons. The question is, change in what direction?', *Probation Journal*, 50 (2): 142–8.

Keith, Mr Justice (2006) *Report of the Zahid Mubarek Inquiry, Volumes 1 and 2*. London: Stationery Office.

Liebling, A. and Price, D. (2001) *The Prison Officer*. Leyhill: HM Prison Service.

McDermott, K. (1990) 'We Have No Problem: The Experience of Racism in Prison', *New Community*, 16 (2): 213–28.

NACRO (2000) *Race in Prisons: A Snapshot Survey*. London: NACRO.

Peart, D. and Le-Faye, P. (2005) *Staff Ethnicity Quarterly Review*. HM Prison Service.

Phillips, C. and Bowling, B. (2003) 'Racism, Ethnicity and Criminology: Developing Minority Perspectives', *British Journal of Criminology*, 43: 269–90.

Philips, C. and Bowling, B. (2005) 'Facing Inwards and Outwards? Institutional Racism, Race Equality and the Role of Black and Asian Professional Associations', in *Criminal Justice*, 5 (4): 357–77.

Thompson, N. (2001) *Anti-Discriminatory Practice*, 3rd edn. Basingstoke: Palgrave.

Wilson, D. (2004) '"Keeping Quiet" or "Going Nuts": Strategies Used by Young Black Men in Custody', in *Howard Journal*, 43 (3): 317–30.

Chapter 5

Prison officers and gender

Sarah Tait[1]

This chapter discusses the relevance of gender to the experience, perceptions and effects of prison officer work. Some twenty years have passed since the introduction of 'cross-posting', and the implications for officer relationships with each other and with prisoners are largely unexplored. Studies on gender and prison staff have tended to focus on questions of the relative competence of male and female officers rather than how gender shapes the accomplishment and experience of prison work. Apart from privacy concerns for women prisoners, little research has addressed male officer work in female prisons. There has been a dependence on surveys and measures of perception rather than qualitative inquiry, such that the role of the institutional environment, or culture, has been missing in the analysis of gender in prison officer work.

In addition to a review of the literature, this chapter reports on findings from two related studies: a survey of over one thousand prison officers in the UK and ongoing qualitative research on prison officer culture in one male and one female prison. Many consistencies in male and female officer perceptions of quality of life were found in both studies, supporting the idea that prison culture may be more important than gender in shaping officer experience. However, gender was a salient issue in some areas of prison officer work. There was evidence of exclusion of women officers by male officers in prisons for men. Officer gender was most relevant to work with prisoners in situations where extreme vulnerability was present (for example, self-harm), and where a particular quality of care was needed. The division of labour between male and female officers in male and female prisons was uneven, and women officers carried the main burden of care. Finally, the sex of the prisoner had important implications for the ability of male and female officers to set boundaries with prisoners and cope with the emotional effects of doing prison officer work.

Cross-posting

In 2005, just over 20 per cent of the 20,000 main grade prison officers employed by the Prison Service of England and Wales were women. The proportion of women employed as officers has risen steadily in recent years due to a rise in the proportion of women working in prisons for men (13 per cent in 1999 to nearly 18 per cent in 2005) and the expansion of the female prison estate. The number of women in prison in England and Wales has risen by about 65 per cent since June 2000 to around 4,248 in January 2006.[2] Accordingly, the number of prison officers employed in female prisons has risen by 27 per cent to almost 1,500. The proportion of male officers working in women's prisons has remained about the same (about one-third) over this period.[3]

Most of the literature on gender and prison officers is concerned with perceptions and experiences of women officers in male prisons following the introduction of cross-posting in English and Welsh prisons in 1982. Initially, only 138 officers were given opposite-sex postings, in limited circumstances. In 1988, cross-posting was broadened to include most duties except for strip searching (Enterkin 1996). In the US, a 1972 amendment to the Civil Rights Act that prohibited sex discrimination by state and local governments enabled women to work in male prisons. Again, this was at first limited to non-contact positions and minimum and medium security institutions, but by 1991 women were allowed to work in maximum security federal prisons (Alarid and Cromwell 2002: 187).

Interest in men working in female prisons has largely been confined to the adverse impact on vulnerable women prisoners with histories of abuse, who may be re-traumatised by invasions of privacy by male officers and left open to sexual victimisation (Chesney-Lind and Pollock 1995: 166). Carlen supported these concerns, but found that women prisoners felt overall that they had benefited from having male staff, whom they portrayed as being less punitive and less petty than female officers in their dealings with inmates (1996: 35). Women prisoners were concerned about the invasion of their privacy regardless of the sex of the officer on patrol.

The privacy rights of male prisoners have generally been subordinated to the rights to equal employment of women officers, with prisoner privacy protected to some degree through the installation of toilet and shower screens (Pollock 1986). Women working in male prisons have met the most resistance from male colleagues rather than from prisoners (Peterson 1982; Hunter 1986; McMahon 1999; Jurik 1985). Researchers have argued that the presence of women in the prison officer role 'disrupts the close association between the prison officer role and the performance of masculinity' (Crawley 2004: 195; see also Crouch 1985; Horne 1985; Owen 1985; Martin and Jurik 1996). Male officers have argued that women's smaller size and lesser strength compromise safety, that women are more vulnerable to sexual assault and that sexual relationships between women officers and male prisoners compromise security (Peterson 1982; Jurik 1985; Zimmer 1986). Women officers have felt 'ignored and shunned or noticed and talked about' (Zimmer 1989: 64). Their mistakes may be excessively scrutinised, and they tend to be judged by the actions and job performance of a minority (Lawrence and Mahan 1998: 66). Zimmer also argues that women officers in male prisons suffer from 'micro-inequities', or forms of discrimination and harassment that are real but too subtle to prove in a court of law. These may include nitpicking, allowing minimal contact with prisoners, impeding prospects for promotions, setting women up for failure, allocating women to unpopular tasks and excluding them from more highly valued tasks (Zimmer 1989: 70; for further discussion of sexual harassment of women officers, see also Pogrebin and Poole 1997; Belknap 1991; Stohr et al. 1998; McMahon 1999).

Recent studies indicate that acceptance of women in male prisons has improved and that women have gained confidence in coping with any resistance they still face. Lawrence and Mahan (1998) found less acceptance of women officers only among older male officers with more experience and men working in maximum security institutions. In their study of cross-gender perceptions of competence in one male and one female prison, Carlson et al. (2004) concluded that the acceptance of women as competent co-workers by male correctional officers within both prisons has improved. Men gave women higher marks at supervision and counselling than they gave themselves. However, women officers seemed to reveal lower confidence in their own abilities, and rated male officers as better at supervising male prisoners and at counselling male and female prisoners. In the UK, Crawley reported that many male officers expressed favourable views towards women officers and found them less threatening to work with (2004: 197). Women officers, particularly those with more Prison Service experience, would not tolerate sexist behaviour from male colleagues, and some used ridicule to assert their dominance among male peers.

Given the barriers that women have faced entering the male prison environment, researchers have been interested in their experience of job stress and satisfaction. Wright and Saylor (1991) reported that while qualitative sources provided evidence of hostility and discrimination, few gender differences were found in survey-reported experiences. In their analysis of the Prison Social Climate Survey, administered to over 3,000 officers working in federal prisons in the US, they found no differences in job satisfaction, but that women reported slightly higher levels of stress. The authors suggested that a sexist environment may cause higher levels of stress in women, that women may feel more at risk of assault or that they may simply be more able to admit to feeling stressed. Fry and Glaser (1987) reported no gender differences on various measures of 'work adjustment', including stress, organisational commitment, evaluation of co-workers and negative impact of the job on self. In their study of prison officer burnout, or loss of care for prisoners due to stress, Carlson et al. (2003) found that women officers reported higher levels of personal accomplishment than men, and suggested that the stressors on women due to the sexist environment reported in earlier studies may have become less relevant since women became more established in men's institutions. Feinman argues that job security, good salaries and benefits and opportunities for promotion are 'strong incentives for women to seek careers in corrections despite the irregular work schedules, the locked-in culture, and the low status of correctional work' (1994: 169–70). Others contend that just as other women in non-traditional work typically enjoy higher levels of job satisfaction, the stress faced by female officers may be ameliorated by the content and income of prison officer work (Wright and Saylor 1991: 508). As flexible shift patterns become the norm in the UK with central detailing being replaced by 'team-based self-rostering' schemes, where staff on each wing sign up for preferred shifts, the ability to manage childcare and family commitments has been improved.

Do women and men do prison officer work differently?

Studies that have aimed to evaluate through self-report questionnaires whether women and men accomplish prison officer work in different ways have generally concluded that there are little, if any, gender differences, and that the influence of occupational culture may be more important. Zupan (1986) detected few substantive differences in the perceptions and attitudes of prison officers and found that men and women officers misidentified prisoner needs in similar ways. Jurik and Halemba (1984) found no difference in punitiveness and concluded that women were no more sensitive to prisoner needs than men. Jenne and Kersting (1998) uncovered no gender differences in the use of reciprocity (defined as overlooking minor rule violation) in men and women officers, and reported that all officers used this selectively.

Women and men may perceive themselves as having different supervisory styles, with women described as having a more personalised, human service approach to prisoners (Crouch 1985; Jurik and Halemba 1984; Pollock 1986; Zimmer 1986; Farkas 1999; Carslon *et al.* 2004). Britton reported that men working in female prisons traditionally have taken on more of the work related to the control and management of violence (2003: 143), while women have been expected to provide a more maternal function. Pollock hypothesised that although individual men and women have unique approaches to the officer role and that the institutional context may influence gendered differences, 'there may be broad difference that can be defined as a *masculine authoritarian approach* and a *feminine personal or caring approach*' (1995: 113; emphasis in original). This hypothesis was based on research on gendered approaches to relationships, where women's relationships are more likely to be care-based, and on research in corporate settings, where women managers tend to reduce the social distance between themselves and other workers to gain compliance (Pollock 1995: 104). Pollock advocated research based on observation of women and men officers rather than self-report in order to tap into the nuances of gendered ways of doing prison officer work.

Some interesting findings support the contention that women and men accomplish prison officer work differently. Farkas (1999) found that both sexes responded similarly in confrontational situations, particularly in situations where training would override any personal decision-making (for example, when an officer is assaulted). However, women tended to report that they would resort to formal authority more often, preferring to 'write-up' a prisoner rather than talk out a resolution, and they were less likely to report that they would use themselves as a physical threat to support another officer, preferring to watch from a distance. Women were cautious not to challenge the authority of their male colleagues. Similarly, Jenne and Kersting (2002) found that women officers tended to state that they would respond more aggressively in particular situations, although for the most part they would handle aggressive encounters in ways ' resembling those of male prison officers. Both studies concluded that differences were attributable to experience and confidence working with prisoners and the need to prove oneself as a female officer and not appear a 'pushover'. Institutional sexism rather than gender role differences appeared to be at the root of these reported differences between women and men. These studies address only situations of confrontation and aggression rather than those where care and personal involvement may be called for, leaving assumptions about women officers adopting a more human service orientation with prisoners in distress untested. Some evidence from the studies reviewed above points to possible bases for greater care by women officers. According to Wright and Saylor (1991), although women perceived themselves to be less safe than their male colleagues, they perceived the prison environment to be safer than men did. If women officers perceive male prisoners to be less dangerous, they may be more able to see them as humans in need of compassion and care. In addition, Fry and Glaser (1987) found that women officers rated services for prisoners lower than male officers did, suggesting that women officers have higher standards for services for prisoners.

The studies

The first study did not set out to examine issues of gender, but the data collected provided a rich source of prison officer views in England and Wales which could be analysed for differences between women and men. As part of an evaluation of new suicide prevention procedures in twelve local prisons, 532 main grade officers were surveyed in 2002 and another 501 in 2004.[4] The survey instrument used in this project was designed to measure staff quality of life and to capture attitudes towards prisoners at risk of suicide, attitudes towards suicide prevention and the impact of working with self-harm and suicide. This version of the Staff MQPL (Measuring the Quality of Prison Life) survey was developed using focus groups with staff and prisoners to identify what matters in prison (Liebling and Arnold 2004). The survey included demographic data (such as gender, age, rank and length of service), and staff were asked to agree or disagree with a list of 109 statements about the quality of their working lives using a 1–5 Likert scale. The dimensions with acceptable reliability scores over .70 in 2002 and 2004 are listed in Table 5.1 and include views on job satisfaction, safety and management. Many individual items pertaining to views on working with prisoners who self-harm did not form reliable dimensions, but have been included in this analysis as stand-alone items. The sample included staff working in eight adult male prisons (n = 713), two male young offender institutions (n = 194), and two women's prisons (n = 126). The prisons were selected in consultation with the Prison Service as those with higher than expected suicide rates and as such are not representative of prisons in England and Wales or even of local prisons. Most were known as 'difficult' prisons in poor physical condition with entrenched traditional staff cultures and highly vulnerable populations. The following discussion of gender and officer work is situated in this context and may be limited in its applicability to prison officer work across the Prison Service.

Surveys were administered during full staff meetings following a brief introduction to the research. This method ensured a high completion rate, with only a few people choosing not to fill in the questionnaire at each meeting as staff were given dedicated time off the wings to complete the survey. Administering surveys in this way carried the risk that officers completing the survey in a group of

Table 5.1 Staff MQPL dimensions

Dimensions	Cronbach's α	
	2002	2004
Relationships with senior management	.94	.93
Work culture/climate	.89	.87
Perception of the Prison Service	.86	.86
Commitment to the prison and Prison Service	.91	.90
Relationships with peers	.89	.88
Relationships with line management	.89	.91
Treatment by line management	.88	.87
Job satisfaction	.86	.85
Role and responsibility	.82	.81
Communication	.72	.68
Distribution of power	.86	.88
Safety/control/security	.82	.83
Relationships with prisoners	.80	.80
Perceived suicide prevention effectiveness	.73	.75

their peers may have responded in similar ways, thereby minimising gender effects. The following results may therefore be considered conservative estimates of differences in perceptions of men and women officers.

The second study was developed as an extension of this project to look more closely at gender, officer culture and care for prisoners.[5] Preliminary analysis of fieldwork notes and interview summaries from 51 officers form the basis of the discussion here. Eleven women officers and 17 male officers at HMP Leeds in Yorkshire, and twelve female and eleven male officers at HMP Eastwood Park in Gloucestershire, were interviewed. Interviewees were recruited opportunistically but achieved a spread of gender, age, length of service and orientations to discipline and care. Participants were asked about pathways into the job, early experiences, important moments, stress and job satisfaction, and experiences with and views on care for prisoners. They were also asked direct questions about gender and working life. The analysis also draws from 'reading' gender from stories and examples that officers gave during their interviews, from observations on the wings and from noting trends in how men and women felt about their work. Interviews were supplemented with shadowing and observation of most of these officers.

Most research on prison officer work has been based in male prisons, or has considered officer experiences in male and female prisons together. There are several reasons for considering the conditions, experiences and outcomes of working with male and female prisons separately. Zupan has argued that research into gender differences should address 'the role that the structural features of the prison organization play in affecting the job orientations of female and male officers' (1992: 339). Women's prisons hold prisoners of all security classifications in one facility; this creates problems in discipline and difficulty in classifying prisoners along either treatment or custody lines (Pollock 1995: 98). Supervising women is reported to be more difficult because women prisoners expect more personal support from officers and are more open in their emotions (Pollock 1986). Imprisonment affects men and women differently: women experience more loss and insecurity while in prison due to their central role in the family (Bosworth 1999; Kruttschnitt 2005); women receive fewer visits; and women coming into prison show higher proportions of vulnerability, including mental illness, drug use and histories of abuse, self-harm and suicide attempts (Liebling et al. 2005). The high level of vulnerability and engagement with women prisoners means that the demands and experience of working in a female prison are qualitatively different from working in a male prison. Observations from the current study suggested that many features of working with prisoners differed in the male and female prison. The staff–prisoner balance of power favoured staff at Leeds, while women prisoners at Eastwood Park were more able to influence officers and the regime by forming strong bonds with one another and working as a group to exert power. Women prisoners were more interested in the staff as people, and were more open about their emotions and opinions. Control tended to be exercised through displays of emotion in the women's prison: officers could rely on expressions of anger or disapproval to promote compliance among prisoners, while at the men's prison, more formal systems of warnings, informal removal of time out of cell and threats of force were the norm. Given these structural differences between male and female prisons, findings presented in this chapter consider male and female prisons separately.

Gender and prison officer quality of life

Table 5.2 summarises the dimensions where significant gender differences were found in officer views of their quality of life in 2002 and in 2004. Of 14 quality of life dimensions, consistent and significant gender differences over time were found on only five. Differences between average male and female officer scores were small, suggesting that overall, male and female officers evaluated their quality of life in similar ways.

Mean dimension scores on a scale of 1 to 5, where 3 is a neutral score, are reported. Note that a higher score indicates a more positive evaluation. Women officers reported significantly higher scores than men did on four measures of their quality of life: 'Relationships with senior management', 'Perception of the Prison Service', 'Commitment' (a measure of commitment and loyalty to the prison and Prison Service) and 'Job satisfaction'. Male officers scored significantly higher than women did on the dimension 'Relationship with peers', although scores for both women and men were high. To explore these dimensions further, the 2004 data set was more closely examined to take into account factors such as length of service and type of prison (holding male or female prisoners), where theoretically relevant. ANOVA results are summarised in Tables A5.1 to A5.6 in the appendix to this chapter and discussed below.

Table 5.2 Officer gender differences on quality of life dimensions in 2002 and 2004

Dimension	2002			2004		
	Mean score men (n=407)	Mean score women (n=122)	t	Mean score men (n=386)	Mean score women (n=113)	t
Relationships with senior management	2.71	2.90	2.17*	2.87	3.02	2.02*
Perception of Prison Service	2.53	2.91	4.99***	2.72	2.99	3.32***
Commitment to prison and Prison Service	3.09	3.36	2.81**	3.27	3.49	2.47*
Job satisfaction	2.98	3.27	3.44***	3.09	3.29	2.34*
Relationship with peers	3.93	3.76	–3.16**	3.95	3.77	–3.00**

The above mean comparisons used independent samples t-tests (*$p < .05$; **$p < .01$; ***$p < .001$).

Orientations towards management

This data was collected in traditional local prisons with a high proportion of long-serving male staff who were often described as holding the most entrenched and vocal anti-management views. The results of two-way unrelated ANOVAs showed that significant effects were found for length of service on the dimensions 'Relationships with senior management' ($F_{1,494} = 24.1$, $p = .000$), 'Perception of the Prison Service' ($F_{1,493} = 47.0$, $p = .000$) and 'Commitment' ($F_{4,488} = 5.30$, $p = .000$), but not for officer sex or for the interactions between sex and length of service. These findings strengthen the argument that women and men share similar views on their quality of life, particularly towards management structures, and that ostensible differences in their reported attitudes relate to other factors. This is unsurprising given the hierarchical nature of the Prison Service, the 'us–them' approach towards managers and the overarching bureaucracy that is an entrenched part of prison officer culture. The longer officers of either sex remained in the job, the more cynical they became. Indeed, interviews also revealed little difference between men and women officers in their attitudes towards management. Most felt a large gap between their work as they saw it and the goals and workings of their managers and the wider Prison Service. Men and women officers expressed equally emotional views on any criticism they had received from managers and the perceived lack of appreciation for the work they did.

Job satisfaction

Many officers in my study who had experience of working in women's prisons reported a higher degree of involvement with women prisoners. It was therefore hypothesised that greater job satisfaction would be found among officers in the women's prisons in this sample, and that the greater number of women working in the women's prisons could account for the higher level of job satisfaction reported by women in the quality of life survey.

No gender differences remained once length of service and the type of prison (holding male or female prisoners) were taken into account. Officers with more than four years of service reported lower scores on 'Job satisfaction' (M = 3.18, SD = .80) than those with less than four years of service (M = 3.49, SD = .65) ($F_{1,482}$ = 6.10, p = .014). Furthermore, officers working in women's prisons (M = 3.48, SD = .70) reported more job satisfaction than those working in men's prisons (M = 3.19, SD = .80) ($F_{1,482}$ = 5.30, p = .022). No significant effect was found for prison officer sex or for any interactions.

Peer relationships: The integration of women officers in a male prison

In interviews at HMP Leeds, many women officers acknowledged that sexual harassment occurred but denied that it was a problem in the prison or that it affected them negatively. They reported having developed a thick skin, having become skilled at and used to brushing things off or 'giving as good as they get'. Younger women often enjoyed flirtation and horseplay with male colleagues. Sexist and sexual banter was accepted as part of the job, unlikely to change and something to adapt to rather than resist.

Women found other aspects of sexism in the workplace more problematic. They felt excluded from Control and Restraint procedures, yet under pressure to prove their ability to control prisoners and scrutinised when dealing with resistant prisoners, particularly early on in their careers. Some described being left alone to deal with escalating incidents while being watched from afar by several male officers. In these situations, they felt 'tested' and hesitated to raise their voice or call for assistance. A few women expressed frustration with the assumption of some male officers that their family concerns would interfere with their job performance. They were aware of criticism if they had to leave work for a family emergency or if they arranged to do part-time work.

The situation in the women's prison was different. There was a more even distribution between the sexes in the use of force and discipline, and exclusion of male or female officers as a group was not evident. As such, only the dataset from male prisons was considered for the dimension 'Peer relationships'. This dimension was viewed as a measure of how integrated and accepted women officers felt by their peers, as it contained items on feeling trusted, respected and treated fairly by peers. Figure 5.1 shows the relationship between officer sex, length of service and peer relationships. There was less variation over

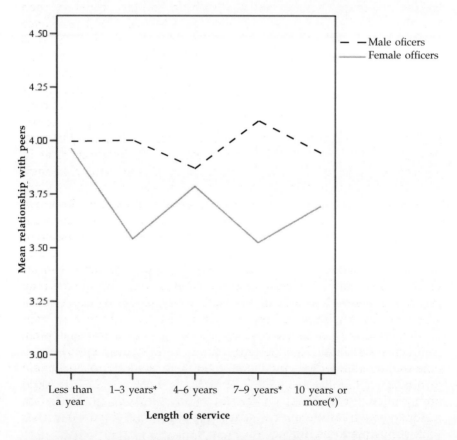

Note: Results of independent samples t-tests of differences between male and female officers at each level of service are indicated (* $p < .05$; (*) $p = .053$)

Figure 5.1 'Relationships with peers', gender, and length of service

time for the male officers, and women's and men's scores tended to fluctuate in opposition, so that when male scores increased, women's decreased, indicating very different career patterns of camaraderie and inclusion for men and women. After starting out with very positive evaluations of peer relationships on a par with their male colleagues, women's scores dropped after one year, and were significantly lower than men's ($t = 2.55$, $p = .013$). They recovered in the 4–6 year service category, perhaps as women gained confidence through experience, and no difference was found ($t = .572$, $p = .569$) but scores dropped again in the 7–9 year category (however, this was a small category for both men and women, comprising only 21 men and five women). The largest group, which contained about 60 per cent of the sample, had served ten or more years in the Prison Service. Scores for men and women appear to converge; however, there was still a difference approaching statistical significance between men and women ($t = 2.02$, $p = .053$).

This data supports the finding from the qualitative research that some women officers in male prisons feel socially and professionally excluded, particularly at *certain stages* of their career. Many officers, men and women, cited the camaraderie of the training programme as one of the best aspects of joining the Prison Service, and this may account for the equal positive scores for men and women new in service. The significant drop in perceptions of the quality of their peer relationships by women officers in the early stage of their careers suggests that women officers may feel they need to prove themselves to older male colleagues, particularly in dealings with refractory male prisoners. Perhaps those who survive this phase and do not leave the service go on to enjoy the equivalent high levels of peer support and loyalty reported by the group of women with four to six years of experience. The drop in later years of service may reflect the perceptions described by Crawley (2005) of experienced women officers who were weary of, but used to, a number of long-serving male officers in their midst who were known to make sexist comments and hold disparaging views of women. It is important to note that overall, women evaluated their peer relationships positively in quality of life surveys, and in interviews most women expressed appreciation for the vast experience of longer-serving officers (the majority of whom were men). Their experience provided other staff with security and confidence on the wing.

In summary, few quality of life differences were found between women and men officers in these prisons. Length of service accounted for differences found in job satisfaction and attitudes towards management and the Prison Service. Only evaluations of peer relationships indicated significant differences in experiences according to sex. Integration of women officers in male prisons varied over their career and was most difficult in the early years following training and for the most experienced women officers.

Gender and the accomplishment of prison officer work

This section turns to the question of how male and female officers accomplished their work in male and female prisons, and discusses the division of control and care work, the establishment and maintenance of boundaries with prisoners and the effects of working with prisoners.

Division of labour

Women officers at HMP Leeds tended to take on more formal care work, or were nudged into it by their male colleagues. They tended to express greater personal responsibility for prisoner well-being and derived job satisfaction from this work. Younger women officers reported being nominated to train as an 'ACCT assessor' (to assess self-harm risk and draw up care plans) for their wing, and many women were sitting on committees for race relations or other 'soft' issues. There was openness about this division of labour on the wings. Of course, some women were not interested in this type of work and were vocal about their disinterest. The struggles that caring male officers faced are described below.

Women officers were often excluded from control and restraint (C&R) procedures, as some men felt women officers were less competent and would compromise the safety of their male colleagues. They could name a limited number of women who they felt were 'just like men' in their approach to C&R, but believed that the majority of women could not be relied on in these situations. These men complained that men were burdened with this type of work, while actively excluding women from it. Fewer men felt that women were equally competent and believed that sending three women to restrain a male prisoner would result in a quick resolution, as there was no pride in fighting with female officers. Again, some women officers enjoyed this form of protection and preferred men to deal with use of force and particularly difficult prisoners. More often, however, women described their exclusion as patronising and limiting.

While the care workload was more balanced between women and men at Eastwood Park, women officers still shouldered more of the burden of care. For many women prisoners, there were limits to what they would share with a male officer, and due to past abuse by men in their lives, these women found it difficult to trust men. At the same time, many women missed male company, and valued their interactions with male officers who were kind and respectful. Male officers who were perceived to be caring by prisoners seemed to fall into either a brotherly or fatherly role. The 'joking around' between women prisoners and male officers sometimes grated on some women officers, who felt that male officers maintained more 'friendly' relationships with prisoners by overlooking infractions. Many women officers felt that, in addition to the burden of care, they also were charged with more of the discipline work. However, banter between women prisoners and male officers could serve to build a rapport that led to important interventions with women who were severely distressed or who prolifically self-harmed, and some male officers worked hard to gain the trust of individual prisoners. The extent of care provided by these men was significant, but overall prisoner relationships with male officers had a less intense quality to them than those with women officers. Women officers were more easily trusted and often received the full brunt of prisoners' distress and anger with little warning.

Staff–prisoner boundaries and the effects of prison work

At Eastwood Park, getting the boundaries right was hard for both women and men officers due to the high level of engagement, interaction and support that many prisoners required. Most men seemed to have gone through an intensely difficult early phase of adjusting to the personal bonds that quickly formed with women prisoners by establishing a more distant wing persona. They worried about being gullible, naive and manipulated by prisoners. To maintain their sense of self, they felt they had to say 'no' more and had to ignore the needs of some women. Many young men officers struggled with sexual harassment and joking from women prisoners when they first started, and were also heavily affected by the women's distress. This may have contributed to their quick establishment of distance. Women officers found it harder to establish this protective distance, and exhibited more ambivalence towards prisoners. Many were exhausted and possibly suffering from compassion fatigue. They tended to express more punitive views of the prisoners they worked with, particularly while feeling worn down during long shifts, and were less likely to excuse disruptive or offensive behaviour. More women resented the 'abuse' (including name calling, swearing, resistance to following orders and sometimes physical attack) they experienced from prisoners, while male officers did not take it so personally. There was a sense that men supervising women prisoners held a degree of 'natural authority' and were more easily bemused than offended by insults from prisoners.

At Leeds, where there was considerable social distance between officers and male prisoners, officers who tended to engage with prisoners shared the sense that they were *the same as* the prisoners held there rather than essentially different. They highlighted that they had similar backgrounds and grew up on the same estates as many prisoners in the jail. Caring officers who were working on more traditional wings were overworked and exhausted. Male officers were sometimes experiencing internal conflicts trying to provide care while attempting to conceal it from their peers. Women officers had more cultural permission to engage with prisoners and provide care, and, as mentioned, often took on a large share of this work. However, those who were too explicitly caring or who were seen to do 'too much for prisoners' could also be bullied and excluded. Some more experienced women officers felt that younger women struggled to develop a rapport with prisoners while maintaining privacy and appropriate distance. They were aware of the scrutiny that women officers were under from some male officers who made continual reference to the rare instances when women officers had been found to be in sexual relationships with male prisoners. A few younger female officers tended to take a firm line with prisoners and were accused by them of being 'worse than the men' in their shouting and aggression. They knew they could 'get away with more' because prisoners were unlikely to assault female officers. Finding the balance between exerting authority and engaging with prisoners was difficult for many young women officers at Leeds (see also Crewe 2006).

Working with prisoners who self-harm

In the Safer Locals Evaluation survey, no statistically significant differences were found between male and female officers on most of their perceptions of working with prisoners, such as placing trust in and feeling respected by prisoners. However, significant gender differences were found on two items relating to self-harm. This supports the notion that officer gender matters most in situations

Table 5.3 Prison officer gender differences in items relating to working with prisoners who self-harm in 2002 and 2004

Item	2002		2004	
	Men % agree/ strongly agree (n=407)	Women % agree/ strongly agree (n=122)	Men % agree/ strongly agree (n=386)	Women % agree/ strongly agree (n=113)
'Prisoners who attempt suicide are usually attention-seeking and trying to manipulate the staff'	41	25	41	24
'Dealing with suicide and self-harm by prisoners is extremely stressful'	67	57	71	66

where a particular quality of care is required. Table 5.3 summarises the percentage of men and women officers who agreed or strongly agreed with these statements. Length of service was not found to have a main or interaction effect for either of these items (see Tables A5.5 and A5.6 in the appendix to this chapter for the summary of ANOVA results). However, there were interesting officer and prisoner gender effects and interactions.

Male officers were more likely to agree with the statement, 'Dealing with suicide and self-harm by prisoners is extremely stressful' ($F_{1,487}$ = 6.76, p = .010); that is, women reported coping better with this distressing aspect of prison officer work than men did. In addition, officers in the women's prisons found dealing with self-harm more stressful ($F_{1,487}$ = 6.84, p = .009), which is in line with the higher rates of self-harm and suicide attempts in women's prisons. But there was also a significant interaction effect between officer and prisoner sex ($F_{1,487}$ = 4.254, p = .040). This interaction is displayed in Figure 5.2 (note that higher scores reflect a more positive evaluation, or the experience of less stress). Male officers were more affected by the sex of the prisoner they were working with, finding it particularly stressful to deal with self-harm by women prisoners.

There was no significant difference between men and women officers on the item, 'Prisoners who attempt suicide are attention-seeking and manipulative' ($F_{1,480}$ = .000, p = .985), although

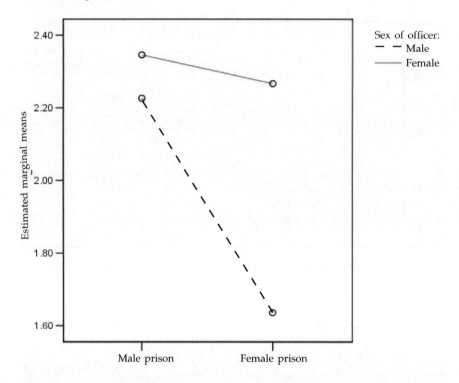

Figure 5.2 'Dealing with suicide and self-harm by prisoners is extremely stressful'

prisoner sex was significant ($F_{1,480}$ = 8.72, p = .003) and there was an interaction effect between officer and prisoner sex ($F_{1,480}$ = 3.79, p = .052). Figure 5.3 depicts this interaction (note that a higher score reflects the perception that prisoners are less manipulative). Prison officers held more sympathetic attitudes towards women prisoners who attempted suicide, and male officers were less likely to believe that suicide attempts by female prisoners were attention-seeking and manipulative. Note that the score for male officers in male prisons was below the neutral score of 3.0, indicating that they held generally unsympathetic attitudes towards suicide attempts by male prisoners.

Women historically have taken on more of the responsibility for care within their relationships and domestic life, and they may be better equipped and more *used to* the experience of becoming emotionally involved with those around them in distress. The findings on male and female attitudes to self-harm support the argument made above that women officers in male and female prisons take on a higher burden of care work. If male officers in female prisons find care work

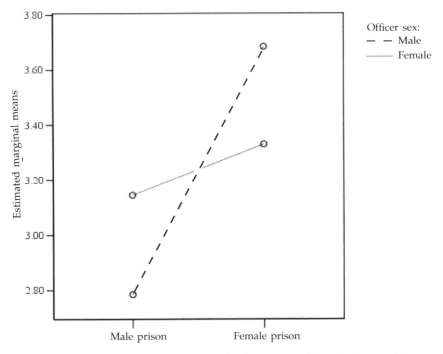

Figure 5.3 'Prisoners who attempt suicide are usually attention-seeking or trying to manipulate the staff'

more stressful, they may seek to avoid it, at least to some extent. In male prisons, on average, male officers report unsympathetic views towards prisoners who attempt suicide and may be more likely to leave this work to women.

Relationships between male officers and female prisoners were often relaxed and 'friendly', perhaps because they did not disrupt the typical power relationships between men and women on the outside. Women prisoners presented little threat to male officer authority. This dynamic was only heightened by the intense and open vulnerability of many women prisoners. Acts of self-harm and attempted suicide are at the extreme end of the expression of distress and despair, and invoked relatively more stress in, and sympathy (and sometimes pity) from, male officers. Women officers, however, were more likely to feel that their authority could be undermined by such acts. This may have modulated the effects of self-harm by women prisoners on women officers. Nonetheless, women officers were still distressed by self-harm, and did not hold punitive views in general about self-harm as attention-seeking and manipulative.

Research directions and policy issues

Future research should incorporate sensitive and nuanced approaches to investigating the role of gender in prison officer work, using both qualitative and quantitative approaches. It is important to consider within-gender differences among male and female officers, and how gender interacts with age and experience in shaping approaches to prison work. Perceptions of both officers and prisoners should be taken into account, and connecting reported attitudes and observed behaviour is a fruitful area of research to further understand how prison culture affects officer work with prisoners.

The research reported on in this chapter is limited in its generalisability, as it took place in Category B local prisons holding constantly changing populations in the early phases of custody with high levels of vulnerability. Gender issues may take a different form in higher performing prisons, higher security prisons, prisons with a more rehabilitative function and prisons with more stable populations, for example. However, several issues raised in this chapter may be relevant to policy-makers throughout the Prison Service. Sexism is still experienced by some women officers in male prisons. Most women who reported these experiences had learned how to cope, but for some the stress this caused had taken its toll. Managers should be aware that in such an environment, where peer loyalty is highly valued and where women often work exceptionally hard to prove themselves, it may be difficult to detect the consequences of subtle and ongoing social and professional exclusion. The tendency for women to take on more duties and hold the burden of care work with prisoners was another dynamic that could place extra stress on women officers. Men and women working in cross-gender postings tended to find establishing appropriate boundaries with prisoners difficult, and some came close to leaving the Prison Service altogether as a result. Some attention should be paid to such difficulties in the training and mentoring of new officers in cross-gender postings. Further, many officers working in women's prisons found their training did not equip them to deal with the specific nature of working in this environment, such as the prevalence of mental illness, the level of prolific self-harm and attempted suicide, and the degree of engagement with prisoners. Again, this calls for appropriate training for officers assigned to work in women's prisons.

While officers working in female prisons have attracted little public and research interest, popular notions about women officers working in male prisons fall into two categories: that they are 'soft' and incapable of standing up to prisoners, or that they are 'power-mad' and relish being in charge of captive men. Women officers faced these assumptions more often from their older male colleagues than from prisoners. To some extent, these assumptions were founded, though they were the outcomes of cultural rather than 'natural' forces. As researchers have hypothesised, women officers did tend to adopt a more caring approach, they were perceived (in general) to be more approachable than male officers and they shouldered the burden of care in male and female prisons. It was also true that some women officers became hostile to prisoners. The cultural pressures women officers were under could foster resentment and alter how they felt about their peers and their work over the course of their career. Between these extremes, however, the majority of women officers were confident, competent and could deliver care without compromising their authority. Equally, male officers faced cultural pressures to be 'hard' and to maintain distance from prisoners. Many battled daily with these pressures and sought to connect with prisoners and provide meaningful care for the vulnerable. These men were in a unique position to work with women prisoners and form new understandings of relationships with the opposite sex.

Appendix: ANOVA results

Table A5.1 Analysis of variance summary table: 'Relationships with senior management'

Source of variation	Sums of squares	Degrees of freedom	Mean square	F-ratio	Probability
sex	4.63	1	4.63	.303	.582
length of service (+/− 4 years)	370	1	370	24.1	.000
sex*length of service	.561	1	.561	.037	.848

Note: The transformation $x \rightarrow x^2$ was applied to the values of this dimension to correct the problem of unequal variances.

Table A5.2 Analysis of variance summary table: 'Perception of the Prison Service'

Source of variation	Sums of squares	Degrees of freedom	Mean square	F- ratio	Probability
sex	.746	1	.746	1.47	.226
length of service (+/– 4 years)	23.8	1	23.8	47.0	.000
sex*length of service	.556	1	.556	1.10	.296

Table A5.3 Analysis of variance summary table: 'Commitment'

Source of variation	Sums of squares	Degrees of freedom	Mean square	F- ratio	Probability
sex	1.498	1	1.50	2.41	.121
length of service	13.151	4	3.29	5.30	.000
sex*length of service	1.774	4	.443	.714	.582

Table A5.4 Analysis of variance summary table: 'Job satisfaction'

Source of variation	Sums of squares	Degrees of freedom	Mean square	F- ratio	Probability
sex	.379	1	.379	.656	.418
length of service	3.53	1	3.53	6.10	.014
sex of prisoner	3.06	1	3.06	5.30	.022
sex*length of service	.005	1	.005	.008	.928
sex*sex of prisoner	.373	1	.373	.646	.422
length of service*sex of prisoner	1.82	1	1.82	3.14	.077
sex*length of service*sex of prisoner	.085	1	.085	.146	.702

Table A5.5 Analysis of variance summary table: 'Dealing with suicide and self-harm by prisoners is extremely stressful'

Source of variation	Sums of squares	Degrees of freedom	Mean square	F-ratio	Probability
sex	5.29	1	5.29	6.79	.010
sex of prisoner	5.35	1	5.35	6.84	.009
length of service	.582	1	.582	.744	.389
sex*sex of prisoner	3.33	1	3.33	4.25	.040
sex*length of service	.626	1	.626	.801	.371
sex of prisoner*length of service	.012	1	.012	.016	.900
sex*sex of prisoner*length of service	1.02	1	1.02	1.30	.255

Table A5.6 Analysis of variance summary table: 'Prisoners who attempt suicide are usually attention-seeking and trying to manipulate the staff'

Source of variation	Sums of squares	Degrees of freedom	Mean square	F-ratio	Probability
sex	.000	1	.000	.000	.985
sex of prisoner	7.99	1	7.99	8.72	.003
length of service	1.19	1	1.19	1.30	.255
sex*sex of prisoner	3.47	1	3.47	3.79	.053
sex*length of service	1.02	1	1.02	1.11	.293
sex of prisoner*length of service	.105	1	.105	.114	.735
sex*sex of prisoner*length of service	.759	1	.759	.828	.363

Seminar questions

1 What might be the implications of different features of the institutional environment for the role of gender in prison officer work? For example, how might officer gender differences vary in rehabilitative environments or in higher security prisons?
2 How do social and historical gender power relations in the wider community shape staff–prisoner relationships in male and female prisons?
3 What are the possible effects of sexism on women officers?
4 Should male and female prisons be studied separately?

Recommended reading

Lynn Zimmer's (1986) *Women Guarding Men* provides a detailed look at the experiences of women officers working in male prisons. Joycelyn Pollock's (1995) chapter, 'Women in Corrections: Custody and the "Caring Ethic"', in Merlo and Pollock (eds) *Women, Law and Social Control*, discusses gender differences in prison officer work and is situated within a collection on women's roles in the criminal justice system, rooting the analysis in socio-historical gender relations. The collection of articles on women officers in Alarid and Cromwell (2002) *Correctional Perspectives: Views from Academics, Practitioners, and Prisoners* offers three interesting perspectives on women officers working in male prisons. Little has been written on male officers working in female prisons, but for a discussion of the role of masculinity in the management of men's prisons, see Carrabine and Longhurst (1998) 'Gender and Prison Organization: Some Comments on Masculinities and Prison Management'.

Notes

1 I would like to thank Ben Crewe and Alison Liebling for their helpful comments on earlier drafts of this chapter.
2 http://www.hmprisonservice.gov.uk/adviceandsupport/prison_life/femaleprisoners
3 Data source: Personnel Corporate Database, HR Planning, HMPS Headquarters.
4 The data used in this analysis is reported on in more detail in Liebling *et al.* (2005).
5 This PhD research conducted by the author began in 2004 and is due to be completed in 2007. The research is independently funded by the Wakefield Foundation (Institute of Criminology, Cambridge University),

the Nightingale Foundation (Trinity Hall, Cambridge University) and an Overseas Research Studentship (Universities UK).

References

Alarid, L. and Cromwell, P. (2002) *Correctional Perspectives: Views from Academics, Practitioners, and Prisoners*. Los Angeles, CA: Roxbury.

Belknap, J. (1991) 'Women in Conflict: An Analysis of Women Correctional Officers', *Women and Criminal Justice*, 2 (2): 89–115.

Bosworth, M. (1999) *Engendering Resistance: Agency and Power in Women's Prisons*. Aldershot: Ashgate Press.

Britton, D.M. (2003) *At Work in the Iron Cage: The Prison as Gendered Organization*. New York: New York University Press.

Carlen, P. (1996) 'Men Working in Women's Prisons', *Prison Service Journal*, 117: 35–7.

Carlson, J., Anson, R. and Thomas, G. (2003) 'Correctional Officer Burnout and Stress: Does Gender Matter?', *Prison Journal*, 83 (3): 277–88.

Carlson, J., Anson, R. and Thomas, G. (2004) 'Cross-gender Perceptions of Correctional Officers in Gender-segregated Prisons', *Journal of Offender Rehabilitation*, 39 (1): 83–103.

Carrabine, E. and Longhurst, B. (1998) 'Gender and Prison Organization: Some Comments on Masculinities and Prison Management', *Harvard Journal*, 37 (2): 161–76.

Chesney-Lind, M. and Pollock, J. (1995) 'Women's Prisons: Equality with a Vengeance', in A. Merlo and J. Pollock (eds), *Women, Law and Social Control*. London: Allyn & Bacon, pp. 155–76.

Crawley, E. (2004) *Doing Prison Work: The Public and Private Lives of Prison Officers*. Cullompton: Willan.

Crewe, B. (2006) 'Male Prisoners' Perceptions of Female Officers in an English Prison', *Punishment and Society*, 8 (4): 395–421.

Crouch, B. (1985) 'Pandora's Box: Women Guards in Men's Prisons', *Journal of Criminal Justice*, 13: 535–48.

Enterkin, J. (1996) 'Female Prison Officers in Men's Prisons'. Unpublished PhD thesis, Cambridge University.

Farkas, M. (1999) 'Inmate Supervisory Style: Does Gender Make a Difference?', *Women & Criminal Justice*, 10 (4): 25–45.

Feinman, C. (1994) *Women in the Criminal Justice System*. London: Praeger.

Fry, L. and Glaser, D. (1987) 'Gender Differences in Work Adjustment of Prison Employees', *Journal of Offender Couseling, Services & Rehabilitation*, 12 (1): 39–52.

Home, P. (1985) 'Female Correctional Officers', *Federal Probation*, 49: 46–54.

Hunter, S.M. (1986) 'On the Line; Working Hard with Dignity', *Corrections Today*, 48 (4): 12–13.

Jenne, D. and Kersting, R. (1998) 'Gender, Power and Reciprocity in the Correctional Setting', *Prison Journal*, 78 (2): 166–85.

Jenne, D. and Kersting, R. (2002) 'Working in a Male-Dominated World: Aggression and Women Correctional Officers', in L. Alarid and P. Cromwell (eds), *Correctional Perspectives: Views from Academics, Practitioners, and Prisoners*. Los Angeles, CA: Roxbury, pp. 197–206.

Jurik, N. (1985) 'An Officer and a Lady: Organizational Barriers to Women Working as Correctional Officers in Men's Prisons', *Social Problems*, 32 (4): 375–88.

Jurik, N. and Halemba, G. (1984) 'Gender, Working Conditions and the Job Satisfaction of Women in a Non-traditional Occupation: Female Correctional Officers in Men's Prison', *Sociological Quarterly*, 25: 551–66.

Kruttschnitt, C. (2005) 'The Politics of Confinement: Women's Imprisonment in California and the UK,' in A. Liebling and S. Maruna (eds), *The Effects of Imprisonment*. Cullompton: Willan, pp. 146–73.

Lawrence, R. and Mahan, S. (1998) 'Women Corrections Officers in Men's Prisons: Acceptance and Perceived Job Performance', *Women & Criminal Justice*, 9 (3): 63–86.

Liebling, A. and Arnold, H. (2004) *Prisons and Their Moral Performance*. Oxford: Oxford University Press.

Liebling, A., Tait, S., Durie, L., Stiles, A. and Harvey, J. (2005) *An Evaluation of the Safer Locals Programme*, Home Office Report. London: Home Office.

McMahon, M. (1999) *Women on Guard: Discrimination and Harassment in Corrections*. London: University of Toronto Press.

Martin, S.E. and Jurik, N.C. (1996) *Doing Justice, Doing Gender*. Thousand Oaks, CA: Sage.

Petersen, C.B. (1982) 'Doing Time with the Boys: An Analysis of Women Correctional Officers in All-male Facilities', in B. Price and N. Sokoloff (eds), *The Criminal Justice System and Women*. New York: Clark Boardman, pp. 437–60.

Pollock, J.M. (1986) *Sex and Supervision: Guarding Male and Female Inmates*. New York: Greenwood Press

Pollock, J.M. (1995) 'Women in Corrections: Custody and the "caring ethic"', in A. Merlo and J. Pollock (eds), *Women, Law and Social Control*. London: Allyn & Bacon, pp. 97–116.

Owen, B. (1985) 'Race and Gender Relations among Prison Workers', *Crime & Delinquency*, 31 (1): 147–59.

Pogrebin, M. and Poole, E. (1997) 'The Sexualized Work Environment: A Look at Women Jail Officers', *Prison Journal*, 77 (1): 41–57.

Stohr, M.K., Mays, G.L., Beck, A.C. and Kelley, T. (1998) 'Sexual Harassment in Women's Jails,' *Journal of Contemporary Criminal Justice*, 14 (24): 135–55.

Wright, K. and Saylor, W. (1991) 'Male and Female Employees' Perceptions of Prison Work: Is There a Difference?' *Justice Quarterly*, 8 (4): 505–24.

Zimmer, L. (1986) *Women Guarding Men*. London: University of Chicago Press.

Zimmer, L. (1989) 'Solving Women's Employment Problems in Corrections: Shifting the Burden to Administrators', *Women and Criminal Justice*, 1 (1): 55–79.

Zupan, L. (1986) 'Gender-Related Differences in Correctional Officers' Perceptions and Attitudes', *Journal of Criminal Justice*, 14: 349–61.

Zupan, L. (1992) 'The Progress of Women Correctional Officers in All-Male Prisons', in I.L. Moyer (ed.), *The Changing Roles of Women in the Criminal Justice System: Offenders, Victims and Professionals*. Prospect Heights, IL: Waveland Press, pp. 323–43.

Chapter 6

Prison staff in the public and private sector

Clare McLean and Alison Liebling

Introduction

The privatisation of prisons has been described as the 'penal experiment of the century', and as 'one of the most important [recent] developments in penal administration' (Harding 2001: 269) but, with a few exceptions, relatively little formal or independent evaluation of its problems and successes has been conducted to date (see James *et al.* 1997; Moyle 1995; Liebling, assisted by Arnold 2004). The two main motivations for privatisation in the UK – increased value for money and improvements to prison staff culture – make it clear that prison staff constitute one of two key experimental variables in this largely sociologically undocumented penal development. The other key variable is management approach and innovation.[1]

It is clear that staff–prisoner relationships are at the heart of prison life (Liebling and Price 2001). It is also the case that 'failures in care and well-being' and weak accountability have been characteristics of the public sector in practice, despite the existence of a clearly stated value base stressing transparency, integrity and public service. In this chapter, we draw on the available literature, on unpublished Home Office and other sources and on comparative quality of life data from staff and prisoners from four private and four matched public sector prisons to explore the following questions:

- Do prison staff in the private sector 'cost less' than in the public sector, and if so, do these cost savings have consequences for staff or prisoner quality of life in prison?

- Is prison staff culture different (that is, 'better') in the private sector, or are variations between prisons in both sectors so large as to make generalisations impossible? More precisely, do staff have different attitudes towards their work, and towards prisoners, in private prisons?

- More tentatively, since we have less evidence on this question so far than on the above matters, do practices differ between public and private sector prison staff? Do officers approach the use of force and authority differently? If so, why might this be the case?

- Where differences in culture, attitudes and practices are found, are these differences due to 'imparted variables' (that is, different characteristics or profiles of the staff concerned) or to 'indigenous variables' (that is, to structural features of private prison environments)? Is unionisation significant in shaping prison staff culture or is it a red herring? What are the implications of these differences?

- Do prisoners regard private sector staff differently?

- How does looking at prison staff in the private sector help us to understand the dynamics of prison life better?

To address these questions satisfactorily, we need to take into account the possibility that the answers may vary over time, as private sector competition has been used since its inception in 1991 to drive through major changes to pay, conditions and working practices in the public sector and as experience accumulates in the private sector. To be successful in its effects, any early differences between the public and the private sector should decline over time: the 'cross-fertilisation' effect (Harding 2001). As private sector staff grow in experience, their initially enthusiastic attitudes towards prisoners may harden. The answers may also vary between companies or prisons run by the same company and according to the sex of the prisoners concerned. We provide here one first look at the evidence, before drawing together the implications of our analysis for scholars of the prison, for policy-makers and for prisoners.

US data suggests relatively low pay and conditions, high turnover, lack of training and low staffing levels in the private sector (Miller 2003: 144–5). On the other hand, design and facilities are often better in the private sector, as private companies have so far only bid for new establishments with modern and purpose-built architecture. What is the case in England and Wales? Can we find systematic, empirical and meaningful differences between staff in the public and private sectors?[2]

On pay and cost, prison officers in the private sector have lower starting salaries, a lower average basic pay and fewer benefits than officers in the public sector (see Shefer and Liebling forthcoming). Staffing levels in private prisons tend to be lean, although since privatisation and performance testing began in the early 1990s, staffing levels in many public sector prisons (and therefore cost differentials) have been considerably reduced. The main benefit of private sector competition, from the taxpayer and Treasury points of view, has been the power it has given to senior managers to control costs elsewhere in the Service. The cost per prisoner place in the public sector has reduced to almost match costs in the private sector, despite better designed buildings available to the private sector. The increase in the size of the prison population since privatisation began, however, has made actual savings to the taxpayer impossible.

Competition on cost has been accompanied by competition on culture: private sector staff are encouraged to deliver as constructive and decent a regime as possible and to avoid the brutalising effects of impoverished and directionless regimes and negative staff attitudes described by critics of the public sector Prison Service throughout the 1980s (see, for example, Liebling 2004: chapter 1; Home Office 1991). The question of whether, and if so how and to what extent this has been achieved remains unanswered in any systematic way (although see National Audit Office 2003, for one attempt to compare quality as well as cost). We look below at some recent evidence on the matter.

Officers in private and public prisons

The following section draws on a survey of 950 staff in four private and four public sector prisons in England and Wales. The surveys were conducted between May and August 2006. In order to draw meaningful comparisons between the sectors a specific sampling frame with detailed inclusion criteria was developed (see Table 6.1).

This framework ensured contrasting performance levels within each sector[3] and a combination of both local and training prisons.[4] To avoid perceptions of bias, one private establishment from each of the four private prison operators in the UK was selected (this necessitated the inclusion of Parc, Group 4 Securicor's only current UK establishment). A public sector comparator prison was then

Table 6.1 Sampling framework

	Local prisons	Training prisons
Medium or low performing	Peterborough (UKDS (now Kalyx)) Highdown	Rye Hill (Global Solutions Ltd) Risley
High performing	Parc (Group 4 Securicor) Cardiff	Lowdham Grange (Serco Home Affairs) Garth

selected, as closely matched on size, performance and function as possible.

The survey formed part of an ongoing PhD study investigating variations in prisoner and staff quality of life and prisoner distress in public and private sector prisons (McLean, in progress).[5] Staff perceptions of the quality of their working life and their attitudes towards prisoners and prison work were investigated using a recent version of a survey developed specifically for this purpose: the Staff Measuring the Quality of Prison Life (SQL) survey. The survey was originally developed in consultation with prison staff (Liebling and Arnold 2002; Liebling 2004). A number of subsequent versions were developed in a series of specific research projects including a Prison Service funded project designed to formulate a version for use by the Prison Service in (for example) establishments undergoing a performance improvement programme. This version was developed and refined over a six-month period in 2005–6. The survey was piloted in six establishments. During this time a number of items were added, removed and reworded following discussions with staff. During this process, two factor analyses were carried out resulting in a 117-item survey grouped into 17 dimensions, including five dimensions designed to assess professional orientation (Klofas and Toch 1982). The dimensions and their reliability scores can be referred to in Table A6.1 in the appendix to this chapter. Following a brief presentation outlining the aims of the research, surveys were administered during full staff meetings at each establishment, which ensured an excellent completion rate.[6] In the following account, only data from uniformed staff is considered. This includes 245 private and 233 public sector officers.

Demographic differences

Public and private sector officers differed on every demographic variable with the exception of self-reported ethnic grouping ($F_{1,458}$ = 2.97, p = .085 – see Tables 6.2 and 6.3). Private sector officers were significantly less experienced than their public sector counterparts; they had been employed for significantly less time in their current prison ($F_{1,460}$ = 83.32, p < .001) and in the service overall ($F_{1,458}$ = 115.67, p < .001). They had worked in fewer prisons throughout their

Table 6.2 Demographic differences between private and public sector staff

		Private sample (n = 245)	Public sample (n = 233)
Length of time in service	Up to 3 years	58%	24%
	4–10 years	37%	28%
	11+ years	5%	48%
Length of time in current prison	Up to 3 years	67%	34%
	4–10 years	32%	35%
	11+ years	1%	31%
Age	Under 25 years	15%	3%
	25–40 years	60%	48%
	41+ years	25%	49%
Number of prisons worked in	1–3 prisons	97%	86%
	4+ prisons	3%	14%
Sex	Male	61%	80%
	Female	39%	20%
Ethnicity	White	96%	99%
	Minority ethnic	4%	1%
Education level	Did not complete high school	5%	7%
	High school	50%	59%
	Sixth-form college (or equivalent)	30%	23%
	University	10%	7%
	Further education	5%	4%

Table 6.3 Analysis of variance summary table: demographic variables

Source of variation	Sums of squares	Degrees of freedom	Mean square	F-ratio	Probability
Length of time in service	169.65	1	169.65	115.67	.001
Length of time in current prison	116.76	1	116.76	83.32	.001
Age	3523.81	1	3523.81	5.55	.02
Number of prisons worked in	132.84	1	132.84	31.45	.001
Sex	4.24	1	4.24	21.01	.001
Ethnicity	3.80	1	3.80	2.97	.09
Education level	4.02	1	4.02	4.89	.03

careers ($F_{1,459}$ = 31.45, p < .001). Private sector officers were younger ($F_{1,442}$ = 5.55, p < .02), more likely to be female ($F_{1,461}$ = 21.01, p < .001) and were educated to a higher level ($F_{1,467}$ = 4.89, p < .03).

Quality-of-life analysis

Officers' views were compared statistically across all 17 quality-of-life dimensions using independent samples *t*-tests. Table 6.4 summarises the dimensions where significant sector differences were found.[7] Officers working in private prisons reported a significantly higher quality of life than those working in public prisons on three dimensions: 'Attitudes towards senior management', 'Perception of the Prison Service/company' and 'Involvement in work'. Officers working in public sector prisons reported significantly higher quality of life than those working in private prisons on three dimensions: 'Treatment by line management', 'Authority maintenance' and 'Views on punishment and control'. Scores above 3 reflect generally positive views on the dimension concerned whereas scores below 3 reflect negative views. Some of these differences were related to the demographic differences reported above.

Views towards management

Officers in private prisons held significantly more favourable attitudes towards senior management (*t* = 4.40, *df* = 447, *p* < .001) and held

Table 6.4 Public-private sector differences in quality-of-life scores

Quality of life dimension	Mean score private (n = 245)	Mean score public (n = 233)	t
Attitudes towards senior management	3.24	2.94	4.40***
Perception of Prison Service/company	3.15	3.00	2.41*
Treatment by line management	*3.45*	*3.62*	*−2.82**
Involvement in work	3.58	3.46	2.09*
Authority maintenance	*3.03*	*3.46*	*−5.58**
Views on punishment and control	*2.44*	*2.55*	*−1.97*

Notes: The above comparisons used independent samples *t*-tests. Dimensions shown in italics indicate a statistically significantly higher score in the public sample. Dimensions shown in ordinary type indicate a statistically significantly higher score in the private sample. *p < .05; **p < .01; ***p < .001.

more positive perceptions towards their prison company than public staff held towards the Prison Service (t = 2.41, df = 455, p < .05). The first result suggests a more marked 'us-and-them' relationship between staff and management in the public sector. Liebling *et al.* (2005) investigated variations in traditional culture among prison officers, where traditional culture was partly characterised by unfavourable views of senior managers. The study took place in eleven public and one private sector prison (but these establishments were not representative). The authors found a smaller percentage of officers in the private prison adhered to this culture when compared to officers in the most comparable public sector prison. Furthermore, when asked to rate their relationships with senior managers, officers from the private prison consistently rated them higher than their public sector counterparts. Logan's comparison of officers in public and private establishments in New Mexico reported similar findings (Logan 1996): staff in the private prison in his study complained half as often about problems with management. Logan attributed this finding to a more decentralised, flatter management structure at the private prison compared to the bureaucratic and hierarchical public sector structure.[8]

If enhanced officer–management relations are, as Logan suggests, a result of structural differences between the sectors, then we would expect the private sector advantage to persist in the long term. If this is not the case, then any private sector advantage could be attributed to the relative inexperience of officers, who are often deliberately selected in order to develop a carefully socialised friendly ethos (as a deliberate counter to the public sector Prison Service traditional culture). Erosion of this more positive ethos over time would suggest that the benefits of flatter management structures are short-lived, and that we cannot demonstrate any deeper differences between the sectors.

This question was investigated using two-way unrelated ANOVA (summarised in Table A6.2 in the appendix to this chapter). In addition to sector, the effect of length of time in service on attitudes towards senior managers was considered. Significant effects were obtained for sector ($F_{1,433} = 7.78$, $p < .01$), but not for length of time in current prison ($F_{4,433} = 1.39$, $p = .24$). Staff in private prisons did therefore maintain their positive attitudes towards senior management over time. In fact, as the significant interaction effect between length of time in service and sector indicated ($F_{4, 433} = 3.81$, $p < .01$), over time, officers in the private sector became more positive towards senior management while officers in the public sector became less positive.

The decentralisation of authority in private establishments may also explain, at least in part, the significantly better perceptions held by officers in private prisons towards their prison companies. In theory, this should lead to officers feeling greater levels of responsibility and control over their jobs (Logan 1996). This was reflected in the individual item t-tests; officers in private prisons were significantly more likely to feel trusted by the company ($t = 2.93$, $df = 441$, $p < .01$), and in return, were more likely to place their own trust in the company ($t = 2.83$, $df = 459$, $p < .01$).[9]

However, these benefits were short-lived. Results of a two-way unrelated ANOVA showed that positive perceptions of the Prison Service/company were actually associated with level of officer experience rather than sector. The length of time that officers had spent in their current prison was significantly and negatively related to positive views of the Prison Service/company ($F_{4,440} = 6.46$, $p < .001$) but sector was not ($F_{1,440} = 0.49$, $p = .49$). The interaction between length of time in current prison and sector was also non-significant ($F_{4, 440} = 2.21$, $p = .07$). The results of this ANOVA are summarised in Table A6.3 in the appendix to this chapter.

As shown in Figure 6.1, officers who had spent less time in their current prison held more favourable views of the Prison Service/company, regardless of whether they were employed in public

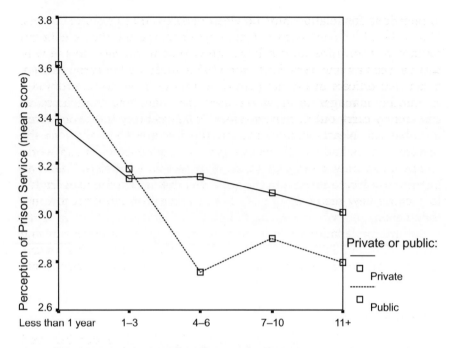

Figure 6.1 Perception of Prison Service, time spent in current prison and sector

or private sector prisons. However, it is clear that as time passes, officers tend to lose their enthusiasm, and their perceptions of their Service or company become increasingly negative. The outcome of the initial analysis, which showed a private sector advantage on this dimension, was attributable only to the fact that officers in the private sector have significantly less experience than officers in the public sector.

Treatment by line managers

Although officers in the private sector produced higher scores for the previous two management-related variables, officers in the public sector scored significantly higher on the dimension which related to the treatment they received from line managers ($t = -2.82$, $df = 449$, $p < .01$). Public sector staff felt that their line managers were fairer, and valued them more than staff in private prisons did.

This difference may be explained by the higher degree of turnover among staff in the private sector.[10] This could have two main implications for relationships between officers and middle managers. First, when turnover reaches a high rate and the workforce changes rapidly, relationships do not have the chance to develop in the way that they can among a stable workforce. Secondly, higher turnover may mean that officers in private prisons are more likely to be promoted to middle manager level when they may lack the experience to confidently carry out their new role.[11] This possibility is demonstrated in Table 6.5. Nearly half of the middle managers surveyed in the private prisons had less than seven years' experience in prison work, compared to only 8 per cent of staff in the public prisons. This may in turn exacerbate turnover problems, as inexperienced managers fail to provide new members of staff with the support and direction that they need.

A third explanation of these findings may be that officers and line managers in public sector prisons are closely bonded in cultural ways and feel a strong identification with each other in their scepticism towards more senior managers.

Involvement in work

Private sector officers reported feeling significantly more involved in their work than those in the public sector ($t = 2.09$, $df = 464$, $p < .05$). This dimension partly relates to the degree of effort that officers feel they are willing to invest in their work, and it appeared that private sector officers were significantly more likely to work hard to achieve their goals and targets ($t = 2.36$, $df = 463$, $p < .05$). This may be attributable to systemic differences between public and private employment. Private sector prison employees are not as strongly unionised as public sector staff, therefore senior managers have much greater flexibility and power in both hiring and firing employees. Logan (1996) has noted that officers in the private sector are highly aware that their career progression (or continuation) is driven by performance rather than the traditional progression through rank that has characterised the public sector (arguably until recently).

Table 6.5 Middle management experience level

	Line managers private sector %	Line managers public sector %
1–6 years in service	45	8
7+ years in service	55	92

Linking performance to progression may be a valuable motivating factor for private sector officers, but the lower private sector score on the item 'It is not worth putting in the extra effort in this prison as it would go unrecognised' ($t = -1.99$, $df = 460$, $p < .05$) suggests that, in this case, private sector officers are more motivated by their vulnerabilities as employees than the promise of wage increases, recognition and promotions. Qualitative research would be required to explore this possibility further.

The second element of the dimension 'involvement in work' relates to a general enthusiasm for work, and viewing it as meaningful, enjoyable and a source of pride. As private sector staff are newer, and newer staff tend to be more enthusiastic about their work, the relationship between sector, involvement in work and length of officer experience was investigated using a two-way unrelated ANOVA and is summarised in Table A6.4 in the appendix to this chapter.

Neither sector ($F_{1,440} = 3.54$, $p = .06$) nor length of time in service ($F_{4,440} = 1.13$, $p = .34$) had a significant effect on involvement in work. However, the interaction between the two factors was significant ($F_{4,440} = 4.11$, $p < .01$). Officers in the private sector became increasingly involved in their work over time, while officers in the public sector became less involved. This finding indicates a structural difference between the sectors that can also be understood in terms of greater degree of job instability faced by private sector staff. As Logan puts it, private sector staff are less 'locked in' (Logan 1996: 69) as their positions are more unstable and their employee benefits are poorer than those provided by the public sector. Over time then, it may be the better and more highly motivated officers that remain in post in private prisons. Alternatively, this may also be related to the tendency in the private sector to promote less experienced officers to middle managers; increased opportunities for development early on in their careers could boost the level of involvement that private sector officers have in their work.

Professional orientation

Significant differences were found for two dimensions which related to officer attitudes to prisoners and prison work. Officers in the private sector scored significantly lower than those in the public sector on authority maintenance ($t = -5.58$, $df = 468$, $p < .001$) and views on punishment and control ($t = -1.97$, $df = 461$, $p < .05$). This meant that officers in private prisons were significantly more likely to feel that personable interactions with prisoners would threaten their level of authority and they also expressed more punitive views towards prisoners.

These findings were in one way surprising, given that the private sector makes concerted efforts to encourage good staff–prisoner relationships via the recruitment of inexperienced but enthusiastic staff and careful socialisation. Furthermore, although there have been few methodical comparisons of private and public prisons in the UK, a number of studies have suggested that staff–prisoner relationships may be more positive in the private sector (NAO 2003; Liebling 2004; James *et al*. 1997). In particular, prisoners appear to perceive private sector staff as more respectful. However, these findings are based on prisoner perceptions of their quality of life and not staff attitudes. Although the two are undoubtedly related, the relationship between the two may not be positive or linear. Shefer and Liebling (forthcoming) have suggested that some elements of prison culture in private prisons that are generally welcomed by prisoners may be underpinned by a lack of staff power and experience. For example, relatively low staffing levels and lack of experience reduces the confidence of private sector officers, thus their willingness to implement the rules regarding order and discipline (see, for example, Liebling 2004: 185–90, 435–6).

Authority maintenance

Undoubtedly, these analyses suggested that officers in the private sector struggled with their use of authority and power, and worried that it could be easily eroded. It is possible that this difference could be related to the demographic differences between public and private sector officers rather than to any structural differences between the sectors. For example, it is possible that younger and less experienced officers, regardless of sector, may have difficulties using their authority appropriately. This possibility was investigated using two-way unrelated ANOVA. The first analysis found that while the relationship between sector and authority maintenance was significant ($F_{1,\,460}$ = 20.72, $p < .001$), the relationship between age and authority maintenance was not ($F_{4,\,460}$ = 1.47, $p = .21$). Additionally, the interaction between age and sector was non-significant ($F_{4,\,460}$ = .23, $p = .92$), confirming that officers in the private sector scored lower on this dimension, regardless of their age.

When the relationship between sector, time spent in service and authority maintenance was explored, significant associations were found between time spent in service and authority maintenance ($F_{1,444}$ = 2.95, $p < .05$) as well as between sector and authority maintenance ($F_{1,444}$ = 6.25, $p < .05$). The interaction between time in service and sector, however, was non-significant ($F_{1,444}$ = 1.63, $p = .17$). Although length of time in service had an effect on authority maintenance (in both cases scores increased over time), sector still had a unique effect on the scores. The results of these analyses are summarised in Table A6.5 in the appendix to this chapter.

So what might explain this lower level of confidence in authority maintenance among private sector staff? There are two possible explanations: factors relating to power and powerlessness and factors relating to training. The first explanation might be that officers in the private sector have less power than public sector officers, and therefore strive to hold onto the authority that they do possess. Their relative sense of powerlessness may arise from a number of sources. Firstly, the line of accountability between the government and the prison officer, which is so clear in the public sector, is less so in the private sector. While the public have directly installed the power to carry out the administration of punishment in public sector officers, in the private sector the existence of the prison company adds an extra link in the accountability chain. Disciplinary cases are heard by the Controller, not by the prison Director, and formal decision-making on early release, segregation and transfer has to be sanctioned by the Controller. These statutory arrangements exist for (good) reasons of principle, but they arguably weaken the power of staff. Secondly, the staff–prisoner ratio in the private sector is lower than the public sector.[12] Although a lower staff–prisoner ratio can facilitate closer staff–prisoner relationships, it can compromise how effectively the prison is run and staff perceptions of safety (see James *et al.* 1997).[13] This trade-off between relationships and safety and order may raise the debate over what is the best level at which to staff a prison. However, as the most commonly reported source of stress for officers in private prisons tends to be low staffing levels, any benefits of this approach are outweighed by the problems that it causes.[14]

Staffing levels may cause a trade-off between relationships between prisoners and staff and perceptions of safety and order. Thirdly, less union power and the relative ease with which officers can be dismissed in the private sector leads to greater job instability.

The second explanation relates to the efforts that the private sector has consciously made to develop a more positive culture, including the deliberate socialisation of new officers through training. At the Wolds Remand Centre, the initial training gave staff a view of prisoner behaviour that was disproportionately optimistic (for example, suggesting, following Woolf, that respectful treatment would lead to compliance). Their training therefore did not focus on the appropriate use of authority. When prisoners chose to stay on their relaxed wings playing pool, cards and other games rather than go to work, there was little that staff could do to encourage more structured activities. Maintaining discipline on these wings became arduous and stressful for officers (see James *et al.* 1997).

Views on punishment and control

Although an overall significant difference was found between the sectors on this dimension, significantly different scores were only found on three individual items. These included 'Prisoners take advantage of you if you are lenient' ($t = -3.84$, $df = 459$, $p < .001$); 'Prisoners should be under strict discipline' ($t = -2.39$, $df = 461$, $p < .001$) and 'Prisoners spend too much time out of cell in this prison' ($t = -5.33$, $df = 465$, $p < .001$). More negative attitudes were reported by officers working in private sector prisons. Further exploration of this dimension revealed that lower scores on this dimension were related to age ($F_{4,453} = 2.95$, $p < .05$) rather than sector ($F_{1,453} = 2.27$, $p = .13$). Older officers in both public and private prisons expressed less controlling or punitive views towards prisoners than younger officers. Similarly, less experienced officers expressed more controlling or punitive views towards prisoners than more experienced officers ($F_{4,437} = 4.30$, $p < .01$) regardless of their sector ($F_{1,437} = 0.04$, $p = .85$).

Sector or performance level?

Many of the significant sector differences persisted even when the demographic differences between the officers were controlled for statistically. This suggests that public and private prisons are structurally different. Unique elements of their management and culture seem to contribute to their strengths and weaknesses. However, to make this argument convincing, prison performance level must also be controlled for. Without controlling for performance level, we cannot confidently conclude that these differences are a result of public versus private prison management.

A series of two-way unrelated ANOVA explored the relationships between sector, performance and the four quality-of-life dimensions where significant differences were found (attitudes towards senior management, treatment by line management, involvement in work and authority maintenance). The results are summarised in Table 6.6. They support the argument that there are clear and measurable differences between the sectors. Sector remained a strong predictor of all four quality-of-life dimensions, but no relationship was found between performance level and staff quality of life.

Prisoners, for their part, tend to have mixed views about private sector staff, seeing them as generally more respectful than many public sector staff they have encountered, but also as inexperienced, having inadequate knowledge to problem-solve and as insufficiently in charge. They appreciate the 'lack of edge', but become frustrated with their lack of expertise (see James *et al*. 1997; HMCIP 2005). Practices and attitudes differ in many respects, but variations also exist within each sector, and over time as establishments mature, making generalisations premature. What is clear is that this penal experiment requires much closer scrutiny that it has received to date.

Table 6.6 Analysis of variance summary: quality of life, sector and performance level

Dimension	Source of variance	Sums of squares	Degrees of freedom	Mean square	F-ratio	Prob-ability
Attitudes	Sector	7.24	1	7.24	14.19	.001
toward senior	Performance	0.19	1	0.19	0.38	.54
management	Sector*performance	11.71	1	11.71	22.95	.001
Treatment	Sector	3.68	1	3.68	8.21	.04
by line	Performance	0.31	1	0.31	0.68	.41
management	Sector*performance	0.23	1	0.23	0.52	.47
Involvement	Sector	1.16	1	1.16	3.70	.05
in work	Performance	0.78	1	0.78	1.79	.18
	Sector*performance	0.85	1	0.85	1.94	.16
Authority	Sector	19.93	1	19.93	28.89	.001
maintenance	Performance	0.80	1	0.80	1.16	.28
	Sector*performance	0.40	1	0.40	0.58	.45

Conclusions

Modern penal practices are undergoing a transformation: criminal justice work is being fundamentally reorganised and, at the same time, the underlying ideologies of criminal justice practice are being refashioned. Some aspects of prison work (the locking up and unlocking of doors and the organisation of the prison day into a routine) remain unchanged, but ideas about who prison staff are, how they should approach their work, its purposes and management, are rapidly changing. This chapter has attempted to take a dispassionate look at some emerging evidence on this transformation, in particular on who prison staff in the public and the private sector are and what they think. By drawing on a relatively large sample of officers, from a number of prisons varying by sector, function and performance level, the findings from the survey reported here indicate that there are some important differences between officers in public and private prisons, both in terms of their demographic composition, their experiences of prison work and their attitudes towards prisoners. While officers in private prisons tend to be younger and less experienced, these differences cannot alone account for a distinctive (but not altogether healthy) attitude towards prisoners and some problems in using their authority. Variations in culture, ethos, management and employment practices clearly exert strong and enduring influences on how officers perceive their work, regardless of how highly or poorly the prison is performing. The paradox that staff in private prisons view managers more positively, prisoners more negatively, but actually under-use their authority suggests that this penal experiment is having complex and unexpected effects on contemporary prison life. There is much to be learned about prison management and penal control in both sectors, and some reflection is needed on the moral as well as practical implications of these changing inner prison dynamics.

For prisoners, the tone and circumstances of their imprisonment matter. How prisoners feel treated, how safe they feel, how carefully staff in prisons use their authority and what efforts are made to provide constructive opportunities for development and change contribute to how legitimate their sentences are. Whether privatisation works for or against legitimacy in the eyes of those subject to it is an open question.

Appendix

Table A6.1 Quality-of-life dimensions and items

	Mean score private (n = 245)	Mean score public (n = 233)	t
I feel a sense of loyalty to the Governor/ Director of this prison	3.48	3.14	3.58***
The senior management team in this prison is competent	3.26	306	2.38*
I have confidence in the senior management team in this prison	3.17	2.96	2.55*
This prison has the right kind of Governor/ Director for current needs	3.83	3.29	2.80**
The Governor/Director is concerned about the well-being of staff in this prison	3.29	3.01	2.81**
I often see senior managers around this prison	3.47	3.25	2.34*
There are times in here where Governors/ Directors fail to support staff when dealing with prisoners	2.56	2.08	5.45***
Attitudes towards senior management	**3.24**	**2.94**	**4.40***
I am trusted by the Prison Service/company	3.57	3.34	2.93**
I trust the Prison Service/company	2.91	2.66	2.83**
I am treated fairly by the Prison Service/ company	3.16	2.99	2.13*
Perception of Prison Service/company	**3.15**	**3.00**	**2.41***
I am valued as a member of staff by senior officers/supervisors in this prison	*3.43*	*3.69*	*−3.66***
I am valued as a member of staff by principal officers/managers in this prison	*3.31*	*3.54*	*−3.21***
I am treated fairly by senior officers/supervisors in this prison	*3.55*	*3.70*	*−2.13***
Treatment by line management	***3.45***	***3.62***	***−2.82***

Table A6.1 continues opposite

Table A6.1 continued

	Mean score private (n = 245)	Mean score public (n = 233)	t
It is not worth putting in the extra effort in this prison as it would go unrecognised	2.87	3.05	−2.00*
I am willing to work hard to meet goals and targets	4.24	4.10	2.34**
I feel that my job is meaningful	3.98	3.73	3.37***
I look forward to coming to work in this prison	3.28	3.08	2.10*
I feel proud of the job I do in this prison	3.92	3.72	2.48**
I get a lot of enjoyment from my work in this prison	3.65	3.30	3.99***
Overall quality of working life	3.38	3.18	2.18*
Involvement in work	**3.58**	**3.46**	**2.09***
The best way to deal with a prisoner is to be firm and distant	3.09	3.54	−4.59***
I tend to keep conversations with prisoners short and business-like	3.06	3.49	−5.09***
Friendly conversations with prisoners undermine your authority	2.95	3.35	−4.24***
Authority maintenance	***3.03***	***3.46***	***−5.58****
Prisoners spend too much time out of cell in this prison	2.56	3.15	−5.33***
Prisoners take advantage of you if you are lenient	2.09	2.41	−3.84***
Prisoners should be under strict discipline	2.28	2.47	−2.39*
Views on punishment and control	***2.44***	***2.55***	***−1.97****

Notes: The above comparisons used independent samples *t*-tests. Dimensions shown in italics indicate a statistically significantly higher score in the public sample. Dimensions not shown in italics indicate a statistically significantly higher score in the private sample. *p < .05; **p < .01; ***p < .001.

Table A6.2 Analysis of variance summary table: Attitudes towards senior management, sector and length of time in service

Source of variation	Sum of squares	Degrees of freedom	Mean square	F- ratio	Probability
Sector	4.03	1	4.03	7.76	.01
Length of time in service	2.89	4	0.72	1.39	.24
Sector*length of time in service	7.91	4	1.98	3.81	.01

Table A6.3 Analysis of variance summary table: Perception of Prison Service, sector and length of time at current prison

Source of variation	Sum of squares	Degrees of freedom	Mean square	F- ratio	Probability
Sector	0.21	1	0.21	0.47	.49
Length of time in current prison	11.24	4	2.81	6.46	.001
Sector*length of time in current prison	3.85	4	0.96	2.21	.07

Table A6.4 Analysis of variance summary table: Involvement in work, sector and length of time in service

Source of variation	Sum of squares	Degrees of freedom	Mean square	F- ratio	Probability
Sector	1.52	1	1.52	3.54	.61
Length of time in service	1.94	4	0.49	1.13	.34
Sector*length of time in service	7.07	4	1.77	4.12	.01

Table A6.5 Analysis of variance summary table: Authority maintenance, sector and age

Source of variation	Sum of squares	Degrees of freedom	Mean square	F-ratio	Probability
Sector	14.25	1	14.25	20.72	.001
Age	4.04	4	1.01	1.47	.21
Sector*age	0.64	4	0.16	0.23	.92

Seminar questions

1 To what degree has the 'cross-fertilisation' hypothesis been supported? Have attitudes, cultures and practices improved significantly in public sector prisons over the past 15 years?
2 Are private sector officers here to 'do business' rather than punish? That is, should they have less power than their public sector counterparts?
3 Is there an optimum staff–prisoner ratio? Are private sector staff protected or made vulnerable by contractual staffing levels?
4 Do prisoners fare better at the expense of staff in private sector prisons?

Recommended reading

Liebling and Arnold's (2004) *Prisons and Their Moral Performance: A Study of Values, Quality, and Prison Life* describes the development of a method of measuring quality of life in prisons, drawing upon an empirical study on 'what matters most' to prisoners and staff in five comparable prisons. Richard Harding's (1997) *Private Prisons and Public Accountability* explores the possible contributions that private prisons, if correctly regulated, could make to custodial standards and practices. By envisaging public and private service providers as two components within a single prison system, Harding suggests that private prisons, if made appropriately accountable, could act as a catalyst for improvement within public prisons. *Privatizing Prisons: Rhetoric and Reality* (James *et al.* 1997) charts the first two years in the life of the Wolds remand centre, the first private prison in Britain, and highlights some of the practical issues facing staff and managers during the early stages of this penal experiment. *The Prison Officer* (Liebling, forthcoming) looks 'appreciatively' at the work of prison officers and draws some comparisons with officers in the private sector.

Notes

1 As far as we are aware, no comparative studies of management style or motivation have been conducted to date.

2 In this chapter we focus exclusively on uniformed officers in both sectors. Data have been collected on other staff and analyses will be reported in McLean, in progress. It is possible that specialist staff (teachers, instructors, drug workers, psychologists, admin grades, and so on) vary less according to sector, but further investigation will be necessary.

3 Performance levels are taken from the Prison Service officially reported Performance Ratings. Prisons are rated on a 1–4 performance scale. Level 4 is awarded to excellent establishments that are delivering exceptionally high performance. Level 1 indicates a poor performer. In this framework, establishments performing at Levels 1 or 2 were defined as low performing, and establishments performing at Levels 3 or 4 were defined as high performing.

4 Initially, only Category B adult male local prisons were included as they have the highest rates of suicide and lowest but most varied levels of well-being (Liebling *et al.* 2005). However, other sampling restrictions meant that it was necessary to widen this to include training prisons.

5 This is an ESRC CASE Studentship with NOMS as the non-academic partner, supervised by Alison Liebling. The study began in 2005 and is due to be completed by October 2009.

6 The completion rates varied by establishment from 60.4 per cent to 100 per cent.

7 Table A6.1 in the appendix to this chapter contains the individual items which comprised these dimensions.

8 James *et al.* (1997) have noted that this key difference in management structure also exists in private establishments in the UK.

9 Officers in the private sector were given a version of the survey which asked them to rate how much they trusted/were trusted by Serco Home Affairs, Global Solutions Ltd, UK Detention Services (now Kalyx) or Group 4 Securicor as appropriate. Officers working in the public sector were asked to rate how much they trusted/were trusted by the Prison Service.

10 In 2005 the overall resignation rate for officers in the private sector in England and Wales was 27 per cent, compared to just 3 per cent in the public sector (Prison Service Pay Review Body 2005).

11 Accelerated promotion may also arise from competition from more highly paid jobs in the public sector. Officers in private prisons often begin with little or no experience but quickly learn skills that are directly relevant in the public sector. Currently, the average basic pay for officers in the public sector is 41 per cent higher than private sector pay (Prison Service Pay Review Body 2005).

12 In September 2005 the staff-to-prisoner ratio in public sector establishments in the UK was 1:1.5. The ratio in the private estate was 1:1.8. (Hansard, 21 November 2005).
13 Logan refers to this as 'staffing efficiency' (Logan 1996: 78) and notes that when the staff–prisoner ratio becomes too low, prison quality begins to suffer.
14 Staff shortages cause staff detailing to change constantly, undermining close staff–prisoner relationships (McLean, in progress).

References

Harding, R.W. (1997) *Private Prisons and Public Accountability*. Buckingham: Open University Press.
Harding, R.W. (2001) 'Private Prisons', in M. Tonry and J. Petersilia (eds), *Crime and Justice: An Annual Review of Research*, Vol. 28. Chicago: University of Chicago Press.
HC Debate, 21 November 2005, c1768W.
HMCIP (2005) *Report on an Unannounced Inspection of HMP Rye Hill 11–15 April 2005 by HM Chief Inspector of Prisons*. London: Home Office.
James, A.L., Bottomley, A.K., Liebling, A. and Clare, E. (1997). *Privatizing Prisons: Rhetoric and Reality*. London: Sage Publications.
Klofas, J.M. and Toch, H. (1982) 'The Guard Subculture Myth', *Journal of Research in Crime and Delinquency*, 19: 238–54.
Liebling, A., assisted by Arnold, H. (2004) *Prisons and Their Moral Performance. A Study of Values, Quality and Prison Life*. New York: Oxford University Press.
Liebling, A. and Arnold, H. (2002) *Measuring the Quality of Prison Life*, Research Findings 174. London: Home Office.
Liebling, A. and Price, D. (2001) *The Prison Officer*. Leyhill: Prison Service Journal.
Liebling, A., Tait, S., Durie, L., Stiles, A. and Harvey, R. (submitted 2005) *An Evaluation of the Safer Locals Programme: Final Report*. London: Home Office.
Logan, C.H. (1996) 'Public vs. Private Prison Management: A Case Comparison', *Criminal Justice Review*, 21 (1): 62–85.
McLean, C. (in progress) 'Wellbeing and Quality of Life in Public and Private Sector Prisons'. PhD thesis underway at Cambridge University.
Miller, J. (2003) 'Worker Rights in Private Prisons', in A. Coyle, A. Campbell and R. Neufeld (eds), *Capitalist Punishment: Prison Privatization and Human Rights*. London: Zed Books, pp. 140–51.
Moyle, P. (1995) 'Private Prison Research in Queensland, Australia. A Case Study of Borallon Correctional Centre, 1991', *British Journal of Criminology*, 35: 34–62.

National Audit Office (2003) *The Operational Performance of PFI Prisons Report by the Comptroller and Auditor General, HC Session 2002–2003: 18 June 2003.* London: Stationary Office.

Prison Service Pay Review Body (2005) *Privately Managed Custodial Services.* London: Stationary Office.

Shefer, G. and Liebling, A. (forthcoming) 'Prison Privatization: In Search of a Business-like Atmosphere?'

Part 2

Prison Officers

Chapter 7

Industrial relations in prisons

Jamie Bennett and Azrini Wahidin

Introduction

Industrial relations (IR) in prisons are widely considered to be in a state of perpetual crisis. The Prison Officers' Association (POA) is often portrayed as a narrow, outdated and militant relic, while managers are seen as either collusive or ineffective in tackling the union. Official reports have condemned IR as being in 'a sorry state' (Woolf and Tumin 1991: 5), and being a block to good performance (Laming 2000). Academic literature has also been critical: prisons have been described as 'The "Jurassic Park" of Public Sector Industrial Relations' (Black 1995; also see Bennett 2004). This perception has only been enhanced by events such as the booing of the Prisons Minister at the POA Annual Conference in 2002, described by the then Director General as 'more appropriate to the Industrial Relations of the 1970s' (Narey 2002).

This chapter aims to look beyond these stereotypical portrayals, discussing prison officer unionisation the history and structure of IR in prisons and identifying some of the key issues and tensions in this area. Through this discussion, the chapter identifies the trend towards greater cooperation in IR, but also highlights the historical and cultural issues that maintain the distinctive antagonistic language and character of prison IR.[1]

Background

The POA represents 96 per cent of all prison officer grades in England, Wales and Northern Ireland. It also represents some middle-ranking governor grades at levels E and F[2] and certain support staff, particularly operational support grades, who carry out non-prisoner work such as gate and control room duties (Calvert 2001). Outside the Prison Service, the POA represents the nursing grades and auxiliary staff in the special hospitals (Broadmoor, Rampton and Ashworth).

Though numerically not large, the almost continuous year-on-year membership increase of the POA has been achieved within its industrial sector and not by extension into other areas of employment (see Table 7.1). This is in contrast to traditional union membership which has gradually declined, although this increase is in line with 'non-affiliated' unions, i.e. independent, narrowly focused unions and staff associations often linked to a particular profession or employer (Farnham and Giles 1995). The current membership comprises 18,156 men and 8,583 women; ethnicity is not recorded (personal correspondence with POA). The objectives of the POA are: to protect and promote the interests of its members; to regulate the conditions of employment; to provide legal advice; to provide death benefit; to publish an official journal; to provide services including employing staff; to promote improvement in prison conditions (POA 2005).

There is a formalised relationship between the POA and the Prison Service, underpinned by the Joint Industrial Relations

Table 7.1 Membership at the end of year

Year	Membership at end of year	% change
1939	2,229	
1949	4,100	84
1959	7,380	80
1969	12,585	71
1979	19,638	56
1989	25,000	27
2006	26,739	7

Source: Personal correspondence with POA (2006).

Procedural Agreement (JIRPA) drawn up in 2004. This is a 'no-strike' agreement, in which the POA has agreed not to induce its members to take industrial action. This agreement provides for consultation on matters that affect the interests of members and a mechanism for dispute resolution including independent arbitration by the Advisory Conciliation and Arbitration Service (ACAS). Annual pay is determined by an independent Pay Review Body (PRB).

The POA has a Facilities Agreement with the Prison Service. This commits the Service to provide facility time for national and local POA officials. For national officials this amounts to full-time union duties, while at a local level it may entail several days a week. The POA has access to promote its service to all newly recruited officers, which means that most sign up without fully understanding what they are doing or why they are doing it (Calvert 2001). Most members join the POA as a form of insurance or individual protection against the actions of managers and prisoners, should they require it during their professional lives, rather than because of overt political unionism (Calvert 2001). One symptom of this is that national POA elections have a relatively low turnout. In the most recent elections, 3,115 votes out of 6,346 cast were required to elect the national chairman in 2002, and 987 votes from a turnout of 5,612 were required to secure a National Executive Committee (NEC) position in 2006 (personal correspondence with POA).

Although it is not recognised by the Prison Service for collective bargaining purposes, the other union to represent prison officer grades is the Prison Service Union (PSU). This was established in 1989 as a splinter group headed by former POA NEC members (see http://www.psunion.org.uk/index.htm). It is not actually an independent trade union but is a satellite of the Financial and Professional Section of the Amalgamated Engineering and Electrical Workers Union (AEEWU). The PSU presents itself as a more moderate and progressive union; for example, it sought members in the private sector long before the POA contemplated this. The PSU claims that it had 4,769 members on 31 December 2004, though the income from subscriptions for the year (£283,387) would suggest that the figure is somewhat less than this. The membership of the PSU tends to be concentrated in individual establishments where central PSU members are based, but it may also have more sympathisers than it has members.

A history of prison industrial relations

Baptism of fire: the creation of the POA

Professor Thomas subtitled his history of the English prison officer (1972) 'A Study in Conflict'. Such a description would equally apply to the history of prison IR. The creation and recognition of prison unionisation was a contested, controversial and protracted process. This baptism of fire 'burrowed deep into the psyche of the association and its membership' (Coyle 2005: 87) and has shaped the relations that have followed.

In the early 1900s, local establishment boards, formed by the then Prison Commission, set the terms and conditions of employment (known as the Bell Scales) (Gatelodge 1989: 27). Although many prison staff sought the right to collective action, the conditions of the early 1900s were not conducive to this and the political, commercial and legal establishments sought to resist the rise and expansion of unionism. For example, the Taff Vale case of 1901 opened union funds to action for damages by employers, making unions financially vulnerable, and the Osborne case of 1909 made political fund-raising unlawful, limiting the political influence of unions. There were also a number of violent confrontations between the state and workers, the most notorious of which was during the miners' strike at Tonypandy, Wales in 1910 (Pelling 1976).

On 15 March 1906 the question of a union for prison officers was mooted for the first time in Parliament and on 5 April 1906, a new Standing Order was introduced, whereby with the sanction of the governor, Commissioner, or on appeal to the Home Secretary, staff were allowed to 'meet and discuss amongst themselves questions relating to their duties and position in the prison service' (Thomas 1978: 28). Two years later, on 28 May 1908, it was asked in Parliament whether that ruling meant that prison staff had the same rights of association as other workmen. A response was never provided. By 1911 Winston Churchill made a definitive statement about unions which remained the official response for many years. He believed that prison officers at all levels had the opportunity to present their grievances in individual prisons, and when asked if Standing Orders could be modified to allow prison officers to hold one general meeting a year, although he agreed in principle, he argued that, as with policeman, soldiers and sailors, it was inappropriate for them to form unions (Cronin 1967; Thomas 1972, 1978).

Covert action was continued by those who sought the right to collective action and by 1910 the *Prison Officers' Magazine* had been founded. It was edited from outside the Service and was called 'the red un' (Thomas 1972). It has been argued that the name was taken from the colour of the front cover, but it also symbolised the radical nature of its content and its oppositional stance to management. By 1913, the first unofficial unions were formed (POA 2000), although members risked being disciplined if discovered (Cronin 1967). In 1918, a major strike was called by police and prison officers in London. The then Prime Minister, Lloyd George, later stated that the country 'was nearer to Bolshevism that day than any day since' (see Reynolds and Judge 1968: 15). There was some initial belief that the right to unionise had been conceded, but this was rebuffed in 1919 with the Police Act, which forbade police and prison officers forming or joining a union. A strike called in August 1919 resulted in the dismissal of everyone participating, including 74 prison officers (Thomas 1972).

The government's response to these crises was to form the Police Federation and a Prison Officers' Representative Board (PORB), which met twice a year. Each prison had a representative at one of the four district PORB meetings, and each district nominated a representative to attend the national PORB meeting. The purpose was to provide a forum for officers to make suggestions, air concerns or share complaints (Cronin 1967; Thomas 1972). However, the PORB was widely derided for its lack of rigour and independence and, as a result, the *Prison Officers' Magazine* flourished and maintained the campaign for union recognition (Thomas 1972). However, this was slow in coming, and it was only in 1939 that the Prison Commissioners finally agreed to recognise the Prison Officers' Association.

The ever-deepening crisis: 1939–92

Following the Second World War, the landslide election of the Labour Party resulted in a revolutionary period of social reform, including the creation of the welfare state. These reforms aimed to reshape social justice and provide support for the weakest and poorest members of society, and they found expression in prisons through the growth of rehabilitative ideals, an idealistic belief that prison could be a place where change was fostered and encouraged. Thomas (1972) argues that the POA resisted this liberalisation, criticising what they saw as a consequent loss of order and increase in violence. This conflict meant that during this period, 'It was only very rarely ... that the Commissioners' account, and the POA account, of what was happening in prison bore any relation to each other' (Thomas 1972: 203).

As prison research emerged in the 1960s, it was clear that IR were a critical aspect of prison life. A study of HMP Pentonville described the POA as conservative, punitive, resistant to change and, above all, 'a militant association' (Morris and Morris 1963: 217). Recruitment from the declining heavy industries had imported a more heavily unionised and radical workforce (Driscoll, cited in Liebling and Price 2001). This all took place against a background of conflict and increased numbers of unofficial strikes throughout the country (Pelling 1976). However, in 1963, the POA published its most radically progressive document, *The Role of the Modern Prison Officer*, which argued that the officer role should not only cover traditional areas such as control and security, but also welfare and rehabilitation. This was an important step in the future development of the officer role, although it may have been motivated primarily by self-interest, preventing the erosion or marginalisation of jobs as the functions of prisons changed (Thomas 1972; Liebling and Price 2001).

Following serious disturbances in high security prisons in 1973, prisons entered a period of increasing industrial and prisoner unrest and growing public concern. This was mirrored in the country generally with a period of serious unrest most clearly illustrated by the three-day week of 1973–4 and the 'winter of discontent' of 1978–9. In prisons, this eventually led to the establishment of a Committee of Inquiry (May 1979). The Committee concluded that while industrial unrest had started in response to prisoner violence, it reached an unprecedented level in 1975 when the POA NEC had recognised the right of branches at individual prisons to take action over local disputes. This had led to a dramatic increase in the frequency, range and extent of disputes. The report recommended that a strong NEC was essential. May (1979) also recognised a wide range of factors that influenced the deterioration in IR, including the changing role of officers, the changing nature of prisoners, the rising population, a more restrictive financial context, poor relationships between managers and staff, inadequate IR procedures and union militancy inside and outside of prisons. This can be seen as a continuing period of serious negative IR that could be characterised as 'classical conflict' or 'continuous challenge' (Fox 1974).

This report led to new IR mechanisms and dispute management procedures, but did not mark a sea change in relations. Further industrial action occurred in 1986, this time a national overtime ban, leading to widespread disorder. These riots affected 40 prisons, causing damage totalling £5.5 million. The subsequent report (Hennessy 1987) identified a number of contextual factors, including overcrowding, poor conditions, the characteristics of the prisoner population and changes to staffing levels that affected both the perception of safety and standards of living. However, Hennessy (1987) placed much greater focus on cultural factors, describing a chronically poor IR characterised by low morale, suspicion and lack of regard for senior managers, negative attitudes of management and media towards the POA, and a feeling among uniformed staff that progress was not being made on matters of concern such as pay and conditions. As a result many believed that industrial action was the only option. Hennessy concluded that the changes to staffing levels and working conditions (including abolition of paid overtime) in the *Fresh Start* agreement of 1987 would help, and his recommendations also led to a new disputes procedure. However, he also called into question the right of prison officers to take industrial action, declaring that 'industrial action should not again be allowed to put lives and property at risk' (Hennessy 1987: 110). This warning was particular significant taking place against a background of Margaret Thatcher's robust curtailment of union power through legislation restricting industrial action by and directly confronting strikes.

Fresh Start was introduced in order to bring fiscal restraint, in particular by abolishing paid overtime, which at that stage accounted for one-third of the pay budget (Coyle 1991). Other changes included the abolition of the chief officer grade, the introduction of a unified structure running from officer to governing governor, increased pay and reduced working hours. The loss of overtime and the failure of the POA to effectively move into representing governor grades began to erode its power (Thomas 1994). As Bryans and Wilson (2000) observed, 'The power of the POA, which at that time had been all-consuming, never again seemed so great' (p. 11).

The most serious disturbances in UK prison history occurred in 1990, starting at HMP Manchester (Strangeways) and spreading to over 20 institutions. The subsequent inquiry, the Woolf Report, focused on prison conditions and the sense of injustice that prisoners felt, but also took a broad view of contributory issues, which included IR (Woolf and Tumin 1991). The report highlighted mistrust between unions and managers and the need for improved cooperation. It considered the call that some had made for industrial action in prisons to be made unlawful, but did not support this, instead optimistically calling for cooperative attempts to improve conditions for both staff and prisoners. However, the report made it clear that this was an opportunity for the POA to show how it would respond to this reform agenda.

During this period, prisons experienced crises, which steadily escalated from the early 1970s through to the catastrophic collapse of order in 1990. The crises of prisoner numbers, conditions and resources also affected working conditions and the IR context. In the 1970s, unions were powerful throughout the country and strikes dominated the political agenda; although this declined in the 1980s, there remained an ongoing power struggle between the unions and managers. While the Woolf report provided an opportunity for a new beginning, there was an ominous public debate emerging about whether more dramatic action should be taken to curtail the POA.

The eclipse of the POA: 1992–2001

The Woolf report led to extensive reforms throughout the prison system, including improved conditions and, initially, a reduction in the prisoner population. There were also reforms in the public sector generally, emerging from the 'New Public Management' (NPM) movement which sought to introduce private sector approaches into the public sector to improve efficiency and effectiveness (Hood 1991; Ferlie et al. 1996). These reforms included explicit performance targets, efficiency savings, the delegation of personnel and financial responsibilities to individual prisons, and the recruitment of private sector managers. The two most controversial reforms were the introduction of competition in the form of private prisons and measures to curtail union power. The decision to introduce private prisons was significantly influenced by the perception that POA militancy presented an obstacle to change (Hurd 2003).

The moves to restrict union power followed a 1993 POA ballot that resulted in a vote in favour of industrial action in opposition to the introduction of private prisons. As a result of this ballot result, the Prison Service took legal action, exploiting the legal anomaly that prison officers did not have the full legal protection of a trade union and could be sued for damages arising from industrial action (Lewis 1997). In making industrial action untenable, this case effectively undermined the power of the POA, and this was confirmed by legislation under section 127 of the Criminal Justice and Public Order Act 1994 which made industrial action unlawful. The NEC was in disarray and throughout the 1990s, significant changes were implemented including the opening of private prisons, extensive regrading of officer posts, and efficiency measures such as reducing staffing levels.

Although conflict continued, including a dispute over the annual pay award in 1998 which resulted in two injunctions being granted to prevent industrial action, none of these seriously threatened order in prisons as in the past. This period therefore appeared to mark the eclipse of the POA as a national force. However, local branches continued to play an important role in individual prisons. While many branches were able to exert a positive influence, supporting establishments through change, the late 1990s saw some branch officials criticised for exerting a malign influence on individual prisons. In particular, the Chief Inspector of Prisons highlighted problems at Wormwood Scrubs where the local branch exercised a virtual veto over management action (HMCIP 1999) and HMYOI Feltham, where it was claimed that individual members of the POA 'mount ritual and continuous challenge to legitimate management and present a consistent obstacle to planned and essential improvements' (HMCIP 2001: 6). In the latter case, this resulted in the controversial compulsory transfer of the branch official, Andy Darkin, in July 2001, a man described subsequently in an independent inquiry as exerting an 'unhealthy influence' on IR at Feltham (Keith 2006: 371).

The 1990s were a period of significant change in prisons. One change in particular, the introduction of private sector competition, developed into a power struggle, which was resoundingly settled in favour of the government and managers. The subsequent curtailment of union power meant that the POA was unable to disrupt prisons in the same way as it had in the past, but there had not been a holistic change in attitudes or beliefs. The changes therefore represented a shift in power rather than the establishment of greater cooperation.

An uneasy partnership: 2001–2006

When New Labour came to power in 1997, there was hope that this would signal a new approach to prisons, including the removal of section 127 and the realisation of a commitment to bring private prisons back into the public sector (Blair 1993). Although this did not happen, the public sector was allowed to compete for private prison contracts when they came for renewal, and in 1998 the Home Secretary signalled his willingness to replace section 127 with a voluntary 'no strike' agreement and to introduce an independent Pay Review Body (PRB). However, negotiations were protracted and it was not until 2001 that these were implemented.

This voluntary agreement marked a significant modernisation in IR procedures. In particular, disputes would ultimately be resolved through independent arbitration via ACAS, where previously they had been settled by the Deputy Director General of the Prison Service. The introduction of an independent PRB was also an important step. Despite these changes, this period still involved conflict. One particular issue was that in 2001, Andy Darkin, who had been compulsorily transferred from Feltham, was elected National Chairman of the POA, leading to a more confrontational and resistant approach. The second issue was that following the first PRB recommendations in January 2002, the Prison Service declared the recommended 6 per cent pay rise was unaffordable, and as a result the rise should be staged, with 3.5 per cent immediately and the further 2.5 per cent effective in January 2003. This was represented by the POA as a case of bad faith. The POA national conference in 2002 was a fractious affair, with straight talking from both the Director General and the Prisons Minister being responded to by booing from the floor.

In 2002, there was a further election for National Chair of the POA, as a nominee had been wrongly prevented from standing at the previous election, ending Andy Darkin's short-lived chairmanship. Colin Moses was elected as Chairman, only the second black national union leader. He was widely seen in the union and by managers as a 'moderniser' and this was seen as an opportunity for a return to more positive IR partnership.

The subsequent period has seen some notable successes. For example, the voluntary agreement was superseded by a Joint Industrial Relations Procedural Agreement (JIRPA) in 2004, formalising the IR framework and restating the partnership approach. This agreement paved the way for the removal of section 127 in 2005. In addition, the Prison Service and POA have cooperated in the performance testing of eight prisons, a process by which poorly performing prisons have an opportunity to develop an improvement plan which, if inadequate, may result in them being offered to the private sector. In addition, there is evidence that in individual prisons, governors and local branches are working successfully in a spirit of partnership, including achieving difficult objectives such as efficiency savings (Bennett 2004). A 'paradigm of cooperation' appears to have emerged, where the interests of the organisation and employees are shared, an important ideological shift.

In 2004, the government announced the creation of the National Offender Management Service (NOMS), a commissioning body for criminal justice services, including prisons and probation, which also has a stake in sentencing guidelines (Blunkett 2004). The aim was to provide improved efficiency and effectiveness in reducing reoffending. One aspect of the brief was to improve 'contestability', in other words to encourage greater competition by identifying wider opportunities for contracting out ancillary services and offering public sector prisons for routine market testing, irrespective of their performance. This would operate in a similar way to how contracts for private prisons currently work. These contracts are awarded for a defined period, at the end of which there is an open competition for the contract. The POA was opposed to the increase in contestability, which it saw as an attempt to introduce 'mass privatisation' and as a direct attack on it as an organisation (Moses and Bennett 2005).

The first competition, for the cluster of three prisons on the Isle of Sheppey in Kent, was announced in March 2005. This was a 'test case' of 'contestability' as none of the prisons had been identified as underperforming. The POA response was a national ballot that supported the local branches at the three prisons refusing to co-operate with the market test. Together, the Prison Service and POA successfully proposed to the Home Secretary that the competition be suspended and that, instead, the prisons have a time-bounded opportunity to present an improvement plan. They also argued for a wider national reform package, known as the Heads of Agreement (Clarke 2005). The Heads of Agreement were to include a prison performance improvement mechanism, a multi-year pay deal for prison officers, a fundamental review of pay using a job evaluation system, revision to grades including reducing the number of middle manager grades and promotion being linked to competences. The improvement plan presented by the three prisons was later accepted, although the Heads of Agreement fell by the wayside due to lack of funding.

The recriminations from this period have resulted in the partnership coming under pressure, particularly from the POA which withdrew from joint training for JIRPA and instructed staff not to cooperate with the developmental work for a new job evaluation system, only rescinding this at the last minute and in the face of potential legal action by the Prison Service. In 2006, the PRB awarded a 1.6 per cent pay rise for prison officers, an award the POA considered derisory. Following this, the POA successfully sought a mandate from their national conference to ballot for industrial action, ostensibly relating to the perceived lack of independence of the PRB. The subsequent ballot in August 2006 was overwhelmingly in favour of strike action, although following this a settlement was agreed and action avoided.

Recent years have not seen any significant shift in the relative power of the POA and Prison Service: the removal of section 127 and its replacement with a 'no strike' agreement is an important symbolic step but has made little day-to-day difference. Nor was there any radical departure in the IR context – increased competition is a continuation and evolution of public policy, and although the prison population steadily continued to rise, there was no return to the chronically poor conditions of the 1980s. However, this period did mark a shift towards a new ideology, which can be described as a 'sophisticated modern' approach (Fox 1974). This is characterised by IR with a strategic purpose where unions are recognised as having a legitimate role as a means of negotiation, consultation and representation and, as a result, membership is encouraged and procedures formalised. For example, the Heads of Agreement, the work on performance testing and the developments at local levels were attempts to collaborate in achieving strategic goals. In addition, the development of JIRPA illustrated a desire to formalise and legitimise IR. Although this period also indicated that change would be slow and faltering, it did nevertheless mark an important step.

Conclusion: IR culture in prisons

During the last century, prison IR has been a source of ongoing conflict, but has also been the subject of significant change. There have been shifts in the nature of IR from early derecognition and covert resistance, to recognition and conflict after the Second World War, to rampant union domination during the 1970s and 1980s, a reassertion of control in the 1990s and, finally, a search for a new legitimacy after 1997. This final section closes by commenting on IR culture in prisons and making observations on recent cultural changes.

The one constant in IR is conflict. As was described at the beginning of this chapter, prisons have a reputation for having particularly poor IR. It is still true that the language of workplace conflict is a feature of prison life, as can be seen in any edition of the POA publication, *The Gatelodge*. This is often heavily critical of management and sceptical about prisoner rights. This is fed by two particular issues: the insular nature of the prison community and the active membership of the POA.

Prison staff have long stated that they feel undervalued by managers and the public (for example, see Thomas 1972), and as a result of this they have reported feeling isolated from the community and becoming drawn closer into the prison world (Crawley 2004). This insularity is also seen in prison unions, which like police unions have been detached from the mainstream union movement due to their own insular concerns, and the perception that they are conservative (Fleming *et al*. 2006). This insularity means that discussion can be characterised by lack of perspective, proportionality or meaningful comparative analysis. As a result, IR may be or may appear to external observers to be more hostile than in other organisations.

In terms of membership of the POA, most prison staff join for self-interested motives, such as personal insurance against the actions of managers or prisoners and the increasing range of financial services and benefits offered (Calvert 2001). They are largely disinterested in national issues and more concerned with the prison they work in and their immediate working environment (Bennett 2004). However, it has also been observed that disaffected and change-resistant individuals naturally seek a home in the POA (Elliott 2006). Where negative individuals gain power, either as managers or union officials, their impact can be damaging. Due to the relatively low level of engagement in POA elections and the higher level of activity among change-resistant people, this can give people with these attitudes a disproportionate voice. As a result, even union officials who do not hold hostile views recognise that they have to display such attitudes in order to appeal to important sections of their electorate (Bennett 2004). There is therefore an element of performance in the conduct of prison IR.

These two factors contribute towards an apparently hostile IR culture. However, it is critical that one distinguish between oral culture (i.e. what a particular group says) and what is done in practice (Waddington 1999). Certainly, the incidence of serious and damaging industrial conflict has reduced significantly in prisons, although the language has retained many features that have been criticised as outmoded. The difference between language and action can be explained, for example, by the fact that while change-resistant staff can have a disproportionate voice they cannot necessarily command the support of the wider membership for more dramatic industrial action, and that while the insularity of prison staff may breed a shared sense of grievance, this may not command wider external support. It is therefore suggested that when the IR culture of prisons is strongly criticised, this is largely as a reflection of an oral culture rather than action.

It has been described that recent years have, in fact, seen the development of IR actions that are more cooperative and progressive. It has been suggested that these years have seen the emergence of what has been termed 'a new paradigm of cooperation' (Bennett 2004), with a greater propensity for managers and unions to work together constructively. This convergence of interests between the organisation and individuals has arisen from structural changes such as commercial competition, and the greater scrutiny and risks arising from NPM techniques such as target-setting, efficiencies and performance testing. Such changes mean that, increasingly, what is good for the organisation is good for individuals. In a sense, this is a mutual pragmatism, or even a mutual powerlessness, between managers and unions, which one governor described as the 'shared anxieties' of implementing externally imposed changes such as efficiency savings (Bennett 2004). This new paradigm is also informed by a pragmatic realisation that the POA has limited ability to both command its members to take industrial action and to do so successfully within the legal constraints under which they operate. However, these changes do also have a more positive aspect, as many staff, managers and union officials have an appreciation of the benefits of greater cooperation and joint working (Bennett 2004). In terms of action, therefore, it can be concluded that the IR culture is becoming more cooperative and consensual, reflecting both a shift in power meaning that the risks of discord and conflict are more significant, and a wider appreciation of the benefits for both the organisation and union members.

Seminar questions

1 How has prison IR changed over time?
2 Do these changes reflect changes in IR more generally or is prison IR distinct?
3 Are the changes simply a result of changes in relative power, or has there been a more fundamental change in attitudes?
4 Why is the POA seen to be resistant to change?

Recommended reading

Andrew Coyle *Understanding Prisons: Key Issues in Policy and Practice* (2005) documents the development of the English prison – how they function, what they achieve and their historical and political context. It looks at who is sent to prison and what happens to them while they are there, explains how the prison system and staff in England and Wales are organised, and offers a future vision of the prison system.

Alison Liebling and David Price (2001) in *The Prison Officer* open the world and work of the English prison officer, showing the centrality of staff–prisoner relationships in the running of the prison and the needs and tensions created between providing a duty of care while at the same time maintaining security.

Notes

1 The research for this chapter included a literature review, examination of documentary sources and interviews with senior managers and POA representatives, and has utilised previous research by one of the authors (Bennett 2004).
2 Manager E and F are what was formerly known as governor grade 4 and 5 respectively. These people will usually manage a large function or department and will, at times, be in operational charge of the prison.

References

Bennett, J. (2004) 'Jurassic Park Revisited: The Changing Nature of Prison Industrial Relations', *Prison Service Journal*, 156: 40–5.

Black, J. (1995) 'Industrial Relations in the UK Prison Service: The "Jurassic Park" of Public Sector Industrial Relations', *Employee Relations*, 17 (2): 64–88.

Blair, T. (1993) *The Perrie Lecture 1993 – The Future of The Prison Service*, republished in Reynolds, J. and Smart, U. (1996) *Prison Policy and Practice: Selected Papers from 35 Years of the Prison Service Journal.* Leyhill: Prison Service Journal.

Blunkett, D. (2004) *Reducing Crime – Changing Lives: The Government's Plans for Transforming the Management of Offenders.* London: Home Office.

Bryans, S. and Wilson, D. (2000) *The Prison Governor: Theory and Practice.* Leyhill: Prison Service Journal.

Calvert, D. (2001) 'The Role of The Prison Officers' Association: What Do Staff in the Prison Service Want from a Union?' Unpublished.

Clarke, C. (2005) *Correspondence with Colin Moses, Chairman of Prison Officers' Association*, 18 May 2005.

Coyle, A. (1991) *Inside: Rethinking Scotland's Prisons*. Edinburgh: Scottish Child.

Coyle, A. (2005) *Understanding Prisons: Key Issues in Policy and Practice*. Milton Keynes: Open University Press.

Crawley, E. (2004) *Doing Prison Work: The Public and Private Lives of Prison Officers*. Cullompton: Willan.

Cronin, H. (1967) *The Screw Turns*. London: John Long.

Elliott, C. (2006) 'Speaking of Performance Improvement', *Prison Service Journal*, 163: 30–4.

Farnham, D. and Giles, L. (1995) 'Trade Unions in the UK: Trends and Counter-trends since 1979', *Employee Relations*, 17 (2): 5–22.

Ferlie, E., Pettigrew, A., Ashburner, L. and Fitzgerald, L. (1996) *The New Public Management in Action*. Oxford: Oxford University Press.

Fleming, J., Marks, M. and Wood, J. (2006) '"Standing on the Inside Looking Out": The Significance of Police Unions in Networks of Public Governance', *The Australian and New Zealand Journal of Criminology*, 39 (1): 71–89.

Fox, A. (1974) *Beyond Contract: Work. Power and Trust Relations*. London: Faber.

Gatelodge (1989) *Prison Officers' Magazine Celebrating Fifty Years 1939-1989*.

Hennessy, J. (1987) *Report of an Inquiry by Her Majesty's Chief Inspector of Prisons for England and Wales into the Disturbances in Prison Service Establishments in England between 29 April–2 May 1986*. London: HMSO.

HM Chief Inspector of Prisons (1999) *HM Prison Wormwood Scrubs: Report of an Unannounced Inspections 8–12 March 1999*. London: Home Office.

HM Chief Inspector of Prisons (2001) *HM Young Offenders Institution and Remand Centre Feltham: Report of an Unannounced Inspections 23–26 October 2000*.

Hood, C. (1991) 'A Public Management for All Seasons', *Public Administration*, 69: 3–19.

Hurd, D. (2003) *Memoirs*. London: Little, Brown.

Keith, Justice (2006) *The Report of the Zahid Mubarek Inquiry*. London: TSO.

Laming, Lord (2000) *Modernising the Management of the Prison Service: An Independent Report by the Targeted Performance Initiative Working Group*. HM Prison Service.

Lewis, D. (1997) *Hidden Agendas: Politics, Law and Disorder*. London: Hamish Hamilton.

Liebling, A. and Price, D. (2001) *The Prison Officer*. Leyhill: Prison Service Journal.

May, J. (1979) *Committee of Inquiry into the United Kingdom Prison Services: Report*. London: HMSO.

Morris, T. and Morris, P. (1963) *Pentonville: A Sociological Study of an English Prison*. London: Routledge & Kegan Paul.

Moses, C. and Bennett, J. (2005) 'The Interview: Colin Moses, National Chair of the Prison Officers' Association', *Prison Service Journal*, 160: 52–7.

Narey, M. (2002) *Director General's Speech to the POA Conference 22 May 2002.*

Pelling, H. (1976) *A History of British Trade Unionism*, 3rd edn. Harmondsworth: Penguin.

Prison Officer's Association (2000) *POA Diary.* London: POA

Prison Officer's Association (2005) *POA Diary.* London: POA

Reynolds, G. and Judge, A. (1968) *The Night the Police Went on Strike.* London: Weidenfeld & Nicolson.

Thomas, J. (1972) *The English Prison Officer Since 1850: A Study in Conflict.* London: Routledge & Kegan Paul.

Thomas, J. (1978) 'A Good Man For Gaoler? Crisis, Discontent and the Prison Staff', in J. Freeman (ed.), *Prisons Past and Future in Commemoration of the Bi-centenary of John Howard's The State of the Prisons.* London: Heinmann.

Thomas, J. (1994) 'Woolf and Prison Staff: Still Looking for "Good Gaolers"', in E. Player and M. Jenkins (eds), *Prisons after Woolf: Reform Through Riot.* London: Routledge.

Waddington, P. (1999) 'Police (Canteen) Sub-culture: An Appreciation', *British Journal of Criminology*, 39 (2): 287–309.

Woolf, H. and Tumin, S. (1991) *Prison Disturbances April 1990: Report of an Inquiry*, Cm 1456. London: HMSO.

Chapter 8

Understanding prison officers: culture, cohesion and conflicts

Elaine Crawley and Peter Crawley

To the general public, we're all mindless morons.
(Long-serving Senior Officer)

Introduction

As the comment reproduced above suggests, prison officers see themselves as part of an unvalued, unappreciated occupational group. Their understanding is that they are regarded by the public as unintelligent, insensitive and sometimes brutal, and that their work is perceived as entailing no more than the containment of society's deviants and misfits. Historically, prison officers were generally ex-military personnel, and like prisoners were physically segregated from the wider community by virtue of living in purpose-built, Prison Service-owned houses located within the prison grounds. In this respect, their lives have resembled those of other 'barrack' groups such as soldiers, another occupational grouping held to have somewhat 'special', and not always pleasant, duties conducted 'for' society. This arrangement prohibited the interchange of ideas and interaction between prison staff and the local community, and gave officers and their families little opportunity to mix with others from different (i.e. non-military) backgrounds and who were engaged in very different types of employment.

For prison officers, the *occupational culture* – and the social interactions which inevitably result – is a significant component of the job itself. In the prison, *how* things are done can be as important as *what* is done, and occupational (that is, informal) rules and norms underpin how officers relate to their inmates, to each other, to their superiors on the wing and to their managers. Occupational norms determine how officers respond (i.e. positively, negatively or with indifference) to institutional changes, how experienced officers accommodate the foibles of new recruits and how male officers accept (or not) the growing numbers of women and ethnic minority recruits entering a traditionally white, male, working-class sphere.

Rather surprisingly, given the range of interesting sociological questions it is possible to ask in respect of prison officers, their social world remains relatively under-researched. This very quickly becomes apparent when we compare what has been written about prison officers with the much larger body of scholarly work into the working lives of the only other blue-collar group employed in the criminal justice system – the police. There is no doubt also that the sociological gaze has more often been directed at prisoners than their 'keepers'; indeed following decades of academic research into the lives of prisoners (notable examples include Serge 1977; Cohen and Taylor 1981; Boyle 1983; Toch 1977; Liebling 1992) we can now be reasonably confident that we have a good understanding of the impact of the prison on its prisoners, the ways in which prisoners attempt to adjust to living in a prison and the ways in which they cope with (and sometimes are unable to cope with) the routines, demands and pressures of prison life.

By contrast, prison officers, their lives and working practices in the prison, their feelings about the work they do and their relationships with prisoners and their fellow officers, have been poorly documented and hence poorly appreciated and understood. Much less is known about the impact of the prison on its uniformed staff, and the psychological and emotional adjustments that ordinary men and women must make in order to become prison officers (though see Arnold, this volume). Despite a great deal of academic interest in the prison *as an institution* (see, for example, Sykes 1958; Foucault 1979) and in the experiences of those sentenced to serve time behind its walls (see especially Serge 1977; Boyle 1977; James 2003, 2005), those whose job it is to keep prisoners captive were, until very recently, more or less ignored in British criminology/sociology. (An exception to this generalisation remains the work of Thomas (1972).) Fortunately, following a lengthy period of neglect, the issue of the prison officer at work has once again begun to be acknowledged as an important one. There is now a significant (albeit relatively small) corpus of research literature from the United States (see especially

Kauffman 1988; Lombardo 1981; Crouch and Marquart 1980; Duffee 1980; Poole and Regoli 1980) and a less pronounced but growing interest among British criminologists (see especially Hay and Sparks 1991; Liebling and Price 2001; Crawley 2002, 2004a, 2004b).

During the past decade or so, the Prison Service of England and Wales has been, and indeed continues to be, subject to rapid institutional change. This has included, *inter alia*, new 'managerialist' rationalisation, the introduction of privately managed prisons and the introduction of new human rights legislation. There has also been a stated desire, on the part of senior managers within the Service, to 'change the culture' of the Prison Service on the grounds that it was preventing the Service from moving forward (Prison Service 1997: para. 10.1). Noting that the Service was shot through with outmoded practices, behaviours and working styles, the review team recommended the urgent implementation of 'a programme of cultural and behavioural change'. Launched against a background of rapid expansion (a result of an unprecedented growth in the prison population) and increasing pressure to become more effective (in both custodial and rehabilitative terms) and efficient (in terms of controlling costs) the review focused on proposals for improving the delivery of prison services.

The 'invisibility' of prison work

When, in the 1940s, American academics first turned their attention to prison staff (see, for example, Barnes and Teeter 1945) the prison officer they portrayed was a stereotype – an unintelligent, brutal and insensitive individual who was capable of little more than shouting orders, carrying a bunch of keys and using his fists. Such portrayals, in common with negative media reports of prison abuses (many of which had, unfortunately, rather more than a ring of truth about them) along with the relative *invisibility* of prison work more generally (all of it still takes place behind high walls) led to the (still) commonly held belief among prison officers that 'nobody cares' about them. This, in turn, has led to their wariness and mistrust of all 'outsiders', i.e. anyone who does not work in a prison. Unsurprisingly, prison officers are generally unaccustomed to talking to researchers about themselves and their work.

To understand the attitudes and behaviours of prison officers it is necessary to understand the conditions under which they work. By 'conditions' we mean not only the physical work environment and their formal contractual obligations but also the character of social relations, including the relations of power (formal and informal) which hold sway in the prisons in which they do their job. Such conditions – the myriad of cultural norms and customs, the perception of being undervalued, the tensions between care and custody and the requirements to deal with new management strategies and a changing employee profile – coalesce to imbue the work with specific meanings for those who do it.

Management theorists – many of whom now bring an anthropological perspective to the problem of organisations – argue that the 'culture' of an organisation is a key component in the capacity of that organisation to deliver on its stated aims and hence make a profit. First then, the notion of what 'culture' *is* must be clearly understood. Generally speaking, definitions of culture tend to deal primarily either with the way we act or the way we think (Williams *et al.* 1993: 14). Writing from an organisational perspective, these authors note that between these two extremes, culture has also been defined in terms of both thought *and* behaviour. A working definition of 'occupational culture' could thus be 'the commonly shared beliefs, values and characteristic patterns of behaviour that exist within an organisation'. In his study of the British police, Holdaway (1983: 134) defines *occupational* culture as '… the officers' construction of what constitutes (and should constitute) police work, i.e. what police officers think they *should* be doing and how they think this can best be achieved'. Such patterns of meanings are, of course, historically transmitted; as people interact the norms and practices of the organisation are continually lived out, enforced and reinforced.

Among the characteristics of prison officer culture are (a) an expectation of solidarity between members; (b) suspicion; (c) feelings of social isolation; and (d) an emphasis on physical courage. The characteristic that is perhaps most frequently identified by prison officers themselves is a strong sense of social isolation, both from their own managers and from society at large.

Social isolation

A common remark made by prison officers – young and older, male and female – is that 'outsiders' (i.e. those who do not work in prisons) either regard them with suspicion and wariness or ignore them altogether. According to Marsh *et al.* (1986: 64), this is because others see, upon prison officers, the miasma of prison, and are keen to avoid contact with it. Research recently conducted by one of us (Crawley 2004a, 2004b) confirms this phenomenon; indeed, prison officers readily volunteer that they are generally treated as if they have been 'contaminated' by their engagement in prison work. One female officer described to us, as an example of this, the attitude of other patients to her while she was waiting in her doctor's surgery:

> If I have to go to the doctors in my uniform, when I sit in the waiting room, people just move. [*How do you mean?*] They physically move away from you … It's as if you smell.

As we shall show in a moment, the issue of 'contamination' arises not only in the context of officers' interactions with the general public but also in the private sphere of the home.

Solidarity

Perhaps the most significant cultural norm prison officers are expected to observe is that of solidarity (Kauffman 1988; Lombardo 1981; Crawley 2004a, 2004b). Officers' need for, and expectation of solidarity between members of their occupational group arises directly from the sense of isolation we describe above. The norm of solidarity performs three central functions for prison officers. First it ensures that they can rely on colleagues in a 'tight spot', i.e. when they are at risk of harm from assailants. The obligation to go to the aid of a colleague is the most important positive responsibility of any uniformed officer; in the prison, as on the police beat, it is 'the norm on which officer solidarity is based, the foundation of their sense of brotherhood' (Kauffman 1988; but see also Lombardo 1981). Secondly, solidarity sustains prison officers against criticism by groups who do not understand the pressures of the job (namely the general public, 'do-gooders', the media, prisoners' legal advisors and prison officers' own managers). It is important to note that staff solidarity '… is very closely related to lack of public support and public apathy' (on this see also Skolnick 1975). Thirdly, staff solidarity ensures that colleagues will maintain secrecy in the face of both internal and external investigations against them, either as individuals or as a group (see, for example, Kauffman 1988; Holdaway 1983).

Cynicism and suspicion

Some of the core characteristics of the occupational culture of prison officers are strikingly similar to those that comprise the occupational culture of rank-and-file police. Albeit to varying degrees, cynicism and suspicion are commonly felt and practised at every rank and in every prison. This has significant consequences. In particular, when an in-group perceives that it is constantly under attack from an out-group, the morale and solidarity within the in-group may, ironically, be increased, along with a sense of isolation. Criticism is considered a prerogative of group members; criticism from outsiders, except in special instances, is fiercely resisted (Goldstein and McGhee 1972). An important effect of criticism from groups as varied as the media, the general public, politicians and prison reform groups has been the development of a 'laager' mindset – a tendency on the part of uniformed staff to 'circle the wagons' against unsympathetic outsiders. Sensing hostility from all sides, prison officers as an occupational group have, over the years, taken an aggressive and confrontational stance to all challenges. Feeling besieged from all sides they turn in among themselves (Crawley 2004a, 2004b).

Humour

In the prison setting, the use of humour is central not only for 'surviving' demanding encounters and events but also for maintaining and increasing staff morale. Humour functions as a defence mechanism (to protect against the emotional distress of specific situations), as a wit sharpener (banter is seen as essential for making officers think on their feet), as a morale raiser (officers allude to this as the pre-shift 'gee up' or the release of tension as staff leave the gate after work), as an 'incorporator' (the joshing of a new recruit to make him/her 'one of us') and as a strategy of exclusion (i.e. to reinforce the belief that 'deviant' officers are *not* 'one of us'). Humour is also therefore a monitor of staff performance on the terms established within the local staff culture. So while humour can be healing (promoting group solidarity and relieving tension) it can also be destructive and divisive (see Crawley 2004a, 2004b).

Much of what prison officers call 'banter' could be described, in anthropological terms, as 'ritual insult exchange' (Zijderveld 1983). Indeed, 'banter' can be tough on new recruits – they may be teased unmercifully (particularly if they make a silly mistake) and become the butt of practical jokes. Ritualised insult exchange must not, of course, be taken too far; in the prison setting officers have to be extremely careful in their verbal joustings with prisoners. Officers claim to be able to gauge which prisoners can appreciate banter and which cannot; this is the kind of knowledge that officers are alluding to when they talk about the 'common-sense' nature of prison work.

The domestic character of prisons

The prevention of escape and the maintenance of order remain the primary tasks of the prison officer. Another component of the 'specialness' of the prison officer role is the capacity for the (legitimate) use of force when required. The capacity to use force is, of course, also required from those working in occupations such as policing and in the armed forces. Unlike the soldier or the police officer, however, prison officers are expected to carry out – in addition to their primary responsibilities – the task of routinely providing care. It is significant that the social world of the prison officer is smaller, more intimate and more *domestic* in character than the world in which the police officer moves. While police officers have high visibility and a wide network of social contacts (they deal with law-abiding members of the general public as well as offenders), prison officers deal, in the main, with people convicted of, or awaiting trial for, a criminal offence. Moreover, the degree of intimacy involved in working with prisoners is considerable compared to that experienced in police work: while a police officer may not have to spend time with an individual he has treated roughly or unfairly, a prison officer may well have to spend months or even years with that individual. For these reasons, prison officers are much more aware of the value of building positive relationships with those in their charge. Moreover, close proximity to prisoners *over time*, in the context of what is, after all, a highly domestic and thus a relatively intimate environment, makes it impossible for staff to maintain – at least for any length of time – the notion of 'them and us', and many *do* develop close bonds with certain prisoners. Like others whose work entails intimate interactions with distressed individuals – Crawley (2002, 2004a, 2004b) compares prison officers' work to that of medical staff, ambulance crews and fire-fighters – prison officers deliberately employ certain coping strategies to get through the working day. These include humour (which we have discussed above), strategies of depersonalisation (e.g. descriptions of prisoners as 'bodies' to be counted) and a rhetoric of coping and detachment (that officers should not get too close to prisoners is an occupational norm).

Machismo

Prison officers work in an occupation that has long been thought to require the traditional male qualities of dominance, authoritativeness and aggressiveness. It is a job in which, for many male officers, the traditional female qualities of nurturance, sensitivity and understanding 'are thought to be not merely unnecessary but actually detrimental' (Zimmer 1986: 3). In most prisons there are officers who continue to stress the importance of 'machismo' for successful job performance, and who claim that the officer who cannot muster some version of this masculine image before both prisoners and other officers is in for trouble (on this see Crouch 1980: 217). This 'cult of machismo' (Ryder 1994: 86), along with the nature of certain tasks inherent in the job itself, does have a tendency to steamroller more sensitive, compassionate and caring individuals. As we shall see, the outcome is that not only do prison officers learn not to *show* sympathy towards prisoners (except in specific circumstances), many also learn not to *feel* it (Crawley 2004a, 2004b).

Occupational culture in prisons

In the interests of brevity, our discussion of prison officer culture here is necessarily simplified, and thus underplays the nuances of occupational culture both in general terms and in specific prisons. Among both staff and inmates, individual prisons have distinctive reputations; while some are known for their harshness or brutality, others are recognised as being innovative and fair. Prison governors, however, particularly 'Number One' governors, have the capacity to set or change the cultural 'tone' of individual institutions, and their reputations can therefore alter in line with changes in management practices, directives and personnel. It is important to note, however, that the occupational cultures of specific establishments evolve over time. Their precise characters are dependent on such things as the type and function of the prison, the prison's history (for example the number of disturbances and the quality of industrial relations), the ratio of young to old and experienced to new staff, the nature of the regime, the ratio of staff to prisoners, the rate of staff turnover and the architecture of the prison itself (see, for example, Bottoms and Light 1987; Home Office 1984; Woolf 1991; Fairweather 1995: 19).

Arguably, external factors such as the political and economic climate are also important. Indeed, the present level of consciousness in any prison (and indeed that of any other institution) can only be understood by reference to the series of historical situations in which it has developed (Cohen and Taylor 1981: 122–3). For this reason, and importantly, the occupational culture of prison officers is not a reified *thing*: rather, it should be thought of as an 'achievement' or 'process' – a 'consequence' of the interplay of various 'materials', including architecture, paperwork, uniforms, rules, jargon, customs, ideologies, technologies and human beings. In consequence, the degree of solidarity, the value placed upon machismo, the nature of the staff–prisoner relationship and so forth vary significantly from prison to prison. Policies and practices designed to 'reconstruct' prisoners therefore inevitably also reconstruct prison staff. In the same way that they impose new demands as to what officers should accomplish, they impose, by extension, new demands on how officers are supposed to conduct themselves.

Becoming a prison officer

Recruitment into the Prison Service of England and Wales is now carried out locally rather than nationally. Since devolution of the recruitment process, each prison is responsible for recruiting the officers they require. Jobs are advertised in local Job Centres, and those wishing to apply must contact the prisons directly. Candidates must be aged between 18 and 62 years at the time of appointment. They must also be fully physically fit (the recruitment process involves a medical and fitness test); however, the Prison Service operates a guaranteed interview scheme for disabled people (as defined in the Disability Discrimination Act 1995) who meet the minimum published criteria for appointment.

A competence-based assessment follows the preliminary application process; this is a structured sifting method where trained assessors, using a standard rating procedure, rate the candidates' accounts of their achievements in specific areas of experience. These areas of activity form part of the key competences required for the job of prison officer. The highest-ranking applicants are invited to an assessment centre where they undertake a series of work-related exercises which do not require experience of prisons. In recent years, the development of the prison officer role has heightened the need for conceptual and analytical skills and the ability to take a theoretical perspective. Applicants are also required to possess a range of interpersonal skills; in particular they require assertiveness, and skills in listening, influencing, negotiating and verbal communication. Following a successful interview, the new recruit must undergo a rigorous – albeit relatively short – period of training. Entry-level training takes place over an eight-week period. After basic training, new recruits are given a brief induction course into the routines and working practices of the prison in which they are to work. They are then supervised by more experienced officers (see Arnold, this volume, for further details)

One of the key lessons taught to new recruits is that they must develop a suspicious mindset when dealing with prisoners. Like police officers, prison officers are specifically trained to be suspicious – to constantly be on the look out for potential, as well as actual, 'trouble'. For the prison officer, the ability to 'read' people and situations is crucial for the maintenance of order and indeed for his/ her own safety, and the new recruit is taught during Basic Training not to trust any prisoner. New recruits are instructed to observe inmates carefully and constantly – to get into the habit of asking themselves, when supervising inmates, 'What is he doing?' 'Why is he doing it?' In short, recruits are advised by their trainers 'never to trust the bastards!' (personal communications, numerous officers). Within the prison setting, officers '… get to think that everybody is out to do you harm if they get the chance … you lose your objectivity a lot' (senior officer). Unfortunately for officers and their families, the development of a suspicious 'mind-set' has certain knock-on effects for officers' relationships *outside* as well as inside the prison. We shall return to this in our discussion of 'spillage' below.

Enculturation

A chief, if largely unacknowledged, aspect of the period of residential training is the way that, in anthropological terms, it acts as the first stage of 'enculturation'. Enculturation is synonymous with 'socialisation'. It refers to the idea that, to be a full member of any 'culture' or 'subculture', individuals have constantly to learn and use, both formally and informally, the patterns of cultural behaviour prescribed by that culture. Initiation rites and other forms of training (formal and informal) are part and parcel of the enculturation process.

It is only in the second stage of this process – the new recruit's sudden immersion into the working practices and informal (or craft) rules of prison work and the day-to-day realities of prison life – that his/her transformation into a prison officer begins to take place.

The process of *becoming* a prison officer, then, only really starts with the new recruit's first posting. Here, he/she will discover that the road to being a prison officer can be a slow, difficult and sometimes painful one, involving a significant degree of culture shock (Crawley 2004a, 2004b). The attitudes, behaviours and work 'styles' of a prison officer are shaped through this process; although the recruit will have some ideas about the kind of officer (s)he wishes to become during his/her basic training, these ideas will inevitably be revised in the light of encounters with established officers, and through their observations of these officers' actions and demeanours as they go about their work. It is only through the internalisation, over time, of the myriad prison rules, values, customs, practices and norms (formal and informal, occupational and cultural) – along with a range of customary 'tips' from experienced officers on how to interact with prisoners – that new recruits learn how to become prison officers themselves.

The pressure to conform: group-think

In the prison setting it is not only prisoners who form cliques to meet the need for social approval; prison officers also coalesce into exclusive social groupings with shared interests, values and beliefs. So while new recruits may feel uncomfortable with certain aspects of the occupational culture – disliking in particular 'the macho side of the job' – in their need to 'fit in' they will find it difficult not to become ensnared. Indeed, the pressure to conform is strong. Most psychologists would argue that all of us have basic psychological needs, including social approval and emotional support, and that much of our behaviour is based on a desire to belong and identify with other persons or groups. Unfortunately the pressure to conform to the values of the group can be so strong as to make people doubt the validity of their own values and experiences.

Workplace stress

New recruits to the Prison Service are particularly vulnerable to workplace pressures. Not only must they learn to deal with the day-to-day problems of prisoners, and to conform to the values of the occupational cultures operating in the prison in which they work, they will also have to cope with the (often disagreeable) attitudes and behaviours of their colleagues. Staff hostility, when it arises, is not only directed towards prisoners – officers often allege intimidation of staff by other staff, directed at keeping in line those unwilling to subscribe to the most dominant norms of the occupational group.

In recent years the Prison Service, like the Police Service, has formally acknowledged that prison work can be extremely stressful (*Prison Service News* 1997; HM Prison Service 1996). However, prison officers do not find it easy to admit to feeling 'stressed'. The long-standing expectation that prison officers will be courageous, resilient, authoritative and fearless in all situations and that they will suppress those emotions thought to be 'non-masculine' (for example, anxiety, fear and depression) often prevents officers who are experiencing such emotions from seeking help. While female officers are also aware of the need to present a confident and authoritative 'front', they are less vulnerable to the pressure to be 'macho' and more likely to share their feelings with colleagues, especially their female counterparts. There is evidence that male officers find women less threatening to work with than other men, and that they appreciate the way that female officers are able to 'cut through the macho bullshit' in ways that they themselves are often unable to do (see Crawley 2004). There is certainly a good deal of sociological evidence that men sometimes *do* find it threatening to be in a group of other men because men often take advantage of any weakness that another man might show (on this see Seidler 1992).

Perhaps surprisingly, officers claim that much of the stress they experience is generated through their interactions with fellow officers and, more particularly, their managers, rather than through their interactions with prisoners. For many officers, a bullying management style is a significant (and routine) workplace stressor. During fieldwork conducted by one of us (Crawley 2004a, 2004b), numerous officers reported being bullied[1] by their managers. Workplace bullying included verbal abuse, pressure to change shifts without notice or to work to unsafe manning levels – all of which can have a devastating effect on staff confidence and morale. Yet some prison officers also bully and harangue fellow officers, particularly those who choose to engage in work that cuts across the (long-standing) cultural norm of 'them and us'. This is particularly evident in the context of officers working in 'specialist' regimes.

Spoiled identity: the 'deviant' prison officer

As we have tried to emphasise throughout this chapter, it is difficult to carry out the duties of a prison officer without reflecting on, and subscribing to, an extremely powerful (and sometimes disagreeable) set of customs, values and norms. Indeed, any officer whose work demands that he/she depart from these norms runs the risk of acquiring a 'spoiled' work identity. That is to say, an officer's willingness to work either with despised groups of prisoners or in regimes which espouse values contrary to traditional occupational norms may expose him/herself to hostility and ridicule from others and to claims that this is not 'proper' prison work. For example, various aspersions are cast on prison officers who work in therapeutic regimes; they are often accused by colleagues of being 'too soft' with prisoners and, consequently, of not being in control of them. Similarly, those working with elderly prisoners – a prisoner population that is relatively compliant and that has a much greater need for personal care – may also be accused of not doing 'proper' prison work. Not only is the work they do seen as too safe and too predictable, displays of machismo – a characteristic perceived by some officers as necessary for working effectively with young, volatile prisoners – are entirely inappropriate for working with frail and elderly men. As one of us has argued elsewhere (Crawley and Sparks 2005), working on an elderly prisoner wing seems to blur the boundaries of what it means to be a 'proper' prison officer – not least because much of the work to be done there represents a threat to professional status in that it is dishonourable, domestic, 'women's work'.

The *management* of a spoiled identity becomes a key concern to officers working in such regimes, and this requires the learning of certain strategies and techniques. The strategy most commonly used involves the employment of socially acceptable 'vocabularies of motive' (Mills 1940). Vocabularies of motive are often called upon by those tainted by the stigma of 'dirty work' (Hughes 1971) and other forms of devalued behaviour. Officers working in Therapeutic Communities and – perhaps particularly – on Sex Offender Treatment Programmes (SOTP), attempt to renegotiate their spoiled identities by asserting the positive value of their role in the face of claims to the contrary (Crawley 2000). The justification most often used is an appeal to higher loyalties (for a discussion of this in the policing literature see Mulcahy 1995). In the context of the Therapeutic Community, officers might stress, for example, the value of their work in terms of helping young prisoners to become drug-free, responsible adults (see

Crawley 2004a, 2004b). In the case of SOTP work, the officer justifies his or her 'dirty work' by asserting that it may prevent further child victims. To varying degrees, these strategies 'work' in the sense that they provide alternative credible identities to otherwise 'deviant' prison staff.

Thank goodness for the police, firefighters, nurses and ...?

As we have already indicated, there is a general understanding among prison officers that they are unvalued by their managers and the general public. That they are not regarded as on a par with other 'public service' workers is a source of deep resentment and disappointment, and this is reflected in the following comment:

> We never get a mention on Christmas day. [On the TV and radio] It's always 'Let's give a thought to the policemen, the nurses, the firemen and the ambulance men who work on Christmas day.' They never mention prison officers. But we give up our Christmas as well to make it a bit better for this lot.

Arguably, negative media portrayals of prisons do little to generate admiration or gratitude for those who work in them. The majority of staff commented that they find the term 'warders' derogatory (although the term 'warder' went out of use in 1924 it is still used widely in the press) because it paints an inaccurate picture of what they actually do. Today, the prison officer role encompasses a relatively high level of rehabilitative work with prisoners, such as the delivery (and in some cases development of) courses oriented towards drug awareness and good parenting. Prison officers resent stereotypical and skewed portrayals of them and their work and largely blame the media for the stereotype that prevails. As this senior officer remarked:

> To the general public, we're all mindless morons. And that's the fault of the papers.

Most prison officers acknowledge that the general public view them in a negative light. Given the public's limited understanding of prisons and the numerous (and sometimes horrendous) accounts of prison regimes over the years, they can to some extent understand this. Nonetheless they are still stung by disparaging attitudes towards them and the general lack of recognition for the positive work that they actually do. The following quote, from a long-serving officer, reveals the intensity of many officers' feelings of hurt defiance:

Public opinion has always looked at jailers a bit warily – [that we] must be strange to be doin' a job like this. The public are not sympathetic to prison officers; never have been, and as far as I can see, never will be. Whether that is purely through ignorance, erm, or an inbuilt unease about people who deprive other people of their freedom, I don't know. We think we should get more [public approval] 'cos its a bloody shitty job, er, and if Joe Public actually wants to be protected from these people, they should be more sympathetic, to us.

Such feelings, shared by many other officers, translate, on a day-to-day basis, into cautious interactions outside the prison setting. Indeed, the prison officer role – and the emotions and attitudes it generates – are extremely difficult to leave at the prison gate.

Changed by the job: 'spillover'

That they have been 'changed' by prison work is a common perception amongst prison officers. Most feel that they have become 'harder' since joining the Prison Service: desensitised to the distress and suffering of others. Those who feel that they had started out as relatively sensitive individuals have noticed that over the months and years they have become blasé and careless in their dealings with prisoners. Interestingly, those who do feel disturbed by the distress of prisoners feel obliged to put on an act:

Everyone's told me I've got harder. Having met death in a variety of ways – through seeing slashings up and so on – it becomes 'So what?' Our warped sense of humour keeps us going. It's a defence mechanism. You grieve privately, not publicly. You can't grieve in this job; people would think you were soft ...

The families of prison officers – particularly spouses and partners – are often deeply concerned by the difficulties officers face in *ceasing* to perform the role of prison officer when they get home. This is evidenced in reports that officers have a tendency to be overly suspicious of their own children (in some cases, children may be 'rubbed down' when things go missing or their rooms searched for 'contraband' such as cigarettes) and that they have an expectation of obedience and a reliance on routines (Crawley 2002, 2004a, 2004b). In short, prison officer culture has a tendency to 'spill over' into personal life. 'Spillover' derives from four key issues: danger, routinisation, desensitisation and contamination. This combination ensures that the potential for role engulfment is high, and officers' ability to come 'out of role' low. Indeed, a striking aspect of prison work is the strain of living in, and moving between, two worlds – only one of which is contained within high walls.

Concluding comments

How officers feel about the work they do, how they think about prisoners, how they see their fellow officers and managers and their perceptions of the 'proper' prison officer role have important implications both for the nature and quality of imprisonment and for officers' satisfaction with their job. The various conflicts we have outlined in this chapter arise, in part, because the prison has to function as an institution concerned not only with security and control but also increasingly, with 'treatment' and 'rehabilitation'. Moreover, these goals are being attempted in an occupational climate which often fails to listen to the voices of uniformed staff. We also need to be aware that when we ask prison officers to take on specialist roles we are, in effect, expecting them to challenge long-established, entrenched occupational norms. Non-mainstream work inevitably makes particular demands on them – demands that can bring long sought-for opportunities, challenges and rewards but which, in the context of prison overcrowding and inadequate resources, can also generate resentment, stigmatisation and high levels of occupational stress.

Seminar questions

1 Why study occupational culture when looking at the working lives of criminal justice professionals such as prison officers?
2 Prison officers become 'enculturated' to a range of characteristics and dispositions in the process of becoming an officer. What are these dispositions? How do they help prison officers carry out their role?

3 Aspects of occupational culture in prisons have a tendency to 'spill over' and affect relationships outside the workplace. Why is this, and what are the implications of spillover for the personal lives of prison officers?
4 How might a prison officer's occupational identity become 'spoiled'? What strategies can officers use to counter this process?

Recommended reading

Crawley's (2004a) *Doing Prison Work: The Public and Private Lives of Prison Officers* is an ethnographic study of prison officers at work. In addition to showing how the job of the prison officer is accomplished on a day-to-day basis, the book explores not only what officers do but also how they feel about their work and how they act when they are doing it. Kauffman's (1988) *Prison Officers and Their World* examines the work experiences of American prison guards. She draws particular attention to their occupational norms – all of which stress the importance of staff solidarity – and the consequences for individuals who breach them. Using an 'appreciative inquiry' approach, Liebling and Price's (2001) *The Prison Officer* presents a study of staff-prisoner relationships and, relatedly, a discussion of prison officers 'at their best'. In so doing they focus on the centrality of discretion in the work of prison officers and on the complexities of the prison officer role.

Note

1 Workplace bullying is a significant problem within the Prison Service, as evidenced by comments from numerous officers, from various articles in the *Gatelodge* magazine and in literature provided by the Prison Service Staff Care and Welfare Service (PSSCWS). Despite the development of anti-bullying programmes for prisoners, management bullying of lower-ranking staff seems to have increased over recent years. Officers in their probationary year are particularly vulnerable to bullying; higher-ranking uniformed grades know that probationers are afraid to refuse because they need favourable progress reports to achieve a permanent contract.

References

Barnes, H.E. and Teeter, N.K. (1959) *New Horizons in Criminology*. Englewood Cliffs, NJ: Prentice-Hall.
Bottoms, A.E and Light, R. (1987) *Problems of Long-Term Imprisonment*. Aldershot: Gower.
Boyle, J. (1977) *A Sense of Freedom*. London: Pan Books.

Boyle, J. (1984) *The Pain of Confinement*. London: Pan Books.

Cohen, S. and Taylor, L. (1981) *Psychological Survival*. Harmondsworth: Penguin.

Crawley, E.M. (2000) 'Reflections on the Sex Offender Treatment Programme', Viewpoint Article, *Howard League Magazine*, February.

Crawley, E.M. (2002) 'Bringing It All Back Home? The Impact of Prison Officers' Work on their Families', *Probation Journal*, 49 (4).

Crawley, E. (2004a) *Doing Prison Work: The Public and Private Lives of Prison Officers*. Cullompton: Willan.

Crawley, E.M. (2004b) 'Emotion and Performance: Prison Officers and the Presentation of Self in Prisons', *Punishment and Society*, 6 (4): 411–27.

Crawley, E. and Crawley, P. (2007) 'Performance and Disorder and the Communicative Quality of Prison Violence', in J. Byrne and F. Taxman (eds), *Prison Violence and Prison Culture*, Boston: Allyn & Bacon.

Crawley, E. and Sparks, R. (2005) 'Older Men in Prison: Survival, Coping and Identity', in A. Liebling and S. Maruna (eds), *The Effects of Imprisonment*. Cullompton: Willan.

Crouch, B.M. (1980) *The Keepers: Prison Guards and Contemporary Corrections*. Springfield, IL: Charles C. Thomas.

Crouch, B. and Marquart, J.W. (1980) 'On Becoming a Prison Guard', in B. Crouch (ed.), *The Keepers: Prison Guards and Contemporary Corrections*. Springfield, IL: Charles C. Thomas.

Duffee, D. (1980) *Correctional Management: Change and Control in Correctional Organizations*. Englewood Cliffs, NJ: Prentice Hall.

Fairweather, L. (1995) 'Does Good Design Help Those Inside?', *Prison Service Journal*, September, No. 101.

Foucault, M. (1979) *Discipline and Punish*. London: Penguin.

Goldstein, J.H. and McGhee, P.E. (1972) *The Psychology of Humour: Theoretical Perspectives and Empirical Issues*. New York and London: Academic Press.

Hay, W. and Sparks, R. (1991) 'What is a Prison Officer?', *Prison Service Journal*, Summer.

HM Prison Service (1996) *Weekly Bulletin*, 1 (18), 6 May.

Holdaway, S. (1983) *Inside the British Police*. Oxford: Basil Blackwell.

Home Office (1984) *Managing the Long-Term Prison System* (Report of the Control Review Committee). London: HMSO.

Hughes, E.C. (1971) 'Good People and Dirty Work', in *The Sociological Eye*. Chicago: Aldine.

James, E. (2003) *A Life Inside Prison: A Prisoners' Notebook*. London: Atlantic Books.

James, E. (2005) *The Home Stretch: From Prison to Parole*. London: Atlantic Books.

Kauffman, K. (1988) *Prison Officers and Their World*. Cambridge, MA: Harvard University Press.

Liebling, A. (1992) *Suicides in Prison*. London: Routledge.

Liebling, A. and Price, D. (2001) *The Prison Officer*. Winchester: Waterside Press.

Lombardo, L.X. (1981) *Guards Imprisoned: Correctional Officers At Work*. New York: Elsevier.

Marsh, A., Dobbs, J. and Monk, J. (1986) *Staff Attitudes in the Prison Service*. London: Office of Population Censuses and Surveys.

Mills, C. Wright (1940) *Situated Actions and Vocabularies of Motive*. Indianapolis, IN: Bobbs-Merrill, College Division.

Mulcahy, A. (1995) '"Headhunter" or "Real Cop"? Identity in the World of Internal Affairs Officers', *Journal of Contemporary Ethnography*, 24 (1).

Poole, E.D. and Regoli, R.M. (1980) 'Work Relations and Cynicism Among Prison Guards', *Criminal Justice and Behaviour*, 7 (3).

Prison Service (1997) *Prison Service Review*, October. London: HMSO.

Prison Service News (1997) 15 (154).

Ryder, R. (1994) 'Violence and the Role of Machismo', in E.A. Stanko (ed.), *Perspectives on Violence*. London: Quartet.

Scottish Home and Health Department (1971) 'Report of the Departmental Working Party on the Treatment of Certain Male Long-Term Prisoners and Potentially Violent Prisoners'. Unpublished.

Seidler, V. (1992) 'Rejection, Vulnerability, and Friendship', in P. Nardi (ed.), *Men's Friendships*. Newbury Park, CA: Sage.

Serge, V. (1977) *Men in Prison*. London: Writers and Readers Publishing Co-operative.

Skolnick, J. (1975) *Justice without Trial*. New York: Wiley.

Sykes, G. (1958) *The Society of Captives*. Princeton, NJ: Princeton University Press.

Thomas, E. (1972) *The English Prison Officer Since 1850*. London: Routledge & Kegan Paul.

Toch, H. (1977) *Living in Prison: The Ecology of Survival*. New York: Free Press.

White, M.E. (1974) 'Therapeutic Communities', *Prison Service Journal*, July, No. 15.

Williams, A., Dobson, P. and Walters, M. (1993) *Changing Culture: New Organisational Approaches*. London: Institute of Personnel Management.

Woolf, Lord Justice (1991) *Report of an Inquiry into Prison Disturbances April 1991*, Cm 1456. London: HMSO.

Zijderveld, A.C. (1983) 'The Sociology of Humour and Laughter', *Current Sociology*, 31 (3).

Zimmer, L. (1986) *Women Guarding Men*. New York: Elsevier.

Chapter 9

Staff and order in prisons

Deborah H. Drake[1]

Order in prisons has been defined by Liebling as: 'the degree to which the prison environment is structured, stable, predictable and acceptable' (Liebling 2004: 291). A prison can appear orderly in terms of its regime, organisation and practices, but orderliness can be achieved through overt control and without the consent of prisoners. The terms 'order' and 'control' can easily be confused in prisons, and the difference between 'orderliness' and an *agreed upon* state of order in prisons is crucial. As King suggests, 'there is always a tendency for prison officials, who are liable to be held to account, to use a lexicon stressing security and control whereas those not so accountable – academic analysts and prison reformers – prefer a vocabulary which emphasises custody and order' (1997: 45). 'Orderliness' can be achieved through a variety of mechanisms (e.g. routines, procedures or rule-enforcement) and the means through which staff achieve 'security and control' differ from approaches that seek 'custody and order'. Control can be a means through which order is restored (if it has been lost) or disorder prevented, but order in prisons (as in society) should be defined in reference to the implicit social contract which exists between the population (prisoners) and the authorities (prison officers). Sparks, Bottoms and Hay (1996) define order, in part, as follows: 'an orderly situation is any long-standing pattern of social relations (characterised by a minimum level of respect for persons) in which *the expectations that participants have of one another are commonly met* ...' (ibid.: 119; emphasis added). This definition is clearly suggestive of a 'social contract' notion of order where prisoners and staff agree to an implicit contract and where the expectations that each group has of the other are generally met. In this way, to achieve 'order' (as opposed to control) in prisons, the pattern of social relations must be acceptable (as Liebling's definition suggests) to both staff and prisoners.

This chapter discusses several issues related to staff and order in prisons. First, it discusses in greater detail the theoretical problem of order in prisons. Second, it considers the traditional role of officers in relation to order. Third, it draws on recent ethnographic and historical-contextual research in two maximum-security prisons in England (see Drake 2007) and describes the specific and general forms of order in these two prisons. Findings from the research illustrate how forms of order can differ depending on how staff emphasise the policies and control mechanisms at their disposal. However, the findings also suggest that although the two prisons studied were quite 'orderly', this state was achieved through control rather than being an 'acceptable' form of order. The chapter then goes on to discuss the contemporary role of officers in relation to order and control. The fifth area this chapter considers is the experience of prisoners in the contemporary context. Through looking more closely at their experiences the importance of the distinction between 'acceptable order' and control is illustrated. Finally, the chapter concludes by suggesting some implications of the emphasis on 'control' rather than 'order' in contemporary maximum-security prisons.

The problem of order in prisons

Order in prisons has been most thoroughly considered in the work of Sparks *et al.* in *Prisons and the Problem of Order* (1996). Their study sought to identify what eroded or contributed to order in maximum-security prisons, which, throughout the 1970s and 1980s had been the sites of minor and major disturbances. Resulting from their exploratory research in two maximum-security prisons in the late 1980s (Long Lartin and Albany), Sparks *et al.* developed a theoretical conceptualisation of how order was achieved and maintained. They suggested that order heavily depended on the appropriate use of authority on the part of staff and on getting relationships right between staff and prisoners. As Sparks *et al.* state: '... the modality of power which stands most in need of legitimation is not democratic discussion, which claims to be inherently self-legitimating, but force' (1996: 86). That is, the relationships between officers and prisoners are especially vulnerable to legitimacy problems because, in a general sense, the authority of prison officers is *imposed upon* prisoners. When power is imposed without consent, authority figures will not be seen as legitimate, making it more difficult for them to achieve compliance or cooperation from those in their charge.

Discussing the inherent difficulty in negotiating order in prisons through cooperation and compliance, Sparks and Bottoms (1995) highlighted that although the official 'Prison Rules' call for an enlistment of prisoners' willing cooperation in the negotiation of control, 'the aspirational language of "willing cooperation" and "getting the relationship right" seem very distant from the realities of prison life' (1995: 51). To achieve these difficult tasks, then, officers need to use their authority in justifiable ways. Officers must walk a fine line between the over- or under-use of their power and use their discretion carefully (of which more below). Yet the pursuit of legitimate relationships should not be confused with a lapse into prisoner appeasement. Citing the work of Tyler (1990), Sparks and Bottoms (1995) argued that assessments of legitimacy are more dependent on procedural fairness, dignity and respect than on outcomes – that is, appeasing prisoners' desires and requests is not akin to legitimacy. As Tyler stated:

> [P]eople obey the law because they believe that it is proper to do so, they react to their experiences by evaluating their justice or injustice, and in evaluating the justice of their experiences they consider factors unrelated to outcome such as whether they have had a chance to state their case and been treated with dignity and respect. (1990: 178)

In a later publication (Tyler 2003), Tyler argued that 'the perceived obligation to obey is the most direct extension of the concept of legitimacy' (2003: 310). Through consideration of Tyler's work it becomes evident that if people perceive that their expectations of social institutions are being met then they feel obliged to meet the expectations society has of them (i.e. to obey the law and maintain social order). Applying Tyler's findings to the prison context would mean that officers should pay special attention to the means through which they try and achieve order because willing compliance and cooperation from prisoners can be gained if officers meet prisoners' expectations of fair, decent and respectful treatment. How, then, might officers seek to meet these expectations? To answer this question it is helpful to take a closer look at previous approaches to order in UK prisons.

The role of officers in relation to order – previous understandings of how order was achieved

For Sparks *et al.* legitimacy is related to two general aspects of prison life: the fulfilment of prisoners' expectations of material standards of daily life and their fair treatment in formal and informal interactions with prison officers. In practice, officers can secure 'order' in prisons by 'getting relationships right'. Although maximum-security prisons were rather disorderly throughout the 1970s and 1980s (see Home Office 1984) and the forms of order sought during those years should not be idealised, there was an understanding among officers that order was built through careful interactions between staff and prisoners. This approach to order sought the cooperation and compliance of prisoners by allowing some level of contribution from them, facilitated through relationships with officers. Officers in Long Lartin in the 1980s, for example, had an understanding of the complex relationship required between staff and prisoners for order to be achieved:

> ... Personality and character will carry you through, not the rule book. You have to point out that we're a living unit, that he's [the officer] got to spend at least two or three years with this inmate. That he's got to live with him daily, and if he makes a decision, then he's going to have to justify it. If he does nick the inmate, then he's got to be certain it's fair otherwise the inmate will never again relate to him for a long period. (Principal Officer, quoted in Sparks *et al.* 1996: 154)

Likewise, in a study of HMP Whitemoor conducted several years later, Liebling and Price (2001) argued that:

> one of the most significant aspects of staff–prisoner relationships was that they constituted the framework within which decisions were made (and discretion exercised) by prison officers and the context in which those decisions were assessed and evaluated by prisoners. Relationships were the route through which everything else was achieved, and through which prisoners perceived the delivery of fairness, respect and justice. (2001: 92–3)

They further stated that:

> there is a continual tension between the intrinsic, caste-like gap separating staff and prisoners, and the bridging of that gap that

is necessary if the task of 'getting through the prison day' is to be accomplished smoothly. This tension is not – and cannot be – controlled by formal rules and structures, but by informal structures that lead to the development of mutual understandings between officers and prisoners. (2001: 94)

Order in prisons was thus achieved by officers seeking to strike a balance between their use of power and discretion and the recognition that prisoners wanted relationships with staff that 'would achieve justice' (Liebling and Price 2001: 92). Staff and prisoners negotiated what each group saw as an acceptable form of order. Although this was an extremely difficult state to accomplish and, historically, many prisons had trouble doing so and thereby lapsed into disorder (for example, Strangeways in 1990 – see Woolf 1991), the idea 'that relations between staff and prisoners are at the heart of the whole prison system and that control and security flow from getting that relationship right' (Home Office 1984: 6) was the dominant understanding in the Prison Service. Order was not generally accomplished through the application of formal rules, a regime structure or through rigid procedures. More recent research in two maximum-security prisons, however, suggests that the mechanisms by which officers now seek order have changed.

Contemporary forms of order in two maximum-security prisons

The research described in this section was carried out in two maximum-security prisons in the UK: HMP Full Sutton and HMP Whitemoor. In addition to ethnographic study of the prisons,[2] the research also included a historical-contextual component.[3] Both the ethnography and the historical re-construction contribute to the characterisations and conceptualisations of each prison which follow.

At the time of the research, Full Sutton had a fairly predictable and an extremely structured and controlled regime. Prisoners who were not engaged in activities (such as work or education) remained locked in their cells for most of the day except during meals or association times. Movements of prisoners around the prison were tightly controlled. Staff had to acquire permission from the 'control room' (from which all movements in the prison were coordinated) at various times throughout the day in order to move groups of prisoners from one location to another (e.g. from a wing to workshops).

Although the regime was fairly consistent, routines were sometimes disrupted. For instance, Full Sutton staff felt it would compromise security, control and safety if there were not appropriate staffing levels and routines were therefore disrupted if a member of staff was late coming to work or if there was not the requisite number of staff present on a wing. This kind of disruption occurred occasionally during the research. In addition, prisoners reported some procedural problems in the prison. For example, there were discrepancies in the amount of time applications took to be processed and delays for prisoners receiving items from reception.[4] Complaints of this nature from prisoners suggested that procedures were not fully embedded in Full Sutton and that staff did not attempt to mitigate the occasional failings of the prison through their relationships with prisoners. Indeed, problems in the prison were exacerbated by the state of staff–prisoner relationships, which were inflexible, distant and contentious. Though there were examples of good relationships between some staff and prisoners, the majority of staff–prisoner relations appeared adversarial. In short, the form of order which had been adopted at Full Sutton might best be described as 'controlled inflexibility'.

In contrast to Full Sutton, at the time of the research Whitemoor had well-embedded systems and procedures which staff followed closely. Whitemoor prisoners did not complain about procedural problems and routines were rarely disrupted. Prisoners' movements and routines were as tightly controlled as at Full Sutton; however, unlike at Full Sutton, Whitemoor staff saw the importance of communicating with prisoners. Although staff–prisoner relationships could be said to be interactive, they were somewhat tainted by the ulterior motive of the intelligence-gathering aspects of dynamic security. The term 'dynamic security' was first introduced into the Prison Service by Ian Dunbar in 1985. In practice, it means that staff should mix with prisoners, talk and listen to them, but while doing so remain alert to the atmosphere and the potential for incidents. Intelligence gathering is an aspect of dynamic security, but its overall purpose should be to reduce the coerciveness of prison environments (Coyle 2005: 139). However, in Whitemoor, the practice of dynamic security appeared more heavily focused on intelligence-gathering than on maintaining positive interactions with prisoners. The form of order in Whitemoor, then, might best be described as 'security-dominant predictability'.

In general terms, both prisons placed a heavy emphasis on security, but Full Sutton staff relied on control and inflexibility in dealing with prisoners, whereas Whitemoor staff focused more heavily on security procedures, maintaining a predictable regime and structured, instrumental relationships with prisoners.

The role of officers in relation to order – the contemporary context

Full Sutton and Whitemoor differed in their forms of order; however, there were also similarities between the two prisons in the approaches the staff took toward achieving it. This was evident when considering the range of duties carried out by staff and the way in which these duties were approached. At both Full Sutton and Whitemoor, staff had to complete a variety of security-related tasks which contributed to the 'orderliness' of the prisons and symbolically reinforced the authority of staff. First, the regular searching of prisoners before movements and the frequent searching of prisoners' cells were both routinised activities, with prisoners seeming to accept the various types of searching that took place each day. The fact that officers carried out procedures like this at such regular intervals meant that their authority over prisoners was symbolically reinforced on a daily basis. The second security-related task undertaken by staff to achieve orderliness was the regularity with which staff patrolled the landings, ensuring frequent, implicit reminders to prisoners that the staff were 'in charge':

> If you patrol a wing now, you patrol it and that means if there are three or four prisoners in a cell, you open the flap, you look in, you open the door and say: are you alright lads? It's about doing your job. We do not shy away from prisoners. (Prison officer)

Third, the use of dynamic security was seen by staff and managers as a crucial component of the contemporary character of order:

> I think the other bonus we got [from the increased security focus in prisons] is in terms of security intelligence. It has improved dramatically, beyond recognition of what it was like before. The sort of skills that we've enabled our staff to develop in those areas and the recognition of our staff of the value of security intelligence, the importance of submitting it no matter how simple it appears has paid huge dividends. And I think, therefore, we are able to predict and anticipate events

159

much more accurately and therefore take pre-emptive action to prevent disturbances, prevent disorder, and certainly prevent serious violence. (Senior manager, Prison Service)

As the above quotation suggests, officers used intelligence information to take pre-emptive action in preventing disorder (or gaining control). The use of intelligence information further reinforced the authority of officers because it gave prisoners the impression that officers knew everything that was going on in the prison. These security-focused practices established a form of 'order' without the careful fostering of compliance that used to characterise staff–prisoner relationships in maximum-security prisons. This shift in the achievement of order is significant.

In addition to the regularised use of certain security tasks and procedures, orderliness was also maintained by staff in Full Sutton and Whitemoor through the use of the Incentives and Earned Privileges (IEP) policy. The IEP policy is a scheme that links prisoners' behaviour and compliance to privilege levels of 'basic', 'standard' or 'enhanced'. Although an early evaluation of this policy conducted by Liebling *et al.* (1997) suggested the policy was 'less successful in reducing misbehaviour than the Prison Service had hoped' (Bottoms 2003: 166), the IEP policy now plays a significant role in the reduction of misbehaviour and the maintenance of order. In 2000, a new national framework for the IEP scheme was introduced and several modifications to the original policy were made, including greater standardisation of the use of the policy across all prison establishments and the linking of the policy to a range of aspects of prison life. As one of the modifications to the policy stated, IEP schemes should aim to be: 'more fully woven into the fabric of prison life and integrated with other initiatives such as sentence planning, anti-bullying, drugs free wings, etc.' (Bottoms 2003: 188). The policy depends on the vigilance of staff in closely monitoring the behaviour of prisoners. Staff use the policy to encourage the compliance of prisoners by reminding them that breaking prison rules can result in the loss of privileges. The policy connects what is important to prisoners in a practical sense (e.g. visits, wage levels, progression through the system, etc.) to what is important according to the prison (e.g. taking offending behaviour programmes, compliant behaviour, drugs testing) and as such it has become a powerful tool for control.

Staff at Full Sutton and Whitemoor also used particular control measures to explicitly reinforce their authority. For example, some longer-serving prisoners reported a change in the control responses of staff in recent years, as the following quotation from a prisoner from Whitemoor illustrates:

> ... there seems to be an increase in security and searching, whereas before if they had to take you off the wing [due to indiscipline] it would be quite informal [and you would be asked to walk down to the segregation unit]. Now they always have to come with the MUFTI[5] stuff and they always rush in at you, they don't give you any opportunity to walk. (Prisoner)

Physical and coercive control over prisoners was thus employed by the staff. For instance, if a prisoner was perceived by staff to be a potential risk to the good order and discipline of the establishment, that prisoner might be subject to a 'planned removal' to the segregation unit. This would consist of several members of staff (usually 7–10, some of whom might be dressed in full riot gear), arriving at the prisoner's cell to forcibly move him to the segregation unit. As the above quotation suggested, the prisoner would not usually be given an opportunity to walk on his own but would be physically restrained and walked there by the removal team. Prisoners argued that heightened control responses such as these were often not required and were over-reactions. As one prisoner at Full Sutton remarked:

> They want this prison to be over-controlled and I think they have got it as well. It is like they are obsessed about it because when a little thing happens the way they [over-] react, you just know that they really, really don't want things to slip so they become very aggressive about it, reinforcing that control. (Prisoner)

Contemporary forms of order in maximum-security prisons are thus achieved in part through procedures, predictability, routines and structure, control over movements and strict adherence to rules and procedures; secondly, through tight control on the behaviour of prisoners via the IEP policy; and thirdly, through the implicit and overt control that staff hold over prisoners, which include the control responses described above. In a practical sense, then, for staff, the maintenance of order in maximum-security prisons involved the fulfilment of a number of tasks, the regularisation of procedures and the formal assertion of control.

The implementation of these tasks, practices and procedures has given staff considerable confidence in their own authority and greater feelings of safety, as the following quotes indicate:

> My personal opinion is that it is a lot easier to work here mainly because of the dynamic security that we've got, there is more control. We now have that authority, there is no question. (Prison officer)

> We're safer now, you feel safe most of the time. We're dealing with prisoners in a different way now. We're dealing with prisoners in a way where you can't hide from issues. The way we're talking to them now, you face them and tell them how it is and you are in control of the situation. You never actually feel that threat anymore, haven't for a long time, which is good. (Prison officer)

This 'culture of confidence' was characterised by perceptions among prison staff and governors that their systems and procedures worked, that they were justified because they were based on well-established knowledge, and that staff had rightful authority over prisoners.

This confidence is a relatively new phenomenon, and can be traced to the greater emphasis on security and control that followed the two high-profile escapes in the mid-1990s (one at Whitemoor in 1994 and one at Parkhurst in 1995) (see Liebling 2002; Drake 2007). As one officer described:

> I was in the Service at the time [after the Whitemoor escape] and it was a big deal and that has shaped the way in which security is used, with the obvious one being about the impetus put on dynamic security as well as the security awareness training which has developed following on from those sorts of things. (Prison officer)

This emphasis stands in stark contrast to earlier understandings of order, based on staff–prisoner relationships, communication and the ability of staff to use their power and discretion carefully. Although this shift was seen by staff as wholly for the better, it is important to consider what the new forms of order mean for prisoners and to reflect upon what has been lost from earlier approaches.

The experience of contemporary forms of order for prisoners

At both Full Sutton and Whitemoor there was some comfort for prisoners in the routine of prison life; however, the strict application of rules and the inflexibility of officers (especially at Full Sutton) were sources of discontent. Prisoners did not dispute the authority taken by the staff, but it was nevertheless a cause for concern. Prisoners often reported feeling that staff over-used their power, which led to a mood of unease. The following quotation on the use of the IEP policy illustrates this point:

> People get punished with it [the IEP policy], for very stupid, stupid little mistakes that they make. For example, you could go and whack an officer, fair enough, you know, you can't complain when they bust you down to standard, it is perfectly reasonable. But if you say to an officer: 'I want to go up to canteen, please.' And he says: 'no you can't.' You say: 'why? There are only a couple of people up there; you are allowed three at a time.' He says: 'well you just can't.' And then you say: 'hold on a minute let me see the PO, this is wrong!' And suddenly you find yourself down to [a] standard [privilege level] with your television being taken away. They use that quite a lot here, as a mechanism for control and basically to say don't question us otherwise bad things will happen to you, you know, you will have a harder life. (Prisoner)

In addition, prisoners felt that the lack of opportunities for them to contribute to decisions or to negotiate the way order was achieved created a coercive environment, one that was repressive and controlling. They perceived themselves as having very little autonomy or avenues to dispute unfair treatment.

Further, prisoners did not, in general, view the behaviour of officers as fair or 'legitimate'. For prisoners, an acceptable form of order would mean being allowed to participate in the resolution of problems, just reason for the use of staff authority, efforts to build trust between officers and prisoners and being treated as individuals worthy of dignity and respect. Contemporary conditions do not allow these kinds of legitimacy-building interactions to occur. The variety of means through which staff can establish structure, predictability and stability mean that there is less of a need for them to use relationships to achieve these outcomes. When staff have other means of controlling prisoners, 'getting the relationship right' is not necessary for order to be achieved or disorder prevented. There is a new knowledge of 'how prisons work' and a new belief among officers in their own rightful authority. This knowledge relies, primarily, on mechanisms of control such as: searching, CCTV, physical and electronic security measures, strict adherence to 'the rules', and policies such as IEP. As a consequence, prisoners feel they have no control over their circumstances or their lives in prison:

> They need to give you a bit of free will. Even, for example, if the exercise yard could be opened at certain set times. What is the problem with like leaving the fucking gate open during association period? You ain't going nowhere. But no it's like they want to control you – robotically. (Prisoner)

The problem of the new 'order' in maximum-security prisons

It is not difficult to understand how the new state of 'order' in maximum-security prisons has come about. For officers, this new state – one of systems, policies and routines – rests on firmer foundations than the negotiated forms of order of the past. Staff–prisoner relationships have become another mechanism of control rather than the 'heart of the whole prison system'. The experience of prisoners raises the question of whether the 'order' of contemporary maximum-security prisons can really be defined as 'order' at all, or whether it might be more aptly described as 'control'. The implications of this are, first, that the 'new problem of order' in prisons is no longer a concern about disorder among prisoners but instead is a question of what forms of order are to be sought in maximum-security prisons. Second, the lack of formalised recognition by staff and in Prison Service practices that authority should be actively legitimated and that control in prisons should be carefully measured suggests that the experience of imprisonment for prisoners is not being fully considered.

The lengths of sentences being handed down by the courts are among the longest in UK sentencing history. The effects of such lengthy terms of imprisonment are, as yet, unknown. The combination of long sentences, non-legitimate treatment and repressive prison experiences may have enduring and irreversible effects on prisoners, the majority of whom will be released back into society. The task of prison staff, then, is a difficult one. Although the strain of serving a long sentence cannot fully be alleviated, recognition of the individuality and agency of prisoners can help provide them with a less repressive, more acceptable prison experience. Delivering a fair system of imprisonment, through the legitimate use of staff authority has far greater implications, however, than simply providing fair and respectful prison experiences.

Prisons as social institutions and prison officers as representatives of the criminal justice system need to adhere to the expected standards prisoners have of them. Prisoners are members of society and rightly expect to be treated with fairness, respect and dignity when they are within social institutions. Prisons are 'institutions of justice' and as such they play an important role in attempting to encourage law-abiding behaviour. If prisons or prison officials do not meet the expectations of prisoners it seems less likely that prisoners will feel obliged to meet the expectations that prisons, officers and society has of them to lead law-abiding lives in prison and on release. As Liebling (2004) has discussed:

> ... is it possible to construct a form of imprisonment whose basic structure and daily practices are more or less acceptable to those who endure it, despite their domination and commonly low social position? Are prisoners slaves or citizens? If they retain their citizenship then certain things follow ... While the imprisoned cannot easily perceive themselves as citizens because of the conditions of their confinement, it is surely important to try and preserve (or try to generate) a notion of citizenship even within the prison. Generating a commitment to civic virtues must be a better strategy, even in the prison, than crowding them out. (Liebling 2004: 491)

The notion of encouraging 'civic virtues' is not an insignificant point for a Prison Service which aims to help prisoners 'lead law-abiding and useful lives in custody and after release'. This is harder to achieve when, in the attempt to achieve orderliness, predictability, security, and safety, prisons substitute notions of order with control.

Seminar questions

1 In what way is order in prison similar to or different from other contexts?
2 What are the compromises involved in ensuring order in prisons? Are there any?

3 In what ways might officers' discretion contribute to or detract from orderliness?
4 How might prison staff find a balance between order and control while encouraging autonomy and responsibility among prisoners?

Recommended reading

Sparks *et al.*'s (1996) *Prisons and the Problem of Order* is an exploratory study of order in two maximum-security prisons in the late 1980s. It identifies the need for legitimacy in prisons and discusses its theoretical implications. John Ditchfield's (1990) Home Office report *Control in Prisons: A Review of the Literature* considers the literature related to aspects of prison regimes that have previously been identified as assisting or detracting from control. Liebling's (2002) chapter: 'A "Liberal Regime Within a Secure Perimeter"? Dispersal Prisons and Penal Practice in the Late Twentieth Century' (in Bottoms and Tonry's *Ideology, Crime and Criminal Justice: A Symposium in Honour of Sir Leon Radzinowicz*) explores the origins, history and more recent experiences of order and control in maximum-security prisons in England.

Notes

1 I would like to thank Professor Alison Liebling for her comments and advice on earlier drafts of this chapter.
2 The ethnography included three months of observations and interviews in each prison. In total, 76 interviews were conducted with prisoners and 74 with staff.
3 The historical aspect of the research included further interviews and the examination of available documents. In total, 38 interviews were conducted with senior managers, former and current prison governors, and long-serving staff and prisoners.
4 When prisoners' families sent items into the prison or when items were ordered through direct order companies, such as Argos, these items needed to be processed through reception, where they were searched and added to prisoners' property cards before they could be moved to the wing and given to prisoners.
5 MUFTI stands for 'Minimum Use of Force Tactical Intervention'. The MUFTI squad was, in effect, an anti-riot team who were dressed in body armour, helmets and shields. These teams have since been replaced by 'Control and Restraint (C & R) Teams'.

References

Bottoms, A.E. (2003) 'Theoretical Reflections on the Evaluation of a Penal Policy Initiative', in L. Zedner and A. Ashworth (eds), *The Criminological Foundations of Penal Policy: Essays in Honour of Roger Hood*. Oxford: Oxford University Press.

Coyle, A. (2005) *Understanding Prisons: Key Issues in Policy and Practice*. Maidenhead: Open University Press.

Ditchfield, J. (1990) *Control in Prisons: A Review of the Literature*. London: Home Office.

Drake, D. (2007) *A Comparison of Quality of Life, Legitimacy and Order in Two Maximum-Security Prisons*. PhD thesis, University of Cambridge.

Dunbar, I. (1985) *A Sense of Direction*. London: Home Office.

Home Office (1984) *Managing the Long-Term Prison System: The Report of the Control Review Committee*. London: HMSO.

King, R. (1997) 'Can Supermax Help Solve Security and Control Problems?', in A. Liebling (ed.), *Security, Justice and Order in Prison: Developing Perspectives*, Institute of Criminology Cropwood Conference Series. Cambridge: Institute of Criminology, pp. 44–51.

Liebling, A. (2002) 'A "Liberal Regime Within a Secure Perimeter"? Dispersal Prisons and Penal Practice in the Late Twentieth Century', in A.E. Bottoms and M. Tonry (eds), *Ideology, Crime and Criminal Justice: A Symposium in Honour of Sir Leon Radzinowicz*. Cullompton: Willan, pp. 97–150.

Liebling, A. (2004) *Prisons and Their Moral Performance*. Oxford: Clarendon Press.

Liebling, A. and Price, D. (2001) *The Prison Officer*. Leyhill: Prison Service and Waterside Press.

Liebling, A., Muir, G., Rose, G. and Bottoms, A. (1997) 'An Evaluation of Incentives and Earned Privileges: Final Report to the Prison Service'. Unpublished report to Home Office, London.

Sparks, R.J. and Bottoms, A.E. (1995) 'Legitimacy and Order in Prisons', *British Journal of Sociology*, 46: 45–62.

Sparks, R.J., Bottoms, A.E. and Hay, W. (1996) *Prisons and the Problem of Order*. Oxford: Clarendon Press.

Tyler, T.R. (1990) *Why People Obey the Law*. New Haven, CT: Yale University Press.

Tyler, T.R. (2003) 'Procedural Justice, Legitimacy, and the Effective Rule of Law', in M. Tonry (ed.), *Crime and Justice: A Review of Research*. London: University of Chicago Press.

Woolf, L.J. (1991) *Prison Disturbances*, Cm. 1456. London: HMSO.

Chapter 10

Creating ghosts in the penal machine: prison officer occupational morality and the techniques of denial

David Scott[1]

A key part of the everyday working life of the prison officer is witnessing the physical manifestation of the suffering of others. Prisons are factories built for the production of suffering and pain, and all who encounter these disrespectful and punitive environments find the experience both 'traumatic and damaging' (Liebling 2004: 166). Imprisonment presents an unremitting challenge to a person's self-respect, autonomy, security and personal safety. Endemic and structurally produced, these pains create in prisoners intense feelings of loneliness, hopelessness, guilt, depression, anxiety, fear and distress. Prison officers often deal with people who have undertaken extreme measures in response to these inherent pains of imprisonment. In any day, an officer may find themselves cutting down a person who has successfully hung themselves; providing resuscitation for a suicide attempter; dealing with a person who has smeared their own excrement over themselves or the cell walls and is refusing to wash, eat or drink; or encountering a person so distressed that they perpetually cut up their arms, their legs or neck, mutilate themselves or attempt to burn themselves alive. More mundanely, but equally disturbingly, officers spend a great deal of time with people so demoralised and damaged by their experience of imprisonment and the outside world that they have become apathetic and unable to cope with the harsh realities of life.

Relationships between prison officers and prisoners cannot remove these structural pains of imprisonment, but they can either mitigate or exacerbate the extent of suffering imparted. Indeed there is evidence that a significant number of prison officers do recognise the suffering imprisonment creates and become actively involved in alleviating its pains, such as through listening to prisoner grievances and troubles, writing positive reports or overlooking minor infringements of the prison rules (Sparks *et al.* 1996; Liebling and Price 2001). However, there is also mounting evidence that many prison officers fail to fully acknowledge prisoner suffering (Kauffman 1988; Scott 2006a). These officers somehow fail to notice or react to the intense suffering experienced by those people in their care and it is these officers who are the central focus here.

The chapter starts with a discussion of Stan Cohen's work on the techniques of denial, and then moves on to consider the studies on prison officer occupational morality by Eric Colvin (1977) and Kelsey Kauffman (1988). These insights are then applied through an empirical study on prison officer occupational culture undertaken by this author in the UK in 2002. The chapter concludes with a summary and consideration of what can be done to enhance wider acknowledgment of human suffering in prison.

The techniques of denial

In his seminal study *States of Denial: Knowing About Atrocities and Suffering*, Stanley Cohen (2001) provides a useful approach to understanding the manner in which human suffering is either denied or acknowledged. For Cohen (2001: x, xiii), *acknowledgment* is understood as occurring when a person has knowledge of human suffering, recognises the full reality of the pain and harm this information imparts, and identifies the personal implications of possessing such knowledge, leading ultimately to some form of action that attempts to mitigate or end the injuries inflicted upon their fellow humans. For prison officers this means knowing the truth about the extent and forms of the pains of imprisonment and doing something about them. When this does not happen, when an officer sees or is aware of human suffering and human rights abuses in prison but somehow is able to reinterpret or recontextualise the implications of these things, then the subsequent gap that develops between cognition of events and possible action to alter the situation should be understood as *denial* (Ibid.: 9).

Following the insights of Cohen (2001: 7–9), there would appear to be three main ways in which prison officers can deny the very real human suffering that occurs in prison: literal denial, interpretive denial and implicatory denial. Strategies of 'literal denial' claim that there is no validity to assertions that human rights infringements or intense sufferings pertain in prisons. This 'denial of knowledge' is not very convincing, especially for those working in prison. A more plausible form of denial in prison is to give the act a different, less problematic explanation. Human rights abuses and prisoner sufferings, when defined through a different interpretative lens, may appear less painful or may be normalised as a 'necessary evil'. A person banging their head against a cell door or wall is not in pain, or mentally ill, or making legitimate protest about their confinement, but becomes merely a pathetic wretch or an inadequate seeking attention; those who self-harm or (successfully) attempt suicide are merely making demands and behaving like spoilt children; those who smear excrement over themselves create their own degrading environment and should be held responsible for those conditions; eating a meal while another person urinates or defecates in the cell toilet is simply an unavoidable reality in times of overcrowding. In other words, what we see is a new meaning being imputed into the events, leading to 'interpretative denial'.

Cohen's third form of denial is to recognise the existence of human suffering but to deny any personal implications arising from such a state of affairs. This entails utilising techniques and rationalisations to provide assurances that there is actually no need to worry about prisoner suffering after all, or if an officer witnesses an incident that is a human rights infringement, there is nothing they can or *should* do to help. Here Cohen (2001) borrows the idea of the 'techniques of neutralisation' from Gresham Sykes and David Matza (1957). For Sykes and Matza (1957), techniques of neutralisation were used to break bonds, ties or constraints that might restrict deviant behaviour. Challenging the subcultural theories that were influential at time of writing, Sykes and Matza (1957) maintained that deviants were the same as everyone else, sharing the dominant ideas, values and morality of the wider culture. Deviance from such norms was only possible when neutralisations were used to justify their breach, without actually denying the legitimacy or validity of these dominant values. Sykes and Matza (1957: 668) argued that:

> The delinquent both has his cake and eats it too, for he remains committed to the dominant normative system and yet so qualifies its imperatives that violations are 'acceptable' if not 'right'.

Sykes and Matza (1957) highlighted five neutralisations that act as means of protecting the individual from blame or weaken their ties to conventional moral values. Cohen (2001: 60–1; 78–101) details how these rationalisations can equally be used to loosen moral principles when witnessing human suffering and human rights abuses.

- *Denial of responsibility.* This technique is depolyed when a person denies that they are fully or even partially responsible for human suffering they have witnessed or created. It is 'not their fault', it is an 'accident' or it is 'not intentional'. It has 'nothing to do with them'. The perpetrator, or observer, can somehow claim ignorance for dealing with the consequences and implications of the suffering.

- *Denial of injury.* This rationalisation leads to the conclusion that what happens to a victim 'does not really hurt'. There is no or only limited harm or suffering imparted through the act.

- *Denial of victim.* Here there is no identifiable victim of the action, or the injured party has lost their claims to being a victim by precipitating the action or undertaking the offence that led to the wrongdoing. In other words they got 'what they deserved'.

- *Condemnation of the condemners.* The person who has suffered should be condemned or share the blame. They are 'hypocrites', 'liars', 'urespectable' or lack the moral authority to complain. Those who have raised concerns may be criticised as 'do-gooders' with little understanding of the real issues, while whistleblowers have performed an 'act of betrayal' or disloyalty to their colleagues. Either way, attention is deflected away from the pain inflicted or the observer's compulsion to help.

- *Appeal to higher loyalties.* This neuralisation promotes the claim that the harm done serves a greater good or favours a group that holds greater demands on our loyalties. The suffering inflicted upon one person may be contrasted with another more vulnerable or 'innocent' person who had been or were also suffering.

Though these techniques provide a highly plausible framework for understanding those people who have allegiance to conventional moral values and then overcome them in a specific situational context, they cannot help us to understand the actions of people who ignore or have rejected normative moral conventions. To address this problem Cohen (2001: 98–101) identifies a further technique of denial that can be adopted to invisibilise human suffering: moral indifference.[2]

Here a person is so committed to the rightness of the human suffering taking place in prison that there are no guilty feelings to be neutralised.

In the prison setting moral indifference necessitates that prisoners have lost the right to be treated like any other human being. In this sense they have been successfully socially distanced or 'othered' (Bauman 1989; Christie 1993). Such psychic distancing arises when prisoners are conceived in terms which place them beyond the boundaries of the prison officer's moral universe and is intimately tied to the ideology of less eligibility.[3] Effectively a more pronounced version of the 'denial of victim', the doctrine of less eligibility dictates that prisoners and other wrong doers deserve and require to be punished, and that their suffering also has further utilities. Prisoner suffering is believed to send a symbolic message to those on the outside that 'crime' does not pay, providing a deterrent effect. Alongside this, so the argument goes, suffering also instills moral fibre and backbone into criminals. If a prison is painful, if it really hurts, the cognitive response of the offender will be to refrain from 'crime'. Through harsh regimes, prisoners will become more responsible, respectable, disciplined and moral people. It is then ideologically justifiable, even desirable, that prisoners *suffer*.

Moral indifference can also imply that people have lost interest in the well-being of others. Rather than the pains of punitive intention, the suffering of others can be justified through the pains of wilful neglect. Given the harsh realities of imprisonment and its corrosive impact upon all who encounter it, for some prison officers distancing may be a mechanism for coping, a means of psychological survival. Officers may become *emotionally detached* as a way of doing their time. This may lead to a situation where other human beings are so far distanced that it is no longer possible to care about what happens to them at all. These officers may become disassociated, non-caring and unconcerned, effectively becoming immune or anaesthetised to the suffering of prisoners.

Prison as a specific moral context

Despite the growing literature on prison officers only a small number of studies have examined the occupational morality or 'moral universe' of prison officers, notably Eric Colvin (1977) and Kelsey Kauffman (1988). Significantly both studies use analytical frameworks which are consistent with Cohen's techniques of denial. In his important study on prison officers at HMP Manchester, Colvin (1977: 143–5) explains how coercive behaviour against prisoners by prison officers could be seen as justified within the boundaries of the prison context. Colvin (1977) argues that though officers still held a sense of conventional morality, within the prison environment they were able to neutralise their normal moral commitments. In a similar vein in a study of prison officers in the USA, Kauffman (1988: 222) found that some officers:

> attempted to neutralise their own feelings of guilt by regarding prisons as separate moral realms with their own distinct set of moral standards or by viewing inmates as individuals outside the protection of moral laws.

From this perspective officer occupational morality is founded upon a distinct construction of the prison, which appears to involve norms, standards of respect and morality which are different from the outside world. For both Colvin (1977) and Kauffman (1988) some officers rationalised morality into two clearly separate moral spheres, allowing demarcations in occupational norms and values from those adopted in everyday life. This allowed the prison officer to conceive of himself as an ordinary, or good, human being, reacting to the specific moral context of imprisonment. Such a construction though could be highly dangerous and breed dehumanisation. For Colvin (1977: 139), it becomes a 'short step' from enshrining the principles of punishment through the 'suspension of rights' and the denial of certain liberties, to denying prisoners 'the status of persons entitled to make any moral claims upon the staff' at all.

However, this kind of moral dualism would appear to be precarious and vulnerable to erosion. Colvin (1977) found evidence of moral confusion and contradictions in prison officer moralities. To maintain a positive conception of (her or him) self, and to somehow overcome a potentially disturbing split in behaviour, officers considered how they could maintain certain aspects of their ordinary morality within the prison situation while suspending other dimensions. Consequently an officer may consider:

> acting reasonably towards his charges, taking an interest in their well being, and treating them with civility. Yet he also learns to value methods of control which involve the ruthless disregard of the personal feelings of his charges. (Ibid: 145)

Kauffman's (1988) in-depth study uncovered three ways in which prison officers attempted to justify their actions: neutralisations, lesser breeds and emotional detachment. Like Colvin (1977), Kauffman (1988) had found that a number of prison officers attempted to overcome inhibitions or neutralised the guilt of prisoner suffering by constructing the prison world as a separate moral realm. However, Kauffman (1988) found that this technique was difficult to sustain as 'actions appropriate to only one realm are susceptible to judgments emanating from the other' (Ibid.: 130). She found that a much more successful technique of denial was to position the prisoners as a class of individuals *beyond* claims of conventional morality. Prisoners, by their *very status as prisoner*, lost all claims to moral evaluation, thus removing all moral obligations from officers to treat them as ordinary men and women. Prisoners were ideologically conceived as less eligible than other human beings, effectively dehumanised as a breed apart, the 'scum of the earth' (Kauffman 1988: 231).

The work of Colvin (1977) and Kauffman (1988) found then that denials of prisoner suffering could be justified 'on all inclusive and damning categorisations of the inmate population' (Colvin 1977: 143). They indicate that prison officer occupational morality is shaped through the distinct environment and moral context of the prison workplace, and imply that prisoners are othered along similar lines to what Cohen (2001) proposes in his techniques of denial. However, given that one study was undertaken over thirty years ago and the other is an American study, would such findings be reproduced among prison officers serving in the UK today?

Prison officer working personalities

The empirical evidence presented below discussing the denial and acknowledgment of prisoner suffering by prison officers is based on a study of a large Category B local prison for men in the North West of England. The fieldwork was undertaken between July and September 2002 and was based on observation and semi-structured interviews with 38 prison officers.[4] The research did not uncover one monolithic or homogenous occupational culture or one distinct prison officer moral universe. Four prison officer working personalities were evident from the interviews: the *careerist*, the *humanitarian*, the *mortgage payer* and the *disciplinarian*. There were clear divisions between those officers who acknowledged, in various different ways, the shared humanity of prisoners and those officers who were either morally indifferent to the plight of prisoners or engaged in a form of moral splitting.

Careerists had relatively positive orientations to prisoners and the two officers interviewed who conformed to this working orientation placed prisoners within the boundaries of their moral universe.

> We should treat [prisoners] decently; we should treat them like human beings, because that is the only way that they are going to change their attitude. (Principal officer 1)

Although primarily interested in prison work as a career, careerists had much in common with the humanitarians.[5] The seven humanitarian officers interviewed did not have any significant problems recognising that prisoners should be treated humanely. Virtually all of the humanitarians embraced the decency agenda and talked of developing positive relationships with prisoners and treating them with humanity, albeit within an inherently dehumanising environment.

> I find myself listening to human beings talking about experiences rather than prisoners. We should look upon them as if they are members of our own family and treating them as though they are our fathers and relatives because that's one way that staff immediately see a way of justifying the humanitarian role. If the prison officer treats somebody the way he expects to have his brother or son treated in prison then it makes them look on prisons in a different light. It does actually work, but it's a matter of how long for, before they forget and go back to the old culture of them and us and calling them shit bags and a different class of person who will never change, and are stuck in a parallel world of crime and immorality. The bottom line is that you are employed by the prison service to be a professional and to use professional standards of decency, regardless of your own personal opinions. (Senior officer 1)

Humanitarian officers looked to treat prisoners the same with the recognition that prisoners were not necessarily that different from themselves.

> You've got to treat all the prisoners the same. We've got to be professional about it … You've got to treat everyone exactly the same. (Senior officer 2)

In this sense 'distancing' between officers and prisoners was under-scored by a universal, inclusionary and humane rationale. In addition there was evidence that humanitarians also showed concern for the suffering of prisoners.

> Some officers really do care, and whenever we lose a prisoner it really does have an adverse effect on staff. They feel as if they've failed that person, and 'if only'. It's not just that that person was a prisoner, he was a human being. (Senior officer 3)

Though both the careerist and humanitarian working personalities acknowledged prisoners' shared humanity and held relatively senior positions in the prison, they were marginalised within the occupational group as a whole. Indeed denial was a much more prevalent finding and characterised the mortgage payer and the disciplinarian working personalities. The six mortgage payer officers primarily approached their job through the cash nexus, working in the prison because their jobs paid for their mortgages. These officers had lost all interest in work and relationships with prisoners, and often other members of staff, and were characterised by emotional detachment. The disciplinarians also distanced prisoners, but they operated through an 'us and them' stereotype and placed much greater emphasis on the ideology of less eligibility. Of the 38 officers interviewed 23 were identified as disciplinarians, collectively comprising the occupational culture. The discussion below focuses primarily on the techniques used by these officers to deny the extent and implications of prisoner suffering.[6]

Creating ghosts in the penal machine

Overall it was found that in the prison officer occupational culture prisoners were constructed as 'ghost' like – that is that their experiences, needs and reality were invisible in the eyes of prison officers. Prisoners were effectively distanced as lesser human beings, constructed as essentially different and beyond the realms of prison officers' understandings of humanity. The five techniques of neutralisation played a key part in rationalising this denial.

1. Denial of responsibility

Prison officers claimed that prison is an 'occupational hazard' determined by a 'rational choice' made by 'habitual criminals'. In this sense even though imprisonment can be recognised as being painful, living conditions poor and services inadequate, this is the responsibility of prisoners not officers. Prison was 'a rod of their own making' (Prison officer 1), or in the words of one officer: 'People in here are society's failures. I haven't put them in. It was their crime that they committed that has put them in prison' (Senior officer 4).

2. Denial of injury

Prison is a soft option. 'Prisons are holiday camps' (Senior officer 5), a place where 'if you can go without sex you can do prison life standing on your head' (Prison officer 1).

> They have no idea of how easy it is in prison. No idea at all. I think we've got to a level now where they've got enough. What else can we give them? It's a prison. (Prison officer 1)

> Well, what else could you give them, apart from conjugal rights, more visits? They've got everything else. You might as well not send them to prison anymore, really. You put a bar in visits, and another couple of beds in there and you've cracked it. You'd get the best of both worlds then. They wouldn't have to deal with the crap out there, and they'd get the beer and the sex in here. They'd be in heaven. You wouldn't be putting them in prison. You'd be putting them in Utopia. They'd have no responsibilities, but they'd be getting all the benefits of life. (Senior officer 6)

From this perspective, prisoners pretend prison is more painful than it really is to get more privileges: 'sometimes they will say "I'm going to slash my wrists" as an excuse to get what they want' (Senior officer 7). Prison conditions 'are better than bedsits' as prisoners have 'their own toilet and wash facilities and three decent meals a day' (Principal officer 2). Expressed in its most extreme form, the *real* 'injured parties' of imprisonment were the 'officers themselves' (Prison officer 1).

3. Denial of victim

This rationalisation denies that prisoners can be 'victims'. Here not only have prisoners lost the rights to such a status, but may be so debased that they lack the ability or judgment to fully comprehend the prison experience and its inherent harms. The following phrases were common in officer descriptions of the treatment of prisoners:

> 'prisoners are relatively docile', 'they are out of their heads', 'they like what happens', 'they don't know any different', 'they don't want to be called by their first names', 'it's the only language they understand', 'get too philosophical with them and they'll take the piss out of you', 'they never asked for half of this stuff', 'they've got everything they need', 'there are no complaints from prisoners about how they are treated'.

Justifications for the notion that prisoners could not be victims could arise when prisoners were perceived as a drug taker, mentally ill or being unaware through cultural deprivation:

> You are dealing with more people with psychological problems. You've been on E2 haven't you? It's the hospital wing. Formally F Wing, and still sometimes referred to by staff as 'Fraggle Rock'. Some of them in there are 'lights on but nobody in' aren't they? (Prison officer 3)

The denial of victimhood may lead to the assumption that prisoners do not have to be spoken to as human beings. 'You say "I'm fucking telling you, you get your arse out of your bed". They understand that' (Prison officer 4).

4. Condemnation of the condemners

Many officers believed that those on the outside fail to fully understand the reality of prison life. Those who criticise the prison, penal pressure groups and those who call for the recognition of prisoners' suffering are dismissed as 'do-gooders' sitting in 'white towers'. For some officers even senior prison service personnel were considered to fall into this category.

> There is too much 'do-gooder' opinion that comes into this job, and these do-gooders don't come and do the job, they don't spend long enough in the jails to have an opinion. You've got to work in here everyday, every week, every month for x amount of years before you know what actually goes on. (Prison officer 4)

Needless to add, this technique also leads to prisoners losing the right to criticise. As the popular saying goes, people in glass houses should not throw stones.

5. Appeal to higher loyalties

The elderly, the respectable poor, children and 'victims' were all groups for whom prisoners' poor conditions were compared by prison officers. These people had *human* rights. Prisoners did not. As one officer stated bluntly, 'human fucking rights! I'll give you human rights! What about victim rights?' (Senior officer 8). Victims 'have as much human rights if not more than the people who are in here', but while there was considerable resources utilised for prisoners, according to those holding this view, victim issues were relatively ignored.

> Now prisoner's rights seem to be that everything is for them and nothing is for the victims. What we have to focus on now is not prisoner's rights. Because they've got a plethora of rights now, we've got to focus on victim issues. If a lot of the victims realised what was going on inside prisons I think an awful lot of them would really start protesting outside. (Prison officer 3)

In the research there is evidence that disciplinarian prison officers could and did breach the techniques of neutralisation. There were often glimpses of acknowledgment of prisoner suffering and human rights abuses. Indeed many staff believed they had a role in preventing human rights abuses. 'We know the culture in prison means that that sort of stuff goes on behind closed doors, out of sight, but staff don't turn a blind eye to it' (Prison officer 5). Further, there was evidence that when officers were presented with prisoners in serious and immediate danger they would risk their lives to protect them.

> There was an incident this dinner time where a lad set fire to his own cell. Now the staff were on their break, but they gave it up to go and save this lad, and also to protect other prisoners. By going in the cell they inhaled the smoke. When they went to the hospital to be checked, the government will say 'why did you go in that cell when you know you should put SDBA[7] kits on first and then go in?' Do you wait to do that? Most staff don't think like that. They just run in without any apparent look to their own safety to save somebody else. (Prison officer 5)

179

One senior officer acknowledged the pains of confinement and the physical and emotional factors contributing to prisoner suffering, highlighting the problems confronting prisoners through overcrowding and the degrading reality of eating their meals effectively in a toilet.

> Prisoners need 24-hour access to sanitation, but they are now eating their meals in the toilet you know. Because there are so many inmates nearly every cell, built as a single cell, is doubled. There is a vanity screen there but it doesn't really hide anything and then there are issues over the smell. You wouldn't want to do it. In theory you could walk down to the canteen, get your meal and get back and your pal would be sat on the loo. (Senior officer 9)

Other prison officers talked in depth about the harm that the poor living conditions in the prison could do to prisoners, especially those who were on drugs or were mentally ill.

> If we're going to talk about the physical conditions lets talk about the DDU [drug dependency unit]. These are probably a group of prisoners who are as vulnerable as anybody. It is an unbearable situation down there. I think either the DDU should be condemned or made decent. Whether it's self inflicted or not, they still have to get through that, the withdrawal and the after effects and so on. You want to say just pull yourself together, but a lot of these just aren't mentally up to it. It doesn't take Einstein to work it out if some one's cutting or setting fire to themselves this isn't the right place for him really, is it? (Prison officer 6)

> We have a lot of mentally ill prisoners, so much so that we are becoming more of a mental institution than a prison. They should be getting help. You can't apply punishment to someone who is mentally imbalanced because they don't understand. So who is that helping? You're keeping them off the streets [but] we're not really doing anything for anyone. (Prison officer 5)

This insight may only bring us back to the insights of Colvin (1977) where officers merely attempt to resolve the problem of splitting and reinforce the notion of themselves as good or moral people. What is clear though is that officers can make connections between human suffering in prison and the outside world.

There is also evidence that prison officer occupational moralities are informed by a further technique of denial: moral indifference. For the disciplinarian officers occupational morality was rooted in a false dichotomy emphasising *sameness* and *otherness*. The 'duty of care' or sense of responsibility for other humans was highly restricted, referring largely to other white male prison officers – in other words people who shared the same social backgrounds as themselves. Prison officers were the 'respectable victims' of the pains of imprisonment. The contours of their 'sameness' were also shaped and defined by otherness, expressed in a profound and deep hostility to prisoners. In this binary opposition prisoners were 'othered' and their suffering considered necessary.

A number of officers interviewed in the study articulated classic restatements regarding the restrictions that less eligibility places on the recognition of prisoner suffering.

> Prison should be a place that you don't want to come back to. Prison now for some of them is a place for 'time out'. So where's the best place to be? It's in here isn't it – three good meals a day, association, the gym. They've got everything. It's really a safe haven. Prison should be a place so bad that you don't want to come back. While they're here let's get some discipline back into them instead of just sitting around watching television all day. It's wasteful. They are just laughing at us. It is just a waste of money. The money that's going in compared to the benefits that are coming out, I just don't think it is worth it. It'd be better spent on things like hospitals for people that have done something good. (Senior officer 6)

Dehumanisation creeps into the psychic constructions of prisoners. They 'become a number in a prison uniform' (Prison officer 7) and this label becomes their new master status. Prisoners are effectively depersonalised and placed at an immense psychological distance. This form of moral indifference also characterised officers who conformed to the mortgage payer working personality.

> Most [prisoners] are just pathetic now. It pisses me off. It's all this 'I want! I want!' It's like dealing with your kids. You're dealing with selfish adults and that's it. If they weren't so selfish they wouldn't be in prison. That's what they're in for, for being selfish. Robbing and thieving instead of going out and getting a job. But then again why should they. They don't

> have to do much to get by. If I had a choice I'd probably come back as a criminal in my next life, because it's a piss easy life. Especially with all this human rights. "Excuse me. I'd like to make a complaint. It wasn't actually hot enough when I got back to my cell." Then you'll get some silly slap arse filling in papers, saying that they'll see to it. (Prison officer 8)

Here distancing was rooted in emotional detachment and a loss of interest in caring for prisoners rather than strategies rooted in reinforcing prisoner inferiority as lesser breeds.

> A lot of the staff are losing interest in the job. And when officers start losing interest that's when prisoners will start losing out. Because the staff just won't be bothered. (Prison officer 9)

The shift between the adoption of different techniques of denial, from neutralisations to less eligibility, to emotional detachment, has been portrayed as evolutionary (Kauffman 1988) but the evidence suggests that this is far from consistent (Scott 2006a). It may be helpful to see these different techniques of denial not as in competition but as acting as a sliding continuum between denial and partial acknowledgment of prisoner suffering. What all the techniques of denial facilitate though is a mechanism through which the doctrine of less eligibility can be institutionalised within the prison officer occupational culture. The techniques provide a justification for the delegitimation of the suffering of prisoners by constructing their suffering as less eligible for our attention, care or concern.

Conclusion: towards the greater acknowledgment of human suffering in prison

The discussion above indicates that there are a number of different prison officer occupational moralities. Some prison officers, especially those who had a humanitarian ethos underscoring their work, were able to acknowledge prisoners' shared humanity and experiences of hardship in prison. In the study these officers were in the minority, but such findings do provide a starting point for thinking about how greater acknowledgment of human suffering can be fostered and the justifications used for its denial. Through the adoption of techniques of neutralisation, it was evident some officers construct the prison as a distinct moral realm from the outside world. This creates a separate, situational occupational morality and understanding of humanity. Rationalisations of different treatment for humans in the *prison world* allow officers to breach human rights and deny the suffering of fellow humans. To avoid undermining their sense of being a good and moral person, officers may transcend their occupational morality and on occasion apply normal moral rules, leading to the partial acknowledgment of prisoner shared humanity.

The literature and empirical evidence cited also indicates that some prison officers go beyond neutralisations as a means of denying the genuine suffering of prisoners. Moral indifference here dominates. The doctrine of less eligibility places prisoners beyond normal conventions of morality altogether. Here prisoners are seen as lesser breeds whose needs and suffering become invisible. Through this occupational morality prisoner suffering is conceived as *essential* to the purposes of imprisonment. The negative construction of the prisoner as a lesser being provides a sense of psychic distance that can justify the deliberate infliction of harm, pain and suffering. Related to this, but a more profoundly dehumanising form of moral indifference, is complete emotional detachment or shut down. Here, officers no longer care about prisoner suffering – it is deemed irrelevant rather than useful. Indeed officers may be so preoccupied with their own misery that they are unable to conceptualise the devastating implications of the pains and suffering of imprisonment for prisoners. Through the social production of moral indifference in the penal environment and wider society, prisoners become almost ghost like, placed beyond the realms of shared humanity.

While there is *physical proximity* between prisoners and prison officers the evidence cited above indicates that this does not necessarily lead to *psychic closeness*, a sense of moral responsibility for the well-being of prisoners or recognition of their shared humanity. Indeed, for many officers the opposite seems to be the case. Perhaps this is because full acknowledgment of human suffering in prison would create an unsolvable moral dilemma for prison officers or make certain functions of the job impossible to complete. For example, the humanitarian acknowledgers discussed in the empirical study looked only to mitigate the harm of imprisonment rather than raise questions about the validity of the infliction of harm through such a dehumanising environment itself. Overall it seems likely that denial is much easier to deal with, can sustain a positive sense of moral identity and inevitably allows the continuation of their daily punishment duties (Scott 2006b).

The application of the label prisoner is predicated on the construction of a negative, dehumanised, one-dimensional caricature of the offender situated solely in the nature of their 'crime'. When prison officers emphasise differences, constructing the prisoner as a lesser being with no legitimate claim to *human* rights, they are tapping into such an understanding. The problem therefore is one of conflating the other, the prisoner, as inherently bad or 'evil'. This is especially so if this leads to the assumption that 'good' people deserve to be helped and that the suffering of bad people should be ignored. If an officer constructs their own moral identity as 'good' and the prisoners as 'bad', the rather ugly outcome is that intense human suffering is denied.

To counter the techniques of denial it seems important then to focus upon what prison officers and prisoners have in common: their shared humanity and the vulnerability of both to suffering in a dehumanising penal environment. This necessitates highlighting, as some of the humanitarian officers cited above, the similarities between those humans who are confined inside and those on the outside of prison walls. This reminds us of the urgent need to raise consciousness of prison's painful realities and of fostering feelings of psychic closeness with prisoners as fellow *human* beings. Acknowledgment requires the visibility of all suffering and a sense of responsibility to do something about it. For social justice we need such recognition, whatever that sufferer has done in the past, good or bad. In the current political climate this may be most successfully fostered by making connections to the inalienable *human* rights of prisoners. Alongside this we must constantly raise the moral question whether the continuation of human suffering that imprisonment manufactures can ever be legitimate. It may be that the deliberate infliction of pain can only be justified through successful neutralisations of, or indifference about, our moral responsibility for ending the suffering of others. Indeed, what kind of moral dilemmas daily confront those officers who do stand by and allow prisoners to be harmed when they think of them as 'one of us', and for other officers, could they continue to perform tasks that intentionally hurt prisoners when their charges are no longer considered to be lesser breeds or are viewed as significantly inferior humans?

Seminar questions

1 Do officers have to be resilient to the suffering of prisoners in order to do

their job? Can such 'denials' be balanced with the moral demands for the prison officer to perform their duties in a fair and decent manner?

2 What can be done to facilitate the greater acknowledgment of human suffering in prison?
3 Can the deliberate infliction of pain ever be considered morally legitimate?
4 What are its implications for those who work in prisons?

Recommended reading

In terms of recommended readings I would suggest that students start with Stan Cohen (2001) *States of Denial*. Kauffman's (1988) *Prison Officers and Their World* provides perhaps the most impressive empirical study of prison officers undertaken to date while Alison Liebling and David Price (2007 Second Edition) *The Prison Officer* provides an excellent overview of the literature. The following books and articles are of great significance in the study of penality: Zygmunt Bauman (1991) *Modernity and Ambivalence*; Stan Cohen (1993) 'Human Rights and Crimes of the State: The Culture of Denial'; Mike Fitzgerald and Joe Sim (1982) *British Prisons*; Richard Sparks (1996) 'Penal Austerity: The Doctrine of Less Eligibility Reborn?' in Roger Matthews and Peter Francis (eds) *Prisons 2000: International Perspective on the Current State and Future of Imprisonment*.

Notes

1 I would like to thank all the editors, and especially Ben Crewe, for their very helpful comments in the preparation of this chapter.
2 A seventh technique of denial is also identified by Cohen (2001): the denial of knowledge. However, this technique is unlikely to be deployed by prison officers given the nature and extent of prisoner suffering.
3 The doctrine of less eligibility transfers the basic premises of neo-liberalism into the realm of punishment. Predicated on the assumption that there exists a universal free, rational and calculating subject, infused with an individual sense of responsibility, criminal activity is understood as a free choice that is based upon weighing up the potential benefits and costs of such behaviour. The logic behind this generic sense of severity is firmly rooted in the utilitarian calculus that to deter the rational offender requires the pain of punishment to outweigh the pleasures derived from the crime. The application of the doctrine of less eligibility broadly ensures that the upper margin of prison conditions are guaranteed not to rise above the worst material conditions in society as a whole, and that in times of social hardships the rigours of penal discipline become more severe to prevent weakening of its deterrent effect. Through its interpretive lens, prisoner

human rights are predicated on certain understandings of human worth and value, themselves intimately linked with the value of labour and subsequent living conditions for the working class (see Scott 2006a).

4 The sample of officers interviewed was determined by staff availability and cooperation. The aim of the research was to uncover prison officer attitudes towards prisoner human rights and in particular their views on the Human Rights Act 1998.

5 The major differences between the two working personalities were that the careerists embraced managerialism and new initiatives as a means of furthering their career.

6 For full details of the four working personalities see Scott (2006a).

7 SDBA is the breathing apparatus that prison officers are required to wear when dealing with a fire.

References

Bauman, Z. (1989) *Modernity and the Holocaust*. Cambridge: Polity Press.

Bauman, Z. (1991) *Modernity and Ambivalence*. Cambridge: Polity Press.

Christie, N. (1993) *Crime Control as Industry*. London: Routledge.

Cohen, S. (1993) 'Human Rights and Crimes of the State: The Culture of Denial', *Australian and New Zealand Journal of Criminology*, 26 (2): 97–115.

Cohen, S. (2001) *States of Denial: Knowing About Atrocities and Suffering*. Cambridge: Polity.

Colvin, E. (1977) 'Prison Officers: A Sociological Portrait of the Uniformed Staff of an English Prison'. Unpublished PhD thesis, University of Cambridge.

Fitzgerald, M. and Sim, J. (1982) *British Prisons*, 2nd edn. Oxford: Blackwell.

Kauffman, K. (1988) *Prison Officers and Their World*. Cambridge, MA: Harvard University Press.

Liebling, A. (2004) *Prisons and Their Moral Performance: A Study of Values, Quality and Prison Life*. Oxford: Oxford University Press.

Liebling, A. and Price, D. (2007) *The Prison Officer*, 2nd edn. Leyhill: Prison Service Journal.

Scott, D.G. (2006a) 'Ghosts Beyond Our Realm: A Neo-abolitionist Analysis of Prisoner Human Rights and Prison Officer Occupational Culture'. Unpublished PhD thesis, University of Central Lancashire.

Scott, D.G. (2006b) 'The Caretakers of Punishment: Prison Officer Personal Authority and the Rule of Law', *Prison Service Journal*, 168: 14–19.

Sparks, R. (1996) 'Penal Austerity: The Doctrine of Less Eligibility Reborn?', in R. Matthews and P. Francis (eds), *Prisons 2000*. London: Macmillan.

Sparks, R., Bottoms, A. and Hay, W. (1996) *Prisons and the Problem of Order*. Oxford: Clarendon Press.

Sykes, G. and Matza, D. (1957) 'Techniques of neutralization: a theory of delinquency', *American Sociological Review*, 22: 664–70.

Chapter 11

'An inconvenient criminological truth':[1] pain, punishment and prison officers

Joe Sim[2]

... the methods that we introduced into the [Special] Unit ... are based on a very simple attitude, that being that we should speak to the prisoners and suggest to them that we should, together, find ways and means best suited for the method where we could live tolerably with each other ... There's never been one single incident of a prison officer being attacked in the Special Unit by a prisoner. (Ken Murray, prison officer).[3]

The culture is in the brickwork in [here]. Staff culture, give them nothing. If an officer is good at his job, and takes things on, people say what is he after? He is ambitious and therefore criticised. (Prison health care officer, cited in Sim 2003: 255)

Introduction

In the summer of 1976, as part of a research project, I visited the Special Unit (SU) in Glasgow's Barlinnie Prison. At that point, the SU had operated for three years, having been opened in February 1973 by the then Conservative government in order to incapacitate those men who had been officially labelled as Scotland's most dangerous and disruptive offenders (MacDonald and Sim 1978). This visit came immediately after spending several weeks in Peterhead, Scotland's most notorious prison, an institution which was dominated by a culture of masculinity which, in turn, sustained, legitimated and reproduced an often desperate culture of violence between prisoners and prison officers and between prisoners and prisoners (Scraton *et al.* 1991). The contrast with the philosophy and atmosphere of the SU was stark, particularly with respect to the relationship between prisoners and staff. Where Peterhead was built on a toxic hostility between the two groups, the everyday interactions in the Unit were based on a very visible philosophy of community support, mutual respect, individual responsibility and collective accountability.

The SU was self-contained and was located in the old women's wing of Barlinnie. This meant that I, and the other researchers, had to pass through the prison's main hall, sometimes when there were shift changes involving prison staff. During these changes, the Unit's officers could be distinguished not only by the white coats they wore (as distinct from normal prison officer uniforms), but also by the often overt hostility shown towards them by the officers from the main prison. They stood alone, away from the majority, a powerful and poignant symbol of workplace alienation. They were regarded as idealistic utopians because of the conscious decision they had made to work with the kind of prisoners who were sent to what was pejoratively labelled by the main staff group as the 'nutcracker suite'. In January 1995, after two decades of sustained media hostility and official belligerence the SU was formally closed. It was a penal innovation which was only ever accorded the status of an 'experiment' whose existence was anathema to a political class whose worldview, in those two decades, became increasingly dominated by an intensified, retributive punitiveness towards offenders, their families and communities (Sim, forthcoming).

Over twenty years later, I interviewed a number of prison healthcare officers in three local prisons in England and Wales. Like Barlinnie's main prison, these prisons were dominated by a culture of prison officer masculinity that legitimated a psychologically lacerating and physically degrading environment for prisoners. Yet in the midst of this brutalisation I interviewed some officers whose behaviour towards prisoners was quite different from the majority of their colleagues. Three officers, who worked in two of the prisons, stood out in terms of their uncompromising respect for, and decency towards, those in their care. They challenged the excoriating discourse of less eligibility in which physically ill and psychologically distressed prisoners were kept and the subservience of medical care both to this discourse and to the insistent and often overwhelming discourses of security and control (Sim 2003). In behaving positively towards prisoners, they also challenged the wider staff culture and, conversely, they felt the burning antagonism of that culture directed towards them. Crucially, because of this antagonism, and the corrosion of their psychological well-being, two were considering leaving the service.

While these events are separated by time and distance they have one hugely significant thing in common which is the question of prison officer culture and its negative impact on prisoners and those staff who show humane empathy towards them. The detrimental and mortifying dimensions underpinning this culture still remain relatively marginal in prison literature. Instead, a theoretically sanitised penology has developed in which this culture, occasionally disrupted by the shame-inducing behaviour of an atavistic 'bad apple', is regarded as functionally benevolent for offenders. This sanitised perspective has been reinforced by an uncritical, political and popular view that prison officers are victimised by an implacable prisoner enemy on the landings intent on violent retribution towards them. Ideologically, these stereotypes have 'become normalised ... [and are] now taken for granted by the majority of academics, politicians, media experts, policy makers and the public' (Sim 2004: 116).[4]

This chapter takes a different position to this sanitised penology. It seeks to provide a critical analysis of prison officers. In taking this position, it is not my intention to present an argument that excoriates *every* prison officer for the work that they carry out in the soul-crunching atmosphere that dominates many contemporary prisons or to engage in a 'politically distracting' exercise as critics of my position on prison officers have alleged (Sparks *et al.* 1996: 308). However, it *is* my intention to differentiate the position taken in this chapter from the emerging consensus around prison officers involving academics and liberal prison reform groups. This consensus has left the politics and processes of prison officer culture relatively unscathed in terms of critiquing its corrosive impact on the lives of both prisoners *and* those officers who are dedicated to responding empathically to them.

The chapter is divided into two parts. First, it outlines a framework for thinking critically about prison officers which seeks to challenge the dominant theoretical paradigm within which their role and culture has been conceptualised and which, implicitly and explicitly, accepts that the majority of prison staff are positive and proactive in their interactions with prisoners. Second, it is concerned with suggesting a number of radical alternatives to the current system which, if implemented, could fundamentally transform prison officer culture, undermine its highly discretionary formal and informal power base and ultimately see it replaced by a different ethical ethos which will not have the same devastating impact on prisoners and demonstrably supportive prison staff.

Thinking critically about prison officers

What would a critical perspective on prison officers look like? There are four dimensions to this perspective that I want to explore which are: first, developing a critical understanding of prison history from below; second, recognising the institutionalised nature of prison officer violence; third, analysing the relationship between the state and prison officers; and finally exploring the interpersonal politics of prison officer masculinity.

Penology from below

I have noted elsewhere, with reference to the history of prison medicine, that accounts by prisoners about their confinement have either been neglected or dismissed. Consequently, 'the construction of penal "truth" in the Foucauldian sense [has] emanated from the powerful whose account of historical events has become the accepted history of penality' (Sim 1995: 105). This specific point can be applied more generally to the history of the prison and to prison officers and their culture. It is their 'truth' which has come to dominate the historical and contemporary debates about prison life and penal policy. Consequently, the punitive and demeaning discourses that have historically underpinned and legitimated the everyday actions of prison officers, and to which prisoners consistently refer, have been neglected in favour of an Enlightenment-based perspective which focuses on the alleged contradictions in their role between custodians on the one hand and responsible, welfare-orientated state servants on the other.[5] In contrast, an alternative, critical history would utilise a 'penology from below', building on prisoners' personal accounts, which would provide a very different starting point for understanding the role and culture of prison officers. As Alyson Brown and Emma Clare have noted, 'numerous prisoner autobiographies have been published since the mid-nineteenth century ...' which have thrown up a number of common 'themes and conflicts' (Brown and Clare 2005: 50). In particular:

> ... in the context of a net-widening penal policy and overcrowded penal institutions of the early twenty-first century it seems

appropriate to re-emphasise the extent to which the experience of the prison can be psychologically and physically damaging. (Ibid.: 50)

Among the common themes to emerge is the use of violence by prison staff (a point I return to below) and the centrality of prison officer discretion in the control and punishment of offenders 'whatever the regulations formally stated' (ibid.: 57). Brown and Clare conclude:

Prison officers have been historically, and remain, the mediators of all schemes and systems within the prison environment and as such they have been identified as one of the most important mechanisms of order and control within the prison ... Historically, in autobiographies, prison officers have been seen as powerful determinants of the harshness or otherwise of life for prisoners as well as of the cultures of different prisons ... (Ibid.: 64)

A comprehensive analysis of the relationship between the social construction of penal truth and regimes of power and domination is beyond the scope of this chapter. Nonetheless, there is one important point to be made. It is often argued by politicians, media commentators and prison officers' representatives that prisoners' accounts should be treated sceptically as they are inherently untruthful. However, given the 'generalised pathology of chronic mendacity' and the 'unprecedented levels of secrecy, obfuscation, dissembling and downright lying that now characterise public life' (Panitch and Leys 2005: vii), it could be argued that state accounts of prison life should *also* be subjected to the same level of scrutiny as prisoners' accounts thereby making state-defined 'truth' around prisons equally problematic and open to challenge. This is particularly relevant to the issue of prison officer violence to which I now turn.

Prison officer violence

Richard Edney has noted that violence has been neglected in criminology to the point where its impact on the lives of prisoners is downplayed (Edney 1997). When it has been discussed it has been conceptualised 'in rigorously positivist terms, the result of an individual, unmanageable state servant deviating from cultural and institutional norms that are otherwise benevolent and supportive' (Sim 2004: 115). In effect, this 'means that the often-insidious role of

prison staff in maintaining the vulpine order of the prison is ignored'
(ibid.). Edney has developed this theme further by pointing out that
the neglect of prisoners' accounts of life inside 'is compounded by
a neglect of the power of the prison culture and institutional norms
and how they may interact with the claims of agency made by prison
officers to produce a phenomenology of violence' (Edney 2004: 37).
He goes on:

> ... there needs to be by criminology an attempt to at least
> theorise and make problematic the nature of violence against
> prisoners. In that sense it requires that the 'stories' of prisoners
> are accepted as legitimate offering as they do the experience of
> those subject to great power and the possible basis for a theory
> of such power ... In comparison with earlier prisons with their
> filth and overcrowded nature, 'modern' prisons are viewed
> in progressive and positive terms. Unfair and brutal practices
> are posited as antithetical to the prison project and contrary
> to penological objectives. Moreover, the implicit assumption is
> that the community has moved *beyond* such prisons. However,
> the prison remains an institution with totalitarian features. A
> necessary by product of such a regime is that prisoners remain
> vulnerable to abuse. (Ibid.: 38–9; emphasis in the original)

Ironically, reports by Her Majesty's Chief Inspector of Prisons come
close to endorsing Edney's argument. In 2006, the Inspectorate noted
that in Pentonville 'only 43% of prisoners ... believed that most staff
treated them with respect' (HM Inspectorate of Prisons 2006a: 5).
Crucially:

> Fewer prisoners than in 2005 felt at risk from other prisoners:
> but many more felt at risk from staff: 40% (compared with 29%
> last time) said that they had been insulted or assaulted by staff
> ... Some prisoners told us that they were reluctant to complain
> formally about ill-treatment by staff, in case of reprisals; and
> the one formal complaint we saw had not been investigated
> properly. Use of force was high, and recording of how and why
> it was used was insufficiently precise. (Ibid.)

The Chief Inspector has also demonstrated how feeling unsafe is
differentiated by race. Of the 5,500 prisoners interviewed in 18 prisons
by the Inspectorate, it was Asian prisoners who faced the greatest
bullying and abuse with 52 per cent indicating that they felt unsafe

'compared with 32% of white prisoners and 18% of black inmates …
while Asian prisoners face[d] most racist abuse from other inmates,
black prisoners felt they were least likely to be treated with respect
by staff' (*Guardian*, 20 December 2005). In Leeds, 'over a third of
prisoners had felt unsafe at some time, and this rose to 43% for black
and minority ethnic prisoners' (HM Inspectorate of Prisons 2005: 5).
At Whitemoor, one prisoner was called a '"fucking nigger". Then
they called my mum a black bitch. I felt frightened that they could
kill me at any time but there was nothing I could do' (*Guardian*, 27
June 2006). Racist disrespect also extends to minority ethnic prison
officers. The fact that in 2006 61 per cent of black and minority ethnic
staff claimed that they had experienced various forms of racist abuse,
and that 43 per cent indicated that their fellow prison officers were
responsible for this abuse (Prison Reform Trust 2006), illustrates that
there is still a serious problem, not only with the formal training
procedures for prison staff (a point I will come back to below) but
also with the informal, landing culture that governs their everyday
actions and interactions.

Prisoners' accounts continue to raise serious issues around prison
officer culture and the routine violence they experience on a daily
basis:

> In our closed environment, mistreatment and punishment have
> become acceptable; it is part of the routine of prison life. Officers
> are ill-equipped; with insufficient training to deal with the
> multitude of problems they encounter … The attitude of being
> 'hard' towards inmates has become part of officers' subculture.
> It is no longer seen as being only necessary in certain situations,
> but as being essential in dealing with everyone. (Tolmaer
> 2006: 3)

Throughout the 1970s and 1980s, radical prisoners' rights organisations
and prisoners themselves consistently, complained about violence in
prisons. This was usually and inevitably denied by those responsible
for the system in the official rush to socially construct the confined
as mendacious fantasists. However, in 2005, Martin Narey, the then
Chief Executive of the National Offender Management Service,
confirmed that in one prison at least it *was* the accounts by prisoners
which were true. In describing his time as a prison officer at Lincoln
prison Narey indicated that he saw 'prisoners in the segregation unit
routinely slapped, it was constant low-level abuse. If you wanted to
do any good you had to do it by stealth. The POA … ran the place.

Assistant governors were derided. I can remember getting a real load of abuse for being seen carrying a *Guardian*' (cited in James 2005: 16).

Thinking critically about prison violence would mean not only recognising its institutionalisation but would also mean developing a wider definition of violent state actions[6] that focuses on processes 'about which people seldom talk: namely *the mechanisms of fear*' that operate in these institutions (Poulantzas 1978: 83, emphasis in the original), a point well made in a recent, autobiographical account which starkly insisted: 'When it came to instilling fear and dishing out brutality, the screws at Wandsworth were experts' (Smith 2004: 325). Again, the Chief Inspector of Prisons endorsed this view in July 2006 when she noted that in Wandsworth:

> over half of those surveyed in the main prison said that they had been victimised by staff and that eight out of the ten most serious concerns identified by prisoners in interviews related to staff; and we saw evidence of poor behaviour and relationships, and an allegation of assault ... it was of some concern that complaints against staff, including racist incident complaints, were not always pursued swiftly and vigorously – or at least there was no evidence that this had occurred. (HM Inspectorate of Prisons 2006b: 5)

Adopting this critical perspective would also mean recognising that violence underpins the consent of the confined to their detention. As Robert Cover notes, behind the 'civil facade' of an autonomous, legal subject acting voluntarily is the spectre of state violence:

> ... most prisoners walk into prison because they know they will be dragged or beaten into prison if they do not walk ... The 'interpretations' or 'conversations' that are the preconditions for violent incarceration are themselves implements of violence ... The experience of the prisoner is, from the outset, an experience of being violently dominated, and is colored from the beginning by the fear of being violently treated. (Cover 1986: 1607–8)

The final point to be made about prison officer violence concerns its individualisation – the 'bad apple' syndrome discussed earlier – and the institutionalised reluctance of the state either to move beyond this syndrome or to offer excuses for this violence. This reached its nadir with the Woolf report which, for liberals, was (and remains) a profoundly important document for articulating a different vision for prisons. However, even here, when there was evidence of violent threats directed at prisoners, it was excused as emanating from a 'small minority' of prison officers who engaged in 'irresponsible behaviour':[7]

> There was no doubt at the time the inmates [at Pucklechurch] were very frightened (I use that word advisedly) and even if the remarks made to them ... were made in jest, they could, and did, cause considerable fear to the inmates. *When considering these criticisms the long hours that management and staff had been on duty should be taken into account. Each member of staff must have been extremely tired and ... close to exhaustion.* (Woolf, cited in Sim 1994a: 36, emphasis added)

State power and prison officers

The third dimension underpinning a critical perspective would involve thinking about prison officers as state servants and not as disembodied, ethereal subjects working in a society where power is pluralised and social control is neutral. This would mean developing an analysis which situates their everyday work within an institutional framework which is concerned not simply with the normalisation of the deviant but also with the reproduction of the deep social divisions that cut across the social and political landscape of this society. However, this does *not* involve reducing complex theoretical arguments concerning their role to crass, conspiratorial assertions but it does mean recognising that prisons are places of punishment and pain and remain part of a state apparatus that is concerned with the reproduction of a deeply divided social order, however contingent and contradictory that process might be. Prison officers play their part in that process, not only through the politics of containment but, more crucially, through the hegemonic construction and objectification of the prisoner as the ultimate and only source of criminality in the society. In turn, this would mean thinking about the Prison Officers' Association as moral entrepreneurs who have played, and continue to play, a primary defining, often invisible role in the debates around law, order and penal policy. As Lucia Zedner has noted, there has been a lack of analysis regarding the relationship between the culture of criminal justice professionals and wider social and cultural processes:

> Culture is typically presented as insulated from the larger social, political and legal environment. Individual actors, be they gang members or criminal justice professionals, are portrayed as the more-or-less passive subjects of an acculturation process that is internal to their group. Interactions between their immediate cultural environment and larger social and political structures are at worst sidelined, at best presented as the subversion of a dominant culture by the codes, values or 'working rules' of the sub-group. (Zedner 2002: 360)

This crucial link has been neglected in criminological and political debates about prison officers in favour of a perspective which has socially constructed their culture, and their organisation, as passive victims at the mercy of unsympathetic governments and out-of-touch bureaucrats. Ironically, it was a link recognised by Harley Cronin, the former General Secretary of the Prison Officers' Association, four decades ago but which has never been fully integrated into the analysis of prison officers. As he noted then:

> ... in the last analysis, the strengthening of the position of the prison officer, and of all authority within prison walls, depends on a drastic strengthening of authority and respect for law and order outside. The erosion of authority and respect has already gone too far. A decisive repair operation has been long overdue. (Cronin 1967: 186–7)

Prison officers and hegemonic masculinity

The final dimension for developing a critical analysis of prison officers would involve thinking theoretically about hegemonic masculinity and focusing on prison officers as men and women rather than men and women as prison officers.[8] As Dana Britton (2003) has argued, in order to fully conceptualise what prison officers do on a daily basis it is important to situate their work within a gendered context which reproduces dominant discourses surrounding masculinity *and* femininity. For Britton, the prison should be understood as a gendered organisation to the point where 'gender is as much part of the edifice of the iron cage that is the prison as its omnipresent walls, bars and fences' (ibid.: 19). Prison officers, male and female, are gendered individuals whose everyday work 'is the outcome of a complex interplay between structure, culture and agency' (ibid.). In England and Wales, the social construction of masculinity and femininity has added a significant new dimension to analysing the operationalisation of penal power and the processes through which prisons reproduce 'normal' men – officers and prisoners – whose hegemonic masculinity then legitimates violent interventions into the lives of subordinate masculinities such as sex offenders. In addition, the masculinity embedded in prison officer culture, contested, contradictory and contingent though it might be, can have very real consequences for those officers who wish to engage in therapeutic work:

> Various aspersions are cast [upon them] … the dominant cultural norms of uniformed prison staff encourage officers to rail against 'deviant' colleagues who are willing to work closely with prisoners seen as 'nonces' and 'beasts'. Similarly, officers who choose to work with elderly prisoners are seen as not doing 'proper' prison work because it is seen as too quiet, too predictable and too safe. (Crawley 2004: 221)

For Eamonn Carrabine, the culture of Strangeways before the disturbance in 1990 was dominated by a structured form of authoritarian fratriarchy manifested in a 'strong canteen culture, actively supported and enjoyed by the former governor and … in the celebration of hard drinking and the associated ethic of hard men doing a hard job' (Carrabine 2004: 113). Crucially, even when there were policy changes at the prison – what he terms an 'uneven transition from authoritarianism to professionalism' – an 'aggressive, confrontational approach to prisoners continued to characterise interactions' (ibid.: 190).

The praxis of prison officer culture is therefore central to the reproduction of the prison as a place of punishment and pain. The often, aggressive, masculine discourses that underpin the discretion-dominated basis of this culture generates and reinforces an everyday politics of moral opprobrium and indifference towards prisoners which is built on the 'neutralisation of moral responsibility for the other' and 'the social production of distance' between them and prison staff as a group (Bauman, cited in Pemberton 2004: 77–8).

Taking these four dimensions together therefore not only raises significant theoretical questions around the conceptualisation of prisons officers and their culture but also brings into focus what policies should be pursued to confront and dismantle this culture. It is to this question that the chapter now turns.

Confronting 'an inconvenient criminological truth'

> Our 'criminal institutions' are every bit in need of assessment
> and 'treatment' as the dangerous people held within them, but
> they are frequently even more resistant. (Cordess 2004: vi)

The working prison

Since New Labour came to power, Tony Blair's governments have
messianically pursued a modernisation agenda for the public services
built on the assertion that 'anything new must automatically be better
than what came before' (Poole 2006: 34). Blair has ruthlessly articulated
this rhetoric, tying it to broader metaphysical and existentialist themes
of respect, freedom, responsibility and community in an attempt to
construct a criminal justice system which is fit to face the problems
confronting the UK in the twenty-first century, problems which he
apocalyptically argues are qualitatively different in nature, intensity
and scope from anything that has gone before (Sim, forthcoming).

For New Labour, the modern prison is a central component in the
ongoing struggle to maintain law and order. However, 'modernisation'
means shifting the institution's overt goals away from the bleak
retribution and frenzied populism of Michael Howard's doctrine of
'prison works' towards the idea of the working prison where the
deviant, deprived and distressed would be exposed to a range of self-
responsibilising strategies designed to normalise them (Sim 2005).

Central to the idea of the working prison, constructed around the
positivist and highly contentious discourse of 'risk', is 'the development
of accredited offender behaviour programmes usually built on the
acquisition of cognitive skills' (ibid.: 220). This development, in turn,
has led to the growth in partnerships between the prison service and
other agencies. In 2000/2001, programmes involving over 1,700 staff
were delivered in over 100 prison service sites and included:

> psychologists, prison officers, educational workers and probation
> officers. At the end of March 2000, over 1300 tutors had delivered
> at least one of these programmes, *41% of whom were basic grade
> officers.* (Blud *et al.* cited in ibid., emphasis added)

What does this development mean for prison officers and their role
inside? Does it herald a new beginning and a shift towards a more
enlightened, less punitive view of prisoners involving *all* prison
officers?

At one level, the involvement of officers in more treatment-orientated regimes is not new. As I indicated at the beginning of this chapter, there are officers who, both formally and informally, have adopted a less militaristic, more empathic stance towards prisoners. Officers working at Grendon Underwood provide a paradigmatic example of this stance (Genders and Player 1995; Jones 2004).

However, there are number of problems with this modernising discourse. In particular, in targeting individual needs, the new programmes are not replacing old strategies of prisoner governance and regulation but are enhancing them. As Pat Carlen has noted:

> ... when this postmodern ideology of multiple programming is cultivated in custodial institutions, its coercive psychological programmes are implemented alongside all the old modernist disciplinarities of placing, normalising and timetabling, and against a backcloth of the even older premodern controls such as lock-ups, body searches and physical restraints, and often in the confused conditions which result from overcrowding. As a result, their possibilities for benign effect are largely neutralised ... the disciplinary transformations in the penal body politic have not supplanted the old disciplinarities designed to keep prisoners docilely and securely in prison. Instead they have added even more layers to the already compacted layers of encrusted disciplinarities. (Carlen 2004: 10 and 17)

New Labour's modernisation of the prison is therefore unlikely to undermine the authoritarian power base of prison officers. Rather, as Carlen suggests, the old discourses will simply be reinforced. This process, with its roots in a reformist political and policy discourse, can be understood as yet another manifestation of the repetitive and self-defeating cycle of reform which Foucault has characterised as intrinsic to the prison since its emergence at the end of the eighteenth century (Foucault 1979: 270). In contrast, what is required are a number of 'negative reforms' which will compete with, and contradict the current baleful system (Mathiesen 1974, 1980).[9] There are three that I want to highlight.

Recruitment and training

One obvious area in need of a 'negative reform' is the recruitment and training of prison officers. As Andrew Coyle has noted, the recruitment procedures are fundamentally problematic: 'due to a series of circumstances' the Prison Service does not have 'a clear notion of the kind of people that it wishes to recruit as first-line prison staff'. Because of these circumstances, recruits do 'not necessarily come to their new role of prison officer with a sense of vocation or of being involved in an important public service' (Coyle 2005: 93).

Even on its own terms, training is a perversely militaristic experience. Jane Coltman has described how:

> Trainee prison officers, as I found when joining, are weaned onto the ideals of the service with the doctrine of order and control at training colleges. Key targets and acronyms become the order of the day, SMART objectives, KPIs ... RESPECT and numerous other uncomfortable examples of corporate jargon were learned parrot fashion. By the time it came to learning to march on a parade ground and daily fitness lessons in the gym, it became apparent that the Prison Service also emulates the military culture ... No one asked why any of us wanted to become prison officers or what we wanted to bring to the role. Certainly being able to march has never helped me when confronted by an inmate giving verbal abuse, or in tears – sometimes both. (Coltman 2004: 143)

In the mid-1990s, training for those officers who wished to engage in therapeutic work was problematic. As one commented, 'I feel like I've been trained as a plumber and given a job as an electrician' (cited in Genders and Player 1995: 123). By the late 1990s, the time allocated for training new staff, was reduced from 11 to eight weeks. In contrast, professions such as mental healthcare, training lasted between two and three years (Coyle 2005: 94). As Coyle notes: 'During this initial training some attention is paid to the development of interpersonal skills but in the short time available the main emphasis is on matters of security and discipline and in the techniques to control violent prisoners ... After eight weeks training the newly minted officers are sent to a prison to begin to supervise prisoners.' Just as crucially, 'no specialized training is given to staff before they are sent to [their] very different working environments' (ibid.: 94–5).

By the turn of the century training was still built on a highly masculinised and intensely sexualised view of human behaviour and included 'games' such as 'shag-tag' which involved trainee officers bending over and touching their knees so that they could 'only be "released" by three thrusts (indicating sexual intercourse from the rear) from another officer (again male or female)' (Crawley 2004: 73).[10]

This was combined with the institutionalisation of moral opprobrium towards the confined:

> ... a female officer commented that 'at training college you're taught never to trust the bastards!' ... Numerous new officers were shocked at the degree of verbal and psychological abuse meted out by their trainers ... They claimed that corporate promotions of 'excellence', 'caring', 'quality' and 'respect' – terms that they had heard a great deal during their initial interviews – were barely evident in the organisational realities that they had experienced during this element of their basic training ... Many of my interviewees, male and female, remarked upon the militaristic, paternalistic and abusive nature of their basic training. (Ibid.: 69–70)

A 'negative reform' would involve the deconstruction of the recruitment and training agenda, underpinned by a radical change of emphasis in the academic curriculum for new recruits through institutionalising and exposing them to: contemporary debates around human rights and social justice; the sociological and psychological research concerning the relationship between power, powerlessness, crime and social harm; the need for anti-racist, sexist and homophobic strategies and attitudes in the workplace; and the importance of psychotherapeutic interventions as practised in institutions such as Grendon Underwood whose regime, while bearing in mind the ever-present dangers of an encroaching medicalised state form particularly for women (Kendall 2002), nonetheless, appears to have positively impacted on many, but not all, of those who have been confined there (Jones 2004).

In addition, being aware of, and committed to, implementing these ideas should become central to the promotion prospects for officers and staff of *all* grades. Clearly, knowledge about security and control is important. However, the formal, often unthinking and uncritical privileging of this knowledge operates to the detriment of other, less militaristic responses to offenders and remains a serious impediment to fundamental individual and institutional change. The current, baleful situation is not lost on serving prisoners:

> While other professions have evolved into the twenty-first century, the prison system remains firmly entrenched in the past. The reality of the role of [the] Prison Officer has become distorted; the central principle seems to be that inmates are

objects to be 'kept' rather than people to be 'cared for'. Perhaps if this inhibitive attitude changed, if officers interacted with inmates, respected boundaries, involved prisoners in their own long-term plans, listened to problems and responded to needs, then the role could be redefined, making the job rewarding and fulfilling. In short, if officers became 'carers' instead of 'keepers' then both sides would benefit greatly. (Tolmaer 2006: 3)

Democratic accountability

Second, prisons should be democratically accountable institutions. Making them democratically accountable would help to breach, and ultimately remove, the informal structure of prison officer power that constitutes a contaminating and castigating presence in many prisons. Despite a plethora of reports from the Prisons and Probation Ombudsman and Her Majesty's Prison Inspectorate, the prison system still remains outside of the democratic processes of accountability which in turn has allowed the landing culture to be sustained and maintained. Thus, even when recommendations by the Prison Inspectorate are implemented, as in the case of Eastwood Park prison in June 2006, the Inspectorate could still report that 'rates of self-harm remained extremely high, averaging 65 a week in 2005' (HM Inspectorate of Prisons 2006c: 5).

If the culture of prison officers is to be radically transformed then the democratic control of prisons should be addressed and put on the criminological and political agenda. This is not as difficult as it seems. Even in the most contentious areas such as the security services, models for their democratic accountability involving 'levels of oversight' have been suggested (Gill and Phythian 2006: 171). Why can the prison system not be subjected to a rigorously enforced system of transparent, democratic scrutiny, one element of which would involve removing the nefarious, centralising influence of the Home Office and creating a system in which individuals would be both accountable *and* responsible for their actions? If one form of contemporary governance is the creation of responsible prisoners why can the same discourse not be applied to penal institutions thereby ensuring the emergence of the responsible, democratically accountable prison?

This development, in turn, would help to control and restrict the unfettered discretion prison staff enjoy, and which many exploit, as a mechanism of individual and collective social control against the confined. In Peterhead in the 1980s, operational practices were obscured, and democratic accountability was denied, which in turn gave the prison a level of autonomy that enabled 'regimes to be developed at the discretion of prison governors but crucially to be interpreted and operationalised at the discretion of prison officers' (Scraton *et al.* 1991: 56). More recently, David Scott has shown how those officers in the prison he studied, who regarded themselves as 'disciplinarians', reinforced their 'personal authority' through:

> the patterning of discretion and decision making based upon the allocation or withholding of prisoner entitlements. Conceived as privileges, prisoner entitlements were either denied or acknowledged dependent upon prisoner behaviour. Entitlements were achieved rather than legally ascribed and the decision to grant or refuse prisoner requests was central to the disciplinarian's power base. (Scott 2006: 247)

In a situation eerily reminiscent of the nineteenth century, Scott identified the discourse of less eligibility as central to the discretionary world of these authoritarian officers who dominated the prison:

> Less eligibility provided the penological logic for the denial of prisoner legal rights and suffering in prison and was institutionalised in the occupational culture. Less eligibility informed how officers treated prisoners and developed relationships with prisoners on a day-to-day basis. (Ibid.: 241)

Us, them and 'non-places'

Finally, and perhaps most difficult of all given the current cynical political climate, it is important to challenge and deconstruct the deeply embedded but disturbing mentality of 'us' – 'the innocent, long-suffering middle-class victims' – and 'them' – 'the dangerous undeserving poor' mentality – (Garland 2001: 182) – that dominates the culture of many prisons and which permeates an increasingly mendacious political establishment and an equally hypocritical popular culture. Garland's argument is important pointing as it does to the role of the 'criminological other' in legitimating the neo-conservative, authoritarian clampdown of the last three decades. However, what is also apparent is that the prisoner has been socially constructed in 'othering' (or, more specifically, 'non-othering') terms long before the rise of the new right in the 1970s.[11] It is this deep-rooted, historical legacy, and the attitudes that sustain it, which has reduced the prisoner to the status of a non-person and the prison to the status of a 'non-place' (Augé 1992) or a 'place of memory' (ibid.: 78) existing on the edges of political and popular consciousness. Paradoxically, relegating prisoners to a 'place of memory' has done little to alleviate the sense of crisis gripping a society which feels itself to be constantly 'under siege' (Bauman 2002). Challenging this process, and recognising the insidious role of politicians and moral lobbyists such as the POA (and the Police Federation) in the construction of the offender as the 'non-other' and the prison as a 'place of memory', would be a small but important step in integrating the prison with, and connecting the prisoner to, the wider society.

In conclusion, I want to point readers back to the comments made by the prison officers at the beginning of this chapter. Their attitudes indicate that it *is* possible to break down the deeply embedded, apparently unyielding cultural edifice of penal negativity discussed in this chapter and develop radical alternatives built on a proactive respect for prisoners. However, if such officers continue to leave the service, or fail to be promoted, or are psychologically lacerated on a daily basis, then the punitive and demeaning discourses which dominate the prison will continue to be reproduced. On the other hand, if they were unequivocally supported and the prison's 'punitive obsession' (Playfair 1971) was deconstructed and replaced, then it is possible to imagine a different model of confinement developing for those who need to be detained. Anything less and the system will remain locked into the discourse of a sanctified 'us' and a despised 'them', offering nothing but daily frustration and denigration to good staff and ongoing humiliation to prisoners while providing little by way of sustained protection to the wider society.

Seminar questions

1 With respect to prison officers and their culture, what differentiates a liberal perspective from a critical perspective?
2 How does a critical perspective conceptualise violence in prison?
3 Whose 'truth' counts when prison violence is discussed? Why is this?
4 Are the radical changes suggested in this chapter to deal with prison officer culture defensible? What changes would you make in order to radically reform this culture and prisons more generally?

Recommended reading

Dana Britton (2003), *At Work in the Iron Cage*, Chapters 1, 5 and 7, provides an important set of arguments regarding how masculinity and femininity is socially constructed and operates to reproduce the power structure of the modern prison.

Richard Edney (1997), 'Prison Officers and Violence', puts the issue of violence at the centre of the work of prison officers. Consequently, it challenges the marginalisation of violence in many of the studies conducted on prison officer culture.

Mike Fitzgerald and Joe Sim (1982), *British Prisons*, Chapter 5, offer a critique of prison officers with respect to their role in the prison crisis in the 1970s and their proactive role during this decade in reinforcing the discourses of security and control as opposed to rehabilitation.

Elaine Genders and Elaine Player (1995), *Grendon: A study of a therapeutic prison*, Chapters 4 and 5, provide an analytical account of prison officers at Grendon Underwood psychiatric prison and the empathic and supportive role of these officers in challenging offending behaviour.

Phil Scraton, Joe Sim and Paula Skidmore (1991), in *Prisons Under Protest*, Chapter 3, are concerned with institutionalised violence in Peterhead prison and the role of prison staff in maintaining and reproducing this violence.

Notes

1 This is a variation on the phrase 'An inconvenient truth' I heard at the time of writing which was used on *Start the Week* on BBC Radio 4 on 2 October 2006. It was also the title of a documentary which was being shown in cinemas at the same time.

2 Many thanks to Paddy Hillyard for discussing this chapter with me, to Eileen Brewer for her technical support with its production and to the editors for their patience. Thanks also to Paul, Teresa and Paul O'Brien for the use of the room.

3 This quotation is taken from an interview conducted by Caroline Jones on ABC Radio on 5 October 1979. It is cited on p. 2 of a letter from Justice Action to the Hon. Mr John Hatzistergos, Minister for Justice, NSW, Australia which can be accessed on www.justiceaction.org.au/actNow/Briefs PDF/InsProp.pdf.

4 This is *not* to say that prison officers do not get assaulted. However, violence against them 'is neither as widespread nor as common as the [Prison Officers' Association] claim' (Sim 2004: 117).

5 The theme of the 2006 Perrie lectures, *Turnkeys or Role Models?*, captured the ongoing influence of this theme very well not just for prison officers but also for probation officers.

6 Liz Kelly's concept of a 'continuum' of violence which she has utilised to develop a feminist, theoretical position on male sexual violence is very useful here. Kelly describes how, many different forms of violence ... *abuse, intimidation, coercion, intrusion, threat and force*, can be understood as a 'continuous series of elements or events that pass into one another and which cannot be readily distinguished' (Kelly 1988: 76, emphasis in the original). This concept can also be applied to the experience of prisoners and challenges the assumption that violence against prisoners can be explained through the individualised lens of positivist determinism. Borrowing the concept, does not, of course, diminish its importance for analysing the specific and widespread nature of violence against women.

7 The 'irresponsible behaviour' involved telling demonstrating prisoners that their arms and legs would be broken.

8 This is a variation on the phrase used in Sim (1994b: 101) which critiqued previous studies of male prisoners for focusing on 'men as prisoners rather than on prisoners as men'. As masculinity is always constructed in relation to femininity (Connell 1985) this framework could also be applied to the study of female prison officers (Britton 2003). Masculinity can also be used to analyse the victimisation of prison officers in the sense that officers who are assaulted will often 'view their victimization through a male frame, the essence of which sees victimization as "weak and helpless"' (Stanko and Hobdell 1993: 413).

9 These reforms are built on securing changes in the wider criminal justice and social policy arena and abolishing prisons in their current form (Sim, forthcoming).

10 The power of the culture to punish deviants also extends to those who speak out against it. Carol Lingard, who complained about the bullying and intimidation of prisoners by officers in Wakefield, was treated as a 'grass' by her fellow officers while managers 'failed to take her complaints seriously'. She lost her job but eventually won a claim for unfair dismissal and received an apology from the Prison Service (*Observer*, 26 June 2005). Her payout amounted to £471,964.26 while the total cost to the Prison Service was £598,021.64. Thanks to John Moore for supplying me with this information.

11 Arguably, there was no major rupture in crime control in the 1970s, rather it was an intensification in state power that occurred (Sim, forthcoming).

References

Augé, M. (1995) *Non-Places: Introduction to an Anthropology of Supermodernity*. London: Verso.
Bauman, Z. (2002) *Society Under Siege*. Cambridge: Polity.

Britton, D. (2003) *At Work in the Iron Cage: The Prison as Gendered Organisation.* New York: New York University Press.

Brown, A. and Clare, E. (2005) 'A History of Experience: Exploring Prisoners' Accounts of Incarceration', in C. Emsley (ed.), *The Persistent Prison: Problems, Images and Alternatives.* London: Francis Boutle, pp. 49–73.

Carlen, P. (2004) *Imprisonment and the Penal Body Politic: The Cancer of Disciplinary Governance.* Paper presented to the Cropwood and Prisons Research Centre Conference, 'The Effects of Imprisonment: An International Symposium', 14–15 April, University of Cambridge.

Carrabine, E. (2004) *Power, Discourse and Resistance.* Aldershot: Ashgate.

Coltman, J. (2004) 'Working at the Coalface', in D. Jones (ed.), *Working with Dangerous People.* London: Radcliffe Medical Press, pp. 143–52.

Connell, R.W. (1985) *Gender and Power.* Cambridge: Polity.

Cordess, C. (2004) 'Foreword', in D. Jones (ed.), *Working with Dangerous People.* London: Radcliffe Medical Press, pp. vii–viii.

Cover, R. (1986) 'Violence and the Word', *Yale Law Journal*, 95: 1601–29.

Coyle, A. (2005) *Understanding Prisons.* Maidenhead: Open University Press.

Crawley, E. (2004) *Doing Prison Work: The Public and Private Lives of Prison Officers.* Cullompton: Willan.

Cronin, H. (1967) *The Screw Turns.* London: John Long.

Edney, R. (1997) 'Prison Officers and Violence', *Alternative Law Journal*, 22 (6): 289–97.

Edney, R. (2004) 'Contested Narratives of Penal Knowledge: H Division Pentridge Prison and the Histories of Imprisonment'. Unpublished, revised version of a paper presented to the 23rd Australian and New Zealand Law and History Society Conference, Perth, Western Australia, 2–3 July.

Fitzgerald, M. and Sim, J. (1982) *British Prisons.* Oxford: Blackwell.

Foucault, M. (1979) *Discipline and Punish.* Harmondsworth: Peregrine.

Garland, D. (2001) *The Culture of Control.* Oxford: Oxford University Press.

Genders, E. and Player, E. (1995) *Grendon.* Oxford: Oxford University Press.

Gill, P. and Phythian, M. (2006) *Intelligence in an Insecure World.* Cambridge: Polity.

HM Inspectorate of Prisons (2005) *HMP Leeds.* London: Her Majesty's Inspectorate of Prisons.

HM Inspectorate of Prisons (2006a) *HMP Pentonville.* London: Her Majesty's Inspectorate of Prisons.

HM Inspectorate of Prisons (2006b) *HMP Wandsworth.* London: Her Majesty's Inspectorate of Prisons.

HM Inspectorate of Prisons (2006c) *HMP and YOI Eastwood Park.* London: Her Majesty's Inspectorate of Prisons.

James, E. (2005) 'A Long Stretch', *Guardian*, 26 October, pp. 16–17.

Jones, D. (ed.) (2004) *Working with Dangerous People.* London: Radcliffe Medical Press.

Kelly, L. (1988) *Surviving Sexual Violence.* Cambridge: Polity.

Kendall, K. (2002) 'Time to Think Again About Cognitive Behavioural Programmes', in P. Carlen (ed.), *Women and Punishment*. Cullompton: Willan, pp. 182–98.

MacDonald, D. and Sim, J. (1978) *Scottish Prisons and the Special Unit*. Glasgow: Scottish Council for Civil Liberties.

Mathiesen, T. (1974) *The Politics of Abolition*. London: Martin Robertson.

Mathiesen, T. (1980) *Law, Society and Political Action*. London: Academic Press.

Panitch, L. and Leys, C. (2005) 'Preface', in L. Panitch and C. Leys (eds), *Socialist Register 2006*. London: Merlin, pp. vii–x.

Pemberton, S. (2004) 'A Theory of Moral Indifference: Understanding the Production of Harm in Capitalist Society', in P. Hillyard, C. Pantazis, S. Tombs and D. Gordon (eds), *Beyond Criminology*. London: Pluto, pp. 67–83.

Playfair, G. (1971) *The Punitive Obsession*. London: Victor Gollancz.

Poole, S. (2006) *Unspeak*. London: Little, Brown.

Poulantzas, N. (1978) *State Power Socialism*. London: New Left Books.

Prison Reform Trust (2006) *Experiences of Minority Ethnic Employees in Prison*. London: Prison Reform Trust.

Scott, D. (2006) 'Ghosts Beyond Our Realm: A Neo-Abolitionist Analysis of Prisoner Human Rights and Prison Officer Occupational Culture'. Unpublished PhD, University of Central Lancashire.

Scraton, P., Sim, J. and Skidmore, P. (1991) *Prisons Under Protest*. Milton Keynes: Open University Press.

Sim, J. (1994a) 'Reforming the Penal Wasteland? A Critical Review of the Woolf Report', in E. Player and M. Jenkins (eds), *Prisons After Woolf*. London: Routledge, pp. 31–45.

Sim, J. (1994b) 'Tougher than the Rest?', in T. Newburn and E. Stanko (eds), *Just Boys Doing Business?* London: Routledge, pp. 100–17.

Sim, J. (1995) 'The Prison Medical Service and the Deviant 1895–1948', in R. Creese, W.F. Bynum and J. Bearn (eds), *The Health of Prisoners*. Amsterdam: Rodopi, pp. 102–17.

Sim, J. (2003) 'Whose Side Are We Not On? Researching Medical Power in Prisons', in S. Tombs and D. Whyte (eds), *Researching the Crimes of the Powerful*. New York: Peter Lang, pp. 239–57.

Sim, J. (2004) 'The Victimised State and the Mystification of Social Harm', in P. Hillyard, C. Pantazis, S. Tombs and D. Gordon (eds), *Beyond Criminology*. London: Pluto, pp. 113–32.

Sim, J. (2005) 'At the Centre of the New Professional Gaze: Women, Medicine and Confinement', in W. Chan, D. Chunn and R. Menzies (eds), *Women, Madness and the Law*. London: Glasshouse Press, pp. 211–25.

Sim, J. (forthcoming) *The Carceral State: Power and Punishment in a Hard Land*. London: Sage.

Smith, R. (2004) *A Few Kind Words and a Loaded Gun*. London: Viking.

Sparks, R., Bottoms, A. and Hay, W. (1996) *Prisons and the Problem of Order*. Oxford: Clarendon.

Stanko, E. and Hobdell, K. (1993) 'Assaults on Men', *British Journal of Criminology*, 33 (3): 400–15.

Tolmaer, I. (2006) 'Prison Officers – Keepers or Carers?', *Inside Time*, 79: 3.

Zedner, L. (2002) 'Dangers of Dystopias in Penal Theory', *Oxford Journal of Legal Studies*, 22 (2): 341–66.

Websites

www.justiceaction.org.au/actNow/Briefs_PDF/InsProp.pdf (accessed 19 August 2006).

Part 3

Prison Managers

Chapter 12

Prison governors: new public managers?

Shane Bryans

Introduction

Prison governors are a key occupational group within the criminal justice system. On behalf of society, governors enforce the state's most severe penalty. It is governors who run the 137 penal establishments in England and Wales, holding in custody over 80,000 citizens, depriving them of their freedom and enforcing the rules and regulations that dictate prisoners' daily lives. Governors exercise considerable personal power within their institutions. Prisoners can be physically restrained, segregated, transferred, confined to their cells, strip searched, refused physical contact with their families and released temporarily, all on the instructions of the governor. Governors manage a 24-hour-a-day, 365-day-a-year organisation which provides various types of accommodation (for staff, prisoners and visitors), a shop, a catering service, a health service, a maintenance department, a sports centre, a college of further education, a library, industrial workshops and possibly a small farm or laundry (West 1997).

The last decade has seen the nature of imprisonment undergo a number of 'relatively radical transformations in terms of its functions, organization, and the size and make-up of the prison population' (Matthews and Francis 1996: 1). Despite these changes and ongoing debates about penal theory, governors have to be grounded in reality and take as their focus the daily operation of their institutions. Governors must balance four functions of penal confinement (Faugeron 1996) – the custodial function (preventing escapes), the restorative function (providing opportunities for rehabilitation and reform), the controlling function (ensuring order, safety and justice) and the maintenance function (providing decent and humane conditions).

The critical contribution that the governor makes to the life of a prison appears to have remained remarkably constant over time:

> The governor is the keystone of the arch. Within his own prison, he is ... supreme ... (Fox 1952: 87)

> A penal institution is the lengthened shadow of the man in charge. (Conrad 1960: 245)

> It hardly needs saying that the most important person in any prison is the governor. (Advisory Council on the Penal System 1968: para. 190)

> Perhaps in no organisation is the position of general manager, and the person who fills it, of such concern to all the organisational participants as it is in the prison. (King and Elliott 1977: 149)

> The key managerial role in the Prison Service is that of Governor ... a well run prison runs more than anything else on the skill and approach of the Governor. (HM Prison Service 1997: paras 4 and 9.14)

> It is difficult to think of a more challenging and important job than governing a prison. Prisons stand or fall by the people who manage ... them. (Lyon 2003: 3)

> The role of governors in shaping the quality of life in prison is crucial ... Their abilities, interpretations of their role, and the values they bring to it influence life in an establishment to a very significant extent. (Liebling 2004: 376–7)

The nature of the work, and the environment in which it is undertaken, has led to the role of the governor being described as unique or *sui generis*. However, in recent years the role has undergone something of a transformation, becoming more managerial and, some believe, less distinct as a *sui generis* profession (see Bryans 2007, for a detailed history of the role of the prison governor). Governors are increasingly seen as general managers and 'the responsibilities of governors and the demands made on them have increased enormously ...' (HM Prison Service 1997: para. 9.34). The view from outside the Prison

Service is similar: '... what governing prisons means and involves will also have changed significantly' (Sparks *et al.* 1996: 134–5) and 'the role of the governor has grown in size and complexity ... governors are increasingly constrained by senior management control and direction, and by a powerful managerialist hold on their actions and priorities' (Liebling 2004: 376 and 381). This chapter looks at how the governor's role and work have changed and considers the current state of prison governance.

New Public Management and governors

It is widely acknowledged that organisations are driven to incorporate the practices and procedures defined by 'the prevailing rationalized concept of organizational work' (Meyer and Rowan 1977: 340). This is certainly true of public sector organisations in this country, which have undergone something of a fundamental reformulation over the last two decades (see Pollitt 1993; Flynn 1997; Clarke *et al.* 2000). The Conservative government in the 1980s, as part of its commitment to lowering public expenditure and redefining the role of the state, launched a major reform programme that affected the Prison Service, like other central government departments. The reform programme was based on the importation of a number of private sector management techniques. This set of tools, ideas, beliefs and behaviours, when applied to the public sector, became known as New Public Management (NPM).

The criminal justice system as a whole was subjected to the full rigours of NPM and radical changes have been implemented across the whole criminal justice system (Garland 1990; McLaughlin and Muncie 1994; see also Cheliotis, this volume).

> To differing degrees, the organisational culture and ways of working of the criminal justice agencies, like all other public sector organisations, have been transformed in recent years by the wave of managerialisation in part promoted and imposed by 'new right' politicians as they have sought to inject private sector principles and practices into the public sector. (Raine and Willson 1997: 82).

What has taken place has been described as an 'ideological process of managerialisation' which has transformed relationships of power, culture, control and accountability in public services (Clarke *et*

215

al. 1994a: 3, 1994b). Managerialisation (defined here to mean the implementation of NPM) has been an incremental process. There was no sudden departure from the ways things had been done previously and, as a result, many practitioners were unaware of the scale or degree of change that was taking place. The lack of a single clearly defined NPM model created a certain fluidity (what Willcocks and Harrow 1992, call its 'contingent' nature) and each public sector organisation took up the NPM mantle in different ways and to varying degrees. It can be argued that managerialism has been the most significant development in the operation of our prisons in recent years. As the chapter will show, managerialism has changed the world of governors in a number of ways: the work they undertake, the way they are managed and the level of discretion they can exercise.

Changes to governors' work and approach

Governors[1] are unanimous in their view that some elements of their work are substantially different from that undertaken by their predecessors:

> In terms of running the establishment I think it is vastly different.

> It has changed beyond all recognition. Quite genuinely beyond all recognition.

> You've got to understand all sorts of things previous governors would have had no idea about.

Governors point to the increase in the complexity of their role, a result of having to take on a broader range of responsibilities. Managerialism emphasises 'decentralising management responsibilities' (Pollitt 1990: 55) and by the 1990s there was a clear view that: 'Governors must be given the discretion to exercise their own judgements and to make a reality of their position as managers of the prison' (Home Office 1991: para. 3.7). With devolution came increased responsibility, as governors were held to account for a range of matters over which their predecessors had no control. The devolution of financial management gave governors the freedom to respond flexibly to changing needs and demands. They were able to move money (and hence staff) from one area to another, and fund new initiatives locally. As one governor put it:

> In the days of Derek Lewis [Director General of the Prison Service 1992–95] much was devolved to Governors, things like budgets and staffing levels. We could pretty much do what we wanted with the money as long as it was within the rules ... It really did feel like we were running our own businesses.

With increased control over budgets came greater accountability for ensuring that the budget was not exceeded and an expectation that 'efficiency savings' would be delivered. The devolution of responsibility for personnel matters also had a major impact on governors' work. Governors found themselves dealing directly with staff recruitment, selection and discipline. Historically all these areas had been the responsibility of Headquarters or regional offices. Provided that governors were able to find the funding from within their budgets they were able to create new posts, select and appoint staff, conduct promotion boards, and discipline or dismiss staff on performance or health grounds.

Devolution took place in other areas such as regime development. Governors were given the freedom to provide, and manage, prisoner work at their prisons. In addition, governors had to generate new sources of funding, rather than rely simply on an allocated budget from headquarters. Like public sector managers in education and healthcare, governors undertook increasing amounts of 'entrepreneurial activity' (see Boyett (1996) for a discussion of the 'public sector entrepreneur'). Some set up innovative joint working with private sector and voluntary sector organisations and in some cases established joint ventures with private sector firms to run workshops and vocational courses within their prisons (Davies 1995; Flynn 1995; Simon 1999).

Governors today not only manage multidisciplinary teams, they also have to manage contractual relationships with a number of service providers from the private, public and voluntary sectors. These contractors deliver a range of services that traditionally were provided in-house. A governor may well be managing contracts for the provision of education, catering, maintenance, library, canteen, laundry, visitors' centre, probation, offending behaviour programmes and drug treatment, each of which may be with a different organisation.

> Life is very different today. I no longer just manage direct delivery of services. I have to manage other organisations managing those services. It gets very time-consuming drawing up the specifications, awarding contracts and then monitoring the delivery of the service.

> My head of activities calculated the other day that we have five different contractors working here and 26 different voluntary sector organisations coming in. That makes things bloody complicated I can tell you.

Governors now also have to undertake partnership working with local bodies, such as Drug Action Teams, Primary Care Trusts, Crime Reduction Groups and victim groups.

One of the most significant developments to result from the implementation of NPM in the Prison Service has been the introduction of a new governance structure, which has reduced the governors' discretion and limited the use of their professional judgment. The introduction of a 'performance management' apparatus has included typical bureaucratic tools such as elaborate written rules and regulations, distortion-proof instructions and the setting and intense monitoring of objective measures of performance. Some thought that the introduction of private sector practices and management techniques would free governors from traditional bureaucratic control. The reality has been somewhat different: 'What might appear at first sight to be a decentralising agenda, the management techniques introduced to monitor better performance of new corporate and individual operatives in the penal field, arguably strengthened the authority of the 'new' system at the centre rather than weakened it' (Ryan 2003: 75). Governors took a similar view:

> It's much more like McDonald's than it was. There are huge manuals setting out standards and how to do things. We must comply with these central directives and all be the same.

> My professional judgment and skills are not needed as much these days. It's about following detailed instructions and doing what we are told.

Governors point to the more corporate approach to planning introduced in recent years, together with auditing to ensure adherence to detailed orders (PSOs) and instructions (PSIs) as resulting in less scope for them as individuals to shape their prison as they would wish. The job of governors is now more about managing the delivery of a service and meeting laid-down standards. The 'professional structure' in which governors were assumed to know what was best for their institutions and their prisoners has changed. The new status assigned to area managers has created tension and has made some governors feel devalued, as their autonomy has increasingly been curtailed.

> I worked for one area manager, who would basically just shout at people and tell the governors what he expected them to do in minute detail on just about everything in the prison.

> Some of these area managers see themselves as 'super governors' and try to run your prison for you.

> They are always bloody interfering. If it is not difficult enough governing, you have now got to keep looking over your shoulder as the bloody area manager is second-guessing you all the time. It has changed the way we do the job.

Each area manager now has a significant area office that includes analysts, auditors, a senior investigating officer and specialist advisers (works, personnel, security, equal opportunities, regimes, drugs, resettlement) providing advice to the area manager on how prisons in their area should be run.

There has therefore been a significant shift in power away from individual governors. Governors are today told: what resources are appropriate for their prisons (by 'management consultancy reviews' commissioned by, and reporting to, area managers); how those resources should be used (ringfenced budgets for various areas such as offending behaviour, education, healthcare); who should provide the service (in the case of maintenance, prisoner offending behaviour programmes, education); what the regime should consist of (PSOs on regime elements such as education, physical education, offending behaviour programmes); what rewards and privileges should be made available to prisoners (the PSO on Incentives and Earned Privileges); and what level of performance is expected (Prison Service Standards). 'Robust' line management then intensively monitors governors, ensures that they do not deviate from laid-down procedures (through monthly visits and standards audits) and holds them to account for the performance of their prison (set out in a personal accountability framework). If management fail to identify any shortcomings, a number of external bodies can scrutinise and challenge a governor's decision (Ombudsman, courts, MPs) and comment on how the prison should be run (independent inspectorate).

Governors made clear that the proliferation in the amount of paperwork in prisons was one of the consequences of managerialism. The production of performance reports, audit documents and action plans, together with having to read weighty and detailed instructions and orders, has, according to governors, added to the administrative burden they face.

> It's a constant battle – the paperwork. I could spend twelve hours a day, seven days a week trying to keep on top of the paperwork. There is so much of it these days. Huge manuals to read, letters to do, reports to write, complaints to deal with. I could spend my whole day in the office and never see the end of it.

Governors believe that paperwork is making them more remote from staff and particularly prisoners, and less aware (from direct personal contact) of what is happening in their prisons. Governors have been forced to limit the amount of time they spend conducting adjudications, hearing applications and touring the prison. It follows that governors are today somewhat less mythical and more managerial than their predecessors. Prisoners and staff are often heard mourning the loss of the highly visible, charismatic and powerful governors of the past, who they compare favourably to the more office-bound managers who now occupy the governor's chair.

A particularly controversial change in the penal environment in recent decades has been the decision to use the private sector to provide custodial services. The involvement of the private sector, and the competition between prisons that has resulted, has had a considerable impact on what governors do. Since 1992, the Prison Service has permitted the public sector to compete directly with the private sector for the management of some existing prisons. (See Bryans (1996) for the detailed early history.) Having to compete with the private sector has pushed down costs and made governors think creatively about how to provide services. Today 'market testing' has been replaced by 'performance testing' whereby poor performing prisons are publicly identified and given six months in which to improve their performance. A failure to improve means that the prison faces closure or being contracted out to the private sector, without the opportunity to do an in-house bid. Governors suggest that this form of performance testing has a direct impact. As a matter of professional pride governors do not want to appear at the bottom of a performance table, or want their prison to be identified as poor performing and thus subjected to performance testing. Governors therefore find themselves operating in a more competitive and less collegiate world. More than ever before, their focus is on how their prison is performing relative to other similar prisons.

> It's been much more about league tables, performance levels and internal competition than about private prisons. All governors, even if they don't admit it in public, try and keep off the bottom of the tables ... it's not the privatisation bit but professional pride. Who wants to be at the bottom of division three and heading for relegation?

The changing nature of the work, the need to conform to a prescribed managerial image and increasing pressures on the holder of the office of governor are also having an effect on styles of governing. There is less room in the Prison Service today for the flamboyant, charismatic and independent governor of the past. Governors continue to bring to the post their individual biographies, personal attributes and values,[2] but the scope for individualism is significantly reduced.

> I think it is fair to say that probably there was a time where you could govern through sheer strength of character. If you had a particular style and you were a very strong-willed person, and perhaps a very charismatic person, then probably you could get away with managing by character and personality, largely anyway, so long as you got things right. I don't think that people can get away with that sort of style nowadays ... the old sort of archetypal Captain on the Bridge bit, is totally redundant. I think that style of management has long gone.

> Governors today are very similar, and we all do the same things. It's a pity really not to have some of the colour and eccentricity that those old governors had.

Governors are now expected to be competent and professional managers who plan and deliver a public service within a set budget and to laid-down standards. They are expected not to be insubordinate, free-thinking, or openly challenging of the current approach to prison management. As one commentator put it: 'Departmental officials look for strong but 'obedient' field leaders in order to maintain cohesion' (Boin 1998: 210). Governors are today less willing to ignore, or fail to comply with, written instructions. This is partly because the chances of their delinquency being found out are higher (through the more intensive monitoring and audit infrastructure), but also because of the increased frequency with which action is taken against those found not to be compliant.

To sum up, therefore, the late 1990s saw: the development of various forms of competition (private sector involvement, market testing, performance testing and league tables); the setting of clear standards of performance; the creation of key performance indicators and targets; the development of robust line management to monitor and assess delivery; and the construction of an audit infrastructure to ensure compliance. Middle management (area managers) have been redeployed to rationalise and regulate the daily operation of the prison system – what Foucault presciently called 'supervising the process of the activity rather than the result' (Foucault 1979: 137). All of these developments have had a significant impact on what governors do and how they do it.

The essence of governing today

A number of aspects of the governors' work have remained remarkably constant over the years. Governors have always been required to: maintain a personal presence by frequently visiting all parts of the establishment; adjudicate on at least some disciplinary matters; sample the prisoners' food on a daily basis; closely monitor prisoners in segregation and hospital; undertake a number of symbolic and ceremonial duties; liaise with the local community; and be effective incident commanders (acting in a 'command role') during incidents such as fires, riots, demonstrations, escapes, hostage-taking and rooftop protests.

> Prisons are very coercive environments. Even today the governor should visit the punishment cells, visit the hospital, I mean areas of vulnerability, is my kind of general point. Areas where there is sensitivity, where things can go wrong, where abuses can occur. So healthcare, segregation ... A good governor understands that ... I think it is also important for the governor to go into what one might call the dark corners.

In addition, governors now perform more generic managerial roles and duties that managers and leaders in many other organisations undertake. These general management tasks relate to finances, planning, human resources, auditing and monitoring. Governors also provide leadership in the form of developing and maintaining the vision of the prison and acting as its figurehead. NPM itself has enhanced the importance of governors by making them general managers who are accountable for the total operation of their prisons (budget, staffing, prisoners and achievement of targets). The governor is now both managerially and institutionally powerful.

Governors, however, will always need to be more than just general managers due to the special social and moral characteristics of their working environment. Governors point to a number of reasons why this is the case: the nature of the custodial institution itself, the historical vestiges in the role, the level of discretion that governors still exercise over individuals and the need for someone to regulate the operation of a prison on a daily basis.

Prisons have a number of characteristics that make them complex institutions in which to manage. Distinctive features of the prison that point to its managerial complexity include: the power disparity between staff and prisoners (the dialectic of domination and subordination is very different from that which subsists in the open parts of society (Cohen 1985); the level of deprivation (liberty, movement, access to goods and services, sexual relations with partners); the high levels of surveillance (in cells, toilets, showers, meetings with family); the limits which are placed on freedom of choice (daily timetable, regime, food); and the requirement that prisons encompass the whole of the lives of their inmates for 24 hours a day, 365 days a year. Perhaps the most significant feature is the dynamic that is created because prisoners are detained against their will. There is always the potential for prisoners to be disruptive, unless prompted and encouraged to conduct themselves well.

Prisons therefore exercise considerable power and influence over the individuals held within them. This power can be used for positive purposes or can be abused. Social systems that may appear stable and permanent are, in reality, in a dynamic state of perpetual reconstruction (Hatch 1997). Prisons are volatile institutions that can quickly degenerate into a state of disorder. While governors' powers have been directed and constrained in many ways, their residual power remains extensive. Governors still exercise considerable discretion in how to exercise their personal power on a daily basis.

The prison environment remains one of great ambiguity in terms of its purposes. As something of a 'Weberian bureaucracy, the Prison Service is ill-equipped for correctly translating vague and conflicting goals into integrated action' (Boin 1998: 66). Coming up with policies that allow governors to achieve all official penal goals in a uniform, efficient and politically acceptable manner is an impossible job (DiIulio 1990; Hargrove and Glidewell 1990). It falls to governors to interpret the aims, purpose and goals of imprisonment. Governors must still balance competing priorities in the light of a proliferation of objectives and tasks which go way beyond governors' functional and financial capacity to deliver (Carlen 2001).

> I think it's more complex, less clear in its aims, contradictory in some areas so that you are facing often in more directions than you've got faces. That gives it a bit of a uniqueness and I think that's to some extent too because of the lack of clarity in that and I don't think it can be clarified. I think it's intrinsically complex and contradictory and, because of that, you're doing much more as a governor. People look to you as the governor to put it all into context, to explain things and to put the pieces of the jigsaw together.

In their daily work therefore governors must exercise their judgment to manipulate the various aspects of the regime in order to ensure security, order and justice on the one hand, and reform, rehabilitation and reintegration on the other. As one commentator put it: 'There can be no simple and invariant solution to all problems of order and legitimacy. Prisons are mercurial institutions' (Rock 1996: 349). Policy instructions, despite their proliferation to cover a greater number of areas, can never be so comprehensive as to cover all eventualities in what is a complex operational environment. Many rules, instructions and orders remain sufficiently 'open textured' (Twining and Miers 1982: 213) to provide considerable scope for interpretation by the governor.

> On the one hand, we are not short of instructions, you know; this office is full of cupboards which are full of manuals; but whether those instructions fully meet, fully advise, fully structure, fully guide governors in order to make the decisions on a day-to-day basis, I'm very doubtful of that. I mean it's down to you as the governor to deal with ambiguity.

Governors believe that they have a central part to play in setting the boundaries for the compromise and accommodation which takes place daily between staff and prisoners, what Mathiesen (1965) referred to as the distribution of benefits and burdens by staff. This involves creating the framework within which prison officers exercise their discretion (see Liebling and Price 2001) and in drawing the line for what is, and is not, acceptable behaviour. Where the governor does not exercise that power, some other individual, or group of individuals, will do so instead.

Governors continue to have a role in assessing and managing risk. Judgments have to be made about what level of risk is acceptable for any given purpose or in any particular situation, what factors should be taken into account and what weight should be given to those factors. Whatever the process for risk assessment, governors continue to have to make the final decision on the risk posed by an individual in various circumstances such as Home Detention Curfew, release on temporary licence, the size of an escort to court or hospital, employment location, segregation, transfer, and security category.

> There is no scientific way of doing a risk assessment when you are working with people and especially cons. You might be able to do a proper risk assessment with a gas boiler or oil rig but with prisoners it's different. You can try and be objective and use all the modern assessment techniques but at the end of the day it's a human judgment – my judgment in many cases.

The governor's role has become vested with a certain amount of mythology, symbolism and power, which continues to contribute to the significance that people attribute to it. One manifestation of this mythology is the way in which prisoners and staff consider the governor to be the ultimate source of power and authority. This is surprising given that a superstructure above the governor makes many decisions and allocates resources. Most governors now have little to do with individual prisoners and their problems (those governors who do adjudications and visit their segregation units have some direct contact with 'troublesome' prisoners but most prisoners see little of the governor and have even less personal contact), and decisions about individual prisoners (such as temporary release, category change or segregation) are often decided on by other managers. However, for most prisoners and staff it is still the governor who they believe can make a difference in their lives and it is to the governor that they turn to address their requests and concerns.

> The role or the office of governor is vested with mythology and power because it has to be I suppose … We have enormous power over people's lives.

> It comes back to the sort of symbolism of the role … It is a total institution. There is a lot of implied danger within it. It's a risk business. It's very people-orientated and complex. Those all make it such that the head is vested with more symbolism than, say, a general manager of a factory.

From interviews with governors it is clear that their work has retained a significant specialist element that involves regulating the operation of the prison, managing emergent tensions and the interface between staff and prisoners, and creating a working balance of the various forces and influences operating in their prisons. Governors have to effectively balance and regulate the use of space, time and the quality of relationships in order to create a 'good' prison. This requires an appreciation of, and ability to manipulate, the 'softer' elements of a prison (such as culture, emotions, tensions, expectations) in order to regulate its daily operation. This aspect of a governor's role – known as 'jailcraft' – has remained ever-present over the years.

Some final thoughts

If the recent past is any indication, prison governance is likely to become even more complex, requiring greater use of professional judgment and discretion. Governors will still shape a prison and dictate by their action, or inaction, the safety, stability, security and justice within that prison. A good governor will still encourage a positive approach to looking after prisoners with humanity, safeguarding prisoners' rights, minimising the negative aspects of imprisonment and providing prisoners with the opportunity to obtain skills and tackle their offending behaviour. Poor governors will still let their prisons 'very rapidly deteriorate into unruly places that can only encourage further delinquent behaviour' (Dunbar and Langdon 1998: 32).

Exactly what a governor should do to achieve a healthy prison will remain a little elusive. As a result, governing a prison will remain an exciting, demanding and complex responsibility that requires enormous dedication and commitment. What is clear is that governors will increasingly be held accountable for all that happens in their institutions, even though they are responsible for matters that they cannot wholly control. As a recent report pointed out:

> President Truman had a sign on his desk in the Oval Office which read: 'The buck stops here.' The sign had been made at a reformatory in Oklahoma, where it had been on the desk of the Warden. The Warden was right. In prison, the buck does indeed stop with the Governor. (Keith 2006: para. 40.1)

There will always be a tension between control from above in the form of rules, regulations and directives (that reduce the governor's autonomy), and the need for governors to exercise their discretion and use 'jailcraft' in managing prisons. So long as this remains the case, the work of a prison governor will remain a form of management that is *sui generis*.

Seminar questions

1 Has NPM really changed the role of the governor or is it fundamentally the same as it always was?
2 Would managers from business or the voluntary sector make better prison governors than the civil servants currently occupying the role?
3 Has the introduction of NPM tools and techniques made our prisons better places to live and work?
4 Is the prison, and its operating environment, so unique that it requires distinct skills, knowledge and experience to effectively run them?
5 Would you agree that the very nature of prisons means that they cannot be safe and productive places, however good the person running them?

Recommended reading

Consideration of prison governance is more limited than its importance suggests that it should be. The literature that does exist is in the form of autobiographies by retired governors (Blake 1927; Rich 1932; Grew 1958; Clayton 1958; Kelly 1967; Miller 1976); practitioner accounts of their work (Bryans and Wilson 1998; Willmott 1999; Bryans 2000; Abbot and Bryans 2001) and in official reports (most recently HM Prison Service 1997 and Laming 2000). Academic consideration of prison governance, and the impact of NPM, can be found in Shane Bryans (2007) *Prison Governors: Managing in a time of change* and Alison Liebling's (2004) *Prisons and their Moral Performance*.

Notes

1 The quotations from governors used in this chapter are taken from interviews with 46 prison governors.
2 For a discussion about penal values and prison management see Liebling (2004: ch. 8).

References

Abbot, B. and Bryans, S. (2001) 'Prison Governors', in S. Bryans and R. Jones (eds), *Prisons and the Prisoner: An Introduction to the Work of Her Majesty's Prison Service*. London: Stationery Office.

Advisory Council on the Penal System (1968) *The Regime for Long-Term Prisoners in Conditions of Maximum Security* (The Radzinowicz Report). London: HMSO.

Blake, W. (1927) *Quod*. London: Hodder & Stoughton.

Boin, A. (1998) *Contrasts in Leadership: An Institutional Study of Two Prison Systems*. Delft: Eburon.

Boyett, I. (1996) 'The Public Sector Entrepreneur – A Definition', *International Journal of Public Sector Management*, 9 (2): 36–51.

Bryans, S. (1996) 'The Market Testing of Prisons: Ideology, Economics and Reality', *Prison Service Journal*, 104: 37–43.

Bryans, S. (2000) 'Governing Prisons: An Analysis of Who Is Governing Prisons and the Competencies which They Require to Govern Effectively', *Howard Journal*, 39 (1): 4–29.

Bryans, S. (2007) *Prison Governors: Managing Prisons in a Time of Change*. Cullompton: Willan Publishing.

Bryans, S. and Wilson, D. (1998) *The Prison Governor: Theory and Practice*. Leyhill: Prison Service Journal.

Carlen, P. (2001) *Governing the Governors: Telling Tales of Managers, Mandarins and Mavericks*, Future Governance Paper 5. London: Economic and Social Research Council.

Clarke, J., Cochrane, A. and McLaughlin, E. (1994a) 'Mission Accomplished or Unfinished Business? The Impact of Managerialisation', in J. Clarke, A. Cochrane, and E. McLaughlin (eds), *Managing Social Policy*. London: Sage.

Clarke, J., Cochrane, A. and McLaughlin, E. (1994b) (eds) *Managing Social Policy*. London: Sage.

Clarke, J., Gerwitz, S. and McLaughlin, E. (eds) (2000) *New Managerialism, New Welfare*. London: Sage.

Clayton, G. (1958) *The Wall Is Strong: The Life of a Prison Governor*. London: John Long.

Cohen, S. (1985) *Visions of Social Control: Crime, Punishment and Classification*. Oxford: Polity Press.

Conrad, J. (1960) 'The Assistant Governor in the English Prison', *British Journal of Criminology*, X (4): 245–61.

Davies, M. (1995) 'Prisons as Social Firms: The Way Forward for Prison Industry?', in Prison Reform Trust, *A Good and Useful Life: Constructive Prison Regimes*. London: Prison Reform Trust.

DiIulio, J. (1990) 'Managing a Barbed-Wire Bureaucracy: The Impossible Job of Corrections Commissioner', in E. Hargrove and J. Glidewell (eds), *Impossible Jobs in Public Management*. Lawrence: University Press of Kansas.

Dunbar, I. and Langdon, A. (1998) *Tough Justice: Sentencing and Penal Policies in the 1990s*. London: Blackstone.

Faugeron, C. (1996) 'The Changing Functions of Imprisonment', in R. Matthews and P. Francis (eds), *Prisons 2000 – An International Perspective on the Current State and Future of Imprisonment*. London: Macmillan.

Faulkner, D. (2001) *Crime, State and Citizen: A Field Full of Folk*. Winchester: Waterside Press.

Flynn, N. (1995) 'Making Workshops Work', *Prison Report*, 30: 26–7.

Flynn, N. (1997) *Public Sector Management*. Hemel Hempstead: Harvester Wheatsheaf.

Foucault, M. (1979) *Discipline and Punish: The Birth of the Prison*. Harmondsworth: Peregrine.

Fox, L. (1952) *The English Prison and Borstal Systems*. London: Routledge & Kegan Paul.

Garland, D. (1990) *Punishment and Modern Society*. Oxford: Oxford University Press.

Grew, B. (1958) *Prison Governor*. London: Herbert Jenkins.

Hargrove, E. and Glidewell, J. (eds) (1990) *Impossible Jobs in Public Management*. Lawrence: University Press of Kansas.

Hatch, M. (1997) *Organisation Theory*. Oxford: Oxford University Press.

HM Prison Service (1997) *Prison Service Review*. London: HMPS.

Home Office (1991) *Custody, Care and Justice: The Way Ahead for the Prison Service in England and Wales*, Cm. 1648. London: HMSO.

James, A. and Raine, J. (1998) *The New Politics of Criminal Justice*. London: Longman.

James, A., Bottomley, A., Liebling, A. and Clare, E. (1997) *Privatising Prisons: Rhetoric and Reality*. London: Sage.

Keith, Mr Justice (2006) *Report of the Zahid Mubarek Inquiry* (Mubarek Report), HC 1082. London: Stationery Office.

Kelly, J. (1967) *When the Gates Shut*. London: Longmans.

King, R. and Elliott, K. (1977) *Albany: Birth of a Prison – End of an Era*. London: Routledge and Kegan Paul.

Laming, Lord (2000) *Modernising the Management of the Prison Service: an Independent Report by the Targeted Performance Initiative Working Group, Chaired by Lord Laming of Tewin CBE*. London: Home Office.

Liebling, A. (2004) *Prisons and Their Moral Performance*. Oxford: Oxford University Press.

Liebling, A. and Price, D. (2001) *The Prison Officer*. Leyhill: Prison Service Journal Publications.

Lyon, J. (2003) 'Managing to Work in Prisons', *Prison Report*, 61, June. London: Prison Reform Trust.

McLaughlin, E. and Muncie, J. (1994) 'Managing the Criminal Justice System', in J. Clarke, A. Cochrane and E. McLaughlin (eds), *Managing Social Policy*. London: Sage.

Mathiesen, T. (1965) *The Defences of the Weak: A Sociological Study of a Norwegian Correctional Institution*. London: Tavistock.

Matthews, R. and Francis, P. (eds) (1996) *Prisons 2000: An International Perspective on the Current State and Future of Imprisonment*. Basingstoke: Macmillan.

Meyer, J. and Rowan, B. (1977) 'Institutional Organizations: Formal Structure as Myth and Ceremony', *American Journal of Sociology*, 83 (2): 340–63.

Miller, A. (1976) *Inside Outside – The Story of a Prison Governor*. London: Queensgate Press.

Pollitt, C. (1990) *Managerialism and the Public Services: The Anglo-American Experience*. Oxford: Blackwell.

Pollitt, C. (1993) *Managerialism and the Public Services: Cuts or Cultural Change in the 1990s?*, 2nd edn. Oxford: Blackwell Publishers.

Raine, J. and Willson, M. (1997) 'Beyond Managerialism in Criminal Justice', *Howard Journal*, 36 (1): 80–95.

Rich, C. (1932) *Recollections of a Prison Governor*. London: Hurst & Blackett.

Rock, P. (1996) *Reconstructing a Women's Prison – The Holloway Redevelopment Project 1968–88*. Oxford: Clarendon Press.

Ryan, M. (2003) *Penal Policy and Political Culture in England and Wales*. Winchester: Waterside Press.

Simon, F. (1999) *Prisoners' Work and Vocational Training*. London: Routledge.

Sparks, R., Bottoms, A. and Hay, W. (1996) *Prisons and the Problem of Order*. Oxford: Clarendon Press.

Twining, W. and Miers, D. (1982) *How to do Things with Rules*, 2nd edn. London: Weidenfeld & Nicolson.

West, T. (1997) *Prisons of Promise*. Winchester: Waterside Press.

Willcocks, L. and Harrow, J. (eds) (1992) *Rediscovering Public Services Management*. London: McGraw-Hill.

Willmott, Y. (1999) 'Governing Women's Prisons – A Qualitative Study', unpublished thesis. Cambridge: Institute of Criminology Library.

Chapter 13

Change management in prisons[1]

Andrew Coyle

Introduction

The management of prisons is an intriguing and largely unexplored subject for study. There is a wide literature on the theory and practice of management in general and also on the management of large public institutions such as schools and hospitals, but comparatively little has been written on the management of prisons. This is partly because the world of prisons itself remains relatively closed. It is also because until fairly recently it was not acknowledged that there is a particular set of skills required to manage prisons properly.

In a number of Western countries the management of prisons was originally a responsibility which was given to retired military officers as a means of enhancing their pensions, a task which was mildly interesting but which still allowed plenty of time for other more gentlemanly activities. The work of the prison governor could be started in mid-morning and finished by lunchtime, leaving more junior staff to carry out the mundane tasks of seeing to the daily needs of prisoners. Many of the junior prison staff were themselves former military personnel and were at ease with this style of light-touch management, which expected little of them other than to maintain a constant routine. In other regions the management of the prison system was, and in some cases such as India remains even today, the responsibility of the police force. A posting to take charge of a prison often came about as an informal sanction as a result of some failing elsewhere. Bright police officers made sure that they completed their spell in charge of a prison as quickly as possible before negotiating a transfer back to mainstream police duties. There was a variation of this model in the Soviet Union where the prison system was part of the Ministry of the Interior and the senior management of each prison was made up of officers in the Ministry of Interior militia.

Currently in some Western European countries such as Germany prison directors must have a legal qualification and their tenure in prisons is only one part of their general training for higher appointments in the public service. In other jurisdictions, such as some parts of the United States, all senior public appointments, including the wardens or directors of jails and prisons, are either themselves subject to election or their appointments are in the gift of elected politicians. In the United Kingdom prison governors are administrative civil servants, most of whom spend their professional careers working in the prison system.

In the majority of countries there is little concept of prison management as a profession or even a skill which requires specific training and development. A newly appointed prison director either is likely to have previous general legal, administrative or military training or will be expected simply to possess intuitively the skills which are required. This is surprising given the complex nature of many prisons. The biggest prisons in the world, such as Tihar in New Delhi and the Rikers Island complex in New York, can hold between 10,000 and 15,000 prisoners, while the smallest may hold no more than a dozen or so prisoners. Managing them requires a defined set of skills, some of which are common to general management and some of which are peculiar to prisons.

The wider picture

The prison as an institution does not attract a great deal of public attention in the normal course of events. Politicians, the media and the public generally become aware of prisons only when something goes wrong, for example when a high-profile prisoner escapes or when there is a major incident such as a riot in a particular prison. Similarly, discussion about the appropriate use of imprisonment usually only occurs in the aftermath of a high-profile crime or when the release of a notorious prisoner is being considered.

Notwithstanding this lack of public attention, prison systems in many countries have undergone a massive process of change over the last twenty years. Between 1980 and 2004, for example, prison administrators in the United States have had to cope with a rise from half a million people in detention to a new figure of almost 2.2 million (United States Bureau of Justice Statistics 2005). In the countries of the former Soviet Union during the course of the 1990s the infrastructure which supported the system of labour colonies all but collapsed. Prison administrators in Russia, for example, have had to grapple with the seemingly impossible task of providing for up to one million prisoners in an environment of a drastic shortage of resources such that there is hardly enough money to pay the salaries of staff or to feed the prisoners (Kalinin 2002). Prisons in a number of countries in Latin America have been places of increasing violence and brutality. Hardly a month goes by without a report of violence in prison systems somewhere in the region. The following report from Brazil is not uncommon:

> Brazilian police have surrounded a jail in São Paulo state, where at least five inmates have been killed in riots between rival gangs. The victims were decapitated and their heads have been displayed on stakes on the jail's roof. The rioting prisoners are holding 11 guards hostage, but they have been negotiating with the state authorities. It is thought the prisoners are unhappy about the transfer of fellow inmates to a different jail. Much of the prison has been damaged, and officials say there could be more bodies inside. The revolt, at the Presidente Venceslau prison 620 km (386 miles) west of the city of São Paulo, began early on Tuesday. Wednesday's newspapers showed photos of rioters on the roof displaying both the severed heads and the live hostages. Riot police are awaiting orders to enter the building (BBC 2005).

Problems such as these have been replicated in many countries around the world.

This increasing pressure on prison systems and the difficulty which they have in coping has been the subject of comment by intergovernmental agencies such as the United Nations through its Special Rapporteur on Torture and the Council of Europe, through its Committee for the Prevention of Torture and Cruel and Inhuman or Degrading Treatment. They regularly publish a series of reports drawing attention to what is happening in many prison systems around the world. Similarly, non-governmental organisations such as Amnesty International, Human Rights Watch and Penal Reform International have reported on the terrible human rights abuses which have occurred, mainly in regard to prisoners but from time to time also in regard to prison staff.

The United Kingdom has not been immune from these pressures. Overcrowding has been an ever-present feature of imprisonment in England and Wales. It reached levels in late 2006 that led the Lord Chief Justice to describe prisons as 'little more than social dustbins to house people with problems' and resulted in the Prison Service putting up the 'house full' notices (Riddell and Doward 2006). The murder of a young Asian prisoner in his cell in Feltham Young Offenders Institution led to unprecedented criticism of the Prison Service by a public inquiry (Keith 2006). In the late 1980s and the beginning of the following decade there was a series of major riots in prisons in England and Wales and in Scotland, culminating in the destruction of Strangeways prison in April 1990 (Woolf and Tumin 1991). More recently an internal Prison Service report discovered evidence of disturbing levels of corruption among staff (Home Office 2006).

Consequences for prison management

To date surprisingly little thought has been given to the implications of these pressures for prison administrations themselves. How does a prison system cope with a 50 per cent increase in the number of prisoners for which it is responsible when there has been no corresponding increase in resources? Or with a situation in which all previous certainties have vanished and in which there is a lack of clarity about what the system is meant to be achieving? Or with a situation in which all control has been ceded to the prisoners? These are major issues for prison management.

And what of the staff who work within these prison systems? In many respects they are a forgotten group of public servants, largely unrecognised in the criminal justice sector. Police have a profile which ensures that the public is aware of their existence and often they are still regarded as custodians of the peace. Prosecutors are powerful figures in many countries, able to take what may well be life and death decisions about which crimes should be taken to court and which should be dealt with in some other manner. Generally speaking, judges are persons of importance in their communities. The story is quite different in respect of prison staff. They carry out their duties away from the public view. In common with prisoners, they are hidden behind high prison walls. In a disturbing number of countries they are poorly trained, badly paid and are given little respect from their governments, from other public officials or from the rest of society.

One can say that to a certain extent prisons reflect some of the values of the society in which they exist. One instance of this is that societies can choose to make more or less use of imprisonment. The United States has a prison rate of well over 700 per 100,000 of its population. In Russia the rate is over 600. Other countries have much lower rates, with Indonesia for example at 25 per 100,000, Iceland at 30, India at 40 and Finland at 50 (ICPS 2006). In some countries imprisonment is used only for those who have committed very serious crimes. Other countries choose to use imprisonment for large numbers of offenders who have committed minor offences, including men and women who are mentally ill, those who are substance abusers and even those who are children or juveniles. These are issues which are very topical in respect of the United Kingdom where recent increases in prison numbers have been fuelled by an increasing tendency of the courts to imprison people whose offence would not previously have attracted a prison sentence. For example, In November 2004 the chief executive of the National Offender Management Service of England and Wales noted that in the previous year 'the courts jailed 3,000 people for thefts such as shoplifting or stealing a bicycle, even though they did not have any previous convictions' (Travis 2004).

The use that a country makes of imprisonment is likely to affect the internal management of prisons. When prisons are overcrowded and under-resourced management may well be restricted to providing the basic necessities of life for those who are under their care. Simply ensuring that prisoners have sufficient food and clean water, have a bed to sleep on and access to fresh air may become a full-time task in some prison administrations. In other jurisdictions there is an attempt to set much higher targets. This may involve doing everything possible to ensure that the damage done to individuals who are imprisoned is kept to a minimum by maintaining family ties and community links. It is also likely to imply encouraging prisoners to face up to the offences which led to their prison sentence and attempting to enhance their personal, social and work skills. All of these activities will be undertaken with the intention of helping prisoners to live law-abiding lives after they are released.

A changing environment

Given that prisons exist to serve the public good, it is inevitable and appropriate that the prison system in each country will be affected to a large degree by the political and social climate in which it exists. The manner in which a society deprives certain citizens of their liberty has to be subject to strict legal and parliamentary control and should be a matter for public and political debate. These controls and this debate may differ, at least in degree, in individual countries and these differences will have a direct effect on the way that prisons are managed. For example, in most countries of Western Europe and North America there has been a traditional expectation that prison should include some form of treatment for individual prisoners. As a result, prison management has often focused on creating an ethos within the prison in which it is possible to influence the personalities of individual prisoners and to change their future behaviour. In less individualistic and more communitarian cultures, for example in many countries of sub-Saharan Africa, a behavioural approach like this is neither appropriate nor practical. In many countries of Eastern Europe and Central Asia, as mentioned above, the collapse of the Soviet model of imprisonment which consisted of exile and industrial work for the state has left a vacuum that has not yet been filled.

Prison management needs to take account of the political and cultural environment which surrounds it. This has been particularly true in the climate of radical change which has existed in so many parts of the world over the last 25 or so years. This implies that good prison management needs to be dynamic rather than static and that any process of improvement has to be a continuous one.

A dynamic institution

Traditionally prison systems have been regarded, particularly by the staff who work within them, as static and hierarchical organisations. They are regarded as static in that their objectives are clear and unchanging. According to this perspective, prisons exist to execute the sentence of the court, which is that the offender should be deprived of his or her liberty. The task of prison staff is to implement that sentence in a decent and humane manner. In so far as this task never changes, the prison system can be described as a static organisation. Secondly, prison systems are hierarchical in that they are disciplined organisations in which orders are passed down from above and the responsibility of staff at lower levels is simply to obey these orders. In a similar manner, prisoners are expected to obey instructions from staff without question. In the prison cliché, 'When I tell you to jump, you should not ask "why?", you should ask "how high?".' According to this perspective, within the prison setting there are no lines of horizontal communication, only vertical ones, and even these go from the top downwards, never from the bottom upwards.

It has sometimes been argued that this organisational structure is necessary because of the operational demands of prison life. Just as in the armed forces, there is no margin within prisons for failure. The first inflexible requirement is that prisoners must not be allowed to escape. The second is that there must be no disorder within prisons. The only way of ensuring that these two requirements are met is if everyone, staff and prisoners, knows their place in the hierarchy and obeys operational instructions without question.

The attempt to impose such an unyielding structure has had two main consequences. The first has been that many junior staff, who are crucial in determining the culture of a labour-intensive organisation like the prison system, have felt undervalued and have not been involved in the change process. The second has been that the bureaucracy of prison systems has usually developed in a highly centralised manner. The story is told of the Chairman of the English Prison Commissioners at the end of the nineteenth century who boasted that he could look at his watch at any time of the day and know exactly what was happening in every prison in the country at that moment. Matters have moved on a bit since those days but in many prison systems there is still an expectation that very little should happen without the approval of the central headquarters. The reality in many countries is quite different from the theory. Prisons often operate on a day-to-day basis as autonomous units, either because of their geographical distance from the centre of the organisation, or as a result of poor communications, or because the governor or director has a high public profile in the local community.

In management terms a static, hierarchical structure can be tolerated when the organisation is stable and not under pressure. In this context the work of the organisation will be predictable, as will be the responsibilities of those working within it and the reactions of those who are affected by it. This is the picture which many long-serving members of staff paint of the prison world in former days. According to this picture, prisons then were not subject to external influence by politicians, government officials, the media or the public. The governor or director of the prison acted, according to one's view, as either a father figure or a feudal baron whose main duty consisted in making a daily tour of the prison to ensure that everything and everyone was in its proper place (in those days all heads of prisons were men). Prison staff came to work each day, knowing what their tasks would be, in the expectation that they would be left to complete their daily business without interference. Finally, prisoners knew their place and would quietly obey instructions from staff without question. This picture is at best only partly true; at worst it is completely mythical.

Whatever the historical reality, in recent years many prison systems have been described as being in a state of permanent crisis. The suggestion that an organisation is permanently in a state of crisis has grave consequences for its inherent stability and for the confidence of the staff who work there. This is what has happened in many prison systems. Anyone who has worked at a senior level in prisons in recent years will have heard staff regularly asking, 'When is the change going to stop?' 'When are we going to get back to the good old days?'

It is questionable whether 'the good old days' ever existed. Even if one allows that they did, the situation in all prison systems has altered in recent years. Organisational change, sometimes of a radical nature, is a fact of life in all institutions. In respect of prison systems this has implications for the work which staff are expected to undertake and for the type of staff which the organisation wishes to employ. In respect of the staff themselves it is likely to imply a change in the way they approach their daily work and their attitude to prisoners. It may also affect job security for both existing and for new staff, who can no longer look forward to a life-time guarantee of employment. Many existing staff can be expected to respond positively to the challenge of change. Others may find it impossible to cope, even though they are willing. A third group may simply be unwilling to try. The organisation needs different strategies to deal with all of these responses.

Provided it is accepted that prison systems are no longer static hierarchical organisations but are dynamic institutions subject to continuous change and development, it is possible to plan appropriate response strategies to the challenge of change. If staff at all levels can be encouraged to recognise this fact, they can be given the opportunity to direct and drive change rather than merely to respond when things go wrong. This will only be possible if there is a change in both the traditional culture and the organisational structure of the prison and the prison system. This means that senior management must be willing to trust junior staff, rather than to assume that they will get things wrong if they are not controlled in all aspects of their work. It also means that junior staff, particularly those who deal directly with prisoners, must be willing to accept responsibility for their actions and to use their initiative in a positive manner when appropriate. There have been a number of examples in recent years, in both individual prisons and national prison systems, where attempts have been made to follow this new model. Some of these have been successful and others less so.

That is not to say that the process of good prison management is purely situational, depending solely on the legal and political environment of each country. There is, for example, an agreed set of international standards, accepted by the vast majority of countries, against which prison management can be assessed (Coyle 2002b). It is also possible to identify a set of parameters within which appropriate models of good prison management can be developed, models that take account of the need for cultural and organisational change.

The need to manage change

Until quite recently most directors and governors of prisons did not recognise themselves as managers of what are often large and complex organisations. By the end of the twentieth century, however, perceptions were changing. In 1991 the author of a report into the management of the Prison Service of England and Wales, who was himself an experienced businessman, wrote that: 'The Prison Service is the most complex organisation I have encountered and its problems some of the most intractable' (Lygo 1991: 2).

This development had been noted earlier in the United States of America. Jacobs in his study of Stateville Penitentiary in Illinois observed that an incoming warden '... brought to the prison a commitment to scientific management rather than to any correctional ideology ... He stresses efficient and emotionally detached management' (Jacobs 1977: 103–4).

If it is true that modern prison management requires a high degree of professional skill and awareness, it will be important that this is acknowledged and that the men and women who are placed in charge of prisons should be capable of management at a high level.

A number of prison systems have given a high priority in recent years to management issues. The National Agency for Correctional Institutions in the Netherlands, for example, requires its prison directors to attend the generic management courses organised for all senior officials in the Ministry of Justice. The topics covered are strategic in orientation and cover issues such as the transformation of organisations, quality management and planning systems. This form of development has made prison directors more conscious of the fact that the prisons that they govern are part of a wider structure and that what happens in one part of the system can affect other parts. Key issues for consideration have been leadership, integrity and how to inspire and motivate staff. Less use has been made of management consultants and greater use of experts who are able to consider issues of principle and values. The main outcome of this approach has been a recognition that management in the public sector in general and in the prison system in particular is every bit as complex as management in the private sector.

The Swedish Prison and Probation Service has identified a particular need to develop the potential of middle managers. Throughout the 1990s the Swedish service placed an emphasis on flattening the management structure, with four levels of staff under the head of the prison, made up of senior managers, unit managers, team leaders and staff members. The unit managers have a key role in this structure. The original intention had been to recruit highly qualified persons from outside the service to take on these roles but this initiative has not been successful and so the alternative has been to train managers from inside the service.

In public sector organisations in many countries the last decade has been marked by an emphasis on managerial issues. The world of prisons has not been exempt from this development. To use its own terminology, this 'managerialism' usually involves a focus on what are called processes and outputs rather than on outcomes. In common language, this means a concentration on how things are done and what the organisation achieves rather than on the changes which result from the activities of the organisation. There is much to be said for such an approach. Properly used, it can ensure that organisations run more efficiently, that they are cost-effective and that they produce what is expected of them. Nevertheless, it is important to recognise its limitations, especially in a prison system.

From a purely managerial perspective the prison system which existed in the former Soviet Union was a model of efficiency. If the prisons and colonies in the Gulag had been measured by modern performance indicators, they would have passed with flying colours. There were virtually no escapes because the penalty of a failed attempt was death. There were few assaults on staff because perpetrators would have faced severe reprisals. As far as the organisation was concerned, the priority for the colony was to deliver a high level of industrial production. This was a simple message for the director of the colony and he made sure that it was delivered. The same could be said of countless other places of detention in totalitarian states.

These considerations apply also to prisons and places of detention in all countries. One conclusion to be drawn from reading the reports produced, for example, by the Council of Europe Committee for the Prevention of Torture and Inhuman or Degrading Treatment is that those responsible for the management of prisons and those who work in them need to avoid taking a purely technocratic approach to their work. It is not sufficient to measure success or failure merely in managerial terms, divorced from any consideration of what effect this has on the people involved, both staff and prisoners. One of the first consequences of such an approach will be that one loses sight of the fact that all the players, including and especially prisoners, are human beings.

In managerial terms it is important that processes and outputs in prisons should be managed efficiently and effectively so as to meet the legitimate expectations of governments, of civil society, of victims and of staff, prisoners and their families. If it is true that prisons reflect the most central values of a society, it is even more important that those with responsibility for prisons and prison systems should look beyond technical and managerial considerations. They also have to be leaders who are capable of enthusing the staff for whom they are responsible with a sense of decency in the way they carry out their difficult daily tasks. If this happens it is more possible that the 'outcomes' from the prison will be of benefit to all members of society.

People management

Put simply, prison management is primarily not about systems and processes but about people: staff and prisoners. If one accepts the contention that prisons are places where the relationships between the human beings involved have a central role to play in determining both culture and organisational direction, an important conclusion follows. This is the need for prisons to operate within an ethical context. If one loses sight of this, there is a real danger that the perfectly proper insistence on performance targets and process delivery will encourage the ever-present danger of forgetting that the prison service is not the same as a factory which produces motor cars or washing machines. The management of prisons is primarily about the management of human beings, both staff and prisoners. This means that there are issues that go beyond effectiveness and efficiency. When making decisions about the treatment of human beings, there is a more radical consideration. The first question which must always be asked when considering any new managerial initiative is, 'Is it right?'.

The one consideration, which must never be forgotten in all of this, is that all prisoners are persons. To use the phrase of one author, they have to be regarded as subjects, not as objects (Duguid 2000). No matter what crime they may be accused or convicted of, they remain human beings, entitled to respect. This recognition should influence prison staff in the way they carry out all their duties. It is also the foundation stone of good prison management. The details of prison management may vary from country to country since they have to be sensitive to local culture and circumstances. However, the need to operate within an ethical context is universal and is also one of the defining features of good prison management.

The same consideration has to be recognised by management in its dealing with prison staff at all levels. If staff are not themselves treated decently and humanely there will be little hope that they will apply such considerations in their dealings with prisoners. In management terms this also implies that management should be willing to trust staff as they carry out their daily duties. The task of management is to lay down clear parameters within which staff must operate, to ensure that staff have the necessary personal and organisational tools and then to allow them to use their initiative in working professionally within the laid down parameters. The reality in many prison systems is that senior management has little trust in junior staff to carry out their tasks efficiently. One reason for this is that success in the prison environment is often measured by absence of failure. The most important measures are negative ones: there must be no escapes, there must be no riots or disorder, violence must be reduced to a minimum. It is more important not to get things wrong than to get things right. These measures are not in themselves sufficient and in recent years the prison services in the United Kingdom have been feeling their way towards a more positive set of management indicators.

Leadership

All of these considerations lead inexorably towards a recognition of the crucial nature of leadership in the prison world. The importance of leadership runs throughout every level of the system. It can be demonstrated in a number of ways. A strong leader will generally have a recognisable charisma which will attract trust and confidence from staff. If the leadership is genuine, it will also be linked to organisational ability in a way that ensures that it does not degenerate into idiosyncrasy. The best leaders will place great emphasis on the ethos within which the prison should operate and will encourage staff at lower levels to use their initiative in implementing the details of the agreed policy.

All of these considerations imply that the governor as leader must also be highly visible within his or her prison. Hardly a day should go past without the head of the prison being seen in all areas where prisoners and staff come together. This visibility should be seen as supportive rather than inspectorial, particularly by staff. It will encourage committed staff to devote themselves wholeheartedly to their work. It will, of course, also have the effect of ensuring that staff who might otherwise hide in offices or behind the ever-present paperwork do not do so. Directors and governors who regularly meet staff and prisoners in the various corners of the prison will have a much better feel for the culture of their organisation.

Conclusions

In brief, a well managed prison is one in which the environment is decent and humane. In practical terms, these features can be measured by the quality of the human relationships between the prisoners who live there, the staff who work there and anyone who comes to visit for any reason. The principle is a very simple one. Its application is one of the most complex tasks in the field of good prison management.

The best managed prison systems are likely to be those which have a clear understanding of their objectives, mission and values. There are at least three key sets of processes, each of which is linked to the other. The first is a series of system issues, including links with other parts of the criminal justice process and public sector agencies. The second is a series of structural issues about how the service is organised so as to recognise its hierarchical nature while at the same time encouraging staff to develop their full potential and use their initiative. The third, which follows from the first two, is a series of what can be called people issues, to do with leadership and the management of all those involved in the system, particularly staff and prisoners. If these processes can be dealt with in the manner which has been described there will be a high possibility that the outcome will be good prison management.

Crucial to all of this is a good communication system, which goes up and down and across the organisation. Staff at all levels have to be aware of and subscribe to the mission and values of the organisation. They have to understand policy decisions, whether they emanate from national headquarters or from local management. They must also feel that they can be heard and will be listened to when they wish to contribute to the thinking and development of the organisation.

Finally, it has to be recognised that good prison management is dynamic. It is a continuous process rather than something which can be achieved once and for all and, very importantly, that it is a means to an end rather than an end in itself. To express this in different terms, it is a journey which never ends. If it ever does come to an end, that will simply be an indication that the culture of the prison has ceased to be dynamic and changing and instead has become fossilised, no longer alive. This journey can without doubt be a dangerous one at times. It indicates a degree of uncertainty, a recognition of the need to change. Prisons as organisations do not like uncertainty; they see it as destabilising and threatening. That is why they need to be set in the context of an agreed set of ethical values linked to clear leadership. If that is the case, the change process will lead to better managed prisons, which are more secure, safer and more effective; in which there is a respect for decency and humanity.

Seminar questions

1 What are the key features that define prison management as a specific skill?
2 To what extent has prison management changed over the last 20 or so years?
3 What new skills are now required of prison managers as a result of these changes?
4 To what extent can individual prison governors act autonomously and what external considerations are likely to influence their way of governing?

5 To what extent can or should prison governors be held personally responsible for the general management of the prison which they govern?

Recommended reading

Some of the key literature on the role of prison managers includes: Grew (1958) *The Prison Governor*; Dilulio (1987) *Governing Prisons: A Comparative Study of Correctional Management*; Boin (1998) *Contrasts in Leadership: An Institutional Study of Two Prison Systems*; Bryans and Wilson (1998) *The Prison Governor: Theory and Practice*; Coyle (2002c) 'Prison Governor'.

Prison officers are well covered in books including: Thomas (1972) *The English Prison Officer since 1850: A Study in Conflict*; Kauffman (1988) *Prison Officers and Their World*; Liebling and Price (2001) *The Prison Officer*; Crawley (2004) *Doing Prison Work: The Public and Private Lives of Prison Officers*.

General prison issues including the development of prison management over the last 15 years are covered in: Lewis (1997) *Hidden Agendas: Politics, Law and Disorder*; Coyle (2005) *Understanding Prisons: Key Issues in Policy and Practice*.

Note

1 Sections of this chapter were first published in Coyle (2002a).

References

BBC (2005) 'Beheadings in Brazil Prison Riot', *BBC News*, 15 June.

Boin, A. (1998) *Contrasts in Leadership: An Institutional Study of Two Prison Systems*. Delft: Eburon.

Bryans, S. and Wilson, D. (1998) *The Prison Governor: Theory and Practice*. Leyhill: Prison Service Journal.

Coyle, A. (2002a) *Managing Prisons in Time of Change*. London: ICPS.

Coyle, A. (2002b) *A Human Rights Approach to Prison Management*. London: International Centre for Prison Studies.

Coyle, A. (2002c) 'Prison Governor', in R. Flin and K. Arbuthnot (eds), *Incident Command: Tales from the Hot Seat*. Aldershot: Ashgate.

Coyle, A. (2005) *Understanding Prisons: Key Issues in Policy and Practice*. Milton Keynes: Open University Press.

Crawley, E. (2004) *Doing Prison Work: The Public and Private Lives of Prison Officers*. Cullompton: Willan.

Dilulio, J. (1987) *Governing Prisons: A Comparative Study of Correctional Management*. London: Macmillan.

Duguid, S. (2000) *Can Prisons Work? The Prisoner as Object and Subject in Modern Corrections.* Toronto: University of Toronto Press.

Grew, B. (1958) *The Prison Governor.* London: Herbert Jenkins.

Home Office (2006) *Tackling Prison Corruption.* See: http://www.homeoffice. gov.uk/about-us/news/prison-officer-corruption.

ICPS (2006) *World Prison Brief.* Online at: http://www.prisonstudies.org.

Jacobs, J. (1977) *Stateville: The Penitentiary in Mass Society.* Chicago: University of Chicago Press.

Kalinin, Y. (2002) *The Russian Penal System: Past, Present and Future.* London: International Centre for Prison Studies.

Kauffman, K. (1988) *Prison Officers and their World.* Cambridge, MA: Harvard University Press.

Keith, Mr Justice (2006) *Report of the Zahid Mubarek Inquiry.* London: HMSO.

Lewis, D. (1997) *Hidden Agendas: Politics, Law and Disorder.* London: Hamish Hamilton.

Liebling, A. and Price, D. (2001) *The Prison Officer.* Leyhill: Prison Service Journal.

Lygo, R. (1991) *Management of the Prison Service.* London: Home Office.

Riddell, M. and Doward, J. (2006) 'Madness of Dustbin Jails – by Lord Chief Justice', *Observer*, 8 October.

Thomas, J. (1972) *The English Prison Officer since 1850: A Study in Conflict.* London: Routledge & Kegan Paul.

Travis, A. (2004) 'Blunkett on Film Sways Judges', *Guardian*, 17 November.

United States Bureau of Justice Statistics (2005) *Prison Statistics.* Online at: http://www.ojp.usdoj.gov/bis/1.

Woolf, H. and Tumin, S. (1991) *Report of an Inquiry into Prison Disturbances April 1990*, Cmnd 1456. London: HMSO.

Chapter 14

Resisting the scourge of managerialism: on the uses of discretion in late-modern prisons[1]

Leonidas K. Cheliotis

Introduction

Over the last three decades or so, or in what sociologists often prefer to call the era of 'late modernity', the postwar transformative rationales for the correctional system are said to have been replaced by a pragmatic, technologically supported and quantification-oriented political rationality widely known as 'managerialism' (Loader and Sparks 2002). Under this critical prism, prisons and their performance are no longer evaluated by reference to individual offenders or any intractable social purposes like rehabilitation and resocialisation, but rather depend upon more feasible and measurable targets like the proper allocation of resources, meticulous record-keeping, streamlined case processing, the reduction of overcrowding and, perhaps most pointedly, the management or even the control (but, at any rate, not the elimination) of the risk of crime (see further Clear and Cadora 2001). Accordingly, prisoners are viewed not as coherent subjects, but as aggregates or mere statistical units within impersonal frameworks of policies, with the criminal justice system now increasingly employing probabilistic risk calculations and statistical distributions applicable to groups of offenders, thereby sorting them by levels of dangerousness and eventually placing them under respective control mechanisms. On the one hand, by protractedly removing large groups of high-risk bearers into prisons, it is purported that significant, albeit still temporary, aggregate crime reductions can be effected (but see Petersilia *et al.* 1986). On the other hand, those classified as lower-risk offenders are distributed (or even *re*-distributed, for that matter) in a wide variety of community-based sanctioning schemes that, disoriented from their originally intended rehabilitative and reintegrative aspirations, serve as low-cost surveillance mechanisms, often by means of frequent drug testing (see further Feeley and Simon 1992).

The villain of the story to date can be traced to the implicit presupposition, indeed, the disturbing presumption that the agency of criminal justice professionals is somehow aligned with the cynical goals of what Rose (1996) would call a strong 'centre of calculation'. Put the other way around, the bulk of contemporary penological analyses seem largely to accept some version of Max Weber's schematic conception of bureaucratic organisations, which claims that officials are made fully to adopt an over-rationalised, nonchalant orientation *vis-à-vis* clients and colleagues. Alas, however, very little has been done to explore the ways in, yet also the actual extent to, which such an alignment (one might go so far as to speak of an 'unholy alliance') is possible. In an attempt to bridge that gap in the literature, this chapter advances an ideal-typical account of the systemic forces, direct as well as indirect, that are meant strictly to determine the *modus operandi* of criminal justice work even in its most hidden recesses, often with severe human consequences for officials themselves. Rather than putting forward any absolute, eternal truths, and admittedly muting the theoretical possibility that managerialism may coexist with, nay, amplify moral, humanitarian ideals (see, for example, Bottoms 1995; Rutherford 1993; Raine and Willson 1997), such an accounting schema offers an alternative heuristic yardstick in comparison to which future research can be undertaken, while at the same time exhorting the reader to be vigilant about the mounting dangers of over-managerialising the penal realm, as these are increasingly felt, before anyone else, among criminal justice professionals. At the risk of seeming to contradict the preceding analysis, a case is then made for the possibility of professional resistance to managerialist reforms: in the world of daily practice, it is argued, penal bureaucracies can hardly be so much the monolithic, static, self-propelled mechanisms delineated in Weberian theory, nor are professionals necessarily calculative, inward-turned actors who adhere blindly to systemic prescriptions with the aim to have their dull compulsions satisfied. Lower-level employees may instead only process work consistent with their chosen preferences and values, and may thus thwart managerialist reforms in a wide variety of surreptitious ways, such as manipulating extant bureaucratic structures (e.g. legal loopholes) and exercising considerable degrees of discretion outside the immediate gaze of their superiors – what one may term 'discreet discretion'.

Risky business

In what follows, I single out for scrutiny, and offer a summary characterisation of, the three basic managerialist forces that, *together*, serve subtly to rigidify the nature and scope of criminal justice work and to mould professionals into patterns of subordination to systemic goals. As the title of this section itself suggests, working in present-day penal organisations largely resembles working in large corporations and conglomerates, not merely in the sense of guiding principles and operational practices, but also in terms of the high degree of professional and existential insecurity for decision-makers and the attendant pressures for social conformity and homogeneity.

The first force, then, is an *increasingly hierarchical division of labour* within criminal justice organisations themselves. In England and Wales, for example, the basic operational responsibilities of the Prison Service flow downwards to numerous subdivisions and officials: from the Director General, to the Prison Service Management Board (comprising the Directors of Resettlement, Operations, Finance and Procurement, Personnel, Health, Corporate Affairs and the Deputy Director), to the Operational Policy Group (consisting of 14 Area Managers and Heads of Group), to prison governors, lower-level managers and officers. Such a firm division of labour may be said to confine professionals to narrow sets of formal tasks, thus not only optimising control over the content of their work, but also preventing them from gaining full comprehension of the overall strategy and the ultimate goals of the organisation. The division of labour also increases workforce expendability and, consequently, discourages lower-level professionals from challenging senior leadership on the ways their work is organised. Discretionary powers are curtailed, decision-making processes are homogenised and powerful mechanisms of accountability like key performance indicators are employed to control front-line criminal justice personnel (see Carlen 2002; Hood 1991; Rose and Miller 1992; Simon 1993; Garland 1996; Liebling 2004). In fact, these techniques bring to mind the 'responsibilisation strategies' applied to imprisoned populations: although heavily restricting individual autonomy, the state still allows for the exercise of a small scale of localised judgment on the part of the professionals, through which to pursue their personal, professional objectives (e.g.

249

upward career mobility), objectives, however, that are only met if in full alignment with the interests of the centralised government (see further Garland 1997).

The second force at play is a *hypertrophic inter- and intra-agency competition*. The situation in Britain, for instance, may be likened to a neo-Darwinian world: at the same time as seeking to enhance inter-agency 'partnerships' (e.g. between the Prison and Probation Services, between the Probation Service and the police, and so forth), the government also exerts significant pressure upon each separate agency to improve its annual expenditure profile, compared not only to past fiscal years, but also to the rest of the organisations. Added to this is the fact that criminal justice agencies also compete for best-quality recruits, programme responsibilities and reputation. As one might expect, inter-agency competition soon evolves into an internal priority, setting in motion the bureaucratic machinery described earlier, with headquarters pressuring senior management teams and lower-level officials to contribute as effectively as possible to the national targets of the organisation. To this end, in 2001, the Prison Service even started producing a quarterly 'weighted scorecard', ranking the cost-efficiency of individual establishments and their performance against a range of indicators like the percentage of positive drug tests, the number of escapes and absconds, and the time spent by prisoners in purposeful activities. And, as Liebling (2004: 65) tells us, '[g]overnors are well aware that their competence is judged by whether or not they succeed in meeting [key performance indicators]'. But that is not all, for with the acceleration of criminal justice privatisation in recent years, especially as concerns corrections, public sector officials are now faced with a new, strong antagonist. In an interview he gave to the *Guardian*, Martin Narey, then head of NOMS, underlined the centrality of 'contestability' to his agency's agenda, defining it as follows:

> Contestability simply means that we will look at the work and give a chance to a range of people to do it. So we ensure that we get the best quality product for the best price ... It's about competition. We're not privatising large pieces of work. If the public sector competes and proves it's best it will keep the work. (Narey, interviewed in Travis 2003: 6)

Finally, the third force pertains to *the breeding of a new, up-and-coming generation of blasé professionals*. If asked to describe the latent organisational stratification of contemporary criminal justice organisations, most insiders (or, at least, most older insiders) would point to the rise of a 'bureaucratic kinship system' (to use Wilbert Moore's (1962) phrase), where pragmatically oriented, upper-level managers tend to recruit, promote and therefore keep control in the hands of their young and culturally similar peers. To give a flavour of this, accelerated promotion schemes now allow young recruits trained in the skills and culture of performance management quickly to climb the ladder of the organisational hierarchy, often even outranking the older generation of criminal justice personnel and undermining the progressive ideology of the past. Because it eloquently reflects the point I wish to make here, let me cite at some length Liebling's account – Liebling describes the ways in which the role of the prison governor has changed with the onset of managerialism:

> It is possible to detect a distinction between older and younger generations of governors, with governors recruited and trained 'in the old days' (i.e. those who attended the pre-managerialist version of the assistant governors' course) more likely to express idealistic aspirations and slightly more liberal perspectives, and younger (new generation) governors more likely to speak the language of performance. Using Alder and Longhurst's characterisation, more prison governors of older generations might have belonged in the 'professionalism-rehabilitation' cell of their means-ends discourse matrix, and more younger prison governors could be characterised as belonging in the 'bureaucracy-control' cell of this matrix today. (Liebling 2004: 399)

So much to say that the criminal justice workforce is now routinely subjected to an ensemble of direct and indirect control mechanisms aimed at replacing traditional (and often anti-authoritarian) values and preferences with a utilitarian concern over craven impulses, thereby eventually turning individuals into mere relays in a hierarchical chain of bureaucratic command. In other words, what the triad of systemic forces which I have described brings in its wake is an increased sense of ontological insecurity, especially for those belonging to older generations of professionals, which in turn fosters exorbitant loyalty to the organisation, acceptance of authority, and conformity to prescribed modes of action. Under the ongoing threat of expendability, or under conditions of what Bourdieu (1998: 85) aptly terms 'flexploitation', professionals are forced to construct a new, market-oriented work identity, often by outgrowing their cultural dispositions, working practices and ideologies, and established alliances in favour of an individualised, mechanistic routine – one which they hardly participate in formatting. Insofar as these techniques have permeated criminal justice, the remark by Simon and Feeley (1995: 173) with regard to offenders that contemporary penality 'has trouble with the concept of humanity' may as well be extended to those who work in the new managerialist culture.

Discreet discretion

So far, I have gone to some lengths to describe the ways in which managerialism extends its reach to those who work at the various levels of the criminal justice system and especially in prisons. This, however, should not lead us to infer that power structures in contemporary penal organisations are axiomatically as monolithic and inescapable as the mechanistic character of managerialism suggests. As Dennis Wrong puts it in his indispensable analysis of the forms, bases and uses of power, '"power over" [or else, an asymmetrical superior-subordinate relation] *may*, not must, constrain the freedom of the subordinate party [or else, its "power to act"]' (Wrong 1988: ix; original emphasis). It follows that professionals' own power *over* prisoners, which is itself a special case of power *to* choose one's actions, *may or may not*, but not *must*, cleave fully to external managerialist constraints. The contention in this section is instead that the potential to overcome the totalising tendencies of penal managerialism derives from the interplay between the inherent deficiencies of bureaucratic structures and the capacity of individuals themselves largely to elude control and act on their own accord, thereby holding true to their chosen worldviews and value commitments, while at the same time satisfying parochial self-interests and the need for self-preservation in particular.

As a general preliminary, one may recall the authoritative treatise of organisational behaviour by Blau and Scott (1962/2003: 34–5), where they argue convincingly that, 'even if it is true that the hierarchy of authority promotes discipline and makes possible the coordination of activities, does it not also discourage subordinates from accepting responsibility?'. A similar point can be made in relation to rules and guidelines, for, however elaborate, they can hardly circumscribe the complexities of all possible contingencies. It is also the case that rules often fail clearly and unambiguously to explicate the goals of the organisation. The profusion of rules 'may actually be an impediment to supervision. They may be so voluminous and contradictory that they can only be enforced or invoked selectively' (Lipsky 1980: 14). Even when job performance is evaluated in terms of the validity and quality of discretionary decisions, numerical output measurements are intrinsically insufficient means of exercising control over professionals, mainly due to the difficulty in outguessing and operationalising the cognitive and emotional processes involved in individual, authoritative decision-making. To add to this, given that professionals often are the primary source of information upper management receives concerning their performance, they are in a position to massage data to make the action taken appear to be responsive to organisational prescriptions when it may not have been (see Lipsky 1980: 162–3). But one may go one step further and speak of the need of the organisation itself for weakening vertical control ties, devolving decision-making down the system and delayering administrative hierarchies, as this need has been consistently demonstrated by social research. For example, James Thompson (1967/2003) identifies three sources of uncertainty that force even the most perfect of machine-like organisations often to rely upon the personal discretion of single individuals rather than on faceless procedures: a lack of cause-effect understanding in the culture at large, which hinders advance planning; contingencies in the environment (e.g. in transactions at the boundaries of organisations) that escape calculation; and the human interconnections inside organisations that can hardly be reduced to programmatic formulae (see also Kanter 1977).

Small wonder discretion is most relied upon in what Lipsky calls 'street-level bureaucracies', that is, in human service organisations such as the schools, police, courts and prisons, whose workers interact directly and regularly with clients and are responsible for dispensing benefits or allocating public sanctions to them. More often than not, street-level bureaucrats work free from close supervision by superiors, in situations that require flexible, on-the-spot decisions on the human dimensions of complicated and diverse issues. Police patrol officers, for example, are given broad leeway to decide who to stop, who to search, who to search intrusively and who to arrest (see, for example, Smith and Gray 1985). Not dissimilarly, prison officers may choose between enforcing the letter of the law and tolerating rule-breaking behaviours on the part of prisoners, '[moving] from tension to peace without incident, [and using] language rather than action to avert the requirement of force' (Liebling and Price 2003: 87). In these and other instances of discretionary power, the interpretation and application of supposedly 'impersonal' rules are matters to be decided by active agents who 'sustain a shared sense of what rules mean by continually working to secure agreement in their practice', and 'authoritatively enact any of the innumerable possibilities that can plausibly be made out as consistent with rules and precedents' (Barnes 1995: 205). Said differently, what escapes the supervisory gaze of the 'system', no matter how Orwellian that may be, is the panoply of personal values and idiosyncratic meanings that individual decision-makers bring to their decisions (or their non-decisions, for that matter) and which eventually coalesce to sustain, form or reform organisational routines.

Criminal justice professionals, then, like their counterparts in other bureaucratic organisations, appear to retain a crucial role in the implementation of policy agendas, often using their discretionary powers to prevent inhumane rationales and processes brought about by the advent of managerialism. To give but an empirical flavour of this, Lucken (1998: 119) examined contemporary penality from the perspective of penal actors in the jurisdiction of Florida, and found that 'objectives, practices and philosophies ... continue to reflect the modern themes of normalization, classification, treatment, rationality, efficiency and progress'. In this respect, while acknowledging the managerialisation of penal system operations on a number of counts, she views 'penality as a balancing act' that embodies both punishment and treatment as complementary, rather than mutually exclusive functions (see Lucken 1998: 113). Similarly, Lemert (1993: 460) demonstrated in his study of probation in California that the rise of actuarial discourse did not signal any 'revolutionary new form of social control'; rather, 'the most conspicuous change has been bankloading [namely processing only the most serious cases], an old practice with a new name' (see also Corbette and Marx 1991; Garland 1995).

Perhaps the most convincing empirical analysis of the 'resistance from the workers in the field to the new penological policies' is that by Mona Lynch (1998: 864, 2000), who conducted an ethnographic study in a parole field office of the California Department of Corrections. Contrary to the statewide effort at the policy-making level to systematise parole as a mechanism for actuarial classification and aggregate management of danger (e.g. through the introduction of a computerised system for tracking parolees), Lynch showed parole agents clung to the traditional notions of law enforcement and rehabilitation of individual offenders. To this end, they circumvented management demands to rely on faceless, bureaucratic risk-assessment techniques like scoring systems based on case histories and chose actively to preserve and, most importantly, to prioritise 'an individualistic approach to the clientele and an intuitive approach to case management' (Lynch 1998: 861–2).

Turning to some evidence from Britain, Robinson (2002) found that, although the Probation Service has now instituted a risk-based approach towards offender governance, having even introduced the use of statistical predictors of reconviction, rehabilitative impulses and clinical decision-making practices still remain salient in the two English service areas she studied. Also, in two Scottish sites, Robinson and McNeill (2004: 295) found that, despite an overarching emphasis on public protection as the official master narrative for probation practice, professionals exhibited a considerable degree of diversity of purpose and approach, to the point that the 'softer' objectives of social inclusion and anti-custodialism were pursued as well.

Similar examples abound (see, among others, McCorkle and Crank 1996; Bayens *et al.* 1998; Brownlee 1998; Kemshall and Maguire 2001; McNeill 2000; Miller 2001). What all this evidence suggests is that, owing mainly to its inherently interactive and therefore affective nature, but also to the capacity of individuals to devise ingenious methods of resistance to power structures, penal practice is more complicated, often also more hopeful, than usually suggested in the penological literature. That is to say, unless our eyes catch the micro-level processes by which 'the ideas that went into policy-making are re-examined and replaced, and the policy conflicts that first surfaced during enactment reappear' (Lin 2000: 17), we are misled to over-dramatise penal currents as being utterly mechanistic and irreversibly inhumane. As for the obvious counterargument that, for one reason or another, those who toe the line of penal managerialism may well outnumber by far and therefore outflank those at odds with it, this should no doubt be a serious cause for concern, but should not lead us outrightly to assume that resistance is futile. This last sanguine point can hardly be expressed better than by Hannah Arendt when she explores humankind from the perspective of the actions of which it is capable:

[P]ower is to an astonishing degree independent of material factors, either of numbers or means. A comparatively small but well-organised group of men can rule almost indefinitely over large and populous empires, and it is not infrequent in history that small and poor countries get the better of great and rich nations. The story of David and Goliath is only metaphorically true; the power of a few can be greater than the power of many, but in a contest between two men not power but strength decides, and cleverness, that is, brain power, contributes materially to the outcome on the same level as muscular force. (Arendt 1958/1998: 200)

Concluding remarks

By and large, and from the standpoint of lower-level professionals (much like from the standpoint of prisoners, for that matter), late-modern prisons are no less 'cultural fields', to borrow Bourdieu's well-known term (see, for example, Bourdieu 1972/1977, 1990), than their modern predecessors. That is to say, they remain sites whose discourses, values and practices are the product not so much of inflexible hierarchies and insurmountable systemic barriers, as of a perpetual, if often silent, conflict between superiors and subordinates over basic assumptions about good and evil, and over what humans should care about most. In other words, one should take care to grasp what historian Jonathan Steinberg (2002: 6) within a different context terms the 'banality of the good', namely the power of human agents to resist and even reverse unfortunate turns, wherever and whenever this power is to be found.

The banality of the good, however, is not the preserve of people at, or near the bottom of, the organisational order. Rather than being abstract, ghostly entities, the upper echelons of bureaucratic organisations may as well consist of agents able and, most importantly, willing to provide countervailing forces to inhumane dominant ideologies or practices. After all, as argued by various analysts, the original impetus towards introducing actuarial methods in criminal justice was to minimise problems of racism, sexism and other biases in discretionary decision-making, and eventually to achieve equity and uniformity in punishment (see Gottfredson and Gottfredson 1988; compare Petersilia and Turner 1987; Tonry 1996). It is in this spirit, I believe, that Feeley and Rubin contend that

> much of what we claim to dislike about bureaucracy – capriciousness, lack of accountability and unresponsiveness – represents the failure to bureaucratise our institutions sufficiently … [B]ureaucracy can also impose a regime of rules and duties that protect, clarify, and standardize, fostering dignity by restraining power and demarcating zones of individual autonomy. It binds people in an institutional framework that

simultaneously empowers the weak and constrains the powerful. Thus, if bureaucracy and law are an iron cage that imprisons, they are also a bulwark that protects. (Feeley and Rubin 1999: 284)

Barry Barnes makes a somewhat similar point when he argues that bureaucratic organisations are 'not so much mechanisms as cultures, which opens the way to seeing them not only as instruments of rationalisation but as targets of it' (Barnes 2000: 86; see further Bottoms 1995; Rutherford 1993; Raine and Willson 1995, 1997).

But insofar as even the moral remainders produced by the rationalised reasoning of managerialism have faded with time, or, to borrow an expression so often used by lower-level prison officials themselves, insofar as 'managerialism has gone mad', professional resistance by means of 'discreet discretion' with the aim to appropriate, reform or even replace overly technocratic agendas appears to be a necessary medium (if not *the* medium) to approximate what criminal justice is ultimately about: progress in the social structure.

Seminar questions

1 Why do contemporary penal organisations endeavour systematically to strip criminal justice work of its inherently affective nature?
2 Which are the structural forces that promote control over officials? Which are the processes by which those forces come into effect?
3 Which are the human consequences of submission to overly managerialised penal milieus?
4 Why, how and to what extent do criminal justice professionals resist managerialist reforms? When is resistance socially progressive and when is it unamiable?

Recommended reading

In their now classic article 'The New Penology: Notes on the Emerging Strategy of Corrections and its Implications' (1992), Malcolm Feeley and Jonathan Simon provide a staunch critique of the various actuarial policies aimed at the effective control of selected risk groups and efficient system management at the expense of the traditional objectives of rehabilitation or punishment of individual offenders. In 'The Philosophy and Politics of Punishment and Sentencing', Anthony Bottoms (1995) helpfully distinguishes between what he views as three separate (albeit interlinked) facets of managerialism: the *systemic*, the *consumerist* and the *actuarial*. Chapter 8 of Alison Liebling and Helen Arnold's (2004) *Prisons and Their Moral Performance: A Study of Values, Quality and Prison Life* analyses in depth the processes and outcomes of the modernisation of prison management in England and Wales during the 1990s. On the daily realities faced by prison staff and prisoners, as these impinge upon how rehabilitation programmes are actually implemented in contemporary prisons, see Ann Chih Lin's (2002) *Reform in the Making: The Implementation of Social Policy in Prison.* For a broader discussion of how discretionary decisions and the routines to which they give rise effectively become the very public policies they are meant to carry out, see Michael Lipsky's (1980) seminal study *Street-level Bureaucracy: Dilemmas of the Individual in Public Services.*

Note

1 This chapter is an abridged version of Cheliotis (2006a). For a more detailed analysis of the managerialist pressures exerted upon criminal justice professionals, see Cheliotis (2006b).

References

Adler, M. and Longhurst, B. (1994) *Discourse, Power and Justice: Towards a New Sociology of Imprisonment.* London: Routledge.

Arendt, H. (1958/1998) *The Human Condition*, 2nd edn. Chicago: University of Chicago Press.

Barnes, B. (1995) *The Elements of Social Theory.* London: UCL Press.

Barnes, B. (2000) *Understanding Agency: Social Theory and Responsible Action.* London: Sage.

Bayens, G.J., Manske, M.W. and Smykla, J.O. (1998) 'The Impact of the "New Penology" on ISP', *Criminal Justice Review*, 23 (1): 51–62.

Blau, P.M. and Scott, W.R. (1962/2003) *Formal Organisations: A Comparative Approach.* Stanford, CA: Stanford University Press.

Bottoms, A.E. (1995) 'The Philosophy and Politics of Punishment and Sentencing', in C.M.V. Clarkson and R. Morgan (eds), *The Politics of Sentencing Reform.* Oxford: Clarendon Press, pp. 17–49.

Bourdieu, P. (1972/1977) *Outline of a Theory of Practice.* Cambridge: Cambridge University Press.

Bourdieu, P. (1990) *The Logic of Practice.* Cambridge: Polity Press.

Bourdieu, P. (1998) *Acts of Resistance: Against the New Myths of Our Time.* Cambridge: Polity Press.

Brownlee, I. (1998) 'New Labour–New Penology? Punitive Rhetoric and the Limits of Managerialism in Criminal Justice Policy', *Journal of Law and Society*, 25 (3): 313–35.

Carlen, P. (2002) 'Governing the Governors: Telling Tales of Managers, Mandarins and Mavericks', *Criminal Justice*, 2 (1): 27–49.

Cheliotis, L.K. (2006a) 'How Iron is the Iron Cage of New Penology? The Role of Human Agency in the Implementation of Criminal Justice Policy', *Punishment & Society: The International Journal of Penology*, 8 (3): 313–40.

Cheliotis, L.K. (2006b) 'Penal Managerialism from Within: Implications for Theory and Research', *International Journal of Law and Psychiatry*, 29 (5): 397–404.

Clear, T. and Cadora, E. (2001) 'Risk and Community Practice', in K. Stenson and R.R. Sullivan (eds), *Crime, Risk and Justice: The Politics of Crime Control in Liberal Democracies*. Cullompton: Willan, pp. 51–67.

Corbette, R. and Marx, G.T. (1991) 'Critique: No Soul in the New Machine: Technofallacies in the Electronic Monitoring Movement', *Justice Quarterly*, 8 (3): 399–414.

Feeley, M.M. and Rubin, E.L. (1999) *Judicial Policy Making and the Modern State: How the Courts Reformed America's Prisons*. Cambridge: Cambridge University Press.

Feeley, M.M. and Simon, J. (1992) 'The New Penology: Notes on the Emerging Strategy of Corrections and its Implications', *Criminology*, 30 (4): 449–74.

Feeley, M.M. and Simon, J. (1994) 'Actuarial Justice: The Emerging New Criminal Law', in D. Nelkin (ed.), *The Future of Criminology*. Thousand Oaks, CA: Sage, pp. 172–201.

Garland, D. (1995) 'Penal Modernism and Post-Modernism', in T.G. Blomberg and S. Cohen (eds), *Punishment and Social Control*. New York: Aldine de Gruyter, pp. 181–209.

Garland, D. (1996) 'The Limits of the Sovereign State: Strategies of Crime Control in Contemporary Society', *British Journal of Criminology*, 36 (4): 445–71.

Garland, D. (1997) '"Governmentality" and the Problem of Crime: Foucault, Criminology, Sociology', *Theoretical Criminology*, 1 (2): 173–214.

Gottfredson, M. and Gottfredson, D. (1988) *Decision Making in Criminal Justice*. New York: Plenum.

Hood, C. (1991) 'A Public Management for All Seasons?', *Public Administration*, 69 (1): 3–19.

Kanter, R. (1977) *Men and Women of the Corporation*. New York: Basic.

Kemshall, H. and Maguire, M. (2001) 'Public Protection, Partnership and Risk Penality: The Multi-Agency Risk Management of Sexual and Dangerous Offenders', *Punishment and Society*, 3 (2): 237–64.

Lemert, E.M. (1993) 'Visions of Social Control: Probation Considered', *Crime & Delinquency*, 39 (4): 447–61.

Liebling, A. (2004) *Prisons and Their Moral Performance: A Study of Values, Quality, and Prison Life*. Oxford: Clarendon Press.

Liebling, A. and Price, D. (2003) 'Prison Officers and the Use of Discretion', in L. Gelsthorpe and N. Padfield (eds), *Exercising Discretion: Decision-making in the Criminal Justice System and Beyond*. Cullompton: Willan, pp. 74–96.

Lin, A.C. (2000) *Reform in the Making: The Implementation of Social Policy in Prison*. Princeton, NJ: Princeton University Press.

Lipsky, M. (1980) *Street-Level Bureaucracy: Dilemmas of the Individual in Public Services*. New York: Russell Sage Foundation.

Loader, I. and Sparks, R. (2002) 'Contemporary Landscapes of Crime, Order, and Control: Governance, Risk, and Globalisation', in M. Maguire, R. Morgan and R. Reiner (eds), *The Oxford Handbook of Criminology*, 3rd edn. Oxford: Oxford University Press, pp. 83–111.

Lucken, K. (1998) 'Contemporary Penal Trends: Modern or Postmodern?', *British Journal of Criminology*, 38 (1): 106–23.

Lynch, M. (1998) 'Waste Managers? The New Penology, Crime Fighting, and Parole Agent Identity', *Law & Society Review*, 32 (4): 839–69.

Lynch, M. (2000) 'Rehabilitation as Rhetoric: The Ideal of Reformation in Contemporary Parole Discourse and Practices', *Punishment & Society*, 2 (1): 40–65.

McCorkle, R. and Crank, J. (1996) 'Meet the New Boss: Institutional Change and Loose Coupling in Parole and Probation', *American Journal of Criminal Justice*, 21 (1): 1–25.

McNeill, F. (2000) 'Defining Effective Probation: Frontline Perspectives', *Howard Journal of Criminal Justice*, 39 (4): 382–97.

Miller, L. (2001) 'Looking for Postmodernism in All the Wrong Places: Implementing the New Penology', *British Journal of Criminology*, 41 (1): 168–84.

Moore, W.E. (1962) *The Conduct of the Corporation*. New York: Random House.

Petersilia, J. and Turner, S. (1987) 'Guideline-based Justice: Prediction and Racial Minorities', in D.G. Gottfredson and M. Tonry (eds), *Prediction and Classification: Criminal Justice Decision Making*. Chicago: University of Chicago Press, pp. 151–82.

Petersilia, J., Turner, S. and Peterson, J. (1986) *Prison versus Probation in California: Implications for Crime and Offender Recidivism*. Santa Monica, CA: Rand.

Raine, J.W. and Willson, M.J. (1995) 'New Public Management and Criminal Justice: How Well Does the Coat Fit?', *Public Money and Management*, 15 (1): 35–40.

Raine, J.W. and Willson, M.J. (1997) 'Beyond Managerialism in Criminal Justice', *Howard Journal of Criminal Justice*, 36 (1): 80–95.

Robinson, G. (2002) 'Exploring Risk Management in Probation Practice: Contemporary Developments in England and Wales', *Punishment & Society*, 4 (1): 5–25.

Robinson, G. and McNeill, F. (2004) 'Purposes Matter: Examining the "Ends" of Probation', in G. Mair (ed.), *What Matters in Probation*. Cullompton: Willan, pp. 277–304.

Rose, N. (1996) 'Governing "Advanced" Liberal Democracies', in A. Barry, T. Osborne and N. Rose (eds), *Foucault and Political Reason: Liberalism, Neo-*

Liberalism and Rationalities of Government. Chicago: University of Chicago Press, pp. 37–64.

Rose, N. and Miller, P. (1992) 'Political Power beyond the State: Problematics of Government', *British Journal of Sociology*, 43 (2): 173–205.

Rutherford, A. (1993) *Criminal Justice and the Pursuit of Decency.* Oxford: Oxford University Press.

Simon, J. (1993) *Poor Discipline: Parole and the Social Control of the Underclass, 1890–1990.* Chicago: University of Chicago Press.

Simon, J. and Feeley, M.M. (1995) 'True Crime: The New Penology and Public Diuscourse on Crime', in T.G. Blomberg and S. Cohen (eds), *Punishment and Social Control.* New York: Aldine de Gruyter, pp. 147–80.

Smith, D.J. and Gray, J. (1985) *Police and People in London: The PSI Report.* Gower: Aldershot.

Steinberg, J. (2002) *All or Nothing: The Axis and the Holocaust, 1941–43.* London: Routledge.

Thompson, J.D. (1967/2003) *Organizations in Action: Social Science Bases of Administrative Theory.* New Brunswick, NJ: Transaction.

Tonry, M. (1996) *Sentencing Matters.* Oxford: Oxford University Press.

Travis, A. (2003) 'Arrested Development', The *Guardian*, 10 March.

Wrong, D.H. (1988) *Power: Its Forms, Bases, and Uses.* Oxford: Basil Blackwell.

Chapter 15

The role of middle and first-line managers

Sue Brookes, Karen Smith and Jamie Bennett[1]

Introduction

The role of middle and first-line managers in prisons is an area that has been almost completely ignored in academic research. This is in contrast to prison officers (e.g. Kauffman 1988; Lombardo 1989; Liebling and Price 2001; Crawley 2004) and governors (e.g. DiIulio 1987; Bryans and Wilson 2000), both of whom have attracted the interest of researchers. However, this group are significant not only in terms of numbers, but also in terms of their potential impact on the management of the prison and the lives of those who live and work there.

This chapter will focus on the work of operational first-line and middle managers, that is senior officers, principal officers and operational managers grade F and E (formerly called governor grade 5 and 4 respectively). These staff carry out a range of roles. Typically, a senior officer will be a shift supervisor, belonging to a small team of senior officers designated to a specific area such as a wing. They will also be expected to act as line manager to a number of officers within that group. Principal officers will line manage a team of senior officers and will be responsible for an area within a prison, such as a wing. An operational manager F will line manage principal officers and will typically head a function within a small prison (such as all of the residential areas, or security or resettlement activities) and be a member of the establishment's senior management team. In a larger prison, an operational manager F may be deputy head of a function or be responsible for part of a function. An operational manager E will head a function in a large prison or in a small prison may take on the role of deputy governor, being the second-in-command. From this brief description, these managers may take on a variety of roles and functions. In terms of numbers, there are 6,234 first-line and middle managers in the Prison Service in England and Wales, out of a total of 25,971 operational staff.[2] Of these, 3,914 are senior officers, 1,281 principal officers, 585 manager F and 454 manager E grades.

This chapter is intended as an introduction to the role of middle and first-line prison managers, an important but overlooked group. It will start by considering the context in which they operate in prisons and the role that they are expected to fulfil, and will highlight the paucity of research available on the working lives and impact of these managers, before considering their own perceptions of their work.[3] The chapter concludes by highlighting some of the key issues and tensions relating to their work, as well as suggesting future research direction.

The management context

The role of first-line and middle managers has altered over the last 15 years, as the pace of change in the Prison Service and the public sector generally has accelerated. This has arisen from the growth of the New Public Management (NPM) movement (Hood 1991; Pollitt 1993; Ferlie *et al.* 1996), which sought to reform the public sector by introducing private sector practices. The NPM approach was a marriage of two ideas: firstly, new institutional economics, moving from the military-bureaucratic model to an emphasis on contestability, user choice, transparency and incentives; and, secondly, a new wave of business-type managerialism (Hood 1991). Within the Prison Service in England and Wales, these changes have been incorporated through approaches such as the introduction of quantitative performance measures, known as key performance targets and indicators (KPTs and KPIs), the development of audit procedures, the delegation of financial and personnel responsibility to prisons, the establishment of efficiency targets, greater controls on union activity and the introduction of private sector competition. These changes have led to changes both in the operating environment and in the means used by prisons to achieve their goals.

These changes have also had an impact on the approach taken towards human resource management in the public sector (Farnham and Horton 1996). First, the personnel function has become more strategic than administrative. This move has led to a greater concern with the softer aspects of human resources, such as customer orientation, personal development, culture management and empowering managers, while also maintaining a close integration with organisational strategy. This can be seen in prisons through the professionalisation of human resources management, the maintenance of Investors in People accreditation and the mandatory production of local people plans. Second, the management style has become more rationalist and less paternalistic. Rather than being led by normative values such as fairness or welfare, managers have become goal-orientated, utilising private sector ideas and techniques. This is most obvious in the development of various measurement methods such as KPTs, KPIs and audits. Third, employment practices have become more flexible and less standardised, with delegation and diversity in recruitment, conditions, promotion and development. The delegation of human resource responsibilities to prisons has led to increasing diversity and flexibility. Fourth, industrial relations have become less collectivist. A preference has developed for dealing with staff issues individually and using direct consultation procedures. Although the Prison Officers' Association remains strong, there have been attempts to contain this (see Bennett and Wahidin this volume). Fifth, state employers have moved from being a model employer to being a 'new mode' employer, with an increasing focus on customers rather than employees, strengthening management control and increasingly mimicking private sector practices. The customer focus can be seen in particular through measures of prisoner perceptions, for example through the Measuring the Quality of Prison Life (MQPL) survey (Liebling, assisted by Arnold, 2004) and the use of community members to monitor the prison through Independent Monitoring Boards.

First-line and middle managers play a significant role in the delivery of this more dynamic strategy of governance. A model for this role has been proposed by Floyd and Wooldridge (1994), suggesting the following responsibilities:

- First-line and middle managers must change themselves to reflect the new strategy and so act as role models.
- They should help and assist their staff in understanding and adjusting to change, acting as mentors or coaches.
- They should translate top-down strategies into practical strategies that work on the ground in their part of the organisation.
- They should act as project managers, delivering the detailed implementation of strategy.

- They should instigate or champion ideas and initiatives. They should take bottom-up issues and influence top management perceptions by the slant they put on that information.
- They should act as guardians of the organisation's performance and reputation, keeping it functioning while new strategies and changes are brought in.

The modern first-line or middle manager can therefore be described as someone who helps achieve strategic aims, goals and objectives through managing people in a positive and developmental way.

In order to realise this new approach, a number of initiatives have been introduced. One of the most important has been the introduction of job simulation assessment centres (JSAC) as the means of selecting staff for promotion. This has replaced unstructured interviews with a series of work-based simulations in which promotion candidates are expected to demonstrate practical competence (see McHugh *et al.* this volume). JSACs provide the gateway for promotion into senior officer, manager F and senior management levels. In addition, a leadership and development team has been established with specialist, expert advisers placed in each area. While much of this resource is allocated towards preparation for JSAC and preparatory training for those who are successful, they also support a number of managers completing management qualifications. There was an attempt during 2005 to rationalise the middle management structure and to link progression to the attainment of nationally recognised qualifications, but this stalled during negotiations with trade unions (Prison Service Pay Review Body 2006).

Middle and first-line managers in prisons

Official reports have frequently highlighted the importance of first-line and middle managers in successful prison management. The Woolf Report, published following the widespread riots starting at HMP Manchester in April 1990, highlighted a range of issues, including the importance and impact of management (Woolf and Tumin 1991). For example, the lack of rigour with which individual managers followed up security information played a key role in the failure to prevent the riot,[4] and the initial response of managers was important in resolving and controlling the disorder.[5] One observation made by the report was that the slow progress that staff could make through the ranks – throughout the Prison Service – hampered the development of an able stratum of middle management. At that stage, a prison officer could not sit the senior officer promotion exam until having served five and a half years and, even if successful, still had to pass an interview which was stacked in favour of seniority based on length of service. The report recommended that selection be more based on ability and that able staff should be able to move into the middle ranks more rapidly.

Following the high-profile escapes of category A[6] prisoners from Whitemoor in 1994 and Parkhurst in 1995, a fundamental review of security was carried out (Learmont 1995). This report highlighted the importance of visible leadership throughout the organisation, building on the popular view that leadership was not simply a senior manager role but was required in all areas and at all levels of the organisation (Schein 1992). It was argued that this leadership was important in establishing the culture or 'philosophy' of prisons (Learmont 1995: 81) – the balance of custody, care and control – and in addressing 'disunity' (p. 84) – the gap between what was intended to be done and what actually occurred. It was recommended that managers were selected on the basis of identified competencies and that they receive specific training in leadership and management.

A further official report, commissioned to examine management in the Prison Service (Laming 2000), criticised the state of first-line and middle management, noting that: 'All too often we heard from Senior Officers who clearly did not identify themselves as part of the management' (p. 13). This issue of the conflict, confusion and uncertainty that uniformed managers, particularly senior officers, experience has also been highlighted by Crawley (2004), who suggested that the transition from officer to senior officer was a particularly difficult one. Senior officers found it hard to take on the managerial responsibilities that came with the grade and struggled with the challenge of having to achieve a degree of detachment from the prison officer group. Senior officers also stated that they were the subjects of resistance from prison officers and thus pragmatically accepted that change would only be successful to the degree that officers cooperated with it.

In considering the experience of these managers, it is worth noting a recent American study of the stress experienced by correctional supervisors, i.e. first-line and middle managers (Owen 2006). This concluded that supervisors experienced less stress than correctional officers, a finding similar to those reported in an earlier UK study (Launay and Fielding 1989). Owen (2006) suggested that this difference was explained by the fact that, while supervisors experienced organisational stressors such as pay and benefits, paperwork and poor communications, they experienced less environmental stressors, which arise from the physical and social nature of the work, because of their reduced contact with prisoners. Many supervisors stated that their most difficult interactions were not with prisoners but with staff. In order to counteract these stressors, it was recommended that job satisfaction could be improved through better communication and training, that improved social support could be provided through physical fitness programmes and workplace counselling, and that an internal locus of control could be developed by allowing supervisors to take an active role in policy and planning. Although this research was carried out in the USA, it nevertheless highlights important issues regarding the concerns of first line and middle managers.

Studies of prison officers and prison work attest to the ability of committed and charismatic leaders to make a difference to the areas in which they work and to those people around them (Liebling and Price 2001; Liebling, assisted by Arnold, 2004), and it is worth giving further consideration to these issues in relation to first-line and middle managers. Here, the academic literature is relatively sparse. Useem and Kimball's (1989) analysis of major US prison riots between 1971 and 1986 argued that, by maintaining uniformity and stability, managers played a central role in creating the conditions of legitimacy that ensured – or, if absent, undermined – institutional order. Thus:

> Fluctuating and unpredictable standards, a multiplicity of competing rules, give the lie to the legitimacy of an order. When every shift commander has a different set of rules, the odds are that they are all wrong; when the administrator says something different every day, all its pronouncements are certainly lies; when corrections officials bicker and fight amongst themselves, they all must be scoundrels: this is how the inmate reasons. (p. 205)

When stability and consistency are absent, prisoners judge their conditions negatively or see prison staff as lazy and incompetent. This can foster a sense of grievance among the prisoner population and can result in significant discontent.

Although not an academic text, Conover's *Holding The Key* (2000) also yields some important insights into prison life. Conover describes most first-line managers as supportive, facilitative people, and some as capable of great compassion towards prisoners. However, they also include people determined to make life hell for new staff and with a deep distrust and hatred of prisoners. Such descriptions reveal the importance of first-line managers in establishing the character of daily prison life both for prisoners and other staff. Research elsewhere confirms that first-line and middle managers play a significant role in determining the experiences of staff. In particular, management has been identified as one source of stress for prison officers (Schaufeli and Peeters 2000). Key issues here include the quality of communication between shifts, the communication of policies and the level of clarity in performance expectations (Launay and Fielding 1989).

Middle and first-line managers in their own words

Little is known about the working lives of middle and first-line managers, particularly in relation to the new mode of prison management detailed above. The following section outlines their views about a range of contemporary issues, including delivering the organisational results expected of them, managing staff effectively and drawing these two elements together in order to achieve results through people.

Delivering results

In relation to strategic aims, first-line and middle managers had a strong commitment towards the achievement of goals. They reported that their most important contributions were meeting targets and standards, delivering the business plan, and monitoring and reviewing practices to ensure audit compliance. The second most frequently stated contribution was maintaining good order and ensuring the safety of the establishment. The promotion of decency was also mentioned, together with contributing to the resettlement agenda and reducing drug supply within the prison, but this was referenced less frequently and was generally seen as less important than meeting targets. This all suggested a clear premium placed by these managers on delivering business objectives.

They reported that senior managers expected them to creatively solve problems, both in the resolution of 'daily crises' and in more developmental management issues. One interviewee stated that 'Middle managers are much more practical – give us a problem and we'll give you a *workable* solution.' They also described their role as being 'the link between SMT [senior management team] and the shop floor', both in terms of implementing strategy and 'keeping the SMT informed of the good and bad things happening in my area of responsibility'. As a result, first-line and middle managers (senior and principal officers in particular) saw their most important skills as having good technical and operational knowledge and having the means to translate strategy into action through approaches such as project management, change management, budget management and business planning.

The aspects of the job from which these managers derived most satisfaction were the opportunity to achieve goals, to operate autonomously and to undertake challenging work. These are qualities that enrich the work experience of these managers.

These interviews suggest that middle and first-line managers are keenly aware of the business imperatives central to New Public Management, and that they are responding positively to the clarity and opportunities that managerialism presents. In relation to the model for dynamic middle management described by Floyd and Wooldridge (1994), these managers particularly emphasised their roles as translators of managerial strategies into action, as guardians of establishment performance, as project managers delivering change and as champions of ideas both from the top down and from the bottom up, acting as a link between the shopfloor and boardroom.

Managing people

In the area of managing people, the responses of the first-line and middle managers suggested that they were less attuned to the needs of staff and felt less skilled than was desirable. When asked to describe what senior managers expected of them, few stated the importance of people management or leadership. When asked to describe the skills they required, senior and principal officers in particular rarely mentioned 'softer skills' such as leadership and teambuilding, inspiring and motivating staff, or resolving conflict and diplomacy. However, these skills were more likely to be mentioned by manager F and manager E grades. This may indicate that leadership and people management is more important for governor grades, perhaps reflecting the hierarchical nature of prisons, with leadership still being more highly valued from more senior staff. The one area in which all managers were in agreement was effective communication, which was described by almost all interviewees as the single most critical skill necessary to perform their role effectively.

The nature of middle managers' approach to managing people was exhibited most clearly in discussions about how they managed their staff and what they found to be the most difficult aspects of their job. All middle managers in the sample reported that first-line managers expected guidance, direction, support and leadership from them. However, there was a blurred boundary between developing and facilitating others on the one hand, and simply doing the job oneself on the other. A number of middle managers complained that they were expected to 'know the answer to everything', and were drawn into decision-making and problem-solving on behalf of their staff: 'first-line managers expect me to make decisions on their behalf'. They were also critical of staff 'who are afraid to make decisions', 'avoid taking personal responsibility' and 'expect me to solve all their problems', or are 'unmotivated' and 'ineffective'. This frustration suggests that middle managers are generally less comfortable with those softer aspects of performance described by Floyd and Wooldridge (1994), such as role modelling, mentoring or coaching. This is particularly important as first-line managers report such difficulty making the transition from officer to manager (Laming 2000; Crawley 2004). Without proper regard to their development and such hostile responses, it is perhaps unsurprising that they more closely associate themselves with the officer group.

Part of the reason for this lack of attention to the softer aspects of people management was the pressure created in an increasingly goal-orientated organisation. A majority of interviewees reported feelings such as 'having too much to do and never enough time to do it', an 'overwhelming number of tasks and priorities', constantly being engaged in 'crisis management', and working in conditions of 'constant change and uncertainty'. In such conditions, there was little time for people management.

This is a major challenge for the Prison Service, one which may be addressed through a major change project known as Phoenix HR, which aims to reduce the amount of human resource support work completed in each establishment through the creation of a central, shared service centre. This change will also require first-line and middle managers to take a more direct role in personnel issues rather than relying on local HR staff. A training needs analysis completed on behalf of the Phoenix HR project revealed that many managers were relying on local HR personnel not only to advise, but to directly manage difficult issues such as poor performance and sickness absence. In general, the analysis found that managers were insufficiently skilled in a range of important areas required for managing people, such as the effective use of appraisal, managing poor performance, identifying and responding to training and development needs and setting and agreeing targets. In addition, it was found that they lacked confidence and competence in tackling workplace conflict, giving constructive critical feedback and dealing with resistance to change. Such findings have important implications, given the impact of management effectiveness on the quality of life for prisoners and staff.

Delivering results through people

The model of a dynamic, modern middle manager proposed by Floyd and Wooldridge (1994) describes a person who is able to achieve results through people. As has been described above, while middle and first-line managers are able to deliver results, this is not always in a way that achieves the right balance with the effective development and support of people. This section describes observations and interviews with middle and first-line managers at highly performing prisons, where a feature of their success appears to be the achievement of this balance between individual and task.

For middle and first-line managers, there appeared to be a link between the level of performance of the prison and their perception of the support and development opportunities they experienced. In higher performing prisons the majority of these managers reported being 'well supported' with 'good development opportunities available'. These included shadowing, coaching, advice and guidance, training courses and secondments. In contrast, those in poorer performing prisons described having 'little support' and 'little development opportunity', and felt that they were 'left to sink or swim'.

In high performing prisons, managers displayed, and were reported to have, particular strengths in relation to communication, clarity of purpose, leadership and staff management. Managers communicated both effectively and regularly with each other, staff and prisoners, using methods including briefings, meetings and written communication. As a result, staff felt 'well informed' and valued. The expressed purpose of high performing prisons was essentially prisoner-centred, and this purpose was widely understood and shared. Managers were clear about the expectations placed upon them, as were staff generally. Given that the purposes of prisons are controversial, contested and sometimes contradictory, the absence of such expectations can lead to role confusion, which can be a significant source of stress (Schaufeli and Peeters 2000). In acting as translators of strategy into action, middle and first-line managers play a particularly important role.

Leadership in these prisons was reported as being widespread and not limited to senior managers. In particular, middle and first-line managers were widely described as being confident and visible, spending time 'walking the floor', engaging with staff and prisoners. In this way, they provided meaningful role models to their staff. They also provided leadership in as much as they accepted responsibility and 'made things happen', following through on actions and promises. This allowed them to act as guardians of the establishment performance and as project managers. In terms of people management, respondents described their approach – and the method they encouraged in their staff – as one that was inclusive and based on teamwork, mutual trust, motivation, inspiration and empowerment. Middle and first-line managers thus acted as role models for appropriate behaviour as well as spending time coaching or mentoring their staff so as to achieve holistic change.

This data suggests that one basis of high performance is the development of the kinds of dynamic middle managers advocated by Floyd and Wooldridge (1994), drawing together both the performance or business aspects of the work and the effective management of people.

Conclusion

Prisons have been through significant change over the last 15 years, and change will continue with the development of the National Offender Management Service, including an increased focus on reducing reoffending, increasing competition through contestability, developments in information technology, the growing prisoner population and the changing demands placed on managers in terms of human resource management arising from the Phoenix HR programme. The role of middle and first-line managers in supporting and achieving these changes will be crucial.

However, this chapter has illustrated that although this group can play an important role in achieving high performance, investment is required to develop the skills and confidence of first-line and middle managers. In particular, greater emphasis is required on the people management aspects of their role and on providing a range of skills to manage areas such as appraisal, personal development, resolving conflict and providing leadership. Organisations are sociotechnical systems (see Trist *et al.* 1963) – they have a technical side relating to equipment, processes, goals and methods, but also socio-psychological aspects in as much as the nature of the work and the way it is carried out has an impact on employees. These two aspects need to be maintained in some kind of equilibrium, indeed an overemphasis on one aspect or the other will be detrimental for the whole: 'The optimisation of the whole tends to require a less than optimum state for each separate dimension' (Trist *et al.* 1963: 7). Although high-performing prisons are better able to achieve this balance, in general the technical aspects of the job appear to dominate most prisons.

This disequilibrium has a number of consequences. For staff, it is likely to feed feelings of resentment and being undervalued, a long-standing complaint of prison officers (Thomas 1972) which is also likely to feed unionism (see Bennett and Wahidin this volume) and contribute towards stress (Schaufeli and Peeters 2000). For prisoners, since there is a clear link between the attitudes of staff and quality of life (Liebling assisted by Arnold 2004), a more engaged and better supported workforce is likely to have considerable benefits. For this to occur, it is clear that more work needs to be conducted on middle and first-line managers, an overlooked but vital group of staff within prisons.

Seminar questions

1 It is often said that there is a difference between uniformed managers (senior and principal officers) and non-uniformed governor grades (manager F and E). What factors may lead to that difference?
2 What strategies could be deployed to develop the dynamic middle managers described?
3 How can more senior managers ensure that middle and first-line managers maintain an appropriate balance between task and people?
4 Why have researchers largely ignored the working lives of middle and first line managers?

Recommended reading

There is little published research on the role of first-line and middle managers. As described in this chapter, the article 'Dinosaurs or Dynamos: Recognising Middle Managers Strategic Role' (1994) by Floyd and Wooldridge is a useful model. In describing the role of these managers in prisons, there is little specific work, although this makes a cameo appearance in several books on prison officers. The best description of senior officers is in Elaine Crawley's (2004) *Doing Prison Work: The Public and Private Lives of Prison Officers*. It is also worth mentioning the article 'Occupational Stress Among Correctional Supervisors' (2006) by Owen as this is the most recent specific research on first-line and middle managers.

Notes

1 The authors would like to thank Paul Kempster for his time and in sharing his knowledge and experience, the Governor and staff at HMP Whatton for their cooperation, time and honesty, Pauline Duff for analysing JSAC results and providing clear comparable data, Eliot Franks (TDP) for providing SOM Development Centre data and Jackie Saunders for her comprehensive HR TNA.
2 Figures are for 31 December 2005 and were produced by HM Prison Service and published internally under the title *HR Planning Staff Profiles and Projections Review – January 2006*.
3 The research for this chapter includes a review of the literature and analysis of documentary evidence including the results of promotion assessments and training needs analysis. Primary research was also carried out through semi-structured interviews with a small sample of middle managers and interviews and observations at high-performing prisons.
4 See Carrabine (2004) for an argument that the failure to effectively manage this security information was a matter of organisational culture rather than individual performance.
5 Boin and Van Duin (1995) describe that it is a feature of incident management that the way the incident is initially responded to plays an important part is shaping the final outcome.
6 Category A is the highest security category and is designed for those prisoners who present the gravest risk to the police, the public or the security of the state and for whom escape should be impossible.

References

Boin, R. and Van Duin, M. (1995) 'Prison Riots as Organisational Failures: A Management Perspective', *Prison Journal*, 75 (3): 357–79.
Bryans, S. and Wilson, D. (2000) *The Prison Governor: Theory and Practice*. Leyhill: Prison Service Journal.
Carrabine, E. (2004) *Power, Discourse and Resistance: A Genealogy of the Strangeways Riot*. Aldershot: Ashgate.
Conover, T. (2000) *Holding the Key: My Year as a Guard at Sing Sing*. London: Scribner.

Crawley, E. (2004) *Doing Prison Work: The Public and Private Lives of Prison Officers*. Cullompton: Willan.

DiIulio, J. (1987) *Governing Prisons: A Comparative Study of Correctional Management*. New York: Free Press.

Farnham, D. and Horton, S., with contributions by Corby, S., Giles, L., Hutchinson, B. and White, G. (1996) *Managing People in the Public Services*. London: MacMillan.

Ferlie, E., Pettigrew, A., Ashburner, L. and Fitzgerald, L. (1996) *The New Public Management in Action*. Oxford: Oxford University Press.

Floyd, S. and Wooldridge, B. (1994) 'Dinosaurs or Dynamos: Recognising Middle Managers Strategic Role', *Academy of Management Executive*, 8 (4): 47–57.

Hood, C. (1991) 'A Public Management for All Seasons', *Public Administration*, 69: 3—19.

Kauffman, K. (1988) *Prison Officers and Their World*. Cambridge, MA: Harvard University Press.

Laming, Lord of Tewin (2000) *Modernising the Management of the Prison Service: An Independent Report by the Targeted Performance Initiative Working Group*. HM Prison Service.

Launay, G. and Fielding, P. (1989) 'Stress Among Prison Officers: Some Empirical Evidence Based on Self Report', *Howard Journal*, 28 (2): 138–48.

Learmont, J. (1995) *Review of Prison Service Security in England and Wales and the escape from Parkhurst Prison on Tuesday, 3 January 1995*. London: HMSO.

Liebling, A. and Price, D. (2001) *The Prison Officer*. Leyhill: Prison Service Journal.

Liebling, A., assisted by Arnold, H. (2004) *Prisons and Their Moral Performance: A Study of Values, Quality and Prison Life*. Oxford: Clarendon Press.

Lombardo, L. (1989) *Guards Imprisoned: Correctional Officers at Work*. Cincinnati, OH: Anderson Publishing.

Owen, S. (2006) 'Occupational Stress Among Correctional Supervisors', *Prison Journal*, 86 (2): 164–81.

Pollitt, C. (1993) *Managerialism and the Public Services: Cuts or Cultural Change in the 1990s?* Oxford: Blackwell.

Prison Service Pay Review Body (2006) *Fifth Report on England and Wales 2006*. London: Stationary Office.

Schaufeli, W. and Peeters, M. (2000) 'Job Stress and Burnout Among Correctional Officers: A Literature Review', *International Journal of Stress Management*, 7 (1): 19–48.

Schein, E. (1992) *Organizational Culture and Leadership*. New York: Maxwell Macmillan.

Thomas, J. (1972) *The English Prison Officer Since 1850: A Study in Conflict*. London: Routledge & Kegan Paul.

Trist, E., Higgin, G., Murray, H. and Pollock, A. (1963) *Organizational Choice: Capabilities of Groups at the Coal Face under Changing Technologies – The Loss, Re-discovery and Transformation of a Work Tradition*. London: Tavistock.

Useem, B. and Kimball, P. (1989) *States of Seige: US Prsion Riots 1971–1986*. New York: Oxford University Press.

Woolf, H. and Tumin, S. (1991) *Report of an Inquiry into Prison Disturbances April 1990*, Cm 1456. London: HMSO.

Part 4

Prison Staff

Chapter 16

The changing face of probation in prisons

Brian Williams[1]

Introduction

By focusing on a few significant historical and contemporary examples, this chapter puts prison probation work into context. It does so in order to demonstrate the influences which moulded the task of prison probation officers, including in the early days the influence of the Church of England, then the probation service's adherence to social and case work, and more recently the impact of managerialism and of public service 'modernisation'.

At times clarity about the role of prison-based probation staff has been lacking. This may have given workers a degree of discretion. However, an examination of more recent developments suggests that the task has become much more differentiated from one prison to another as a result of the increasingly contractual relationship between governors and outside service providers including probation areas. The chapter concludes with some speculation about the likely impact of the introduction of 'contestability' and the National Offender Management Service (NOMS) for prison probation work.

Historical context

Prisons began as places of containment prior to the execution of the death sentence, and at that time they were privately run and the proprietors cared little for the welfare of their inmates. This began to change in the early nineteenth century with the introduction of salaried staff and an independent inspectorate (Cheney 2005; McConville 1981).

Of the 'civilian' staff groups working in prisons in England and Wales, probation staff have a relatively long history. While the place of the chaplaincy was securely established from the very early days of state-run prisons, and medical men also played a role from the beginning, the precursors of probation officers had firmly established the legitimacy of their access to inmates by the mid-nineteenth century (but initially as outsiders rather than prison-based staff). Like the chaplains, 'welfare' workers had close connections with the established church, which had enormous influence upon the running of state prisons from their foundation until the early twentieth century, and later with other denominations and religions. Chaplains' standing in the hierarchy of prisons diminished from the second part of the nineteenth century (McConville 1981: 357; see also Serge 1931: chapter 10) but they continued to sit on important committees such as discharge boards, and to filter and refer cases to discharged prisoners' aid societies.

The 'missionaries' and 'agents' who were among the early forerunners of the probation service were employed by the discharged prisoners' aid societies with a view to preventing released prisoners from returning to a life of crime, helping them find employment and accommodation in some cases and encouraging them to return to their home towns rather than taking up residence near the prison. From the late 1850s they began to take over statutory supervision of released convicts from the police, and prisoners released under police supervision under the ticket-of-leave system also became the responsibility of an 'appointed society' from 1948. Police court missions and discharged prisoners' aid societies (established by Temperance Societies, part of a huge social movement supporting abstinence from alcohol in the second half of the nineteenth and early part of the twentieth centuries) began to work with selected prisoners' families from the 1870s. At times their agents also met prisoners on their release and acted as bankers for their discharge grants in an effort to prevent 'back-sliding'; many campaigners for teetotalism were also involved in penal reform activities. Some societies also helped offenders to emigrate to the colonies (Cranfield 1982; Priestley 1999). Most of their activity involved visits to prisons (often from 'missions' just outside the gates) rather than employing staff based inside. However, the prison gate mission in Durham was commandeered to accommodate troops during the Second World War, and from 1942 the prisoners' aid society agent was based inside the prison (Cranfield 1982). By 1953, when the Maxwell Committee reported, at least eight prisons had a 'resident welfare officer' (Maxwell Committee 1953: para. 43).

Elsewhere, discharged prisoners' aid societies first employed welfare officers – many of them trained social workers – to work inside prisons as a result of the recommendations of the report of the Maxwell Committee in the period from 1955 until 1966–9. Their salaries were comparable to those of probation officers. In the late 1960s, these staff were transferred to the renamed probation *and after-care* service (Monger 1967; Foren and Bailey 1968; Cranfield 1982; Williams 1995a). Some subsequently left prisons for fieldwork and many continued in post until they retired, as prison or community-based probation officers.

Thus the religious influences which permeated field probation work until at least the 1980s also had a powerful effect upon prison probation work. To some extent, casework-trained welfare workers were involved in the administration of prisons alongside the governors, chaplains and doctors who had hitherto served as prison managers, albeit in a subordinate role. Monger (1967: 67) stated that:

> In most prisons, the welfare officer's day revolves around the various boards: the Reception Board, the Applications Board, the Review Board, and so on. Besides these, the work involves dealing with the results of the various applications ...

made by prisoners. The account continues with 'paper work ... correspondence and telephoning ... diagnosis', liaison with colleagues outside the prison and with the governor and the chaplain, and 'acting as mentor to other members of prison staff' who worked directly with prisoners (Ibid: 76; this is an issue discussed further below).

Clearly, prison probation officers' priorities and tasks have changed in many ways in the past 40 years – and yet aspects of this job description remain recognisable today, not least the need for prison probation departments to be represented on committees making decisions about individual prisoners. Many prisoners, particularly those serving long sentences, avoided prison-based probation officers for this very reason, seeing them as 'inextricably part of the prison bureaucracy' (Williams 1992: 270; see also Priestley 1972). The original Home Office Circular setting out the tasks of the new prison welfare service in 1967 described its tasks as planning after-care, acting as a 'channel of communication on social problems with the outside' and as 'the focal point of social work' in prisons (Home Office 1967).

However, institutional pressures tended to mean that they got caught up in a 'welfare cycle' of reacting to applications by prisoners – many of them relatively trivial – and undertaking routine administrative tasks to meet the needs of the system, leaving little time for other work (Haxby 1978; Ashe 1993).

Increasingly, this problem has been addressed by delegating 'welfare' work to others and undertaking group work, both because it is more economical in terms of time usage and because group dynamics can be utilised to encourage change. Some groups exist mainly to share information (Ashe 1993, gives the example of HMP Lindholme's Parole Information Group) while others form part of accredited programmes with therapeutic or desistance from offending aims (NPD 2002; Maguire and Raynor 2006).

Prison probation officers' main tasks, according to one probation area's website, currently include:

- running group work programmes designed to address offending behaviour and reduce the likelihood of further offending;
- working with voluntary and other specialist agencies offering advice and support to prisoners;
- liaison with probation staff in the community in relation to supervision of individual prisoners post-release;
- 'supporting prison staff in the preparation of sentence plans';
- preparing risk assessments on prisoners being considered for early release;
- working on offending behaviour as part of planned sentence management;
- involvement in bail information schemes;
- helping to avoid self-harm by prisoners (ASPA 2006).

The emphasis given to these tasks varies according to the type of prison; for example, those housing long-term inmates will not be involved in bail information and local prisons have considerably less involvement with group work because of the transient nature of their population. Most prison probation staff also spend time on prison wings talking to staff and prisoners, and much informal work goes on as they walk around the prison. The probation team is also normally represented at parole hearings, lifer assessment and review panels, security meetings and so on. In some teams, much day-to-day work is undertaken by probation service officers.

Field probation officers have been less and less likely to be able to visit prisoners in recent years, and in urgent cases they may ask prison colleagues to prepare pre-sentence reports on inmates. While very few field probation officers currently attend sentence planning boards, this is expected to change once they become responsible for chairing such meetings under new arrangements introduced by the Offender Management Model from November 2006.

The privatisation of prison escort arrangements has meant that prisoners' papers rarely accompany them from court (except in the case of documentation relating to suicide risk), so administrative staff in remand prison probation teams now spend a good deal of time chasing up PSRs and risk assessments.

Shared working between prison and probation officers

A question which has resurfaced periodically over the years is the extent to which uniformed prison staff should be involved in 'welfare' work with prisoners. In one sense, it is inevitable that they sometimes are: they talk to prisoners, often come from similar backgrounds to the majority of inmates and in many cases choose to engage with their problems. Whether some prison officers should be expressly trained for this work has been a matter of controversy. Back in the 1960s, it was understood that any involvement by prison officers in welfare work was 'auxiliary' to the role of trained staff (Monger 1967: 78) and any professional partnership would be informal. However, moves were afoot by that time to introduced 'shared working' between prison and probation officers in some establishments.

The Prison Officers' Association had called for a greater role for uniformed staff in the rehabilitation and aftercare of prisoners at its 1963 annual conference. The Home Office responded by setting up a joint working party on the issue which met for 18 years without any practical consequences, which suggests that the POA's commitment to the idea may not have been strong at that time or may have been largely rhetorical. However, in the late 1980s a number of 'shared working' schemes were set up with central prison service support, allowing probation officers to dispense with some routine tasks and to train prison officers for direct work with inmates and supervise them (Williams 1991). Prisoners who were prepared to use a welfare service provided by uniformed staff found them easier to get hold of than probation staff, but not always as helpful, according to one study (Evans et al. 1988); however, another local evaluation found that prisoners were equally willing to talk to probation or prison officers (Williams and Eadie 1994). There tended to be a lack of continuity due to shift patterns, and prison officers reportedly found it frustrating that time did not permit them to provide as good a service as they would have wished.

Part of the motivation of the POA and of prison governors for encouraging these developments was that they allowed at least a minority of prison officers to develop professionally and to undertake more fulfilling tasks than the traditional 'turnkey' role. These aspirations were encapsulated in the 'better jobs' initiative in the early 1990s (Williams and Eadie 1994). The Woolf Report on the riots in Manchester and other prisons in 1990, published in 1991, argued that job satisfaction for prison officers was an important and neglected issue (see Player and Jenkins 1994) and recommended a greater involvement by uniformed staff in negotiating contracts or compacts with prisoners (an idea greeted with considerable scepticism by many experienced commentators – see, for example Sim 1994 – but encouraged by HM Inspectorate of Prisons).

Much of the energy devoted to such arrangements was subsequently diverted to specialist provision such as legal aid and bail information schemes inside prisons, provided primarily by uniformed staff and originally supported by 'hypothecated' (ring-fenced) funding (Williams and Eadie 1994). As a consequence, prison-based probation officers regained responsibility for most 'welfare' work with individual prisoners, except in a small number of specialist 'therapeutic' regimes such as that at Grendon Underwood (see Genders and Player 1995: 110–16). However, prison officers nowadays also routinely share responsibility for certain types of group work, notably the Short Duration Drugs Programme and the Sex Offender Treatment Programme. In some prisons, shared working on issues of prisoner welfare remains a live issue, with uniformed staff undertaking the majority of duties such as initial contact with outside housing providers, initiating contact with field probation staff and basic welfare work with prisoners. In others, senior probation officers are now much more integrated with prison management than in the past; senior probation officers (SPOs) have taken on the role of Head of Resettlement in a number of institutions, giving them responsibility for managing prison officers and civilian prison staff as well as the probation team. In such cases senior probation officers form part of the prison's senior management team.

Sentence planning, aftercare and throughcare

Another issue which resurfaces from time to time is sentence planning. The Advisory Council on the Treatment of Offenders recommended to the Home Secretary in 1963 that:

> After-care, to be fully effective, must be integrated with the work of the penal institutions in which the offender serves his sentence, and must be conceived as a process which starts on the offender's reception into custody, is developed during his sentence, and is available for as long as necessary after his release. (Quoted in Monger 1967: 2–3)

Except in the case of life-sentenced prisoners, and later with some high-risk sexual offenders, this was never effectively implemented. The probation service developed the notion of throughcare in recognition of the need for greater collaboration between prison- and community-based staff to provide an individualised service to prisoners, but the task was a huge one requiring enormous institutional changes and resources which were not forthcoming (Haxby 1978). The institutional setting made it unlikely that a high priority would be given to establishing a bespoke service aimed at creating the conditions for prisoners to discover ways of setting realistic objectives for themselves with a view to motivating them to change, as envisaged by the Younger Report in 1974. Indeed, the National Association of Probation Officers (NAPO) adopted a policy in 1981 of supporting the withdrawal of probation officers from working in prisons in order to free up resources for wholehearted provision of throughcare by community-based probation officers. This policy resulted partly from the view that the probation presence in prisons had failed to exert any significant positive influence upon regimes (Williams 1991; NAPO 1994).

Indeed, aftercare or throughcare work was explicitly downgraded with the publication of the Statement of National Objectives and Priorities by the Home Office in 1984. Throughcare became increasingly bureaucratised and impersonal (Williams 1992), characterised in particular by 'poor preparation for release, lack of effective communication between prison and probation, limited practical assistance and a strong focus on the enforcement of attendance requirements' (Maguire and Raynor 2006: 21). However, it remained obvious that:

> To the offender, any helper who arrives on the scene after sentence is all over, arrives at precisely the time when he wants help least. (Monger *et al.* 1981: preface)

Not surprisingly, then, the idea of throughcare re-emerged subsequently. Under the 1991 Criminal Justice Act, every prisoner serving over 12 months should have been interviewed early in their sentences to agree a set of targets which would then be reviewed annually. This was seen as over-ambitious even for the more serious, long-term offender (Hirschmann 1996) and it was not implemented consistently in England and Wales,[2] despite the publication of national standards (Prison Service 1994). Effective implementation of this policy would have required an enormous injection of extra resources which was never forthcoming. In some areas it was introduced for longer-term prisoners, but this depended upon the commitment of senior staff both in prisons and in probation areas, which was not always in place (Williams 1995b).

Throughcare had another apparent revival at the turn of the century, partly as a result of the findings of academic research and a joint report by the inspectorates of prisons and probation, but more due to the influence of a report by the Social Exclusion Unit published in 2002 (Maguire and Raynor 2006). Part of the justification for the introduction of the National Offender Management Service in 2004 was prisoner throughcare, now under the guise of the 'seamless sentence' which is supposed to integrate interventions with offenders in prison with those available post-release (Gough 2005). One wonders whether it will have any greater success in being implemented on this occasion than in the past, particularly given the controversy surrounding the most recent reorganisations of the probation service and the 'potentially negative impact of "contestability" on relational continuity' between prisoners and community-based service staff (Maguire and Raynor 2006: 19; see also Burke 2005; Mantle 2006; PBA 2005).

The impact of managerialism

Since the early 1980s public services have been subjected to:

> a regime of efficiency and value-for-money, performance targets and auditing, quality of service and consumer responsiveness ... [as part of] an explicit ... attempt to inject into public criminal

justice agencies private sector 'disciplines' and ways of doing things. (Loader and Sparks 2002: 88)

In the context of prison probation work, these trends have manifested themselves in the long gestation of the National Offender Management Service (NOMS) which, while ostensibly intended to introduce integrated service delivery (or 'seamless offender management') by prison and probation services, may be more likely in practice to lead to 'fragmentation of services [… by] introducing a purchaser/ provider split' (Burke 2005: 21).

There has also been a continuous process since the 1980s of reducing the autonomy of professional staff such as prison and field probation officers and requiring them to enforce increasingly inflexible government national standards which can impede their ability to form fruitful relationships with the offenders under their supervision. Field probation officers are increasingly required to return ex-prisoners to court for technical breaches of the requirements of their supervision, to such an extent that some commentators fear that:

We will not so much be promoting desistance as making the 'revolving door' an official requirement. (Maguire and Raynor 2006: 33)

This has, inevitably, constrained probation officers' freedom to deliver what they view as an appropriate, high-quality service in the prison setting as elsewhere. However, the introduction of increased competition between service providers ('contestability') is presented by the Home Office as providing opportunities for innovation, better coordination and improved services to prisoners (Home Office 2006). This is discussed in the following sections.

Programmes and one-to-one work: relationships with prisoners

At one time, it was often difficult to fill prison probation officer vacancies: many qualified staff preferred to work in the community, where they could employ their training to devise and deliver treatment packages aimed at keeping offenders out of custody. Partly because of the impact of changes in the 'field' probation task, this has changed since the 1990s: indeed, many probation officers volunteer to undertake secondments to prison establishments because they feel that they have more flexibility to engage with prisoners in constructive professional relationships.

The use of the discourse of 'relationships' has fluctuated over the years: for a time in the mid-1990s this terminology was frowned upon (in the period when probation was trying to avoid incurring further wrath from politicians, such as Michael Howard during his time in office as Home Secretary, who seemed to see social work trained probation officers as part of the crime problem rather than part of its solution). It has more recently come back into fashion, however, with the growing realisation that many of the objectives of cognitive-behavioural work depend upon a degree of trust and respect being developed between workers and their clients:

> We know that some of the key features of successful programmes, for example prosocial modelling and reflective listening, are dependent on the quality of the relationship. (Vanstone 2000: 176; see also Rex 1999, Farrall 2002 and Burnett and McNeill 2005)

Prison probation officers have almost always had high caseloads and been forced to be selective about providing services to prisoners. In some cases, they have chosen to work intensively with high-risk offenders, even dealing with issues relating to prisoners' own previous victimisation where this might be a way into working on the impact of their crimes upon victims (Webb and Williams 2000).

As mentioned above, many prisoners want little to do with the probation service, but they may see the benefits of cooperating when (for example) parole and home leave reports are needed, or when required to take part in accredited group work. Non-uniformed staff who carry keys are often viewed with suspicion despite their relative independence of the prison hierarchy. Recent changes dictated by managerialist imperatives have increasingly meant that the probation role is more one of 'case manager' than direct case worker.

There is some evidence, though, that probation officers faced with the introduction of NOMS are reluctant to 'accept a case management role' at all (Burke 2005: 21, citing Minkes *et al.* 2005), but prison-based probation staff have little discretion in this respect, although it is far from clear how prisons will be accountable to regional offender managers or how integrated working arrangements between prison and field staff will be ensured. The government's 'contestability prospectus' does, however, give some indications of possible implications for practice (Home Office 2006). Arguing that partnerships offer prospects for improved and better-coordinated services, it gives examples of existing successful partnership arrangements. The possible implications of 'contestability' are discussed in the final section below.

Relationships with uniformed staff

Prisons are slow to change, even in response to legislation. An obvious example of this was in relation to 'cross-posting', the policy whereby male uniformed staff were increasingly sent to work in female establishments and vice versa in response to equal opportunities legislation and legal cases after 1988. The POA resisted this process of integration, ostensibly on the grounds of protecting the privacy and decency of prisoners. The assumptions underlying this opposition went largely unchallenged and cross-posting was implemented, at least at first, in a tokenistic way. Meanwhile, 'female officers [were] often only conditionally allowed into the pervasive [male] officer subculture' (Enterkin 1998: 34). Thus any attempt at substantial change within prisons has to involve negotiation with the powerful interests involved (often including prisoners themselves) and tends to result in a compromise.

Prison probation teams, once predominantly male in both male and female prisons, have more recently come to reflect the balance of the probation service as a whole more accurately, with a preponderance of female officers. Thus more than half of all probation officers, including those working in prisons, are women. The great majority of psychologists are, too. This has major implications for work with male prisoners. There is a dissonance between working, in groups and individually, to challenge male sexual offenders' derogatory attitudes towards women and children, while they are living in the sexist male culture of a men's prison. 'Pro-rape attitudes' (Cowburn 1998: 240) are common enough outside prisons (Amnesty 2005), but they are widespread in men's prisons. Combined with a minority view among male staff that women have no place working in male prisons and with the widespread acceptability of sexist remarks to and about women staff, such attitudes can present a major barrier to effective group work in prisons:

> Separating programme content and programme delivery from the culture and ambience of the prison as a whole may merely indicate to sex offenders on programmes that they have to learn

one language for the therapy group and retain another for their daily life inside the prison and beyond its gates. (Cowburn 1998: 246; see also Genders and Player 1995)

Working in prisons is stressful, for uniformed and other staff. Factors such as aggression from inmates, staff shortages and poor communication have long been known to contribute to low morale among prison officers. More recently, poor publicity about corruption and drug smuggling cannot have helped prison officer morale (*The Times* 2006). Another factor is the need to suppress one's feelings, leading to 'emotional dissonance' (Rutter and Fielding 1988; Abraham 1998: 138). Ultimately, experiencing such dissonance day in and day out can lead to emotional exhaustion and burn-out. This is likely to apply almost equally to probation staff and prison officers – but probation officers at least have regular opportunities to get out of prisons during their working day (although less so than at one time in some institutions, now that prison governors have so much control over their work).

The differences in occupational culture already touched upon can themselves produce emotional dissonance, or what in sociological terms is called role strain: one of the groups probation officers may decide they have to be careful about showing their true feelings to the uniformed staff. The traditional hostility of a minority of prison officers towards 'civilian' workers (which goes back at least to the 1950s; see Foren and Bailey 1968; Priestley 1972) has to do partly with prison officers' 'canteen culture', which is a way of promoting solidarity and preserving safety in a hostile environment. Probation officers work to promote particular values which may be at variance with prison officers' occupational culture; there may well be differences of view, for example, about the relative importance of prisoners' opportunities for contacts with their families, or the likelihood that individual or group work with prisoners can ever lead to positive change. Probation officers are highly likely to be more sceptical about the usefulness or positive potential of imprisonment; prison officers may well view them as 'soft' and easily manipulated by inmates. Nevertheless, probation officers have security responsibilities which may produce further dissonance for them.

Prisons vary enormously. In some institutions probation officers act as treatment managers and as such they directly supervise the work of prison officers. Where senior probation officers serve as Head of Resettlement, the same applies.

Relationships with other specialist staff

Perhaps inevitably, relations between prison probation staff and prison psychologists are characterised by some tensions in certain institutions. The two groups have different occupational cultures. While they can and do work harmoniously together, there is scope for conflict over issues such as who is qualified to do what kinds of work, the relative importance of risk to the public and risk to individual prisoners, and the need to service the prison bureaucracy. From a probation perspective, psychologists tend to regard themselves as treatment professionals, implying that they can legitimately avoid sitting on boards and committees; they see prisoners as their clients and may consequently be less inclined to emphasise risk to the public than probation staff, and they sometimes feel that they are uniquely qualified to act as treatment managers, regardless of the experience probation staff may have in this field.

Despite these tensions, probation officers and psychologists work as co-tutors on groups such as Enhanced Thinking Skills and the Sex Offender Treatment Programme (Clarke *et al.* 2004; Friendship *et al.* 2003) and they are jointly involved in the risk assessment of individual prisoners. In certain prisons without a full-time senior psychologist presence, probation officers provide professional supervision to junior psychologists delivering group work programmes with uniformed staff.

What might the future hold?

The precise role of probation officers working in prisons has been unclear for some time. As the historical discussion above has shown, it has changed enormously over the years. A probation inspectorate thematic report in 1996 expressed concern about the lack of specific terms of reference; as a result, a working group was set up and in 1998 a prison service instruction and a probation circular were published. Among other things, they required prison governors to define the work of seconded probation officers in their establishments (Home Office 1998: 2). This document is no longer widely available within prison probation departments, however; in practice there appear to be very wide disparities between practice in one prison and another. A good deal is at the discretion of prison governors, who reach service level agreements with probation management to define the probation team's role. In practice, field probation officers considering moving into prison work find out what is involved in discussion with the team's senior officer.

The prison probation officers with whom the content of this chapter was discussed were enthusiastic about their role and compared it favourably with field probation work, which they saw as considerably more circumscribed by detailed and prescriptive national policies than their own jobs.

As noted above, the NOMS contestability prospectus highlighted a number of areas in which effective partnerships were said to be operating between prisons and outside agencies in the delivery of resettlement programmes, with the particular examples of Blakenhurst and Bristol prisons cited (Home Office 2006: 8–9).

Given the history recounted earlier in this chapter, it is hardly surprising that prisoner resettlement remains under-developed. Despite the glowing words in the Home Office prospectus, for example, praise for resettlement provision in Blakenhurst has to be seen in the context of a recent unannounced inspection report which praised the 'extensive' resettlement programme but expressed concern about its lack of targets or measures of success, the selectiveness of its provision and its heavy reliance upon external funding. The report also noted that the prison's resettlement strategy 'contained nothing specifically for the short-term population' (HMIP 2006: 69), which is a particular concern given the greater risk of reoffending among this group (Harding and Harding 2006). The resettlement project praised by the Home Office appears to emphasise meeting prisoners' housing needs on release, although the partnerships formed include links with Relate, Citizen's Advice, job centres and Reed Learning (Allender et al. 2006). This suggests that probation staff, along with others working in prisons, may in future find themselves spending much more time brokering such partnership agreements than delivering direct services to inmates or even coordinating the sentence planning in relation to individual prisoners.

The partnership at Bristol and Eastwood Park prisons is with a private company. A pilot drug intervention project 'run by UKDS (part of the Sodexho Alliance group of companies) works with challenging offenders who need intensive support post-release' (Home Office 2006: 9). The short-term prisoners who volunteer to take part in the project are met on release and escorted to the project's hostel where they undertake a full-time 12-week programme, during which they undergo regular drugs tests. All being well, they then move on to a social housing tenancy, supported in the community by project staff for a further six months. The local probation service had some involvement in setting up the scheme at the outset, but appears to be only peripherally involved now that it is established. However, it is about to extend its eligibility criteria to prisoners serving up to 18 months, at which time prison probation officers may need to become more centrally involved.

In some prisons, the European Social Fund matched prison service funding to provide new employment and resettlement services ('Prison Service Plus') from 2004. The new services are provided mostly by voluntary sector agencies and are applicable only to certain categories of inmates. Managing these contracts has proved complex and time-consuming, and some in the probation service feel that they duplicated services already provided by prison probation teams. Some prisons are believed to have been financially penalised because the projects failed to meet their performance targets. If this was an experiment in 'contestability', it appears to provide a rather unfortunate precedent in some ways.

The private sector is clearly keen to become more involved in the delivery of offender services, including those for prisoners. Indeed, in the summer of 2006 the Confederation of British Industry expressed its impatience at the slow pace of 'harnessing the strengths of providers from all sectors through extending competition' since the establishment of NOMS two years earlier (CBI 2006: 1). The following month, the government's contestability prospectus was published, containing some of the same examples of partnership working as the CBI document. It is clear that the Home Office shares the enthusiasm of industry for these developments, so this is likely to lead to substantial changes in the role of the prison probation officer and senior probation officer – along with changes in the roles of other public sector workers – in the immediate future.

Seminar questions

1 How influential has the historical development of prison probation work been upon the nature and type of services delivered to prisoners?
2 There are passing references in the chapter to the respective roles of prison psychologists and prison probation staff. What consequences are the competing claims to expertise of these two disciplines likely to have for the delivery of effective group work within prisons?
3 How might the introduction of 'contestability' and the creation of NOMS ensure that prisoners are finally provided with 'seamless' services such as accommodation and employment advice – and supervised effectively upon release?

Recommended reading

Perhaps significantly, very little has been written about prison probation work in the last decade. There is a particular lack of accounts by practitioners. However, the chapter by David Webb and Brian Williams (2000) 'Violent Men in Prison: Confronting Offending Behaviours Without Denying Prior Victimization', in Hazel Kemshall and Jacki Pritchard, *Good Practice in Working with Victims of Violence*, was an attempt to fill part of that gap.

The literature on desistance and resettlement, although rarely referring directly to the role of prison probation officers, has clear implications for their possible part in contributing to successful resettlement: see, for example, Maurice Vanstone's (2000) 'Cognitive-Behavioural Work with Offenders in the UK: A History of Influential Endeavour' and Mike Maguire and Peter Raynor's (2006) 'How the Resettlement of Prisoners Promotes Desistance from Crime – or Does It?'

The references to work with prisoners in the Home Office 'contestability prospectus' may prove significant in terms of the future direction of the work, as suggested in the final section of the chapter, above: see Home Office (2006) *Improving Prison and Probation Services: Public Value Partnerships.*

Notes

1 I should like to thank Paul Allender, Roy Bailey, Rob Canton, Matt Muller and Maurice Vanstone for their assistance in the preparation of this chapter, as well as the prison probation officers who did not wish to be identified.
2 Specifically in relation to sexual offenders released from custody in Scotland: see Spencer (1999): chapter 10.

References

Abraham, R. (1998) 'Emotional Dissonance in Organizations: A Conceptualization of Consequences, Mediators and Moderators', *Leadership and Organization Development Journal*, 19 (3): 137–46.

Allender, P., Brown, G., Bailey, N., Colombo, T., Poole, H. and Saldana, A. (2006) *Prisoner Resettlement and Housing Provision: A Good Practice Ideas Guide.* Coventry: Centre for Social Justice, Coventry University.

Amnesty International UK (2005) 'UK: New Poll Finds a Third of People Believe Women who Flirt Partially Responsible for Being Raped'. Press release, 21 November at http://www.amnesty.org.uk/news_details. asp?NewsID=16618 (accessed 2 August 2006).

Ashe, M. (1993) 'Meeting Prisoners' Needs Through Groupwork', in A. Brown and B. Caddick (eds), *Groupwork with Offenders.* London: Whiting & Birch.

Avon and Somerset Probation Area (2006) 'Prisons', including section on 'What probation staff do in prison'. Available at: http://www.aspa-online.org.uk/Main/default.asp?t=prisons&a=view (accessed 21 September 2006).

Burke, L. (2005) *From Probation to the National Offender Management Service: Issues of Contestability, Culture and Community Involvement*. ICCJ Monograph 6. London: NAPO.

Burnett, R. and McNeill, F. (2005) 'The Place of the Officer–Offender Relationship in Assisting Offenders to Desist from Crime', *Probation Journal*, 52 (3): 221–42.

Cheney, D. (2005) 'Prisons', in C. Hale, K. Hayward, A. Wahidin and E. Wincup (eds), *Criminology*. Oxford: Oxford University Press, pp. 547–66.

Clarke, A., Simmonds, R. and Wydall, S. (2004) 'Delivering Cognitive Skills Programmes in Prison: A Qualitative Study', *Findings*, 242. London: Home Office RDSD.

Confederation of British Industry (2006) *Protecting the Public: Partnership in Offender Management*. London: CBI.

Cowburn, M. (1998) 'A Man's World: Gender Issues in Working with Male Sex Offenders in Prison', *Howard Journal*, 37 (3): 234–51.

Cranfield, R.E.G. (1982) *One Hundred Years of Prisoners' Aid in County Durham 1882–1982*. Durham: North Eastern Prison After Care Society.

Enterkin, J. (1998) 'Prison Service Cross-Posting Policy and Female Prison Officers', *Prison Service Journal*, 117: 32–5.

Evans, R. *et al.* (1988) *Prisoners' Welfare and Social Work Procedures: An Evaluation of the Shared Working Scheme at Stocken Prison 1985–1988*. DPS Report, series 1, no. 30. London: Prison Department.

Farrall, S. (2002) *Re-thinking What Works with Offenders: Probation, Social Control and Desistance from Crime*. Cullompton: Willan.

Foren, R. and Bailey, R. (1968) *Authority in Social Casework*. Oxford: Pergamon.

Friendship, C., Mann, R. and Beech, A. (2003) 'The Prison-Based Sex Offender Treatment Programme – an evaluation', *Findings*, 205. London: Home Office RDSD.

Genders, E. and Player, E. (1995) *Grendon: A Study of a Therapeutic Prison*. Oxford: Oxford University Press.

Gough, D. (2005) '"Tough on Probation": Probation Practice under the National Offender Management Service', in J. Winstone and F. Pakes (eds), *Community Justice: Issues for Probation and Criminal Justice*. Cullompton: Willan.

Harding, A. and Harding, J. (2006) 'Inclusion and Exclusion in the Re-housing of Former Prisoners', *Probation Journal*, 53 (2): 137–53.

Haxby, D. (1978) *Probation: A Changing Service*. London: Constable.

Hirschmann, D. (1996) 'Parole and the Dangerous Offender', in N. Walker (ed.), *Dangerous People*. London: Blackstone.

HM Inspectorate of Prisons (2006) *Report on a Full Unannounced Inspection of HMP Blakenhurst, 30 November – 9 December 2005*. London: HMIP.

Home Office (1967) *The Role and Functions of the Prison Welfare Officer*, Home Office Circular 130/1967, 31 July. London: Home Office.

Home Office (1984) *Statement of National Objectives and Priorities*. London: Home Office.

Home Office (1998) *Prison Service Instruction on Effective Implementation of Throughcare*, Probation Circular 63/1997, 19 January. London: Home Office Probation Unit.

Home Office (2006) *Improving Prison and Probation Services: Public Value Partnerships*. London: National Offender Management Service.

Loader, I. and Sparks, R. (2002) 'Contemporary Landscapes of Crime', in M. Maguire, R. Morgan and R. Reiner (eds), *The Oxford Handbook of Criminology*, 3rd edn. Oxford: Oxford University Press.

McConville, S. (1981) *A History of English Prison Administration Volume 1: 1750–1877*. London: Routledge & Kegan Paul.

Maguire, M. and Raynor, P. (2006) 'How the Resettlement of Prisoners Promotes Desistance from Crime – or Does It?', *Criminology and Criminal Justice*, 6 (1): 19–38.

Mantle, G. (2006) 'Counterblast: Probation: Dead or Dying?', *Howard Journal of Criminal Justice*, 45 (3): 321.

Maxwell Committee (1953) *Report of the Committee on Discharged Prisoners' Aid Societies*, Cmd. 8879. London: HMSO.

Minkes, J., Hammersley, R. and Raynor, P. (2005) 'Partnership in Working with Young Offenders with Substance Misuse Problems', *Howard Journal of Criminal Justice*, 44 (3): 254–68.

Monger, M. (1967) *Casework in After-Care*. London: Butterworths.

Monger, M., Pendleton, J. and Roberts, J. (1981) *Throughcare with Prisoners' Families*, Social Work Studies No. 3. Nottingham: University of Nottingham Department of Social Administration and Social Work.

National Association of Probation Officers (1994) *Draft Policy on Throughcare*, Professional Committee paper P63-4. London: NAPO.

National Probation Directorate (2002) *The Treatment and Risk Management of Sexual Offenders in Custody and in the Community*. London: NPD. Available at: http://www.probation.homeoffice.gov.uk/files/pdf/The%20Treatment%20and%20Risk%20Management%20of%20Sexual%20Offenders (accessed 21 September 2006).

Player, E. and Jenkins, M. (eds) (1994) *Prisons After Woolf: Reform Through Riot*. London: Routledge.

Priestley, P. (1972) 'The Prison Welfare Officer: A Case of Role Strain', *British Journal of Sociology*, 23: 221–35.

Priestley, P. (1999) *Victorian Prison Lives*. London: Pimlico.

Prison Service (1994) *National Framework for the Throughcare of Offenders in Custody to the Completion of Supervision in the Community*. London: Home Office.

Probation Boards' Association (2005) *PBA Response to 'Re-structuring Probation'*. London: PBA.

Rex, S. (1999) 'Desistance from Offending – Experiences of Probation', *Howard Journal of Criminal Justice*, 38 (4): 366–83.

Rutter, D.R. and Fielding, P.J. (1988) 'Sources of Occupational Stress: An Examination of British Prison Officers', *Work and Stress*, 2 (4): 291–9.

Serge, V. (1931/1977) *Men in Prison*. London: Writers and Readers Publishing Cooperative.

Sim, J. (1994) 'Reforming the Penal Wasteland? A Critical View of the Woolf Report', in E. Player and M. Jenkins (eds) *Prisons After Woolf: Reform through Riot*. London: Routledge.

Spencer, A. (1999) *Working with Sex Offenders in Prisons and through Release to the Community*. London: Jessica Kingsley.

The Times (2006) 'Prison Take: Corruption Threatens the Foundations of the Criminal Justice System', leading article, 9 September, p. 4. Available at: http://www.timesonline.co.uk/article/0,,542-2349381.html 9accessed 2 October 2006).

Vanstone, M. (2000) 'Cognitive-Behavioural Work with Offenders in the UK: A History of Influential Endeavour', *Howard Journal of Criminal Justice*, 39 (2): 171–83.

Webb, D. and Williams, B. (2000) 'Violent Men in Prison: Confronting Offending Behaviours without Denying Prior Victimization', in H. Kemshall and J. Pritchard (eds), *Good Practice in Working with Victims of Violence*. London: Jessica Kingsley.

Williams, B. (1991) *Work with Prisoners*. Birmingham: Venture Press.

Williams, B. (1992) 'Caring Professionals or Street-level Bureaucrats? The Case of Probation Officers' Work with Prisoners', *Howard Journal of Criminal Justice*, 31 (4): 263–75

Williams, B. (1995a) 'Social work with prisoners in England and Wales: from missionary zeal to street-level bureaucracy', in J. Schwieso and P. Pettit (eds), *Aspects of the History of British Social Work*. Reading: Faculty of Education and Community Studies, University of Reading, pp. 21–65.

Williams, B. (1995b) 'Towards Justice in Probation Work with Prisoners', in D. Ward and M. Lacey (eds), *Probation: Working for Justice*. London: Whiting & Birch.

Williams, B. and Eadie, T. (1994) 'The Contribution of Prison-based Bail Information Schemes to Better Jobs', *Prison Service Journal*, 93: 27–30.

Chapter 17

Teachers and instructors in prisons

Phil Bayliss and Shirley Hughes

Introduction

Teachers and instructors in prison can help to motivate, support and encourage some of the most vulnerable people in this country. HM Chief Inspector of Prisons has stated that more people are being treated for substance misuse problems, helped with mental health difficulties and taught basic skills in our prisons than in any other public institution (Owers 2005). Combined with the paramount importance of security, these are just some of the challenges that demand more than patience, understanding and good humour from staff. High-level quality training is essential for all educators in prisons if they are to facilitate the cause of learners, who, as Uden states, are: '... likely to have the most to gain by engagement in education and training, while being the least likely to have benefited [in the past] or to benefit in the future' (Uden 2003: 2).

In this chapter, we discuss the training, professionalisation and motives of this sometimes forgotten group of teachers and instructors whose motivation for working in prisons is examined. The particular nature of education in prison is analysed in relation to its recent history while identifying benefits to the institution and the prisoner learners. We argue that emphasis on basic skills and the focus on efficiency targets has narrowed the curriculum. However, this trend is contrasted by some imaginative activities developed by dedicated teachers and instructors. The chapter is drawn from an accumulation of data from several years of teaching and researching in male local and training prisons in the South West of England. Semi-structured interviews, focus groups and questionnaires were carried out with teachers, managers, instructors and prisoners. Pseudonyms are used to protect individual respondents and their institutions.

The recent history and development of prisoner education

Changes in the range and content of learning opportunities in prison over several decades have resulted from tensions between financial resources and political interventions which relate to shifts in thinking about the function of prisons and the purposes of learning.

Two-thirds of prisoners are unemployed at the time of imprisonment (DfES 2005), and an estimated 60 per cent of people in prison suffer from what Moser (DfES 1999: 10) terms 'functional illiteracy and/or innumeracy'. Sixty-one per cent of all released prisoners reoffend within two years (DfES 2005), and this failure to halt reoffending costs the criminal justice system an average of £65,000 per person up to the point of reimprisonment and, subsequently, about £37,500 per year in prison. If the government's target to reduce reoffending by 10 per cent is achieved by 2010, it will save £1 billion a year (Gamble 2006). Although, given the overall social needs and profiles of most prisoners, education is only one of many factors that is likely to aid desistance and resettlement – it is important to emphasise that a prison sentence is a debilitating experience and should never be used as an excuse for rehabilitation (Coyle 2005) – raising levels of literacy and numeracy among prisoners seems likely to assist them greatly in finding stable employment and desisting from crime (Social Exclusion Unit 2002). It is with such aims in mind that the government's budget for education and training in prisons has risen from £56.7 million in 2001/2 to £151 million in 2005/6 (DfES 2005).

Only recently have education and training been brought together under the same planning body, the Learning and Skills Council (LSC). In the 1940s a Prisoners' Education Advisory Committee report separated vocational training and physical education, which was taught by Prison Service staff, from what was then known as Education – liberal education or learning for pleasure (Elsdon 2001). Education departments were staffed by employees of local education authorities (LEAs), most of whom worked for further education (FE) colleges. When a Director of Education was appointed by the Prison Service in 1961, there were full-time education officers in 29 institutions for an education service of evening classes only. All other organisers and teachers in prisons were part-time or volunteers. As recognition of the value of education in prison rose over the years (Baynes and Marks 1996), so the range and availability of classes increased. However, the curriculum content and divisions of staffing created some resentment, as one prison officer illustrated:

> When I first joined the Prison Service in 1987, education was looked on as an inconvenience by most of the [prison] staff, and this took a long time to change. The officers were against the idea of education for prisoners, and most avoided the Education Block ... The courses on offer were limited to Art, Pottery and Music, with none geared towards rehabilitation or gaining employment on release. Education seemed a way for prisoners to get out of their cells. (Edwin)

Circumstances changed when the 1992 Further and Higher Education Act removed FE colleges from the control of LEAs. Learning then became a competitive commodity, with prison education contracts put out to tender and the majority won by FE colleges. Liberal education, mainly arts and crafts, began to be replaced by accredited academic courses until 1997 when a Core Curriculum was introduced. This focused on Skills for Life – literacy, numeracy, English as a second or other language (ESOL), information and communications technology (ICT), key work skills and social skills. With the advent of this new functional curriculum, it was a natural progression to introduce centralised targets. The first Key Performance Indicator aimed for a reduction of 15 per cent of prisoners being discharged at Level 1[1] or below by March 2002. This national target (KPT) was exclusively focused on the numbers of prisoners to achieve Level 2[2] Communications and Numeracy in each prison. Criticism led to 'a more rounded set of targets' (SEU 2002: 45) where Level 1 and Entry Levels were included, but none for Level 3 or Higher Education. Pursuit of these targets for efficiency and hence funding gains led to widespread abuse (Bayliss 2003), where, for example, graduate prisoners would be included in Basic Skills assessments.

In a national prison survey it was these targets that raised more responses than any other issue (Braggins 2002). Governors, education managers and contractors generally considered that these changes had enhanced the importance of education and created greater cooperation within the prison. Others criticised this adherence to value-free managerialism where what can be measured becomes valorised at the expense of recognising the worth of what *should* be assessed, for example:

The *new effectiveness-plus* agenda consists of standards for all
aspects of work; ... regimes and programmes which are subject
to accreditation; reducing reoffending as a key outcome (by
certain restricted and 'approved' methods); best value from
resources ... (Liebling 2004: 40; emphasis in original)

This prevailing target-setting agenda was identified by Rutherford
(1993) as the 'efficiency' credo, along with two others: a 'punishment'
credo based on moral condemnation and a 'care' credo which
emphasises humanitarian values. All three credos can fluctuate
according to current political and social climates, yet the caring values
of the third credo, prevalent among teachers and instructors, can sit
uncomfortably with the other two beliefs. This was exemplified by
the stripping of educational provision to the point where in many
prisons there were no courses beyond the core curriculum, a situation
exacerbated by the burgeoning psychology programmes that drew
on a North American correctional ethos. An education manager
illustrated the effects of this development in 2002:

There has been an enormous amount of funding for Offending
Behaviour courses. So they have proliferated and cut across most
other activities that are happening. A Psychology department of
nil has grown to 20 plus; so now it is a large activity within
prison. In that same period we've seen a catering course, a
builders' course and an IT course disappear. (Horatio)

To redress the balance in the curriculum a new partnership between
the Home Office and the Department for Education and Skills (DfES)
called the Prisoners' Learning and Skills Unit (PLSU) was formed
in 2001. Its aim was to combine the DfES objective of widening
participation with the Home Office's drive to reduce reoffending.
    Ringfencing the budget allocation for education in prisons was
one of the PLSU's first duties. The PLSU evolved into the Offenders'
Learning and Skills Unit (OLSU) which initiated Project Rex, a
programme to introduce new contracts alongside education and
vocational training courses in prisons for the first time. However,
following the publication of the Carter Report (2003) a new National
Offender Management Service (NOMS) was established in 2004.
Project Rex was curtailed and replaced by a new regional Offender
Learning and Skills Service (OLASS). Around this time new Heads of
Learning and Skills (HoLS) were appointed to Prison Service senior
management positions in each prison to oversee the education contract

and to promote learning and skills throughout their institutions. At the present time, offenders both in custody and the community are the responsibility of OLASS with their education and training planned and funded by the LSC, the agency accountable for all non-higher post-16 learning.

The focus of OLASS is to give the offender an initial assessment, then advice and guidance leading to the production of an individual learning plan. *The Offender's Learning Journey* (DfES 2004), with separate juvenile and adult versions, outlines what has been described as a 'broader, deeper curriculum' (Halsey *et al*. 2006: 9). The intended outcomes are that half of all offenders will participate in education and training which should enhance their employability, though problems need to be addressed here, including the lower pay in some establishments for education compared to jobs in the workshops. The current education provision, which was described as 'unacceptable' by a Select Committee (HoC 2005), allows access to learning for less than one-third of prisoners. Moreover, leadership and management in more than half the prisons inspected were considered poor by the Adult Learning Inspectorate in their annual report (ALI 2006a). Initial evaluations of the implementation of OLASS (Halsey *et al*. 2006) indicate that the transfer of offender education records and communications between the various agencies involved will need to be improved, and prisoners' access to learning through the Internet should be enhanced/explored. However, other aspects of the curriculum are becoming more creative.

Innovations within the curriculum

Within this functional curriculum, imaginative teachers and trainers have brought innovations in offender learning. Many of these are celebrated as case studies in Nashashibi *et al*. (2006) where they are classified as 'motivation', 'partnership and collaboration' and 'supporting transition'. Examples of the projects include running a radio station, a National Gallery art programme, and a kitchen-fitting course. The curriculum has been inspected by the Adult Learning Inspectorate (ALI) – or Ofsted in the case of juvenile offenders – since 2002, whose website details inventive prison projects in its Good Practice section (ALI 2006b). These include *Storybook Dads* where stories are read by prisoners, professionally recorded with music and sound effects, then sent home to their children, and the Toe-by-Toe peer tutoring scheme where prisoners teach others to read, offering skills and increased self-esteem to both mentor and mentee.[3] There are also many examples of how learning is embedded into other activities such as fitness testing to improve ICT skills and challenging racist attitudes through sport. Some sessions have subtle ways of teaching social skills such as a unit with a high proportion of travellers[4] which started a pilot horse-whispering scheme. Here, prisoners were taught to manage their own anger before learning to work with horses (McDonald 2006). These innovative projects take learning beyond the arid and narrow demands of education-as-rehabilitation and the new effectiveness-plus agenda to offer the humanitarian values of the 'care credo' vision of prisoner education.

The benefits of education and training

Education and training should foster personal development opportunities for prisoners. Added to the benefits already described, further advantages of adult learning include better physical and mental health and greater happiness (Schuller *et al*. 2004). A distinction can be made between the 'hard' outcomes of learning – gaining certificates, achieving qualifications and getting employment – with 'soft' outcomes concerned with emotions and attitudes. It is these 'soft' outcomes that McGivney (2002) argues are most frequently mentioned as learning gains by adults. This is illustrated by a prisoner who explained his feelings after passing an Access to Higher Education programme:

> Yes, I think it's an achievement passing the Access course. It doesn't really count for a lot … for me personally, with a 20-year criminal record with a history of drug abuse – I'm not very highly desirable. But it's given me more hope for the future, do you know what I mean? And it's given me self-esteem and confidence, and it's hard to say, but it's still pretty bad now, but it's increasing a little bit. (Cuthbert)

Although this prisoner underplayed the hard outcomes of passing the course, this had not deterred him from enrolling in a Natural Science degree with the Open University. Opportunities such as this should be extended to cater for the 56 per cent of prisoners with a sentence of four years or more (APPG 2004: 10) and other prisoners who might have learning requirements beyond Level 2. In addition a wider curriculum, which includes, say, creative arts, might encourage disaffected learners back into education and develop those soft outcomes of self-confidence and esteem as well as showing how leisure time can be spent.

For educators to inspire all learners in this way requires a particular view of learning. The concept of 'banking education' where information is transferred to a passive learner was dismissed by the Brazilian educator Paulo Freire (1996). In contrast, Freire espoused 'conscientization', the notion of actively constructing concepts and understandings through a process of problem-solving and reflection. The American humanist, Jack Mezirow (1991), has developed these ideas of critical education and argued that learning occurs through a series of changes of meaning and accumulates to form new outlooks, or what he calls 'perspective transformation' which can lead to major life changes. This mode of learning is important for prisoners who want to transform their lifestyles or identities. Equally, teachers and instructors in prison should be aware of these effects:

> Critical education is not merely concerned with the acquisition of skills and the upgrading of qualifications, but with significant change in capacity and understanding. (Costelloe and Warner 2005: 17)

When active, supportive, learning such as this is continued in other parts of the prison it can have a calming influence through activity and good communication: 'An establishment with an active education and training programme tends to be more peaceful and easier to manage' (Forster 1998: 2).

This notion of learning offering hope and relief for the prisoner as well as contributing calm to the prison was illustrated by an education manager who described her prison education department as 'an oasis in a pretty bleak environment' (Ada). Nevertheless, Wilson (2000) warns that education should not be considered as a management tool – a means of simply 'preventing idle hands from making mischief' (p. 11). This requires vigilant and enthusiastic staff.

Teaching and instructing in prison

Most teachers in prisons who are employed by FE colleges are part-time, hourly paid or on fixed-term contracts, in a sector which is becoming increasingly casualised (NATFHE 2006). They tend to work longer hours than their counterparts on the college campus, without the typical advantages of out-of-term-time holidays, and on average earning £5,000 per annum less (Sellgren 2006). This follows a pattern of teachers in prisons being overlooked within the education sector where they were omitted from a sector pay review, and no mention was made of prisoners' education during the establishment of the Learning and Skills Council (Uden 2003).

Added to these disadvantages, the teaching conditions in prison can be challenging. Behavioural problems can arise from prisoners with substance dependencies, learning difficulties and mental health problems. An extreme example of difficult conditions is a cookery teacher in a Close Supervision Centre (CSC) for the management of dangerous and disruptive prisoners, who had to explain recipes to her students while passing ingredients through the bars of their cells.

Generally, overcrowding leads to disruptive movements of prisoners known as 'the churn' across the estate with little warning, so that in local prisons, in particular, a quarter of an enrolled class can change every week. In addition, other programmes and appointments can compete for prisoners' time in classes. All of these factors can impede teachers' efforts to maintain continuity in learning. Since the typical length of stay in prison is about nine months for men and about six months for women (Uden 2003) the planning of short-term courses is necessary. For example, ten-hour modules in hairdressing, industrial cleaning, and painting and decorating are held at HMP Leeds which has an annual turnover of prisoners five to six times its total population.

Many prisoners might be sceptical about participating in learning having had little success with education at school: 52 per cent of male prisoners and 71 per cent of female prisoners have no qualifications (DfES 2005). Teachers therefore need to motivate prisoners with tact and sensitivity. Sometimes this requires taking the learning out to the wings for those who are wary of revealing any inadequacies to their peers. These are demanding conditions, which require 'imagination to create a positive learning space for a unique learner group. We must be constantly looking to develop our curriculum and develop our pedagogy' (Behan 2005: 6).

Such recommendations were discussed in a major research project into the role of the prison officer in supporting education in prisons (Braggins and Talbot 2005). The project found that in more than two-thirds of the prisons visited, officers were involved in encouraging and supporting prisoner education. Prison officers' recommendations included: more regular communication between them and the education department; targeting those prisoners who need help with basic skills or who show a commitment to learning; career development for those officers who want to teach; and dedicated time to support education and to assist in informal learning. Examples of good education and training practice by prison officers abound in the report including: organising Duke of Edinburgh Award Schemes; running gym-based junior leadership skills courses; and taking 'Prison Me No-Way!!' presentations to local schools.

In everyday terms, prison officers can and do support learning in different ways, as one prisoner stated:

> They've respected that I've been studying in my cell time. So when they come in to do cell searches they see that there's paper everywhere. And I've said, 'Please don't touch that because it's in a certain order and what not.' And they haven't. (Cecil)

Prison officers perceived their role (Braggins and Talbot 2005) primarily in terms of security and discipline. Most officers were timetabled for classes and programmes as part of their operational duties. These included offender behaviour programmes, induction and pre-release courses and drugs programmes. Among other detailed duties could be: suicide awareness, voluntary drugs testing and OASys (Offender Assessment System) management. Despite the pressures of staffing, time and coping with some disturbed and dangerous prisoners, they also had an essential pastoral duty:

> Officers' day-to-day contact with prisoners and the opportunities afforded, as they saw it, to impart a wide range of social and life skills, including communication and inter-personal skills, was clearly seen as an important and integral part of their role. (Braggins and Talbot 2005: 23)

However, a conflict between these disciplinary and education roles has been highlighted for many years (Council of Europe 1990).

In addition to prison officers, civilian teachers and instructors employed by education contractors, there are many others who teach in prison. Foremost among these are the prisoners themselves, often orderlies who assist in Skills for Life and ICT classes, and vocational training workshops, such as Industrial Cleaning, or who teach in the Toe-by-Toe reading scheme. There are other organisations such as the National Association of Prison Visitors (NAOPV) who befriend and support prisoners on request, and charities such as UNLOCK (the National Association of Reformed Offenders) who run financial advice sessions on obtaining and using bank accounts. Moreover, there are a number of groups such as storytellers and actors who teach in prison through drama and music. These people who work with offenders now have the opportunity to develop their own skills and qualifications.

Teacher education and training

There is a government target to accredit teachers and instructors employed by colleges so that: 'By 2010 we would expect only new entrants to FE teaching would not be qualified' (DfES 2002: para. 84). Additionally, the government recommends that all teachers and instructors in prisons should update their skills and gain qualifications (DfES 2005).

In 2001, the University of Plymouth started a teacher education and training programme in a prison in the South West. During that academic year, a government bursary of £6,000 was introduced for all full-time student teachers, prompting a rise in demand for places on university programmes in the UK for a national teaching qualification: the Post-Graduate Certificate in Education (PGCE) or Certificate in Education (Cert. Ed.). A partnership between the University, Strode College (the education contractor) and the Prison Service was created. This was the first time that the Cert. Ed./PGCE student teachers would spend some of their teaching practice in prison. In a brief encounter with the prison regime, each applicant to the programme was invited inside an establishment for an interview, not only to experience the environment but also to meet tutors and prisoners. Some potential teachers changed their minds after finding the episode unnerving, but those accepted on the programme were given a comprehensive course on security by prison officers.

After overcoming some teething problems, the programme was so successful that a specialist module for Teaching and Instructing in Prisons was written by the Education Manager at the prison. It included 'the purposes and values of prisoner education' and the 'roles and duties of teachers and instructors'. Subsequently, part-time Cert. Ed./PGCE programmes were developed which attracted teachers and instructors who were already teaching in prison. These teaching groups then included civilian staff from classrooms and workshops, prison officers and prisoner orderlies who would be teaching their peers. In order to adhere to adult education ideals of teaching among equals, some semblance of equality was engendered. As the prisoners were always last to arrive, the officers (who would remove their epaulettes) and civilian teachers always left a space between them so that the prisoners would mingle among them. Mutual ground rules for the class were created by the members. For the orderlies, the programme presented an opportunity to drop the identity of 'prisoner' and adopt the role of higher education student. The programme was enhancing professionalism, introducing new ideas and raising awareness of education and training within prisons through a range of shared perspectives.

The success of the programme led to a Master's module entitled, Education of Offenders: Teaching and Learning Issues. Prison officers, education managers, experienced teachers, HoLS and other suitably qualified participants who successfully completed the assessed academic study could choose to receive 30 CATs points at MA level or a Certificate in Advanced Professional Studies (CAPS). Policy and practices of education were critically analysed from a spectrum of collective experiences. As well as confirming their professional development, the qualification entitled participants to teach the Cert. Ed./PGCE specialist module in prisoner education so that they could cascade their learning to staff in their own prisons. This is one way of achieving staff development for teachers and managers, raising awareness of prisoner education and engendering professionalisation. Throughout the courses that we taught, we were interested in the participants' reflections on the teaching profession.

Views of teachers and instructors in prison

Stephen Brookfield (1995) states:

> We teach to change the world and our efforts as teachers are about helping students not just to learn but to treat each other and the environment with compassion, understanding, and fairness. (p. 1)

This might sound ambitious, particularly if put into the context of prisoner education, and yet this could be especially relevant to the Statement of Purpose displayed at every prison gate, which states that:

Her Majesty's Prison Service serves the public by keeping in custody those committed by the courts. Our duty is to look after them with humanity and help them lead law-abiding and useful lives in custody and after release.

If Brookfield (1995) is right in his assertion about what motivates people to teach then those working in prisoner education have possibly a greater opportunity to effect change. In teaching the Cert. Ed./PGCE groups we noticed high levels of motivation and commitment to the education of offenders from novice trainees, experienced teachers and instructors alike. Many student teachers, entering prison for the first time to teach, quickly became 'hooked'. Considering some of the issues and constraints previously discussed, such as the lack of resources, limits of the curriculum and the frequent use of short-term contacts, why would anyone continue to teach or instruct in this closed setting? Is this work more rewarding in some way? We decided to explore the issues further with initial focus groups followed by interviews to discover if it *is* about 'changing the world' or having a greater opportunity to make a difference.

The first focus group consisted of teachers within an education department (past and current students). Asked about the constraints of the job, their responses included: a sense of isolation from the 'provider college'; lack of access to the resources available in FE settings; the lack of opportunity for further professional development and support from the employer; feeling 'cut off from decision-makers'; and a feeling that change was imposed 'from above' without consultation. Those participants on short-term contracts (who are paid by the hour) felt that they were treated as supply teachers and that even more demands were made on their time. They sometimes felt that they were used as 'babysitters' to cover when other full-time teachers were absent. Generally, there was a lack of opportunity to learn from more experienced colleagues. Prison staff and educational staff did not often mix together and were not always mutually supportive, although one teacher suggested that attitudes were changing as education was increasingly valued as part of the life in prison. Some of their responses to questions about motivation were as follows:

The rewards of seeing men of all ages lose their fear of Maths and as a by-product improve their self-esteem. To see and hear them rejoice in small successes is a wonderful feeling. (Colin)

I am highly motivated knowing that what I do can make a vast difference to someone's life, not all, but if what I do can make a difference to one it is worthwhile. (Anne)

Good – positive response from students mostly let down by school education. (Jay)

But he thanked me and that made it all worth while ... Will I carry on? I've started now so I'd better finish! There is a very important job to be done. Who else would be crazy enough to do it? (Sue)

In a smaller focus group at another prison with instructors who were prison officers (they had just started on the course), there was a clear consensus that they were officers first and foremost, that they were primarily responsible for security, and that they were governed by codes of conduct which seemed to create a greater distance between them and their prisoner-students. Their teaching, or instructing, was work-skills related, either in workshops or through vocational qualifications, for example in industrial cleaning. This group was generally cynical about the benefits of education in relation to recidivism. All agreed when one officer suggested that money should be spent much earlier in educational careers before children dropped out of school. They also felt that money was wasted on prisoners of a younger age who had no intention of changing their offending behaviour. Many thought that education and training was only of use once a person had decided to change, often in their late thirties or forties. Their views should be balanced with awareness that they were regarding education in the conventional sense of 'schooling' and work training, yet they were well aware of the soft outcomes of the vocational work they were doing, and of themselves as important role models.

Eventually these officer-instructors talked about their motivations, such as achieving successes 'against all the odds':

Seeing the look on their faces when they get it, they've suddenly ... you know ... done something for the first time, something they've been struggling with. They'll bring it and show you if it was in class. That was worth the effort. (John, but all nodded agreement)

This focus group also raised the issue of the obstacles/frustrations related to prisoners who self-harmed, suffered from mental health problems and who were at risk for various other reasons. As officers, they were more directly involved with this part of the job than those teachers working in the education departments. Much time was spent on one-to-one support, as these prisoners were more likely to be in workshops than in education. This was a role for which they often felt ill prepared and unsupported.

The officers who taught in different capacities, either on Offending Behaviour Programmes such as Enhanced Thinking Skills (ETS), or in Physical Education, had more positive and supportive attitudes towards all forms of education. While most courses follow a highly structured pattern the officers considered themselves as facilitators of learning and were specifically trained to deliver the courses. Equally, the Physical Training instructors reported aims and difficulties similar to those of the teachers' group. They were highly motivated and positive about the benefits of physical education and the accredited courses they ran, and believed that the courses they ran had the potential for 'changing lives'.

It would seem from our discussions with the teachers and instructors that they themselves benefited from being able to make a difference and from helping some of the most deprived people in the country to lead more fulfilling lives despite the inherent constraints of the prison environment.

The development of teaching and instructing in prison

Enthusiastic teachers and instructors who are working in difficult conditions are vital for effective prisoner learning.

> The people who know the service users are key. They should be highly skilled, highly trained, well-paid, with high morale, good support with a wide ranging set of programmes to draw upon, as they see fit. (Feinstein 2005: 21)

These principles, which should attract and retain talented staff, refer to teachers in the FE sector and therefore include those involved in prisoner education. Education programmes, which have developed over many years, are no longer restricted to the classrooms; they are in the gym, the workshops and out on the wings attracting some of the least confident learners in society. Additionally, through encouraging staff to continue learning by developing their skills, the value of education might be recognised by all strata within the prison. However, this worth of education programmes should be considered not just within the contexts of targets, efficiency and hard outcomes, but also according to a care credo which values the softer outcomes that they foster. By permeating all prison activities a culture of learning could be engendered throughout the institution with supportive interactions between all departments. In the future, there could be specialist prisons attracting particularly talented teachers and instructors on academic and vocational programmes where prisoners could be transferred to learn a trade or study for a specific qualification. The linking of this improved learning in prison to education in the community after release could be a significant factor in lowering reoffending rates. Any of these developments will need the passion of determined educators who really want to make a difference in the lives of the prisoners they are helping to change.

Seminar questions

1 Prison officers who teach might experience tensions between security needs and the requirements of teaching prisoners. What are these tensions and how might they be alleviated?
2 Civilian education staff in prison appear to be part of a forgotten sector in the education system with lower pay and conditions than those who teach elsewhere. How are these staff to be retained and recruitment levels raised?
3 Prisoners, particularly those with Skills for Life needs, require certain teaching strategies and techniques. Why do prisoners require these approaches and how might teachers satisfy their needs?

Recommended reading

The most significant book in recent years on education in prisons has been a collection of writings from academics, educators and prisoners: David Wilson and Anne Reuss (eds) (2000) *Prison(er) Education*.

For a comparative perspective on education in prisons in a range of countries throughout the world see William Forster (ed.) (1998) *Education behind Bars: International Comparisons*.

An informatively wide-ranging book which considers the various aspects of prison design that impinge on the activities of staff and prisoners is Leslie Fairweather and Sean McConville (eds) (2000) *Prison Architecture: Policy, Design and Experience*.

A warmly entertaining autobiography by the playwright Brendan Behan, set in the 1950s, an era when he describes avuncular staff running borstals as if they were secure public schools is Behan (1967) *Borstal Boy.*

A cogent argument for the efficacy of education in prison is made in the journal article by Clements (2004) 'The Rehabilitative Role of Arts Education in Prison: Accommodation or Enlightenment?'.

Notes

1 Level 1 is the standard expected of an average 11 year old.
2 Level 2 is the standard expected of an average 16 year old. This is the equivalent of a General Certificate in Secondary Education (GCSE) at grade A*–C.
3 Storybook Dads (and now Mums) began as a small project in HMP Dartmoor by Sharon Berry. Toe-by-Toe was begun by Christopher Morgan with the help of a prison officer from HMP Wandsworth. Both projects now occur in prisons throughout the country.
4 Travellers are also known as Romanies who often use horse-drawn wagons to journey around the country.

References

Adult Learning Inspectorate (2006a) *Annual Report of the Chief Inspector 2000–05.* Coventry: ALI.
Adult Learning Inspectorate (2006b) *Good Practice: Prisons.* Available online at: http://www.ali.gov.uk/GoodPractice (accessed 1 September 2006).
All-Party Parliamentary Group on Further Education and Lifelong Learning (APPG) (2004) *Inside Track: Prisoner Education in 2004 and Beyond.* Available online at: http://www.fpe.org.uk/filestore/insidetrack.pdf (accessed 15 September 2004).
Bayliss, P. (2003) 'Learning Behind Bars: Time to Liberate Prison Education', *Studies in the Education of Adults*, 35 (2): 157–72.
Baynes, P. and Marks, H. (1996) 'Adult Education Auxiliaries and Informal Learning', in R. Fieldhouse (ed.), *A History of Modern British Adult Education.* Leicester: NIACE, pp. 308–32.
Behan, B. (1967) *Borstal Boy.* London: Hutchinson.
Behan, C. (2005) *'Vigilance, Imagination, Courage': The Role of the Teacher in Prison Education.* Conference Paper for the European Prison Education Association, Sofia.
Braggins, J. (2002) *Shared Responsibilities: Education for Prisoners at a Time of Change.* London: Association of Colleges/NATFHE.

Braggins, J. and Talbot, J. (2005) *Wings of Learning: The Role of the Prison Officer in Supporting Prisoner Education*. London: Centre for Crime and Justice Studies.

Brookfield, S. (1995) *Becoming a Critically Reflective Teacher*. San Francisco: Jossey-Bass.

Carter, P. (2003) *Managing Offenders: Reducing Crime*. London: Home Office Strategy Unit.

Clements, P. (2004) 'The Rehabilitative Role of Arts Education in Prison: Accommodation or Enlightenment?', *Journal of Art and Design Education*, 23 (2): 169–78.

Costelloe, A. and Warner, K. (2005) *Beyond 'Offending Behaviour': The Wider Perspective of Adult Education and the European Prison Rules*. Conference Paper for the European Prison Education Association, Oslo.

Council of Europe (1990) *Education in Prison*, Recommendation No. R (89) 12. Strasbourg: Council of Europe.

Coyle, A. (2005) 'Foreword', in A. Liebling and S. Maruna (eds), *The Effects of Imprisonment*. Cullompton: Willan, pp. xix–xx.

Department for Education and Skills (1999) *A Fresh Start: Improving Literacy and Numeracy* (The Moser Report). Suffolk: DfES Publications.

Department for Education and Skills (2002) *Success for All: Reforming Further Education and Training*. London: DfES.

Department for Education and Skills (2004) *The Offender's Learning Journey: Learning and Skills Provision for Adult Offenders in England*. London: TSO.

Department for Education and Skills (2005) *Reducing Re-Offending Through Skills and Employment*, Cm 6702. London: TSO.

Elsdon, K. (2001) *An Education for the People? A History of HMI and Lifelong Learning 1944–1992*. Leicester: NIACE.

Fairweather, L. and McConville, S. (eds) (2000) *Prison Architecture: Policy, Design and Experience*. Oxford: Architectural Press.

Feinstein, L. (2005) *The Wider Benefits of Further Education: Theory, Evidence and Policy Implications*. London: DfES/Centre for Research into the Wider Benefits of Learning.

Forster, W. (1998) 'The Prison Service in England and Wales', in W. Forster (ed.), *Education Behind Bars: International Comparisons*. Leicester: NIACE, pp. 59–74.

Freire, P. (1996) *Pedagogy of the Oppressed*, rev. edn. Harmondsworth: Penguin.

Gamble, J. (2006) 'Breaking the Cycle of Crime Through Learning and Skills', *Talisman*, 55: 8.

Halsey, K., Martin, K. and White, R. (2006) *The Implementation of OLASS: Assessing Its Early Impact and Examining the Key Challenges – Phase 2 Report*, Research Report 794. London: DfES/National Foundation for Educational Research (NFER).

House of Commons Education and Skills Committee (HoC) (2005) *Prison Education*, Seventh Report of Session 2004–05, Vol. I. London: TSO.

Liebling, A. and Arnold, H. (2004) *Prisons and Their Moral Performance: A Study of Values, Quality and Prison Life*. Oxford: Oxford University Press.

McDonald, S. (2006) 'Teaching Behind Bars: Beyond the Classroom', *Times Education Supplement: Jobs*, 27 January, p. 1.

McGivney, V. (2002) *A Question of Value: Achievement and Progression in Adult Learning*. Leicester: NIACE.

Mezirow, J. (1991) *Transformative Dimensions of Adult Learning*. San Francisco: Jossey-Bass.

Nashashibi, P., Boffey, K., Harvey, S. and Rowan, T. (2006) *Just Learning? Case Studies in Improving Offender Education and Training*. London: Learning and Skills Development Agency (LSDA).

NATFHE (2006) *Motions for Annual FE Sector Conference 2005*. London: NATFHE.

Owers, A. (2005) 'Rights Behind Bars: The Condition and Treatment of Those in Detention', *Prison Service Journal*, 158: 63–71.

Rutherford, A. (1993) *Criminal Justice and the Pursuit of Decency*. Winchester: Waterside Press.

Schuller, T., Preston, J., Hammond, C., Brassett-Grundy, A. and Bynner, J. (2004) *The Impact of Education on Health, Family Life and Social Capital*. London: Institute of Education.

Sellgren, K. (2006) 'Prison Teachers "Lose Out on Pay"', *BBC News*, 2 April. Online at: http://www.bbc.co.uk/news/education (accessed 5 May 2006).

Social Exclusion Unit (2002) *Reducing Re-offending by Ex-prisoners*. London: Social Exclusion Unit/Office of the Deputy Prime Minister.

Uden, T. (2003) *Education and Training for Offenders*. Leicester: NIACE.

Wilson, D. (2000) 'Introduction', in D. Wilson and A. Reuss (eds), *Prison(er) Education: Stories of Change and Transformation*. Winchester: Waterside Press, pp. 9–23.

Wilson, D. and Reuss, A. (eds) (2000) *Prison(er) Education*. Winchester: Waterside Press.

Chapter 18

Psychologists in prisons

Graham Towl and David Crighton

This chapter discusses the recent history of psychological services in prisons, a case study of change leadership and finally an outline of some key challenges for the future. The focus is on developments within England and Wales. Since the 1990s, the provision of services in prisons has become something of a 'mixed economy' involving public, voluntary and private profit-making organisations and psychologists have been employed directly across all of these sectors. Public sector prisons are by far the largest single employer of psychologists within the National Offender Management Service (NOMS) but coverage here extends across prisons managed by public sector prisons and private providers too.

An understanding of the recent history of psychological services is important in giving a context for more recent developments and the chapter therefore begins with a short summary of key events in the development of the increased professionalisation of psychologists in prisons. Some of the key developments since the 1980s in psychological services in prisons are covered. Following this a case study is outlined looking at some of the key inherited staffing challenges and opportunities and how they were addressed and taken forward. The areas of work undertaken by psychologists in prisons are also touched upon with a commentary on future likely directions.

Recent history

Historically within professional psychology circles so called 'prison psychology' was frequently frowned upon for its lack of adequate postgraduate training, poor or non-existent continuing professional development (CPD) arrangements and the curious practice whereby psychological staff were generally required to turn their hands to everything psychological and beyond. Underlying these concerns for some were the professional challenges presented by the coercive environment of a prison. At a more prosaic level many within the profession in prisons believed that their pay and conditions were behind those of colleagues elsewhere in applied psychological practice, for example in psychological services in healthcare environments.

In the late 1980s two professional developments stand out as key in applied psychological practice in prisons: first, the advent of a new postgraduate master's degree programme in Applied Criminological Psychology at Birkbeck College, University of London; secondly, the advent of professional Chartership introduced by the British Psychological Society (BPS). Both of these developments contributed to the development of professional standards in psychological practice in prisons. Psychologists in prisons now enjoyed the benefits of being put on an educational par with colleagues across the applied psychological spectrum. The second change, driven by the professional body, served as a lever for areas of applied psychological practice, as each professional area could potentially benefit from 'Chartered' status. Such status was taken to be proof of qualification (and, broadly, parity of qualification) as a qualified applied psychologist across all branches of psychology.

In the 1990s the University of London MSc was dispensed with, and psychologists in prisons looked increasingly vulnerable in comparison with colleagues in other areas of applied practice which were thriving. However, two developments served to offset this and contributed to both the status and growth of psychology practice in prisons. The professional division of the BPS, which represented most psychologists in prisons, had been called the Division of Criminological and Legal Psychology (DCLP). This was changed to the Division of Forensic Psychology (DFP) in 1999, which served to broaden the remit of the division and soon dramatically expanded membership. Within prisons, there were also major injections of cash from the Treasury for psychological therapies to reduce levels of criminal reoffending, most of which was directed into manualised interventions, many of which had generous levels of psychological staffing. The other major direction for additional funding was towards a range of interventions to reduce drug misuse (Lee and George 2005; Towl 2006). Psychology staff were involved in this area of work to some extent, although the provision of psychology staffing was less evident.

The change in name of the Division gave rise and legitimacy to the use of the professional title of 'Chartered Forensic Psychologist'. This was important partly because it clearly conveyed to the broader professional psychology community and beyond that much of the work undertaken in prisons remains as forensic psychology. At the time, there was much internal professional wrangling about how appropriate (or inappropriate) the use of the term 'Forensic' was, but the vast majority of DCLP members had voted in favour of the change to the naming of the Division and the associated functional professional title. Most accepted the democratically expressed wishes of the professional community although a very small number of primarily court and hospital-based psychologists left the newly named division. Following the change, the new professional title of 'forensic psychologist' was almost universally adopted by this group of psychologists in prisons, significantly improving the status of the specialisim within the profession and outside it.

The manualised groupwork interventions introduced in the 1990s using new Treasury funding, and deriving from psychological models of behavioural change, contributed to a growth in interest in the employment of psychological staff. Interestingly in terms of staffing, the notion of using 'psychological models' was often conflated with requiring psychologists for actual delivery. This misleading notion served to wholly unnecessarily make the organisation and implementation of such work more difficult. It also led to largely fallacious claims that sufficient numbers of psychologists could not be recruited. Indeed the related myth of a 'shortage' of psychological staff was to prevail for a short while early into the following century. This contributed to a professionally unseemly growth in such staff with a lack of appropriate due regard for the needs of such trainees. Increased funding for psychologically based approaches therefore appears to have been, quite unnecessarily, associated with a 'dumbing down' of the training of psychologists (Towl 2006). There was unfortunately no national or local link between the numbers of qualified staff and the number of trainees being recruited. This was professionally untenable and unsurprisingly staff turnover surged with 'trainees' increasingly dissatisfied with the professional inadequacy of their training. Many lacked identified professional supervisors and funding for professional training, or indeed clear plans for them to get to the point of qualification. Professionally, this state of affairs was simply indefensible.

A case study of change leadership

At the beginning of the twenty-first century, psychological services in prisons were at a turning point and faced growing professional problems, which necessitated a multi-pronged solution. The first of these was the need for a national, organisationally and professionally endorsed, strategic approach. This was delivered and, for the first time, the development and delivery of psychological services in prisons was to be based on an agreed national strategy. This in turn was underpinned by clear ethical and professional standards (HM Prison Service and National Probation Service 2003; Towl 2004, 2006).

The inherited staffing position at the end of the twentieth century had a number of strengths. First, there was a high demand for and value placed on the knowledge and skills of psychological staff. Second, for staff there were greater promotion opportunities than before with the rapid expansion of posts which characterised the late 1990s. In growth terms the field was booming, although as noted above this expansion held the potential seeds of its collapse (Towl 2006).

It was decided to make a joint appointment in 2000 to provide professional leadership for psychological services in both prisons and probation. The post was located, largely for historical reasons, in the personnel directorate of HM Prison Service. The pressing case for the post remaining within the personnel directorate was based upon the growing psychological staffing problems in prisons. Arguably the post could have been placed within another directorate within the organisation such as the operations directorate, health or rehabilitation/resettlement. However, given the scale and depth of the problems it was probably wise for the post, certainly initially, to be firmly located within the personnel directorate of HM Prison Service.

A number of staffing concerns were central to this interesting period in the development of applied psychological services. From an organisational perspective in terms of corporate risk management, there was the concern that psychological staff would leave prison work in large numbers. It was claimed by some, albeit implausibly, that psychologists would be better paid in the probation service. Such expressed concerns, were used in support of arguments to very significantly raise the pay costs of psychologists. In large part, such apparent concerns most plausibly reflected professional self-interest.

Surprisingly, there had been no systematic analysis of pay data, and when this was completed a number of themes emerged, suggesting a rather more complex picture than that initially suggested. First, in comparison with other organisations at that time (for example the NHS) the Prison Service was over-paying trainee psychologists. Some qualified staff though, had fallen behind comparison groups. The 'market' for trainees was strongly in favour of employing organisations with many good quality candidates for each trainee post. By contrast the 'market' for qualified staff was markedly tighter, with comparatively small numbers of applicants for 'qualified psychologist' posts. Particularly in view of the 'market' there was a clear need to make short-term and longer-term changes to the pay structure for psychologists. As a first step the minimum pay levels for qualified staff were significantly enhanced and maximum pay levels for trainees were reduced. These changes probably contributed to achieving marked year-on-year improvements in staff retention (see Table 18.1).

While the salary levels for trainee psychologists appeared generous against levels across other branches of applied psychology this needed to be set against the quality of professional training and support available. In this area, practice was generally poor with standards frequently falling below professionally acceptable levels. The Professional Psychology Advisory Group (PPAG) (as it was named at the time) financially supported some trainees undertaking

Table 18.1 National Workforce Planning Data

		2000/2001	2001/2002
Sickness days	4.2 days		
% of women	81%		
% of ethnic minority staff	7.5%		
% of part-time workers	1.8%		
Retention level of qualified psychologists		82%	93%
Retention level of training grade psychologists		76%	90%
Retention level of psychological assistants		70%	75%

Source: Derived from PMG data for 2001/2002.

their training while others were not given such support. Sometimes individual governors ensured that trainees in their prisons received appropriate financial support for their training, others did not. Some individual governors appeared more concerned with the delivery of their manualised groupwork targets, and did not appear so concerned about professional standards and the training requirements of individual psychologists. The 'system problem' for the organisation was that there was no link between the decision to employ a trainee psychologist in a prison with a responsibility for resourcing and enabling their professional training. This is a problem professionally for a staff group characterised by well above average training and supervision needs given the demanding nature of such roles. This systemic problem was addressed by making a direct link in policy and practice terms between recruitment and the resourcing of a trainee psychologist's training.

In summary the strength of the inherited position has been the popularity, growth and valuing of psychological knowledge and skills; the fundamental weakness has been a distinct lack of basic professional standards, particularly in the areas of training and supervision of trainees, effective workforce planning and the restricted range of work undertaken.

In terms of the emergent issues 'the market' for the training of forensic psychologists was expanding with the emergence of a number of university postgraduate courses, both full time and part time. In parallel to this, the British Psychological Society had introduced a Board of Examiners in Forensic Psychology to develop standards for professional training. All those seeking to qualify as forensic psychologists would need to meet the standards set across a common academic and practice syllabus, developed in line with broader professional occupational standards for all areas of applied psychology. Prospective trainees would need to demonstrate the academic knowledge and skills required for independent practice. The academic component of training would be demonstrated by completion of professional (Part 1) examinations, or by completion of a professionally accredited master's degree in forensic psychology. The practice component would need to cover a broad range of experience across forensic contexts and settings. The expansion of the market in university-based courses and the numbers of candidates taking the professional examinations allowed for more flexible training routes for trainees employed in prisons.

Also on the horizon was (and still is) the advent of the Statutory Registration of professional psychologists. The British Psychological

Society had campaigned for this for a number of years as a means of improving standards of professional psychological practice. These likely changes influenced the policy decision to cease the previous practice of referring to staff who were effectively 'trainees' as 'psychologists' or 'higher psychologists'. The 'higher psychologist' grade for trainees was not cost effective or professionally defensible and hence it was dispensed with. The 'psychologist' grade was retitled 'trainee psychologist'. The shift in designations for trainees was an important professional development in that grade titles now reflected professional roles in a more transparent and unambiguous manner. This is an important ethical issue because previously there had been a danger that recipients of services including prisoners, governors and others may have incorrectly been led to believe that individuals in such roles were qualified psychologists. This was also an important step in protecting trainees, making it less likely that too much would be asked or expected of them professionally. A similar process of change in designations was also made for qualified staff with the introduction of the 'psychologist' grade below that of 'senior psychologist'. Previously, 'senior psychologists' were often just qualified, and in that sense in no way 'senior'. Again there was a danger that the recipients of services would not necessarily be aware that in professional terms a 'senior psychologist' would, in practice, often be a relatively junior and inexperienced member of staff. This served to provide psychological staff particularly more junior staff with a new level of professional protection too.

The new national strategy for the professionalisation of psychological services in prisons involved a number of key practical elements. First, the establishment of a national network of area-based psychologists mirroring the existing organisational structure of HM Prison Service. Thus 'area managers' had 'area psychologists' introduced to their teams, with a strategic and professional responsibility for the organisation and delivery of professional psychological services across the area. Pay and training arrangements, as noted above, had fallen out of step with professional counterparts elsewhere and were changed accordingly. In addition, and unlike in the NHS, a promotion route for psychological assistants to the trainee grade was introduced. This contributed to improvements in the continuity of service delivery in individual prisons and also appears to have had some positive impact on retention levels.

In 2003 the strategic framework document for psychological services in prisons and probation was formally issued after an extensive consultation process (HM Prison Service and National

Probation Service 2003). The strategic framework reflected both the broader public service reform context and developments within applied psychological practice. Crucially the framework had support at the most senior management levels within both HM Prison Service and the National Probation Service.

> ...The renewed focus on training, supervision and continuing professional development is very important in the maintenance and development of an appropriately high quality service. We are confident that this will be a useful framework to inform the development of applied psychological services in probation and prisons. We welcome and endorse the approach. (Foreword by P. Wheatley and E. Wallis, in HM Prison Service and National Probation Service 2003).

Three themes underpinned the strategic framework: first, the broad public service context. Thus it was, and is, important that psychological service staff have a broad understanding of the political environment within which they work. One example here was the need for more flexible working patterns as part of a two-way process, whereby employing organisations needed to be more flexible about working patterns to suit the changing needs of staff, while staff needed to work more flexibly in response to the needs of employers.

Second, there was a need for a renewed focus on some basic professional standards with the introduction of much more structured supervision and training arrangements. Perhaps too little had been done in the past for qualified psychologists working in the prison service in terms of the need for their continuing professional development (CPD). Again this is a two-way process. Psychologists benefited from a more receptive and supportive organisational environment in which to develop professionally, but also, from an organisational perspective, clearer policies supporting CPD contributed to the more robust management of the corporate risks associated with professional malpractice.

Third, there was a clear focus on meeting 'business needs' through the improved organisation and targeting of psychological work. Nationally there were widely differing professional practices in terms of what work different grades of staff did. One financial consequence of this was that sometimes services were costing as much as twice what they needed to.

Perhaps the major strength of the strategic framework though was the recognition that a 'one size fits all' approach to service developments and delivery would not be effective. The framework provided just that, an enabling structure for the new area psychologists and other senior managers to take a more strategic approach to the organisation and delivery of psychological services in response to local needs.

The change leadership approach outlined was implemented from 2000 to 2005. Strategically, decisions, policies and areas of work could be tested in terms of the extent of their 'fit' with the framework. Thus the framework was a comparatively modest element of the strategy for change, but an essential signpost nonetheless. Another principle of the implementation was that if something appeared to be going wrong, the policy team assumed that it was going wrong and quite possibly to a far worse extent than was initially evident. This 'iceberg' principle proved a very helpful pragmatic approach throughout the implementation, for example where it became evident that, as part of obtaining 'informed consent', a number of psychologists had been giving potentially misleading descriptions of some psychological assessments. The basis of the misrepresentations were chiefly ones of omission, with the assessed prisoner not being fully informed that they were being assessed, for example, for 'psychopathy', but rather that the assessment was a 'personality test'. This example perhaps also reflects the danger of an over-reliance upon applied psychologists with an exclusively forensic focus. This is an important ethical point which we will return to below.

Such unethical professional practices perhaps reflect a number of potential conflicts or tensions: first, the potentially challenging relationship between policy and advice and their relationship to professional codes of conduct, in this case the British Psychological Society Code of Conduct; second, the marked propensity for forensic psychological staff to be compliant. Psychologists should, arguably, among all staff, be particularly aware of the dangers of unreflective and uncritical obedience to authority. Simple awareness of the research base on obedience to authority, though, is clearly no guarantee of appropriate behaviour, highlighting the importance of robust professional standards based on a strong ethical framework (BPS 2006a). This was one of the reasons why there was such an emphasis in the strategic framework document on the need for the use of a range of applied psychologists delivering services in prisons. Thus increasingly there are clinical, counselling, health, educational and occupational psychologists delivering services too. Intra-professional differences and commonalities of approaches to ethical policies and practices are likely to provide a better test and challenge of the ethics of particular professional decision-making. Sometimes the various applied psychologists are directly employed by public sector prisons, but increasingly there is a growing range of employers of psychologists with responsibility for the delivery of services to prisons, e.g. Primary Care Trusts (PCTs). There is much scope for intra-professional learning then, perhaps particularly in relation to ethical issues.

In sum, the change leadership approach adopted for psychological services needed to be robust, focused, clearly communicated and consistently implemented. This process contributed to enhancing the quality of both policy and practice in psychological services. Additionally, and no less importantly, professional developments within the British Psychological Society from the 1980s onwards set the context for greater professionalisation and improving standards of psychological services in prisons to thrive.

Issues in professional psychological practice

Unsurprisingly the professional horizon has moved on. Professionally though, three current issues are perhaps most pertinent. First, the implementation of statutory registration of applied psychologists is increasingly likely. All professional specialisms across applied psychology are likely to sit together, alongside a diverse group of other health professions. Second, it seems likely that the distinctions between different specialist branches of applied psychology will diminish, following the long-term efforts of the British Psychological Society to establish core professional competencies and commonalties across the profession (see BPS 2006b). This is likely to have very marked impacts on the ways applied psychologists are trained and for the professional lives of practitioners. For example, it may well be that in the future all trainee psychologists will start with a generic training in applied psychology and only once they have completed this will they specialise. On fruition, such an approach would have major advantages to recipients of services, employers and to the professionals themselves. Overall it creates the potential for both more skilled practitioners but also more flexible practitioners, able to respond more effectively to emerging needs. Third, the organisational needs of prisons seem likely to change rapidly. Prison managers will need to be able to draw on a more flexible and better skilled professional workforce if they are to effectively respond to emergent demands placed on them. For example, demand is likely to increase for psychological risk assessments with indeterminate sentenced prisoners.

The organisational horizon

The broader context of the work of psychologists in prisons has also changed with the advent of the launch of the National Offender Management Service (NOMS). The new approach to service improvements has a number of characteristics that will have a direct impact upon psychological services. It seems likely that there will be an increased number of 'service providers' who will effectively compete against each other. The balance between costs and quality of services will be crucial in the award of psychological work. Psychological services will therefore come under scrutiny in terms of both the quality and cost of services in comparison with alternative service providers. As ever, this will have both benefits and disbenefits for psychological staff: benefits in demonstrating that psychological services provide good value for money, where this is so; disbenefits where services are provided at unnecessarily high costs. In financial terms this aspect of NOMS is nothing new, area psychologists were put in place, in part, to ensure appropriate value for money in service delivery. But current notions of 'contestability' seem likely to bring with it a renewed focus on such matters.

Increasingly there is, and will continue to be, a greater range of applied psychologists delivering services employed by different providers. Individual providers are likely to increase the range and types of applied psychologists they employ too. This will help them ensure that they don't suffer recruitment problems and also will improve the diversity and flexibility of the psychological workforce. However, there are some potential barriers to such growth, particularly perhaps with regard to those psychological staff employed through the NHS. Already there are concerns that salary inflation may result in a decrease in the number of (trainee) psychological posts in the NHS (Miller 2006). However, there is still likely to be a general increase in the number of applied psychologists providing services to prisoners where they are not directly employed by public sector prisons. Public sector prisons may well continue to employ an increased range of applied psychologists diversifying to improve the quality and range of services.

Perhaps, the major challenge will be the repositioning of psychological staff to ensure that not only do psychologists do psychological work but also that they, arguably most importantly, expedite the organisation and delivery of psychological interventions including therapies.

Traditionally many psychologists in prisons have delivered work that does not require a psychologist, for example the tripartite team roles in relation to manualised interventions. With the increase in demand for psychological reports on indeterminate prisoners this may well, rightly, draw such staff away from roles not requiring a psychologist. There is plenty of scope for freeing up such staff in this manner. There is likely to be an increased need to keep careful track of the proportion of trainees to qualified staff if the professional infrastructure is to remain fit for purpose. This will help ensure appropriate professional standards and reduce corporate risk associated with poor quality professional services.

The need to facilitate the organisation and delivery of psychological interventions including therapies will be one test of the efficacy of organisational arrangements. It is important that psychologists avoid the pitfall of being precious about claims to need to be always directly involved in delivering psychological therapies. A more constructive and effective approach for prospective recipients of such services will be to contribute to the development, strategic direction, organisation and evaluation of such interventions, helping to ensure that needs are appropriately prioritised and that evidence-based and informed interventions are appropriately organised and delivered (Crighton 2005; Towl 2005). This may well mean a greater involvement in staff training, but also a much greater need to have a fuller awareness of the broader evidence base in support of particular interventions.

The recent history of psychological services in prisons has been characterised by increased professionalisation and rapid growth. Expenditure on psychological therapies has expanded dramatically (more than doubling) over the last decade and, in this, developments in prisons have mirrored those in health services.

Such rapid growth of services has presented a number of significant opportunities and problems and, at least initially, these were not generally effectively addressed. To date the growth of psychological services has been maintained with more effective strategic professional policy both within the prison service and within the profession. In ensuring the ongoing development of services an increased diversity in both the range of employers and professional specialisms employed in psychological work in prisons has been important and seems likely to become more so. The future of psychological services in prisons will perhaps be best judged by how successful or otherwise psychologists are in ensuring that psychological approaches are most effectively used in helping contribute to positive behavioural changes among prisoners and staff, as opposed simply to the expansion in the number of psychologists employed.

Seminar questions

1 How do we prevent abuses of professional power?
2 What could psychologists contribute to addressing racism and homophobia in prisons?
3 What do the different applied psychology specialisms (e.g. counselling, clinical, educational, health and forensic) have to offer children and young people in contact with criminal justice staff?

Recommended reading:

Camila Batmanghelidjh (2006) *Shattered Lives: Children Who Live with Courage and Dignity* is a remarkable book which is beautifully written and will have a resonance with the lives of many children, young people and adults that we imprison. As one reviewer put it, 'It's so clear, it hurts' (Ruby Wax).

Tom Murtagh (2007) *The Blantyre House Prison Affair: Lessons from a Modern-day Witch-hunt* is a highly readable account of the mushrooming of parliamentary interest into a prison search and governor move at a resettlement prison in Kent. It provides some fascinating insights into the culture and politics of prison management.

Graham Towl (ed.) (2006) *Psychological Research in Prisons* covers much of the key psychological research undertaken in prisons in recent years. Ultimately it is a book about more ethical and effective policy and practice.

References

Batmanghelidjh, C. (2006) *Shattered Lifes: Children Who Live with Courage and Dignity*. London: JKP.

British Psychological Society (2006a) *Code of Ethics and Conduct*. Leicester: British Psychological Society.

British Psychological Society (2006b) *National Occupational Standards for Psychology*. Online at: http://www.bps.org.uk/document-download-area/document-download$.cfm?file_uuid=B5649668-1143-DFD0-7E2C-D2987DA035BF&ext=pdf (retrieved 18 September 2006).

Crighton, D.A. (2005) 'Applied Psychological Services', *British Journal of Forensic Practice*, 7 (4), 49–55.

HM Prison Service and National Probation Service (2003) *Driving Deliver: A Strategic Framework for Psychological Services in Prisons and Probation.* London: HM Prison Service & National Probation Services.

Lee, M. and George, S. (2005) 'Drug Strategy Unit', *British Journal of Forensic Practice*, 7 (4), 39–48.

Miller, R. (2006) 'President's Column', *The Psychologist*, 19 (7): 395.

Murtagh, T. (2007) *The Blantyre House Prison Affair: Lessons from a Modern-day Witch-hunt.* Winchester: Waterside Press.

Towl, G.J. (2004) 'Applied Psychological Services in Prisons and Probation', in J.R. Adler (ed.), *Forensic Psychology: Concepts, Debates and Practice.* Cullompton: Willan Publishing.

Towl, G.J. (2005) *Risk Assessment, Evidence-Based Mental Health.* London: BMJ Journals.

Towl, G.J. (2006) 'Introduction', in G.J. Towl (ed.), *Psychological Research in Prisons.* Oxford: Blackwell.

Chapter 19

The prison drug worker

Michael Wheatley

Introduction

The Prison Drug Worker (PDW) is a relatively new role within the Prison Service, and as policy and strategy have developed so the role has become clarified. Fundamentally, the role relates to drug treatment interventions and administration, although awareness of security and supply reduction are also relevant to the job. The PDW helps address problems related to problematic drug use largely associated with the consumption of illicit supplies of heroin, cocaine, crack cocaine, benzodiazepines, barbiturates, amphetamine, ecstasy, cannabis and volatile substances such as gases and solvents. The abuse of prescription medications is also a subject of intervention. Alcohol dependency is only treated when part of a poly-drug-using profile, as funding for alcohol-only interventions has yet to be identified and allocated. The Youth Justice Board (YJB) has developed services for young people in custody that will address all substance-misuse needs, including alcohol, tobacco and solvents as well as drugs. The arrangements for these services are set out as standards and service requirements in the 'National Specification for Substance Misuse Services for Juveniles in Custody' and should be referred to specifically for further information (Youth Justice Board 2005).

This chapter mainly pertains to PDWs within the adult prison system and within the public sector in England and Wales. What PDWs do varies between jurisdictions, but how they do it is essentially the same. This chapter is divided into three sections: first, the context in which the role of the PDW has developed; second, what PDWs do; and, third, some essential attributes of a PDW.

Background

Legislation

Drug use and supply became increasingly political issues in the 1980s, and by the mid-1990s had gained further significance with the publication of *Tackling Drugs Together* (HM Government 1995) which introduced a strategic framework for agencies and drug misusers to work together to address problematic drug use. *Tackling Drugs to Build a Better Britain* (HM Government 1998) detailed a ten-year plan to address social exclusion, through community-orientated drugs prevention and drug-related education and treatment via law enforcement and crime reduction endeavours (South 2002). It is worth noting that policy priorities and resources were not directed towards alcohol.

To coincide with government strategy, the Prison Service reviewed its drug services and published *Tackling Drugs in Prison* (1998) which established a strategy and emphasised that:

> The Prison Service has a key part to play in the national strategy because it holds a particularly damaged and potentially damaging population of problem drug misusers. (HM Prison Service 1998)

This strategy was regarded as a progressive step in making imprisonment an opportunity for reducing offenders' involvement with drugs (Home Affairs Committee 1999).

The government's national drug strategy was updated in 2002 (see Home Office 2002). For the Prison Service, this meant more community drug workers present in custody suites to offer support and referral opportunities, more persistent offenders being targeted for treatment via the extension of drug testing in police custody, an expansion of and improvement in prison-based treatment programmes and, for those leaving prison and treatment, a new throughcare and aftercare service called the Drugs Interventions Programme (DIP) which ensures that prisoners receive the support and treatment needed to minimise the likelihood of drug misuse and offending (Home Office 2005).

The National Offender Management Service drug strategy

The National Offender Management Service (NOMS) was created in 2004 following a review of correctional services (Carter 2003; Home Office 2004). NOMS brings together the work of the prison and probation services as a new single service to oversee the management of offenders. The NOMS drug strategy is an integral part of the government's national drug strategy and succeeds the specific Prison Service strategy. Its aim is 'to address the needs of problematic drug users during their engagement with the correctional services' (NOMS 2005a).

Prevalence – problematic drug use and prisons

Approximately one-third of all problematic drug users are serving custodial or community sentences (NOMS 2005a) and there is evidence that the levels of drug use among prisoners tend to be much higher than the general population (Farrell *et al.* 1998). Many studies estimate that approximately 60 to 70 per cent of prisoners have misused drugs in the twelve-months prior to imprisonment (Burrows *et al.* 2001; Mason *et al.* 1997; Ramsay 2003; Singleton *et al.* 1998; Swann and James 1998).

NOMS (2005a) estimated that around 136,000 offenders are imprisoned per annum. Using the lowest estimate of problematic drug use (60 per cent), this means that 81,600 problematic drug misusers pass through the prison system annually, with around 47,000 being present at any one time. As the prison population increases, so does the presentation of prisoners with problematic drug use, establishing the Prison Service as having the greater concentration of problematic drug misusers than the healthcare system or wider criminal justice system at any one time (NOMS 2005a).

The NOMS drug strategy is part of the national government drug strategy that contributes to the Home Office Public Service Agreement (PSA) targets of: reducing the harm caused by illegal drugs, including increasing the number of drug misusing offenders entering treatment via the criminal justice system; increasing the participation of problematic drug users in treatment programmes by 100 per cent by 2008 (with a progressive increase in numbers retained and completing treatment); and reducing the use of Class A drugs and frequency of use of any illicit drug among all young people under the age of 25.

The Prison Service response

The Prison Service offers a comprehensive range of drug interventions for problematic drug users while in custody. These address low, moderate and severe drug dependency in both sentenced and remand prisoners. The interventions comprise the following:

- Clinical services (detoxification and/or maintenance prescribing programmes) available presently in all local and remand prisons and being developed in other prisons. This service delivery is informed by Department of Health guidelines (DoH 1999) PSO 3550 (HMPS 2002a) and Clinical Management of Drug Dependence in the Adult Prison Setting (DoH 2006).

- CARATs (Counselling, Assessment, Referral, Advice and Throughcare services) are available to all prisoners who are 18 years or older in every prison (see PSO 3630: HMPS 2002b). The rationale for CARATs is as follows:

  Through the use of counselling techniques such as brief intervention work and motivational interviewing and based on quality assessment which appropriately screen, prioritise and inform effective care planning, the service will build on information from, and make referrals to other services both in custody and in the community. It will provide timely advice and support to minimise harm from drug use to self and others and ensure the provision of effective throughcare by ensuring continuity of care before, during and after release (NOMS 2005a)

  The CARAT service contributes to the Drugs Intervention Programme (DIP), which aspires to effectively case-manage all problematic drug users. DIP aims to break the cycle of drug-related crime by engaging problematic drug users at all stages of the criminal justice system, directing them into treatment, and retaining and supporting them during (throughcare) and after (aftercare) sentence.

- Drug rehabilitation programmes have been established in 114 prisons across the country (National Drug Programme Delivery Unit (Prison Service) 2006: personal correspondence). These programmes have been accredited by the Correctional Service Accreditation Panel and meet key evidence-based ('What Works') criteria for effective interventions. There are approximately seven types of programme which vary in intensity depending on prisoner risk and need; the shortest is the Short Duration Programme (approximately 45 hours' therapeutic intervention) delivered in 40 prisons for remand or short sentence prisoners and the longest is the FOCUS programme (approximately 130 hours of therapeutic intervention) delivered in five high-security sites for long-term high-risk/need prisoners. Programmes have three philosophical orientations – cognitive behavioural (97 sites), twelve-step (13 sites) and therapeutic community (four sites).

Treatment interventions are supported by a range of other initiatives such as Voluntary Drug Testing (see PSO 3620: HMPS 2000), Mandatory Drug Testing (see PSO 3601: HMPS 2005) and supply reduction services (such as use of CCTV, drug detection dogs, mobile phone detection) designed to deter, detect and disrupt illicit drug-related activity in prisons (see Wheatley 2007). Prisoners also have access to a number of non-drug-specific services including education, employment, housing, spiritual support and physical education to complement drug strategy-related interventions.

Approximately 1,500 PDWs are currently working in prisons. This includes both CARATs (850 staff) and other prison drug treatment staff (650 staff). A recent survey estimated that approximately 60 per cent of PDWs were women and 40 per cent men (NDPDU 2006: personal correspondence). PDWs can be from 'contracted-in' drugs agencies, directly employed, psychologists, probation officers and prison officers, all of whom work in partnership to deliver a consistent multidisciplined service. Initially, PDWs joined prisons from existing drugs agencies and brought with them the experience gained in these contexts. However, as drug treatment provision expanded rapidly within the prison service, the pool of qualified workers quickly dried up. Now, PDWs join from a variety of backgrounds (not necessarily drug or criminal justice in orientation) and get 'on-the-job' training to reach the levels of competence required. Further developments and expansion of drug treatment services in prisons are planned and there is likely to be an increase in the number of qualified staff required. Current figures estimate that the Prison Service will require up to 400 additional PDWs by 2008 (and 450 clinical staff) to meet the demand for substance misuse services in prison. This will bring the total PDW staff group to approximately 1900 people (NTA/HO 2006).

PDWs are recognised within the Prison Service as a staff group in their own right with a salary scale ranging from £18,000 to £22,000 depending on qualifications and experience. They are managed by a senior staff member who is usually a recognised manager (usually grade G or F level). This team is accountable to the Establishment Drug Strategy Coordinator who is required to be a local senior management team member. The Area Drug Strategy Coordinator supports prison teams at a regional level and is accountable to a Prison Service Area Manager or representative for drug strategy service delivery. The status of PDWs within establishments is dependent on local circumstances and varies within areas.

What does a prison drug worker do?

In order to achieve the aims of the government, Home Office and NOMS, PDWs deliver a range of services, identified above, that help bring the drug strategy into effect. Essentially, a PDW either actively delivers the CARAT service or facilitates other treatment interventions such as rehabilitation programmes.

PDWs perform five key tasks. First, after receiving a referral (from any source) the PDW begins an assessment process. This identifies areas of risk and need which informs referrals to and deployment of treatment interventions. The PDW uses a range of standard assessment instruments including a triage or basic assessment and a comprehensive assessment which can include drug dependency measures such as the Severity of Dependency Scale (SDS) and Alcohol Use Disorders Identification Test (AUDIT). The standard assessment instruments collect background demographic information and details of drugs used (including frequency and quantity), gather criminal conduct explanations and identify potential areas of treatment need by pulling together particulars associated with mental and physical health, housing, education or training, employment and family. Upon completion of an assessment, a care or treatment plan is formed where treatment goals are formulated and agreed. The care plan is regularly reviewed following further assessment as treatment progresses or new needs are presented.

Second, where low-intensity treatment interventions are required (these are brief, basic and simple) the PDW, as part of the CARAT service, may offer and deliver a limited number of individual or group support sessions. The CARAT Good Practice Guide suggests up to six sessions being offered in any one intervention at the end of which the Care Plan should be reviewed (NOMS 2005b). The aim of these sessions will be to support or achieve treatment goal attainment. Work in this area may include interventions such as individual motivational enhancement or harm minimisation and overdose prevention advice.

Third, for clients requiring more intensive interventions often known as drug rehabilitation programmes, the PDW can help refer to, provide information relevant for and deliver a range of treatment services to address identified need. These programmes require the prisoner to undergo further assessments for suitability which vary from programme to programme. PDWs, who meet strict selection criteria, receive additional specialist training to facilitate these programmes.

Fourth, as prisoners participate in treatment programmes, PDWs monitor contributions and attend the case reviews that occur upon programme completion. These actions contribute towards the 'case worker' function of the PDW's role; they become a key worker for a particular prisoner and take on specific roles and responsibilities associated with that person, noting any progress made or issues outstanding. This insight can facilitate a Care Plan review and new goals for treatment. PDWs are actively encouraged, with clients' consent, to contribute to the Offender Management Process within prisons which helps plan regime activities and further interventions while in custody. This fulfils an essential throughcare role by ensuring the continuation of treatment and support while in prison.

Fifth, to help reduce reoffending by ex-prisoners, a number of socially orientated variables were identified that are predictive of reoffending (Social Exclusion Unit 2002). These variables informed the NOMS Reduction Reoffending Action Plan (NOMS 2004) which identified seven 'treatment' pathways to reducing re-offending: (1) accommodation; (2) education, training and employment; (3) mental and physical health; (4) drugs and alcohol; (5) finance, benefits and debt; (6) children and families of offenders; and (7) attitudes, thinking and behaviour. Drug-using offenders have complicated needs, linked to all or some of these pathways, which require a coordinated response sustained over time. 'It is therefore essential that services that impact on offending work collaboratively in order to promote reform' (NOMS 2004: 7). This requires a national strategy, strong regional partnerships and effective local interventions. The Drugs Interventions Programme, as part of community Criminal Justice Intervention Teams (see Home Office 2005), provides a national strategic framework within which the action plan can be effectuated, integrating a variety of organisations and agencies that can address issues related to each pathway. PDWs contribute to this process by delivering interventions locally, assessing outstanding treatment needs and referring prisoners to community DIPs for continued psycho-social support. This function is an essential component of the PDW's role.

PDWs report participating in many other tasks relating to individual and organisation management, usually originating from local arrangements. These tasks can include staff training (substance and service awareness), delivering auricular acupuncture, meetings, networking and liaison both in and out of the prison.

PDWs have limited administrative support and a considerable amount of paperwork associated with the CARATs and Programmes casework records. A significant proportion of their time is spent on administrative tasks, completing such paperwork and liaising with different departments or agencies within and outside of the prison. The administrative burden is frequently reported as restricting the quantity of direct client contact.

Essential attributes of a prison drug worker

A good PDW should blend many ingredients to promote change in prisoners. Bringing all these ingredients together in practice is one of the biggest challenges a PDW will face. The essential ingredients are described below.

1. Knowledge

There are two important areas associated with the knowledge base of prison drug strategy service provision.

Understanding the causes, development and maintenance of drug use
Michael Gossop (2000) provided a framework to help drug workers understand and explain why people take drugs. He describes three separate, but intrinsically linked, rationales for drug taking: the specific pharmacological properties of the drug (chemical reactions within the body to ingestion), the psychology of the users (intrinsic belief systems held) and the social setting (extrinsic environment and relationships experienced) in which drug taking occurs. These rationales interact with each individual to produce a unique drug-taking profile. Drug users are a diverse group of people with different reasons for using and PDWs need to look at individuals holistically, focusing on these pharmacological, psychological, social, economic and familial factors.

Matching prisoners to appropriate interventions

Recent developments in the area of effective 'correctional' treatment have identified three primary principles that are essential to determining the development of appropriate treatment responses. This 'Risk Needs Model' (Andrews and Bonta 2003) proposes that treatment will be most effective in reducing recidivism if it adheres to three important principles: risk, need and responsivity. The risk principle states that higher-risk offenders should receive a higher dose of treatment and low-risk cases have less intensive services. The need principle states that treatment targets should focus exclusively on criminogenic needs; that is, factors which are empirically predictive of criminal behaviour and may be changed through treatment. The responsivity principle states that the style in which treatment is presented to the offender should be one to which offenders are receptive, and should take account of individual differences such as intellectual ability, learning style, cultural issues and interpersonal sensitivity (Andrews and Bonta 2003). The 'Risk Needs Model' stems from the notion that not all problematic drug-using prisoners require the same type of treatment nor is every treatment appropriate for every individual (CCSA 2004). Accurate assessment of risk and treatment need is required to conceptualise intervention goals and match prisoners with the most appropriate intervention:

> No single treatment is appropriate for all individuals. Matching treatment settings, interventions and services to each individual's particular problems and needs is critical to his or her ultimate success in returning to productive functioning in the family, workplace and society ... Effective treatment attends to multiple needs of the individual, not just his or her drug use. To be effective, treatment must address the individual's drug use and associated medical, psychological, social, vocational and legal problems. (NIDA 1999: 1)

2. Skills and personal characteristics – building a therapeutic alliance

Knowledge of therapeutic techniques and relationships can maximise treatment benefits. Many writers claim that successful therapeutic outcomes depend not only on technique but also on the therapists' interpersonal skills (Beck *et al.* 1979; Egan 1998; Frank 1971; Kleinke 1994; Rogers 1975). Seligman (1990) found that positive outcomes were significantly related to (a) the acceptance by the therapist of the clients beliefs and values, (b) an emphasis on client support,

(c) moderate therapist self-disclosure, (d) a display of interest in the client, (e) the therapist's confidence, and (f) the ability to engage clients, keep them task-focused and motivate them to make positive changes. It is vital that PDWs are aware of their behaviours during interventions and consider how their actions influence the client and affect the therapeutic climate. Valle (1981) examined styles of therapists working with alcohol-dependent clients and found higher levels of interpersonal skills in therapists were related to fewer incidents of relapse assessed two years later.

Marshall *et al.* (2001), having reviewed a wide range of psychotherapeutic literature, listed the major features of therapists who facilitate high-quality treatment. These features are equally applicable to PDWs who deliver treatment interventions (Marshall 2006: personal correspondence). The 14 therapist features he identified are described below (see Marshall *et al.* 2001 for all supporting citations).

- **Empathy** – an attempt to understand and relate to the feelings of a client without being overwhelmed or subjectively experiencing the emotions. The expression of accurate empathy has been shown to be the most clearly effective element of treatment.

- **Genuineness** – being yourself, not pretending or acting within a role and behaving in a real and consistent manner. A PDW who is non-defensive, comfortable with themselves, actively participates in sessions and behaves in a honest and interested manner often gets better results.

- **Warm** – behaviour that is accepting, caring and supportive. Clients being treated by a warm and friendly therapist show greater reductions in fear following treatment, feel understood and are more willing to explore difficulties.

- **Respect** – modelling a type of behaviour expected in return that conveys the client is valued. It is important to distinguish between the person and their offending acts and to indicate respect for the person and disapproval of their offending conduct. Being disrespectful to clients is predictive of poor outcomes.

- **Support** – emphasising and reinforcing positive effective behaviour. Clients show less aggression and resistant behaviour when therapists provide high levels of support and positive feedback.

- **Confidence** – client confidence in a therapist is crucial. Therapist credibility and confidence are positively correlated with good outcomes.

- **Emotional responsivity** – if a client is asked what his views are when calm and rational, this often will not reflect his actual core beliefs when, for instance, he is depressed or angry. Therefore it is essential to permit and perhaps encourage a range of emotions to be expressed during treatment. Role play is a good technique to facilitate emotional responsivity.

- **Self-disclosure** – moderate therapist disclosure and sharing of some personal experiences, as illustrative examples, can increase client disclosure, trust and positive regard. It is important for PDWs to present themselves as coping models with flaws rather than as models of mastery, otherwise clients may not attempt to emulate them.

- **Open-ended questioning** – clients tend to feel more understood and respond more openly (often with insight) to open-ended questions than to questions that prompt only yes or no answers. Problematic reactions by clients are reduced in frequency and intensity when open rather than closed questions are posed.

- **Directiveness** – clients often expect direction, especially at the beginning of interventions and this can provide a positive structure for submissive and dependent clients. Thereafter, clients may respond better to a more flexible approach.

- **Flexibility** – tailoring a style of interaction to fit the changing goals and needs of different clients at different points in therapy is likely to optimise effectiveness. A reflective style often works best with aggressive or defensive clients.

- **Encouraging active participation** – clients who engage in the therapy process have enhanced levels of commitment to and compliance with therapy, reduce reactance and promote positive outcomes. Active participation encourages social skill acquisition, facilitates empathic displays and can promote self-esteem as well as consolidating learning.

- **Rewarding** – where goals are achieved, client behaviours should be reinforced or encouraged. Initial progress should be rewarded before moving to reinforcing a range of behaviours.

- **Use of humour** – helps create a therapeutic atmosphere of openness, releases tension and decreases anxiety, thereby promoting client–therapist cohesion as long as an empathic relationship exists. Humour can also promote social interest, reduce feelings of inferiority and help clients recognise the value of humour in their lives as long as they don't feel ridiculed or the focus of a joke.

It is not sufficient for PDWs to convince themselves or their managers that they have the necessary competencies or characteristics of a good therapist. They must also ensure that clients actually recognise and respond to these features.

The most significant impediment to change is a confrontational style (Marshall *et al.* 2001). A PDW who adopts an intrusive, aggressive approach characterised by harsh, confrontational challenges of clients can damage the therapeutic relationship and impede progress. Other behaviours associated with negative effects on clients include rejection by the group or facilitator, feedback overload, low levels of therapist skills (lack of warmth, empathy and genuineness), manipulation to meet the needs of the PDW, boundary problems and low levels of interest. Outcomes studies report more positive effects when an empathic style is adopted.

The quality of the therapist–client relationship has been shown to account for approximately 25 per cent of the variance in treatment effectiveness (Martin *et al.* 2000; Morgan *et al.* 1982). McLeod (1990) suggests that clients view the therapeutic process (having someone to talk to and trust) as being more important than the actual therapeutic techniques. Evidence suggests that the therapeutic relationship or alliance is all important (Ackerman and Hilsenroth 2003; Beck *et al.* 1979; Luborsky *et al.* 1985; Yalom 1985). Poor quality alliances affect the rate of treatment attrition (Marshall *et al.* 2001). Clients are drawn to people who understand them, instil hope, offer encouragement and who are genuinely interested in them. Horvath and Symonds (1991) found a consistent and positive relationship between the quality of the alliance and treatment outcomes across a variety of treatments. It is clear that the therapeutic alliance is the glue that makes treatment work for a range of problematic behaviours. Ackerman and Hilsenroth (2003) found that therapist personal attributes such as being flexible, honest, respectful, trustworthy, confident, warm, interested and open were found to contribute positively to the alliance. Techniques such as exploration, reflection, noting post-therapy success, accurate interpretation, facilitating the expression of affect and attending to the client's experience were also found to contribute positively to the alliance.

Marshall *et al.* (2001) conclude that therapist skills and personal characteristics are highly influential in producing benefits beyond the effects produced by treatment techniques. PDWs who integrate the two are likely to maximise treatment benefits.

3. Commitment to high professional standards and continued practitioner development

Confidentiality and code of practice

PDWs deliver individually planned, tailored interventions either as part of the CARAT service or through rehabilitation programmes. This requires drug teams and other prison departments to work closely together to treat the prisoner holistically. Clarity about issues of confidentiality and codes of practice are of paramount importance to ensure high standards of service delivery.

The boundaries and limitations of confidentiality should be explained clearly before any service is provided. Information disclosed to a PDW either as part of the CARAT service or a rehabilitation programme is regarded as being confidential to the individual worker and the team delivering the service within the establishment (NOMS 2005b). It is essential that PDWs make prisoners aware of this, at the earliest possible opportunity, to ensure there is no difficulty in sharing information. If this basic level of consent is not given, confirmed by the prisoner's signature, access to the particular service is either limited or terminated because of the restrictions imposed by the client.

PDWs also need to work closely with all other relevant service providers in the prison and the wider community. This should be discussed with the prisoner during the first meeting, and consent to the exchange of information with these teams should also be secured. If permission is not given, restrictions on service delivery will be imposed. For example, if a CARAT worker is not given permission to liaise with a community DIP team this will inevitably limit the aftercare support that can be offered following release.

In certain circumstances, information may be shared by a PDW even when consent has not been obtained. This is when either the security or safety of the prison and those within it may be compromised, when there is a perceived risk of self-harm or harm to others, or because of concerns related to the welfare of any children who may be in the prisoner's care (as detailed in the Children Act 1989).

PDWs should also be governed by and adopt a specific code of practice. Since HM Prison Service does not have one, many prison areas have adopted the codes of practice of professional organisations from the drugs and alcohol treatment services, such as the Federation of Drug and Alcohol Professionals Code of Practice (see FDAP 2006a).

Competence development

National Occupational Standards (NOS) specify standards of performance that people are expected to achieve in their work and the knowledge and skills needed to perform effectively. The Drugs and Alcohol National Occupational Standards (DANOS) are a suite of competency standards specific to the drug and alcohol field. Some are generic, such as communication, analytical or negotiating skills, while others are more specific, such as knowing different substances and their effects or being able to carry out a comprehensive substance misuse assessment (DANOS 2006).

PDWs require a particular set of competences. A service specification prepared by the NOMS Drug Strategy Unit identifies 16 competence sets, made up of 34 integral task units, which a PDW should be able to demonstrate or be working towards (NOMS 2005b). Various certification schemes exist to facilitate demonstration of the required competencies. An example of a certification scheme is provided by the Federation of Drug and Alcohol Professionals (see FDAP 2006b).

The National Treatment Agency/Drug Strategy Directorate–Home Office (2006) introduced some interim workforce development targets covering the training and qualifications for practitioners and managers working with adults. These include, by 2008, 75 per cent of non-professionally qualified practitioners having or undertaking an NVQ Level 3 award in Health and Social Care or equivalent; 60 per cent of professionally qualified staff undertaking a programme of continuous professional development relevant to their work; and at least 90 per cent of managers undertaking or having completed an appropriate management training course or qualification. A PDW should commit to achieving the level of competence required through continued professional or practitioner development which could include self-study, training and participation in clinical supervision.

Conclusion

PDWs form a large staff group within the prison service, whose purpose is to address problematic drug use within the prison population, thereby promoting health and reducing the likelihood of reoffending.

Problematic drug use stems from a combination of factors. Drug users are not a homogenous group and therefore require different interventions to facilitate change. This is dependent on levels of presenting risk, need and individual responsivity issues. A need exists for prisoners to be appropriately matched to treatment interventions, be offered adequate time in treatment and given effective throughcare and aftercare. This adds weight to the claims that the treatment needs of problematic drug using prisoners are clearly diverse and a single approach is unlikely to be effective. PDWs have therefore to be proficient in several critical areas:

- completing a comprehensive and ongoing assessment of prisoner need;
- facilitating the delivery of a range of treatment services;
- providing a continuum of treatment interventions;
- case managing and monitoring the engagement of clients in appropriately intensive services; and
- providing and integrating continuing social support opportunities.

To succeed in these critical areas PDWs should be highly knowledgeable, well skilled, have the desired personal qualities, demonstrate competence and be committed to continued practitioner development. Being able to efficiently build and maintain positive working relationships with clients is essential. The challenge for the PDW is to be eclectic and blend together the essential ingredients of the job and deliver a level of service that is engaging and motivational, retaining clients in treatment for as long as necessary while promoting the acquisition of treatment goals.

In the future, PDWs face many challenges such as taking a more holistic approach to drug abuse and incorporating alcohol-only and tobacco dependency into their practice. These two substances alone account for the vast majority of health and offending problems in the UK. The Prison Service has a responsibility to financially resource and provide policy mandates to support this work. Strengthening PDW, involvement in regional Reducing Reoffending Action Plans, which promote social integration via recognised support services thereby improving the maintenance of treatment effects and drug-free lifestyles, is strongly recommended. Improving aftercare provision in the community must be prioritised to support prison drug work. Finally, research into the effectiveness of PDWs, interventions needs to be commissioned to build and contribute to an evidence base to legitimise and justify service provision. PDWs have a considerable role to play in facilitating research and should seek to blend research opportunities into their practice and publish their findings to inform future service delivery.

The prison drug worker has a vital role to play in the modern Prison Service and what it aims to deliver and address.

Seminar questions

1 What difference can treatment make to a problematic drug user?
2 Should drug use be legalised?
3 To be a good drug worker must you be an ex-user yourself?
4 Do drugs in prison make users easier to manage and give staff an easier time?

Recommended reading

For an introduction to the issues regarding substance misuse and criminal conduct generally, Michael Gossop (2000) *Living with Drugs* and Philip Bean (2004) *Drugs and Crime* provide a good introduction. In understanding the challenges of dealing with this client group and as an exploration of a particularly valuable technique, William Miller and Stephen Rollnick (2002) *Motivational Interviewing: Preparing People for Change* is recommended.

A good introduction to issues in prisons, including drugs is, Yvonne Jewkes (2007) *Handbook on Prisons*. In relation to drug use in prisons, Steve Gravett (2000) *Drugs in Prison: A Practitioner's Guide to Penal Policy and Practice* is a useful text.

References

Ackerman, S.J. and Hilsenroth, M.J. (2003) 'A Review of Therapist Characteristics and Techniques Positively Impacting the Therapeutic Alliance', *Clinical Psychology Review*, 23: 1–33.
Andrews, D.A. and Bonta, J. (2003) *The Psychology of Criminal Conduct*, 3rd edn. Cincinnati, OH: Anderson Publishing.
Bean, P. (2004) *Drugs and Crime*, 2nd edn. Cullompton: Willan.
Beck, A.T., Rush, P.J., Shaw, B.F. and Emery, G. (1979) *Cognitive Therapy and Depression*. New York: Guilford Press.

Burrows, J., Clarke, A., Davison, T., Tarling, R. and Webb, S. (2001) *Research into the Nature and Effectiveness of Drugs Throughcare*, Occasional Paper 68. London: Home Office.

Carter, P. (2003) *Managing Offenders, Reducing Crime. A New Approach.* London: Home Office.

CCSA (2004) *Canadian Centre on Substance Abuse – Substance Abuse in Corrections: FAQs.* Canada: CCSA.

Department of Health (1999) *Drug Misuse and Dependence: Guidelines on Clinical Management.* Online at: http://www.dh.gov.uk/assetRoot/04/07/81/98/04078198.pdf (retrieved 15 September 2006).

Department of Health (2006) *Clinical Management of Drug Dependence in Adult Prison Setting including Psychosocial Treatment as a Core Part.* Online at http://www.dh.gov.uk/en/Publicationsandstatistics/Publications/PublicationsPolicyandGuidance/DH_063064 (retrieved 15 January 2007).

Egan, G. (1998) *The Skilled Helper: A Problem-management Approach to Helping.* Pacific Grove, CA: Brookes/Cole.

Farrell, M., Howes, S., Taylor, C., Lewis G., Jenkins, R., Beddington, P., Jarvis, M., Brugha, T., Gill, B. and Meltzer, H. (1998) 'Substance Misuse and Psychiatric Comorbidity: An Overview of the OPCS National Psychiatric Morbidity Survey', *Addictive Behaviors*, 23 (6): 909–18

FDAP (2006a) *The Federation of Drug and Alcohol Professionals: Code of Practice.* Online at: http://www.fdap.org.uk/ethics/newcode.html (retrieved 9 September 2006).

FDAP (2006b) *The Federation of Drug and Alcohol Professionals: Drug and Alcohol Professional Certification – Overview.* Online at: http://www.fdap.org.uk/certification/dap.html (retrieved 15 September 2006).

Frank, J.D. (1971) 'Therapeutic Factors in Psychotherapy', *American Journal of Psychotherapy*, 25: 350–61.

Gossop, M. (2000) *Living with Drugs.* Aldershot: Ashgate.

Gravett, S. (2000) *Drugs in Prison: A Practitioner's Guide to Penal Policy and Practice.* London: Sage.

HM Government (1995) *Tackling Drugs Together.* London: Stationery Office.

HM Government (1998) *Tackling Drugs to Build a Better Britain.* London: Stationery Office.

HM Prison Service (1998) *Tackling Drugs in Prison.* London: HM Prison Service.

HM Prison Service (2000) *Voluntary Drug Testing Units and the Framework for Voluntary Drug Testing*, PSO 3620. Online at: http://pso.hmprisonservice.gov.uk/PSO_3620_voluntary_drug_testing.doc (retrieved 15 September 2006).

HM Prison Service (2002a) *Clinical Services for Substance Misusers*, PSO 3550. Online at: http://pso.hmprisonservice.gov.uk/PSO_3550_clinical_services.doc (retrieved 15 September 2006).

HM Prison Service (2002b) *Counselling, Assessment, Referral, Advice and Throughcare Services*, PSO 3630. Online at: http://pso.hmprisonservice.gov.uk/PSO_3630_carats.doc (retrieved 15 September 2006).

HM Prison Service (2003) *Drug Strategy General Briefing Note – 17.12.03.* Online at: http://www.hmprisonservice.gov.uk/assets/documents/10000157drugstrategyGenBriefingNote171203.doc (retrieved 23 June 2006).

HM Prison Service (2005) *Mandatory Drug Testing*, PSO 3601. Online at: http://pso.hmprisonservice.gov.uk/PSO_3601_mandatory_drugs_testing.doc (retrieved 15 September 2006).

Home Affairs Committee (1999) *Drugs and Prisons.* Online at: http://www.publications.parliament.uk/pa/cm199900/cmselect/cmhaff//271/27103.html (retrieved 9 September 2006).

Home Office (2002) *Updated Drug Strategy* Online at: http://www.drugs.gov.uk/ReportsandPublications/NationalStrategy/1038840683 (retrieved 15 September 2006).

Home Office (2004) *Reducing Crime – Changing Lives. The Government's Plans for Transforming the Management of Offenders.* London: Home Office.

Home Office (2005) *The Drug Intervention Programme.* Online at: http://www.drugs.gov.uk/WorkPages/DrugInterventionsProgramme (retrieved 15 September 2006).

Horvath, A.O. and Symonds, B.D. (1991) 'Relation Between Working Alliance and Outcome in Psychotherapy: A Meta-Analysis', *Journal of Counseling Psychology*, 38 (2): 139–49.

Jewkes, Y. (2007) *Handbook on Prisons.* Cullompton: Willan.

Kleinke, C.L. (1994) *Common Principles of Psychotherapy.* Pacific Grove, CA: Brooks/Cole.

Luborsky, L., McLellan, T., Woody, G.E., O'Brien, C.P. and Auerbach, A. (1985) 'Therapist Success and Its Determinants', *Archives of General Psychiatry*, 42: 602–11.

McLeod, J. (1990) 'The Clients Experience of Psychotherapy: A Review of the Research Literature', in D. Mearns and W. Dryden (eds), *Experiences of Counselling in Action.* London: Sage, pp. 66–79.

Marshall, W.L., Fernandez, Y.M., Serran, G.A., Mulloy, R., Thornton, D., Mann, R.E. and Anderson, D. (2001) 'Process Variables in the Treatment of Sexual Offenders: A Review of the Relevant Literature', *Aggression and Violent Behaviour*, 2: 1–30.

Martin, D.J., Garske, J.P. and Davis, M.K. (2000) 'Relation of the Therapeutic Alliance with Outcome and Other Variables: A Meta-analytic Review', *Journal of Consulting and Clinical Psychology*, 68: 438–50.

Mason, D., Birmingham, L. and Grubin, D. (1997) 'Substance Use in Remand Prisoners: A Consecutive Case Study', *British Medical Journal*, 315 (7099): 18–21.

Miller, W.R. and Rollnick, S. (2002) *Motivational Interviewing: Preparing People for Change*, 2nd edn. London: Guilford Publishing.

Morgan, R., Luborsky, L., Crits-Christoph, P., Curtis, H. and Solomon, J. (1982) 'Predicting Outcomes of Psychotherapy by the Penn Helping Alliance Rating Method', *Archives of General Psychiatry*, 39: 397–402.

National Treatment Agency/Drug Strategy Directorate – Home Office (2006) *Joint National Treatment Agency and Drug Strategy Directorate Workforce Development Plan for the Substance Misuse Field*. Online at: http://www.drugs. gov.uk/publication-search/drug-strategy/workforcedevelopmentplan (retrieved 27 September 2006).

NIDA (1999) *Prinicples of Drug Addiction Treatment: A Research Based Guide*. Rockville, MD: NIDA.

NOMS (2004) *Reducing Re-offending: National Action Plan. Reference Document*. Online at: http://www.noms.homeoffice.gov.uk/downloads/noms_ reducing_reoffending_national_action_plan.pdf (retrieved 9 September 2006).

NOMS (2005a) *Strategy for the Management and Treatment of Problematic Drug Users within Correctional Services*. Online at: http://www.hmprisonservice. gov.uk/assets/documents/100008E3NOMS_drug_strategy_jan_05.doc (retrieved 9 September 2006).

NOMS (2005b) *CARATS Practice Manual*. London: National Offender Management Service.

Ramsay, M. (2003) *Prisoners' Drug Use and Treatment: Seven Research Studies*, Home Office Research Study 267. London: Home Office.

Rogers, C.R. (1975) 'Empathic: An Unappreciated Way of Being', *Counseling Psychologist*, 1: 2–10.

Seligman, L. (1990) *Selecting Effective Treatment*. San Francisco: Jossey-Bass.

Singleton, N., Meltzer, H., Gatward, R., Coid, J. and Deasy, D. (1998) *Psychiatric Morbidity among Prisoners in England and Wales*. London: Stationery Office.

Social Exclusion Unit (2002) *Reducing Re-offending by Ex-prisoners. Report by the Social Exclusion Unit*. London: Office of the Deputy Prime Minister.

South, N. (2002) 'Drugs, Alcohol and Crime', in M. Maguire, R. Morgan and R. Reiner (eds), *The Oxford Handbook of Criminology*, 3rd edn. Oxford: Oxford University Press.

Swann, R. and James, P. (1998) 'The Effect of the Prison Environment upon Inmate Drug Taking Behaviour', *Howard Journal*, 37 (3): 252–65.

Valle, S.K. (1981) 'Interpersonal Functioning of Alcoholism Counsellors and Treatment Outcome', *Journal of Studies on Alcohol*, 42: 783–90.

Wheatley, M. (2007) 'Drug Misuse in Prison', in Y. Jewkes (ed.), *Handbook of Prisons*. Cullompton: Willan.

Yalom, I.D. (1985) *The Theory and Practice of Group Psychotherapy*, 3rd edn. New York: Basic Books.

Youth Justice Board (2005) *National Specification for Substance Misuse for Juveniles in Custody*. Online at: http://www.yjb.gov.uk/Publications/ Downloads/Nat%20Spec%20Substance%20Misuse%20Juveniles%20in%20 Custody.pdf (retrieved 16 October 2006).

Chapter 20

Health professionals in prisons

Morag MacDonald and Paul Fallon

Prison context

Providing healthcare to patients detained in prison is a crucial and challenging task. Some of the challenges arise from the complex medical and social needs of the patients and the difficulty of establishing and maintaining therapeutic relationships with them. Other challenges relate to environmental and structural factors such as: high levels of staff and patient turnover, overcrowding, facility fitness for purpose, regimen and lack of patient empowerment. The task is none the easier for having been transferred from Her Majesty's Prison Service (HMPS) to the National Health Service (NHS), for although the latter may be better placed to help obviate the challenges, its recent restructuring has meant that the pace of development has been slower than anticipated.

This chapter explores the difficulties experienced by healthcare staff, whether HMPS, private healthcare company or NHS employees, locums or independent contractors (some GPs, dentists, pharmacists and opticians). It also sets out the developments that have taken place affecting prison health professionals over recent years. We conclude that in spite of the difficulties, the last few years have witnessed gradual improvements in workforce recruitment, retention and development, and in the provision of services and facilities in prisons, including the growing use of information technology as an aid to prisoner healthcare.

The challenges of meeting prisoner needs

There are nearly 72,000 prisoners in public sector prisons receiving primary care services at an annual cost of some £189 million (letter from Richard Bradshaw and Michael Spurr, 1 March 2007, to Prison Service Area Managers). About half the prisons have 24-hour health centre cover. In the light of increased sentence lengths, a burgeoning prison population and the consequent turnover of prisoners, the population receiving healthcare each year amounts to approximately 150,000 individuals. As a result of these issues and the increase in the number of prisoner transfers *between* prisons (100,000 per annum), the annual number of prison 'admissions' is in the region of 250,000.

On admission to each establishment, it is an HMPS requirement that a prisoner is assessed by the healthcare team, thus posing an enormous daily task. Healthcare staff assess their patients against the risk of self-harm and yet some 23,000 self-harm incidents occur each year (of which about 90 are fatal). Healthcare staff also identify which patients require assessment for treatment at facilities outside prison, requiring them to be transported or transferred to a secure secondary care hospital. The Twelve-Month Study commissioned by the Department of Health and Her Majesty's Prison Service (2006) of escort and bedwatch activity showed that the 75–80,000 daily total prisoner population between April 2004 and April 2005 resulted in 48,000 referrals to NHS hospitals, of which about 2,600 prisoners were transferred to mental hospitals for further treatment.

The Annual Prison Healthcare Statistics (1998–99), when the prison population was less than 65,000, gives details about the number of consultations per annum. Extrapolating for 2006 population figures, the figure is nearly 3 million, some forty times the daily prisoner population (see Table 20.1).

As well as the volume, the *nature* of healthcare in prisons raises a number of challenges for staff, for example dealing with a lack of trust from a client group unable to choose his or her own doctor. Healthcare staff also have to be aware of the potential of being manipulated by prisoners and have to be able to balance ethical professional practice in relationships both with prisoners and custodial staff. Within prisons, challenges may also arise as a result of the conflict between roles of control and care and moral and value judgments made about what prisoners should be entitled to. In order for prison healthcare staff to meet these conflicting demands and to avoid misunderstandings it is essential that 'prison physicians and health care workers stick to solid medical ethics and that these are

Table 20.1 Estimated number of consultations, with nurses, doctors and visiting specialists

Daily prison population	77,800 (June 2006)
Annual prisoner throughput	304,000
Annual number of consultations	2,900,000
Of which, undertaken by:	
Nurses	1,894,000 (65%)
Prison doctors	743,000
NHS visiting specialists	304,000

Source: Prison Service Staff Profiles and Projections Review (January 2006).

made known to and accepted by the whole prison community, i.e. the prisoners and the prison administration' (Pont 2006: 259).

Human rights standards and guidelines call for prisoners to receive healthcare provision at least equivalent to that in the community, with an emphasis on equivalence rather than equity because prisons are closed institutions with a custodial role. However, prisoners are generally in a poor state of health at admission thus requiring greater care and treatment than that required by many people in the community (Reyes 2001). Structural factors, such as overcrowding, may hinder efforts to improve prison living standards and prison healthcare services, such as preventing the spread of HIV, hepatitis and other infections among prisoners. Overcrowding also makes the implementation of harm reduction and prevention initiatives much more difficult and creates the conditions for increased prison violence (including sexual coercion and rape), which in turn places additional pressure on prison healthcare staff.

The type of prison will also make the problems more or less acute. For example, staff in remand prisons may face more severe problems due to the high turnover of a client group that has in many cases come straight off the street not having had access to medical care.

English and Welsh prisons are currently experiencing overcrowding and this increases the difficulty for prison staff to provide high-quality healthcare as a report by the European Committee for the Prevention of Torture (CPT 2005: 2) highlighted:

The issue of prison overcrowding has received considerable attention in the course of the ongoing dialogue between the CPT and the United Kingdom authorities over the past decade. The CPT has stated that an overcrowded prison entails, inter alia, cramped and unhygienic accommodation; a constant lack of privacy (even when performing such basic tasks as using a sanitary facility); reduced out-of-cell activities, due to demand outstripping the staff and facilities available; overburdened health-care services; increased tension and hence more violence between prisoners and between prisoners and staff. These effects were clearly visible in the establishments visited by the CPT's delegation in 2003. As the Committee has pointed out, for as long as overcrowding persists, the risk of prisoners being held in inhuman and degrading conditions of detention will remain.

The nature of the prison population is such that there are particular needs that have been consistently highlighted as being particularly important. Specifically, these include mental health, self-harm and suicide, problematic drug use and an ageing prison population.

There is a high incidence of mental illness amongst prisoners in the UK demonstrated by numerous studies (Reed 2003). The Prison Reform Trust and MIND, a leading mental health charity, argue that the rates of severe mental illness are more than ten times higher among male prisoners than the general population (Public Health News 2004). Although it is government policy that, wherever possible, mentally disordered offenders should receive care and treatment from health and social services (Reed Committee Report 1992), in reality mentally ill prisoners, once detained, frequently fail to receive appropriate psychiatric care (HM Inspectorate of Prisons 2004).

A report from the Joint Committee on Human Rights (2004) warned the UK government that more needs to be done to protect the right to life of prisoners, especially those who are 'vulnerable' as a result of mental illness or addictions. An assessment of the incidence of suicide in English and Welsh prisons from 1978 to 2003 (a total of 1,312 suicides) found that:

> The overall suicide rate was five times greater than that of the general male population of similar ages. The suicide rate among young offenders aged 15–17 years was particularly high – around 18 times that of the general male population of the same age. (Fazel 2005)

The fear of a suicide in custody drives HMPS and ministerial interest and this is another key area that prison medical staff must deal with. As staff from the Archway Surgery (contracted to provide medical services in the light of the new NHS approach) stated:

The Prison Service has a touching faith that the medical profession can define the risk of suicide in all cases. We are dealing with some angry impulsive young men with personality disorders. They may self harm, but not often clinically depressed, and can be dangerously impulsive. (http://www.careprovider. com/prison.htm)

It is interesting to note that HMPS procedures have done little to reduce the suicide rate compared to successful initiatives implemented in other correctional systems. For instance, prisoner suicide rates in local jails throughout the USA dropped in the period 1983 to 2002 from 1.27 to 0.47 per thousand and in US state prisons from 0.34 to 0.14 per thousand (Bureau of Justice 2005). In England and Wales the prisoner suicide rate between 1978 and 2003 increased (Shaw *et al.* 2004) and, more specifically, the self-inflicted death rate among male prisoners in England and Wales increased between 1982 and 1997 from 0.54 to 1.15 per thousand (Kelly and Bunty 1998).

Another key issue that impacts on healthcare staff is the high number of prisoners with a history of problematic drug use. The results of a survey (Ramsey 2003) addressing problematic drug use showed that nearly three-quarters of prisoners in the sample had taken an illegal drug in the twelve months prior to incarceration and of these, over half (55 per cent) reported that they had committed offences connected to their drug taking. The need for money to buy drugs was the most commonly cited factor. Findings such as these indicate the importance of drug treatment being available to prisoners and the need for drug use related healthcare and treatment from prison heathcare staff. One response by a GP contractor in one prison to the treatment of drug users was to avoid prescribing any drugs that might have had a market on the wings. In addition the Health Centre followed:

… the British National Formulary to the letter, so 'co-anything' was hardly used, and diazepam did not have any role. The difficulty was to detect the patient that must have morphine related drugs for their pain. Our policy was well known to the prisoners and this made life easier all round. (http://www. careprovider.com/prison.htm)

Finally, with increasing sentence lengths, healthcare staff are now also beginning to address health-related issues presented by older prisoners who are growing old in prison or will die in prison (Wahidin *et al.* 2006).

The structural and environmental challenges

There is a range of problems that Primary Care Trust (PCT) healthcare staff may encounter when they start to work in a secure environment. Many of these relate to overcrowding and the availability of appropriate facilities. These can both have a significantly detrimental impact on the quality of life for staff and prisoners and the quality of the service provided. There may be a cultural tension between practice in the community and practice in the prison environment, reflecting the complex balance that needs to be maintained between care and security or control. This is not necessarily located only at the shopfloor level: for example, the former Home Secretary, David Blunkett (2001–04), set the tone in respect of prisoner suicide when his first response to the death of Harold Shipman at HMP Wakefield was to ask: 'Is it too early to open a bottle?' (Press Association 16 January 2004). A more routine example of this culture clash is a recent court case where a group of ex-prisoners won a settlement from the Home Office because their community drug treatment (methadone substitution) was stopped by HMPS and they were made to 'go cold turkey' (*BBC News,* 13 November 2006).

The tension between care and control can be played out in the most fundamental aspects of healthcare provision, such as access to health professionals. It is not always a simple procedure to obtain a healthcare appointment in prison. For example, the Archway Surgery, which provided medical services within a prison, found that:

> [Prison] staff assumed that access by prisoners to the doctors had to be actively discouraged. NHS Primary Care's 24-hour and 48-hour access targets to NHS professionals, obligatory for GPs, was considered to be a sign of weakness. It often took three weeks or more simply for a prisoner to make an appointment to find out his blood test result. There was no other mechanism for him to get the result. Before we attempted to put an end to it, many emergency presentations were sent away because the prisoner had not made the formal application. (http://www.careprovider.com/prison.htm)

Dental waiting times are another area where standards are often compromised. The recommended guideline of two days for prisoners who need an urgent appointment is often exceeded. The average waiting time for all 140 prisons in England and Wales was 5.1 days (155 per cent under target, during the quarter to September 2006), and the time ranged from 1 to 21 days (DoH 2006). For routine appointments, for which the guidelines state that the waiting time should not exceed 42 days, the average wait for an appointment was 57 days (36 per cent under target), ranging from 6 to 304 days (DoH 2006). These figures demonstrate that many prisons are failing to comply with the recommended waiting times for both urgent and routine dental care.

There are of course excellent examples of good practice where NHS intervention has significantly improved prisoner access. For example, HMP Full Sutton, a high-security prison, trialled in 2004 an NHS Walk in Centre, which allowed prisoners more or less immediate and unquestioned access to nurse led primary care during working hours. The prison is currently building on this initiative by developing telehealth as a means of improving access by prisoners to clinical consultation at a distant hospital. This illustrates that innovation is possible, but such developments are currently inconsistent.

Organisation and reform of prison health

This section will briefly outline the cost, organisation and staffing of prison healthcare services. Prison healthcare costs, as well as escort and transport costs for prisoners, are understandably high. Based on the public sector Prison Healthcare Allocations for 2007/08 (letter from Richard Bradshaw and Michael Spurr, 1 March 2007, to Prison Service Area Managers), the £189 million sum equates to around £2,600 per prisoner per annum. The NHS will spend around £90 billion in 2007/08 (http://www.dh.gov.uk), equating to around £1,500 per patient. This difference reflects the frequency with which prisoners are required by HMPS procedure to be health-assessed, higher prisoner morbidity levels and consultation rates as well as the difficulties posed by providing healthcare within a secure setting.

Currently, prisoner healthcare is going through a period of change and consolidation due to its commissioning having been transferred from HMPS to the NHS. Delivery is provided from a variety of sources – the NHS, independent primary care contractors, private sector suppliers and still some by HMPS itself. These changes were brought about through the development of national and local partnerships between HMPS and the NHS (DoH 2000a).

The effectiveness of these changes is dependent on a range of factors within both the NHS and the prison environment – the degree to which PCT commissioners embrace the challenge, NHS priorities and resources, the robustness of local prison and NHS partnerships, HMPS overcrowding, culture, security considerations, staff recruitment and turnover of care staff. The transfer of these functions for public sector prisons has meant in practice that some PCTs have assumed the role of the provider as well as the commissioning function, whereas other PCTs have insisted on having responsibility for commissioning alone. The transition, which took place gradually between April 2003 and April 2006, has led to a significant number of HMPS-employed healthcare staff transferring into the NHS. Thus the 1,428 Healthcare staff employed by HMPS in December 2003 was reduced by 24 per cent to 1,086. Healthcare staffing is the only sector of HMPS personnel to have reduced in numbers as the prisoner population has risen.

The distribution of healthcare staff employed by HMPS on 31 December 2005 was as shown in Table 20.2 (HMPS 2006a). The number of healthcare staff involved in prison health but employed by non-HMPS providers is not routinely collected and is therefore unknown.

The HMPS Staff Profiles and Projections Review (HMPS 2006b) confirms that, unlike the gender composition of HMPS employees (two-thirds of whom are male), healthcare staff within prisons are chiefly female (three-quarters). The Working Party on Doctors Working in Prisons, recognising a shortage of female GPs, recommended that GP recruitment policies should ensure that female prisoners

Table 20.2 Distribution of healthcare staff employed by HMPS at 31 December 2005

Staff role	Distribution
Healthcare managers	7
Nurses	932
Doctors	50
Pharmacists	29
Pharmacy technicians	68
Total	**1,086**

had a choice to see a female doctor, which may in part explain this composition.

In addition to nurses (including mental health nurses), doctors and pharmacists, there is a range of primary care healthcare staff involved in caring for prisoners. This includes opticians, physiotherapists, occupational therapist, dieticians and health promotion professionals. It is also important to note that prison officers are often 'first on the scene' to incidents and may have to administer first aid or emergency care if required. As a result of this a prison-employed group of staff are responsible for some aspects of prison healthcare provision (DoH 2005b).

The providers of primary healthcare within prisons come from several sources: HMPS itself, the NHS (including some PCTs but by no means all) and independent healthcare enterprises such as 'independent contractors' (GP practices), locum agencies, out-of-hours GP enterprises and private healthcare companies. Currently, PCTs, who act as commissioners, continue to contract about 60 per cent of provision from the traditional provider, HMPS. This may suggest that PCT commissioners have not fully embraced the challenge of modernising prisoner health provision.

Nurses, doctors and pharmacists working in prisons

Following the publication of *The Future Organisation of Prison Healthcare* (DoH 1999), a number of concerns were raised about the professional isolation of prison nurses and doctors and difficulties in their recruitment and retention. In light of these concerns, Ministers commissioned a report on nurses (DoH 2000b), doctors (DoH 2001) and pharmacists (DoH 2003) working in prisons.

Nurses

The Nursing in Prisons Report (2000b) examined the development of prison nursing with particular reference to healthcare officers. This report made 35 recommendations to bring nursing in prisons in line with NHS practice in the wider community. The report concluded that prison healthcare services must make best use of available skills, mirror the changing direction recommended for NHS nursing strategy set out in *Making a Difference* (DoH 1999b) and acknowledge that nursing in a secure setting, with high turnover and prisoner variations, has different features and challenges from those found in the wider community. The report also recognised the important contribution that good nursing occupational standards could make to improving prison healthcare.

Nurses working in the prison environment should be able to access clinical supervision. The purpose of clinical supervision and performance appraisal is to encourage and promote continuous professional development and assure standards of care (Health Care Standards Unit 2006). A number of reports have highlighted how a lack of management support can create difficulties in the implementation of clinical supervision, which can lead to, in some instances, professional isolation (Health Care Standards Unit 2006; DoH 2000a).

Doctors

The Report on Doctors Working in Prisons in December 2001 made 50 recommendations in relation to the training, recruitment and retention of prison doctors, as well as increasing the links between HMPS and the NHS. In order to develop the medical workforce and provide the same level of care as that offered in the community, it was recognised that doctors must receive the same training, support and career development opportunities as their counterparts in the community. The report suggested that professional qualifications should be mandatory and that systems be developed that addressed poor performance. Doctors working in prisons are obliged to work at least one session per week in a relevant NHS setting.

The above report identified 713 doctors working with prisoners in England and Wales. These were a mix of prison-employed doctors (138 and mainly full-time medical officers), visiting GPs and NHS hospital specialists (mainly sessional or part-time) and doctors employed by private healthcare providers. By December 2005 the number of medical officers employed by prisons had decreased to 50 thus showing that the mainstreaming process was taking place.

Individuals held in custody have the same rights to and expectations of medical care as any other patients, including the right to privacy, dignity and confidentiality. Nevertheless, the role of prison doctors is particularly sensitive as they have a dual role both to their patients and to assist the authorities who employ them in the efficient and economic running of the prison (BMA 2004). Prison doctors may encounter obstacles in exercising their clinical judgment:

It is common for prescribing protocols to be agreed in many areas of medical practice in order to make best use of scarce resources. In some prisons, however, doctors feel that they have been excluded from the process of drawing up and agreeing suitable protocols that balance prisoners' needs with economy. They are in the very difficult position of being accountable to their professional body, the General Medical Council, for the standard of care, which includes the medications they prescribe, but at the same time they are often restricted by prison budgets in exercising their clinical judgement about prescribing. (BMA 2004)

Some doctors have complained of extreme professional isolation, due to a lack of support from colleagues working in the NHS:

Not all the blame can be attached to the prison system and the authorities that run it. Lack of support from colleagues in the NHS can put prison doctors at risk of feeling extremely isolated professionally. NHS hospitals are often reluctant to take prisoners who need more specialised services than are available in prison hospitals. For this reason, and because of the prison service's obsession with security, there are often delays in securing admission of prisoners to hospitals which can adversely affect the prisoners' health. These delays are extremely demoralising to the doctors caring for those prisoners, their patients. (BMA 2004)

Like all other doctors, prison doctors have to fulfil the requirements of revalidation and show that they are keeping clinical skills up to date in order to remain on the Medical Register. It is unclear, however, how the system will make the necessary facilities available for HMPS-employed doctors to maintain their professional skills, nor is it clear that this will be maintained consistently. Prison doctors' ability to engage in continuing professional development activities alongside their NHS colleagues has been a long-standing problem.

Pharmacists

A Pharmacy Service for Prisoners (DoH 2003) recognised that there were wide variations in the quality of the delivery of the pharmacy service, that there was an absence of any service framework and that the services that were available did not reflect prisoner needs. The establishment of the new NHS partnership was seen as an opportunity to provide a service equivalent to that available to patients in the community through maximising the use of existing resources and expertise, reducing professional isolation and ensuring a patient-focused service with added consistency and continuity.

The report identified that about 25 per cent of prisons had in-house, HMPS-employed pharmacy staff who served another 50 per cent of satellite prisons. Only 25 per cent received services from the NHS (hospitals and community pharmacists). The report made 30 recommendations for redressing professional workforce deficits and for mainstreaming the service into the NHS. As the work on modernising pharmacy for prisoners allowed for local determination in its implementation without a national survey, it is unclear how extensively the recommendations have been implemented.

Issues for healthcare staff

There are a number of key issues that impact on healthcare staff in prisons. Two are dealt with in this section: job satisfaction and absenteeism.

Job satisfaction and sickness rates

Although HMPS staff turnover rate is high for the public sector (8.6 per cent), the prison healthcare staff turnover rate is the highest among permanent HMPS employees, even after adjusting for those healthcare staff transferred out to PCTs, as shown below:

- All prison staff   8.6 per cent turnover
- Nurses   21.2 per cent turnover
- Other healthcare staff   18.8 per cent turnover

As mentioned previously, the frequency with which prisoners are required to be health-assessed impacts significantly on staff turnover. High healthcare staff turnover is likely to adversely affect both the clinician and the patient experience. This may be further exacerbated by the higher use of locum clinicians in some prisons than would be normal in the wider NHS community. However, PCTs can do much to ameliorate staff isolation and Spurgeon et al. (2004) noted that in one NHS Trust (Huntington PCT), collaboration between prisons and the PCT enabled both the recruitment and retention of high-quality staff to work within the prison.

The Nursing in Prisons Report (DoH 2000b), argued that sickness absence results in increased agency and overtime costs, compromised standards of healthcare, lowered staff morale and in addition challenged recruitment and retention. The report recommended that effective sickness management would benefit the whole healthcare team.

As a consequence of high staff turnover and sickness rates within HMPS, there is an effective shortfall in all prison staff numbers. For example, in December 2005 there were approximately 1,850 HMPS staff vacancies on a requirement of 48,868 (3.8 per cent). In contrast, HMPS-employed healthcare staff vacancies accounted for 237 of these staff, a disproportionate amount (19 per cent). HMPS is taking active steps to redress staff absence due to sickness and the figures for 2004/05 and 2005/06 show a promising improvement in some areas (HMPS 2006b) (see Table 20.3).

Bringing standards of healthcare in prison up to that of the general population

A key means to bring prison healthcare up to the standard of that available to the general population is for PCTs to see prison healthcare as 'just another GP practice'. This necessitates that prisons work in partnership with community healthcare providers and where transfer to the NHS is seen as an opportunity to improve healthcare delivery and to bring services up to NHS standards (Spurgeon *et al.* 2004). In order to do this the educational and training needs of all healthcare staff (including security staff) need to be evaluated. Healthcare staff coming from the outside community need to be made aware of the constraints and special requirements needed to work in secure environments. Security officers are not healthcare staff but in many

Table 20.3 Absence due to sickness

Employee	Sickness days lost per employee 04/05	Sickness days lost per employee 05/06
All prison staff	12.7%	12.2%
Nursing staff	16.4%	15.1%
Other health staff	9.4%	14.8%

situations, e.g. accidents or attempted suicide, they may be the first member of staff on the scene. It is important therefore that they should be given appropriate training and support to enable them to respond to emergency situations as they occur. In 2003 the DoH created the Justice and Offender Services Health Education and Development Group (JOSHED) to review the training available to staff working in custodial environments, with a particular focus on substance misuse, communicable diseases and mental health (DoH 2005a).

Prison healthcare staff also require continuing staff development that requires resources being made available in order to meet the postgraduate education and practice requirements of, for example, such bodies as the United Kingdom Central Committee for Nursing and Health Visiting (UKCCNHV).

The Prison Service needs to minimise sending prisoners to hospital because of the security risks involved and because the escort and security costs are immense. The Twelve-Month Study of Prison Escort and Bedwatches (DoH/HMPS 2006) showed that the annual non-clinical costs were nearly £17 m (£140 per escort and £3,731 per bedwatch). Staff shortages meant that outpatient appointments were often cancelled. The study made 18 recommendations for optimising this area of prison health activity which, when implemented, will improve matters significantly.

Conclusion

It is somewhat naive to imagine that the desirable quality of care in all prisons can be achieved when 60 per cent of NHS trusts admit care failings in the community, as demonstrated by the first self-assessments 'of light-touch regulation' introduced last year by the government (*Guardian*, 10 July 2006). These assessments of 570 NHS Trusts showed that there was 'widespread non-compliance with government guidance to ensure that treatment is safe, effective and well managed' (ibid.). A key breach identified was 'uncertainty about whether staff have taken part in mandatory training' and this raises a fundamental question as to whether healthcare staff working in the prison environment are receiving the training required to work both effectively and professionally in prison to provide a high quality of care (*Guardian*, 10 July 2006).

The challenges of ensuring quality healthcare for England and Wales' burgeoning prison population are many, with the added dimension of having roots in both NHS and HMPS systems. Owing to the recent reorganisation of NHS PCTs and Strategic Health Authorities (SHA), allied to the retrenchment brought about by pressures on NHS budgets, there is growing recognition within the NHS that getting 'more for less' is not going to be easy. Some SHAs and their PCTs with prisons are exploring the notion of rationalising the PCT commissioning bodies in order to develop expertise, e.g. one PCT could commission prison healthcare for, say, five or six in its region, thus gaining expertise and efficiencies. It follows that the plethora of provider organisations, with more robust and specified commissioning in place, could be rationalised further in order to streamline provision and enhance quality.

Prison transfers and security procedures can also lead to difficulties in delivering prison health services, often having a detrimental impact such as increased waiting times. Commissioners are beginning to realise the need for a clear 'Memorandum of Understanding' with HMPS in order to minimise the number of adverse practices that affect the quality of healthcare delivery. This proposal was first put forward by the Northumberland Care Trust which commissions for two prison establishments.

Prison healthcare has made gradual but positive progress since the transfer of management to NHS PCTs was first proposed in 2002. There are pockets of excellent practice in some establishments, along with examples of better professional engagement (e.g. doctor and nurse recruitment). The future of prison healthcare looks promising. It is only through more effective and transparent practice that significant gains will be made in the quality of healthcare for prisoners which in turn will minimise the endless procedural and systemic challenges faced by healthcare staff every day.

Seminar questions

1 Providing healthcare in prisons raises a number of challenges for healthcare staff, for example dealing with a lack of trust from a client group unable to choose his or her own doctor and the clash between security and healthcare for a prisoner patient. What key strategies would you suggest to overcome this lack of trust?
2 In your group design a training module for prison staff about harm reduction. You will need to consider issues such as provision of needle exchange in prison, substitution treatment, condoms, bleach and health and safety measures.
3 Is prison an appropriate place to house those with mental health problems or problematic drug use? What is the alternative?

4 Prison healthcare staff shortages are common in many countries. What initiatives would you introduce to (a) attract healthcare staff to come to work in prisons and (b) overcome cultural differences between working within prisons and in the community?

Recommended reading

In terms of recommended readings we suggest that students should read Walmsley (2005) *Further Developments in the Prison Systems of Central and Eastern Europe: Achievements, Problems and Objectives*, as this provides an excellent overview of not only the issues that impact on healthcare but the structure of prison systems in other European countries. In addition MacDonald (2005) *A Study of Healthcare Provision, Existing Drug Services and Strategies Operating in Prison in Ten Countries from Central and Eastern Europe*, provides a detailed analysis of the delivery of health care in a range of European countries. For a more in-depth discussion of the key issues of harm reduction and problematic drug use refer to the information provided by Lines, Jürgens, Betteridge, Laticevschi, Nelles and Stöver (2006) *Prison Needle Exchange: Lessons from a Comprehensive Review of International Evidence and Experience* and the Prison Reform Trust and National AIDS Trust (2006) provide excellent coverage. For more detailed readings specifically about prison healthcare in England and Wales please refer to the references provided in this chapter.

References

Archway Surgery – see online: http://www.careprovider.com/prison.htm.

BBC News (2006) 'Where Drugs Are Withdrawn or Cut Short', Monday, 13 November.

British Medical Association (2004) *Prison Medicine: A Crisis Waiting to Break: Pressure to Compromise Clinical Judgement*. See online at: http://www.bma.org.uk/ap.nsf/Content/Prisonmedicine.

Bureau of Justice Statistics (2005) US Department of Justice Press Release, 21 August.

Committee for the Prevention of Torture (2005) *Report to the Government of the United Kingdom on the visit to the United Kingdom and the Isle of Man carried out by the European Committee for the Prevention of Torture and Inhuman or Degrading Treatment or Punishment (CPT) from 12 to 23 May 2003*. Strasbourg.

Department of Health (1999a) *The Future Organisation of Prison Healthcare*. London: Department of Health.

Department of Health (1999b) *Making A Difference*. London: Department of Health.

Department of Health (2000a) *Prison Health Handbook*. London: Prison Health Policy Unit and Task Force/Department of Health.

Department of Health (2000b) *Report on the Working Group on Nursing in Prisons*. London: Department of Health.

Department of Health (2001) *Report on the Working Group on Doctors Working in Prisons*. London: Department of Health.

Department of Health (2003) *A Pharmacy Service for Prisoners*. London: Department of Health.

Department of Health (2005a) *Care Services Improvement Partnership*. London: Justice and Offender Services Health Education and Development Group (JOSHED).

Department of Health (2005b) *Prison Health: An Education and Training Framework for Staff Providing Healthcare in Prisons*. London: Department of Health and Elaine Sauvé Associates.

Department of Health (2006) *Prison Health Traffic Lights/Performance Assessment*. London: Department of Health.

Department of Health and HM Prison Service (2006) *A Twelve-Month Study of Prison Healthcare Escort and Bedwatches*. London: Department of Health.

Fazel, S. (2005) 'Male Prisoners 5 Times More Likely to Commit Suicide than Males Not in Prison, UK', *Mental Health News*. See online at: http://www.medicalnewstoday.com/medicalnews.php?newsid=17772.

Health Care Standards Unit (2006) *DRAFT Signpost C5b: Health Care Organisations Ensure That Clinical Care and Treatment Are Carried Out Under Supervision and Leadership*. See online at: http://www.hcsu.org.uk/index.php?option=com_content&task=view&id=152&Itemid=111 (accessed 20 July 2006).

HM Inspectorate of Prisons (2004) *Annual Report of HM Chief Inspector of Prisons for England & Wales 2002–2003*. London: HMSO.

HM Prison Service (2006a) *Human Resource Planning*. London: HMSO.

HM Prison Service (2006b) *Staff Profiles and Projections Review*. London: HMSO.

Joint Committee on Human Rights (2004) *Too Many Dying in UK Prisons, Mainly Through Suicide*. See online at: http://www.hda-online.org.uk/html/about/phnews.asp?ItemID=7316812.

Kelly, S. and Bunty, J. (1998) 'Demography and Health, Population Trends'. Office of National Statistics (92), Summer.

Lines, R., Jürgens, R., Betteridge, G., Laticevschi, D., Nelles, J. and Stöver, H. (2006) *Prison Needle Exchange: Lessons from a Comprehensive Review of International Evidence and Experience*, 2nd edn. Canadian HIV/AIDS Legal Network; also available in French and Russian (see: http://www.aidslaw.ca).

MacDonald, M. (2005) *A Study of Health Care Provision, Existing Drug Services and Strategies Operating in Prisons in Ten Countries from Central and Eastern Europe*. Helsinki: HEUNI (see: http://www.heuni.fi/12542.htm).

Pont, J. (2006) 'Medical Ethics in Prisons: Rules, Standards and Challenges', *International Journal of Prisoner Health*, 2 (4).

Press Association (2004) *Blunkett Tells of Joy at Shipman's Death*, 16 January.

Prison Reform Trust and National AIDS Trust (2005) *HIV and Hepatitis in UK Prisons: Addressing Prisoners' Healthcare Needs*. London: Prisoner Reform Trust (see: http://www.nat.org.uk/HIV_Testing_&_Care/Prisons_&_ detention).

Public Health News (2004) 'Mental Health Crisis Growing in Prisons', 17 May. Online at: http://www.publichealthnews.com.

Ramsay, M. (ed.) (2003) *Prisoners' Drug Use and Treatment: Seven Research Studies*, Home Office Research Study 267. London: Home Office Research, Development and Statistics Directorate.

Reed Committee Report (1992) *Review of Health and Social Services for Mentally Disordered Offenders and Others Requiring Similar Services. Volume 2: Service Needs – Community Advisory Group Report*. London: HMSO.

Reed, J. (2003) 'Mental Health Care in Prisons', *British Journal of Psychiatry*, 182: 287–8.

Reyes, H. (2001) 'Health and Human Rights in Prisons', extract from *HIV in Prisons: A Reader with Particular Relevance to the Newly Independent States*, chapter 2, pp. 9–18, World Health Organization – Europe 'HIPP' (Health in Prisons Project).

Shaw, J., Baker, D., Hunt, I., Moloney, A. and Appleby, L. (2004) 'Suicide by Prisoners, National Clinical Survey', *British Journal of Psychiatry*, 184: 263–8.

Smith, R. (1997) 'Prisoner's Health: A Test for Civilisation', *British Medical Journal*, 315: 1.

Spurgeon, P., Tyler, S., Woodin, J. and Lemiech, R. (2004) *Prison Health Development Network: Key Themes and Case Study Reports*. University of Birmingham.

United Nations Office on Drugs and Crime (2006) *HIV/AIDS Prevention, Care, Treatment and Support in Prison Settings: A Framework for an Effective National Response*. New York: United Nations, co-published with the World Health Organization and the Joint United Nations Programme on HIV/AIDS.

Wahidin, A., Farney, L. and Aday, R. (2006) *Adapting to Life in Prison: From The Voices of Older Female Prisoners*. Paper presented at the annual meeting of the American Society of Criminology (ASC), Los Angeles Convention Center, Los Angeles, CA, 1 November (see online at: http://www. allacademic.com/meta/p125422_index.html).

Walmsley, R. (2005) *Further Developments in the Prison Systems of Central and Eastern Europe: Achievements, Problems and Objectives*. Helsinki, HEUNI.

Part 5

Developing the Human Resources of Prisons

Chapter 21

Recruitment and assessment of prison staff

Martin McHugh, Jim Heavens and Keith Baxter

Introduction

Effective recruitment is essential to any organisation, not only to ensure that it has the right number of employees, but also to ensure that it has employees with the appropriate skills and attitudes. Failure to get recruitment right can have significant consequences in terms of reduced performance and increased turnover and absenteeism (ACAS 1999). The aim of this chapter is to provide an overview of the crucial practices of recruitment and promotion assessment in the public sector Prison Service. The typical recruitment process will involve a number of elements including: identifying the requirements of the role; attracting potential employees; methods of selection; and review of effectiveness. However, this discussion focuses particularly on the methods of selection for key groups of staff including prison officers and managers.

The approach of the public sector to people management has changed significantly since the 1980s. The main development has seen the public service opened up to commercial competition and adopting practices from the private sector, including the wide use of performance targets. This approach has been described as New Public Management (NPM) (Hood 1991; Ferlie *et al.* 1996). Some of the practices imported from the private sector have related to people management. In particular, the philosophy of human resource management (HRM) has become increasingly important. Traditional personnel work has been focused on employee welfare, whereas HRM works from the needs of the organisation and is therefore more closely aligned with business strategy (Torrington 1989). In prisons, this focus was particularly notable when HMPS launched its People Strategy Programme in 2004. This programme aimed to centralise transactional personnel work for all prisons into a single shared service centre, while having specialist and strategic support available to prisons through area teams and establishment-based business partners. The aim was to make HR more strategic and direct it towards providing the people aspects of the five-year strategy Securing the Future (2007). These strategic changes have had an impact on the practice of recruitment and selection. In particular, this has become integrated with other elements of HR including appraisal, development and performance management, with recruitment seen not just as a bureaucratic task that provides the right number of staff, but a strategic, business-orientated process in which people add value to an organisation (Evenden 1993). The way in which this has taken shape in relation to the recruitment and promotion of prison staff will be described below.

Recruitment in prisons – general principles

The Prison Service employs almost 50,000 people, covering a wide range of grades and specialisms (see Chapter 1). The majority of staff undertake 'operational' duties involving direct contact with prisoners or the public, while a significant number are employed in administrative and support functions. In a typical year the Prison Service recruits around 6,000 staff. In 2005, for example, the following staff were recruited: 1,707 prison officers, 1,646 operational support grades, 1,371 administrative staff, 262 psychology staff, 298 healthcare staff, 384 industrial staff, 32 chaplains and several hundred into other grades (figures provided by HM Prison Service).

Recruiting staff suited to work in the custodial environment is crucial if the service is to fulfil its business objectives. The custodial environment is unique in the pressures and challenges it poses. Moreover, recruiting unsuitable staff is expensive and damaging to the organisation and individuals. As well as these contextual contraints, recruitment must conform to the principles outlined in the Civil Service Commissioner's Recruitment Code (2004). This distinguishes the public sector service from its competitors.

Over the last decade, the Prison Service has attempted to place recruitment closer to the point of service. This marks a shift from a largely centralised model of recruitment in the 1980s which involved nationwide advertising campaigns, a national training course and assigned newly trained officers based on national staffing needs rather than candidate preferences. Although the devolution of responsibility enables greater flexibility in responding to local needs, this model poses challenges in terms of maintaining national standards. Many prisons are geographically isolated and although the introduction of local pay allowances (i.e. additional payments where housing costs are high or recruitment difficult) has had some beneficial effect, the labour pool is limited in some areas. This is an important factor when attempting to attract a diverse workforce which reflects the range of prisoners in the care of HMPS. Demonstrating respect for ethnicity and diversity is a crucial attribute for prison personnel. In 2001 the Prison Service became the first public service employer to require all new recruits to sign a declaration indicating that they have no affiliation with racist organisations. There are also national and local targets that aim to ensure that the number of black and minority ethnic staff reflects the diversity of the local community.

Prison officer recruitment

The main drawback of the selection process in the 1980s was the weight given to the unstructured interview – the least reliable of selection tools (Taylor 1998). In the light of this weakness, a new selection tool was developed in the mid-1990s. The basics for this were found using in-house techniques developed to train staff in incident command and hostage negotiation, i.e. practice simulation. The theory of simulations is that they create the opportunity for candidates to demonstrate the skills that would be required in real settings. Although well established in settings which require high skill levels, simulations had been less widely used in basic-grade recruitment.

The selection technique was based on the results of a job analysis of the core behaviours required for the prison officer role. These have been refined over the last decade to include: non-verbal listening, assertion, showing understanding, suspending judgment, exploring and clarifying, and holding appropriate attitudes to diversity-related issues. In order to demonstrate these behaviours, applicants are invited to attend a local assessment centre where they are assessed in four role-play simulations set in a non-prison context, one of which tests attitudes to diversity. In 2004, a separate simulation was introduced to specifically test the core behaviours relevant to a juvenile context (with offenders under the age of 18). Performance is assessed against standardised and defined behavioural criteria. The simulations are video recorded, which allows independent quality control and the reassessment of individuals who are close to the pass threshold.

The use of simulations represents a significant improvement over the unstructured interview. Candidates can be presented with a diverse range of tasks – and different types of role players – in which inappropriate attitudes and behaviours are likely to be exposed. Little of this behaviour is captured in a standard interview. There are, of course, limitations on what can be assessed through role-plays. Some staff within the Prison Service have argued that candidates can merely play act through the process. However, the feedback from those administering and participating in the process suggests that the range of simulations that the candidates encounter makes this unlikely. In fact, it is demonstrably much easier for a candidate to deceive the interview panel than the simulations (Taylor 1998). However, one constraint on what can be assessed during the selection process is the requirement of affordability and cost-efficiency. Keeping time to hire down to a minimum is crucial to avoid high drop out rates; adding elements to the recruitment process may add to its robustness but may be simply too expensive.

It is important that prospective prison officers possess the levels of basic literacy and numeracy skills necessary for the job. During 2006, the Prison Officer Selection Test (POST) was introduced to check for the presence of such everyday skills using a work sample test. As well as providing face validity, tests drawn from such work samples have been shown to be more effective than other forms of standardised test (Taylor 1998). The test tasks are placed within a custodial context that gives candidates an insight into what they will face in their daily role. The test includes: numeracy, listening and recall, checking information, applying rules, reading comprehension, writing clearly and visual recall. The test has been extensively piloted and has been subject to external independent scrutiny. A practice version is available to prospective applicants via the Prison Service website (http://www.hmprisonservice.gov.uk), which also includes detailed information about the role of the prison officer and the qualities required for the job.

The recruitment process is managed either by individual prisons or clusters of establishments in an area. In cases where there are high numbers of applicants, a competence questionnaire may be used as a method to filter the number of applicants proceeding to the POST test. A number of establishments arrange familiarisation events at the start of recruitment campaigns to give prospective candidates the opportunity to gather information about the selection process and the job itself. For example, these events provide information about the POST and the assessment centre (a video example of a role-play is played) and what is involved in the fitness and medical tests. Often, prison officers and trainers give presentations at these events, describing the role and the training involved in becoming a prison officer, so as to provide a realistic job preview.

Some areas have conducted outreach work to encourage a more diverse range of applicants, for example by developing local contacts and becoming involved in community events. This is particularly important given the aim of increasing the number of staff from black and minority ethnic (BME) communities. Recent years have seen a significant improvement in the ability of the Prison Service to attract such applicants, although naturally the picture varies across the country. During 2005/06, 352 staff from a BME background joined the Service representing 8.2 per cent of all recruits (figures provided by HM Prison Service). This compares to an average BME population of 7 per cent within the communities surrounding Prison Service establishments. Nine out of the 13 operational areas recruited proportionately more BME staff than are resident in their local communities (figures provided by HM Prison Service).

Recruitment of other staff

The majority of non-officer recruitment uses a standard competence-based application form followed by a competence-based interview conducted by a panel of at least two members, an approach that has a higher level of reliability than unstructured interviews (Taylor 1998). Applications are sifted where the number of applicants are high.

The placement of job vacancies on the Prison Service website has made recruitment more transparent and accessible. For example, in a typical month (July 2006) the website received 65,126 visitors to the careers and jobs page (http://www.hmprisonservice.gov.uk). In addition to operational roles, the site lists jobs in the following areas: administration, agricultural work, catering, building, chaplaincy, finance and procurement, healthcare, instructional officer work, managerial positions and psychologist jobs. In the majority of cases, selection takes place through a competence-based interview. There are, however, a small number of roles which involve a more substantial assessment process. These are described below.

Specialist staff

From time to time, recruitment drives are conducted for specialists posts such as human resources professionals, accountants and psychology staff. Depending on the scale of recruitment, selection may involve attendance at an assessment centre consisting of in-tray exercises, psychometric tests and role-plays.

One example of the use of assessment centre techniques can be found in the recruitment of prison chaplains. The Prison Service employs just over 300 chaplains of whom just under 40 per cent work part-time. They represent a wide range of faith traditions, including Buddhism, Church of England, Free Church, Hinduism, Judaism, Islam, Roman Catholicism and Sikhism. Recruitment into full-time posts in the chaplaincy is centrally managed. The selection process assesses competencies specific to the prison environment, an area for which not all ministers will be suited. The process includes a short pre-prepared sermon for a custodial audience and delivered to an audience of assessors and candidates, a role-play within a prison setting and a panel interview. Assessment is based on a competence profile. These exercises require candidates to reflect on the prison context, and provide them with some understanding of what it is like to work in a prison.

Graduate recruitment: fast-track managers

Over the last 20 years, the Prison Service has provided direct, annual entry for graduates onto its Intensive Development Scheme (IDS), previously known as the Accelerated Promotion Scheme. Currently, the scheme consists of a three-year development programme including a year as a prison officer, a year as a senior officer (first-line manager) and a year as a trainee operational manager (junior governor). On graduation from the scheme, candidates take on middle management roles with the prospect of speedy progression for those who are the most able.

The scheme has proved increasingly popular. The campaign in 2005/06 attracted just under 1,400 applications, with 23 final offers made. The scheme attracts more applicants from women (on a ratio of about 65–35 per cent) (figures provided by HM Prison Service), which seems to reflect the higher levels of interest from graduates studying subjects that have a greater proportion of female students. The scheme has historically been less successful in attracting high-quality applicants from BME communities. Although there may be a number of reasons for this, chief among them is the perceived low status associated with the custodial sector compared with the more traditional professions such as medicine and the law. In recent years, effort has been devoted to targeting universities and colleges with higher proportions of BME students and to more generic outreach campaigns highlighting the attraction of the Prison Service as an employer. In the 2005/06 campaign, 18 per cent of applicants were from BME backgrounds – a higher figure than the average of 14 per cent BME students in universities/colleges. This particular campaign resulted in 11 per cent of offers being made to BME candidates (figures provided by HM Prison Service).

A number of improvements have been made in order to attract good quality candidates, including the award of a non-consolidated bonus of £2,500 to graduates during their first six months to assist with debt and expenses. Although the starting pay for graduates is tied to prison officer pay (£17,774 in 2006) and compares unfavourably with the public sector generally, where the median starting salary is £23,136 for graduates (Association of Graduate Recruiters 2006), the pay progression prospects are good, with £28,654 offered by the second year on progression to senior officer. Additional local pay allowances of up to £4,250 may be payable according to geographical location. Prospective applicants may register interest by e-mail on the Prison Service website at any time. The scheme is also open to internal candidates, with or without a degree. Retention rates on the programme are very good (over 90 per cent) and compare favourably with the norm for graduate schemes. A sizeable proportion (27 per cent) of current in-charge governors are graduates of fast-track programmes.

The selection process for the Intensive Development Scheme has typically been modelled around the traditional Civil Service selection procedure, involving a written sift followed by an assessment centre. The final stage assessment centre typically includes four or five exercises, such as group tasks, oral briefing and panel interview. A number of improvements have been made to this stage including the adoption of a matrix using competence assessment, ensuring that each assessor only assesses a candidate once in one exercise and using a competence profile for the pass/fail threshold to ensure a better fit between outcome and candidate performance. All exercises are video-recorded to allow independent review where candidates fall into the borderline–fail category. These changes have reduced the likelihood of bias through either a horns/halo effect or factors irrelevant to the competencies under consideration. In particular, the panel interview is entirely competence-assessed and is given equal weighting to the other exercises. Feeling that they have been treated fairly and objectively through the assessment centre process is important to participants and to a wider audience of potential recruits (Woodruffe 2000). As Kandola *et al.* (2001) observe, graduates discuss their recruitment experiences with their peers and decisions about applying to the Prison Service will be influenced by such discussions.

Direct-entry recruitment of managers

The Prison Service has historically recruited managers from external routes and this has been seen as essential to bring in managers from diverse backgrounds. During the 1970s and 1980s, graduates and experienced managers were directly recruited onto the assistant governors' training programme. This programme was superseded by the Accelerated Promotion Scheme in the late 1980s. At the end of the 1990s, some limited direct-entry recruitment at middle manager level was undertaken. Although this was small scale it successfully provided a more diverse talent pool. It is anticipated that routes at middle manager level will be opened up further in the future. A number of limited competitions have also been held for administrative and specialist staff already employed by the service who have wished to move into operational management (see Wilson and Bryans 1998, for a historical overview of prison governor recruitment during the twentieth century).

Senior managers

The Prison Service has recently introduced, for the first time, a scheme to recruit experienced managers directly into senior prison management roles. First piloted in 2005, the programme is aimed at attracting managers who have the experience and skills required to quickly be ready to take on the role of deputy governor of a large establishment or an in-charge position in a smaller one. Since the majority of senior governors have traditionally come up through mainstream routes and have accrued substantial operational experience, this is a challenging programme.

Application for the scheme was fully facilitated online and consisted of an application form including a competence questionnaire. The four

376

main competencies for which candidates were required to provide examples were decision-making, communicating and influencing, leadership and drive for results. The campaign micro-site (changeitnow. co.uk) described the skills and experience which successful candidates were likely to need to be ready for such a senior level programme. They included people management, business performance management, financial management, working with stakeholders, strategic planning and working in a duty-of-care environment.

The selection process consisted of three stages, each of which were pass or fail: consideration of the applicant's initial application and competence form; undertaking a senior operational manager job simulation assessment centre (JSAC); and a final assessment day which included personality assessment, verbal and numerical reasoning tests, and a structured panel interview.

Psychometric and ability testing yield valuable supplementary evidence to the skills profile provided from the JSAC and the structured interview. The structured interview, when used correctly, is a powerful tool for assessing candidates' motivation, experience and values (see Dipboye 1997, for an overview of the most effective design in structured interviews). The extent to which psychometric data should be used in the final decision-making is still the subject of debate but studies of the predictive validity of cognitive ability tests have generally found a positive correlation between scores on general mental ability tests and future job success (Bertua *et al.* 2005).

A second round of recruitment onto the programme was conducted in 2006 with wider advertising. It is too early to assess the impact and effectiveness of this programme but it represents a bold step in creating a new entry route at a hitherto untapped level.

Assessment of staff in mainstream progression

The first part of this chapter has focused on recruitment and selection of staff externally. The remaining sections will cover assessment used internally for staff promotion, particularly for operational staff, i.e. prison officers (including senior and principal officers) and governor grades.

It may first be helpful to describe the current grading structure for operational staff, which has been the subject of substantial change over the last decade. Operational grades form part of a unified grading structure, with the prison officer rank as the base (see Figure 21.1).

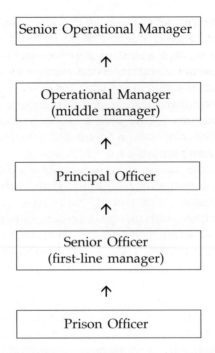

Figure 21.1 Operational grading structure

The key progression points are: from prison officer to senior officer (this involves a first move into line management); from principal officer to operational manager (this involves a move out of uniform into what was formerly described as a junior governor role); and from operational manager to senior operational (this involves a move from middle management as head of a function into a senior role such as deputy governor or governor).

Robust assessment processes have been introduced for these key progression points. For each, an assessment centre has been introduced based upon the methodology used for prison officer recruitment, using job simulations pitched at the level to which prospective candidates are applying for promotion. As a tool in promotion assessment, simulations were developed by the police in the mid-1990s (Bligh 1994), and the similarities between the police and prison roles suggested that this approach might also be appropriate for prison officer recruitment. Testing candidates in the context of a job simulation is as close to testing candidates in the real setting as is possible (see Baxter *et al.* 2004, for a fuller account of the JSAC methodology).

For each managerial level a job analysis is conducted to identify behaviours crucial to good performance. This provides the material for the construction of a series of realistic problems or scenarios. Unlike the simulations used in recruitment, the promotion JSACs simulations are set in a prison context. Typically, a JSAC will consist of eight simulations, each lasting between 15 and 20 minutes. The scenarios are road-tested and benchmarked with operational staff to ensure that they are both realistic and representative of work demands at the higher grade.

Job analyses have identified the following core skills: briefing, inquiring, caring, developing, acknowledging achievement, giving constructive criticism, persuading, managing conflict, incident management, writing skills and analysing statistical and written information. These skills become increasingly strategic at higher levels. In addition, candidates are assessed on valuing diversity and upholding equal opportunities.

To increase reliability, each JSAC is constructed so that core managerial skills are tested at least three times across different simulations. In each scenario, the candidate will encounter a trained role-player(s) with whom they have to interact to deal with the particular problem(s). All role-players receive training and are prepared on how to respond to candidate performance in a systematic and standardised way. Each scenario is assessed in real time and is video-recorded to allow quality control and case-by-case review. This is of particular importance where a candidate's performance is borderline. The assessor panel is organised so that each scenario is assessed by a trained assessor working independently on a single scenario. Thus, in a typical JSAC, a candidate will have been observed by eight independent assessors. This significantly reduces the possibility of assessor bias and adverse impact.

Prior to arrival at a JSAC, a candidate will typically have received pre-reading materials which contain information relevant to the particular set of scenarios they will face. On arrival, they will receive a further briefing and additional materials, including their timetable/schedule of appointments for the day. Each candidate is then allocated their own room, where they have opportunity to prepare for the role-plays. The candidate stays in that room for the rest of the period and the role-play staff appear on schedule. The candidate will have 15 to 20 minutes to explore the issues with each role-player and take appropriate action to deal with the matters presented.

The JSAC process has been subjected to a number of independent reviews. These have concluded that it is a robust and transparent process which is objective and fair, meets best-practice standards in assessment design and meets occupational standards on assessment.

The JSAC process also plays a useful function as an organisational development tool. First, the specific choice of scenarios sends out a clear statement to staff about priorities. For example, one scenario requires a candidate to reach a successful resolution with a prisoner while demonstrating care and compassion. A successful candidate shows a commitment to decency and anyone not showing this commitment is unlikely to be successful. In this sense, the JSAC is a tool with substantial power to drive organisational change. Second, each JSAC functions as an organisational diagnostic tool by providing data on the skill level of candidate cohorts. This diagnostic analysis can be conducted at a range of levels, from national to area down to individual units within prisons. Essentially, this provides a training needs analysis for the organisation which can be used to identify skill deficits and act as a barometer to assess the impact of training.

An integrated selection and organisational development model

The Prison Service has undergone a number of strategic changes over recent years. For example, the development of the decency agenda (Coyle 2003) and the introduction of measurements in the quality of prison life (Liebling, assisted by Arnold, 2004) have placed greater emphasis on the treatment of prisoners by staff. There have also been externally imposed changes, some in response to incidents, such as the Mubarek Inquiry (Keith 2006), while others have been more planned, such as the creation of the National Offender Management Service (NOMS). NOMS was set up following the publication of the Carter Report (2003). The aim was to draw together organisations delivering services to offenders, such as prisons and probation, into a single organisation, and to reinvigorate the idea of contestability, including promoting competition and benchmarking services.

In meeting these strategic challenges, the Prison Service has had to develop its people management approach. The developments have also reflected changes in people management itself, including the move to more strategic HRM, providing an integrated HR framework directed towards achieving organisational strategy. Four major developments are highlighted below as examples of the next steps in developing recruitment and selection.

First, a new Competency and Qualities Framework (CQF) is being developed for implementation in 2007. The framework takes account both of specially commissioned research and findings from research on prison life (for example, Liebling and Price 2001). It will be in line with Professional Skills for Government (see http://psg.civilservice. gov.uk/), a strategy for people management across the Civil Service. The framework comprises twelve behavioural competencies: achieving a safe and secure environment; showing resilience; acting with integrity; respecting others; persuading and influencing; building relationships and team working; communicating effectively; caring; problem-solving and decision-making; organising and maximising performance; embracing change; and developing yourself and others. The framework will provide the basis for recruitment and promotion, individual and team development, and individual feedback from managers or peers. Leadership development will be based on an enhanced version of the CQF, called the Leadership Qualities Framework, which includes cognitive as well as behavioural descriptors.

Second, assessment will be integrated with staff development. An example of this was the introduction in 2006 of a development centre as a mandatory element of senior operational manager accreditation (JSAC) All candidates attended a two-day development centre and undertook a number of psychometric and personality tests. They were given advice about self-development, were provided with feedback on their test results and participated in a career development interview. The development centre was not part of the assessment. Each candidate subsequently received a detailed report on their results and individual advice about their suitability for the role of a senior operational manager. Those candidates who were not eligible for progression were provided with advice as to whether to defer, look for wider experience or re-evaluate the possibility of becoming a senior manager. The matter of whether to proceed further then became a matter for the candidate and his or her area manager. The report was also to be used as the basis for a personal development plan.

This approach is likely to be used more extensively in the future so that development becomes accessible prior to promotion. In making decisions about suitability, the individual's managers will be given information upon which they can make judgments about development. Development centres at every level of promotion are unlikely to be affordable, but a close integration of development with assessment can be achieved through less formal structures, including a more informed dialogue between the individual and their manager. The establishment of Organisational Development (OD) within the Service will assist this change, with OD advisers working alongside area managers and HR business partners.

Third, planning will be improved. Increasingly, HR planning tools are being used to inform management decisions. However, *workforce planning* is constrained by the inadequacies of IT systems. This should be significantly addressed though the People Strategy Programme, one element of which is to provide integrated systems for the collection of workforce information. At more senior levels, the Service has improved *succession planning* arrangements. A Succession Planning Committee (SPC) oversees the appointment, promotion and recruitment of all senior operational managers and, increasingly, other senior managers and operational managers. It is supported by the Succession and Management Unit which has collated information about senior staff from operational manager upwards to provide a more detailed picture of the senior workforce. This information, taken with assessments by area managers and the SPC, has enabled the Service to develop a succession plan for governor-in-charge and deputy governor levels at all establishments. This identifies those who are considered able to take over either immediately or in one or more years' time.

While women are rapidly gaining ground in terms of their numbers at senior operational manager levels, the number from black and minority ethnic backgrounds remains low. The Service recognises that it needs to move more quickly in addressing this shortfall and ensuring greater diversity at this level. This effort has highlighted some other key issues for future planning decisions, not least the fact that managers at operational and senior operational levels are increasingly inexperienced, are not attracted by the prospect of mobility (even to take up a more senior post) and have frequently paid little attention to their own development or those reporting to them. The work has also suggested that prisons, like many other organisations, will struggle to fill all of their vacancies with suitable managers at a senior level. This has led to the Service embarking on a new direct entry scheme for senior prison managers in 2005, as described earlier.

In regard to individual development and the need to ensure capability from within the potential senior management cadre, the work of succession planning will be increasingly seen as one of *talent management*. The planning for and availability of managers to take on more senior roles will be linked more closely to judgments about readiness to progress and the level of individual personal development that has taken place.

Fourth, a revised appraisal system, the Staff Performance and Development Report (SPDR), was introduced in 2006, with the intention of simplifying procedures and concentrating on the most significant areas of work for each individual. A Performance Management Improvement Project has recently been launched with a wide brief to consider and, if accepted, to introduce measures that will assist managers to boost and maintain improved performance. Again, this work is likely to be effective only if it provides both practical and easily digested measures that give prison managers the tools, skills and knowledge to help them lift performance.

Conclusion

This chapter provides an insight into the recent advances made by the Prison Service in selection and assessment. Over the last 15 years, there have been major changes in prisons, including the impact of NPM, the development of more value-based strategies such as the decency agenda, and the move towards integrated offender management within a competitive criminal justice environment. Human resource management has an essential role to play in ensuring that the Prison Service can respond successfully to these challenges.

This chapter has illustrated how the practice of recruitment and selection has become more integrated. This is both in the sense that it has become more internally integrated – joined up with other HR practices such as appraisal and development – and more closely aligned with strategic objectives, with changing priorities being reflected in recruitment practice. To reflect these changing needs, the practices of recruitment have also become more flexible and less bureaucratic. For example, recruitment is being aimed at a much more diverse range of potential recruits, with direct recruitment routes being opened up through the removal of unnecessary barriers. Methods of recruitment are also becoming more diverse, and now range from competence based interviews to work sampling and assessment centres. As reflects a view that people are a 'vaule-adding resource', these are designed to optimise effectiveness rather than simply meet procedural guidelines. In coming years, the challenge for recruitment and selection will be to continue to meet the demands made on prisons in a rapidly changing penal environment.

Seminar questions

1 How do recruitment methods reflect organisational strategy?
2 What are the risks and benefits of recruiting people directly into senior prison management positions?
3 How can prisons attract more recruits from BME communities?

Recommended reading

The chapter by Evenden (1993) 'The Strategic Management of Recruitment and Selection' provides a useful introduction to the role of recruitment and selection in achieving organisational strategy. In terms of more specific work about prisons, the chapter by Baxter *et al.* (2004) entitled 'The Contribution of Job Simulation Assessment Centres to Organisational Development in HM Prison Service' is the only recent description. Given the importance of assessment centres to the recruitment approach in prisons, this is a particularly important chapter.

References

ACAS (1999) *Recruitment and Induction.* ACAS Advisory Booklet.

Association of Graduate Recruiters (2006) *Graduate Recruitment Survey.* Hobsons Planning & Research Division.

Baxter, K., Davis, K., Franks, E. and Kitchen, S. (2004) 'The Contribution of Job Simulation Assessment Centres to Organisational Development in HM Prison Service', in A. Needs and G. Towl (eds), *Applying Psychology to Forensic Practice.* Oxford: Blackwell.

Bertua, C., Anderson, N. and Salgado, J. (2005) 'The Predictive Validity of Cognitive Ability Tests: A UK Meta-analysis', *Journal of Occupational and Organizational Psychology,* 78 (3): 387–409.

Bligh, D. (1994) *Assessing Professional People by OSPRE.* London: Police Review Publishing.

Carter, P. (2003) *Managing Offenders – Reducing Crime: A New Approach.* London: Home Office Strategy Unit.

Civil Service Commissioners (2004) *Civil Service Commissioner's Recruitment Code,* 5th edn. London: Civil Service Commissioners.

Coyle, A. (2003) *Humanity in Prisons: Questions of Definition and Audit.* London: International Centre for Prison Studies.

Dipboye, R. (1997) 'Structured Selection Interviews: Why Do They Work? Why Are They Underutilized?', in N. Anderson and P. Herriott (eds), *International Handbook of Selection and Assessment.* Chichester: Wiley.

Evenden, R. (1993) 'The Strategic Management of Recruitment and Selection', in R. Harrison (1993) *Human Resource Management: Issues and Strategies.* Wokingham: Addison-Wesley.

Ferlie, E., Pettigrew, A., Ashburner, L. and Fitzgerald, L. (1996) *The New Public Management in Action.* Oxford: Oxford University Press.

HM Prison Service (2007) *Securing the Future: A Five-Year Strategy for Her Majesty's Prison Service (Public Sector Prisons).* London: HMPS.

Hood, C. (1991) 'A Public Management for All Seasons', *Public Administration,* 69: 3–19.

Kandola, R., Wood, R., Dholakia, B. and Keane, C. (2001) *The Graduate Recruitment Manual.* Aldershot: Gower.

Keith, Mr Justice (2006) *Report of Zahid Mubarek Inquiry, Volumes 1 and 2.* London: Stationery Office.

Liebling, A. and Price, D. (2001) *The Prison Officer.* Leyhill: Prison Service Journal.

Liebling, A., assisted by Arnold, H. (2004) *Prisons and Their Moral Performance: A Study of Values, Quality and Prison Life.* Oxford: Clarendon Press.

Taylor, S. (1998) *Employee Resourcing.* London: Institute of Personnel and Development.

Torrington, D. (1989) 'Human Resource Management and the Personnel Function', in J. Storey (ed.), *New Perspectives in Human Resource Management.* London: Routledge.

Wilson, D. and Bryans, S. (1998) *The Prison Governor: Theory and Practice.* Leyhill: Prison Service Journal.

Woodruffe, C. (2000) *Development and Assessment Centres,* 3rd edn. London: Institute of Personnel and Development.

Chapter 22

Training and developing prison staff

Maggie Bolger and Jamie Bennett

Introduction

The coordination, design and delivery of training for almost 50,000 staff in the Prison Service is a complex and challenging task. This is due in part to the diversity of roles that are undertaken by staff throughout the Service at prisons and headquarters. It is also due to the vast geographical spread of the organisation across England and Wales. Prison staff are broadly categorised into three main groups: operational staff, who have direct contact with prisoners on a daily basis, non-operational staff who generally support the administrative functions of a prison, and specialist staff, such as psychology, health care, education, trades staff and chaplaincy.

The Training and Development Group (TDG), part of the Directorate of Human Resources, is the largest provider of education and training for the Prison Service. TDG is responsible for the strategic direction of learning across the Service, including training needs analysis, the development of curriculum, evaluating the effectiveness of training, quality assuring course materials and trainer delivery, as well as maintaining the central records of training undertaken by the various grades of staff throughout the Service. The Prison Service College provides training on a diverse range of subjects including: leadership and management development, security, offender management, personnel management, prison administration, IT, control and restraint, and physical education, as well as construction and technical training. The main focus of TDG's training portfolio concerns the preparation and development of new entrants into the Service in order to fulfil the role of the prison officer.

Each prison will also have its own training department which manages the delivery of delegated courses, such as control and restraint refresher training, suicide prevention and diversity awareness. Training for staff is also provided by other headquarter groups, reflecting the specialist nature of prison work. Examples of this type of training include finance, offender behaviour programmes, drug treatment programmes and sentence management. The Service will also 'buy in' training from external providers where appropriate, for example management development, health and safety, and specialist trades training.

Training for prison staff has traditionally been instructor-led, concentrating on technical training directly related to operational functions and linked to policy initiatives driven by Prison Service Orders (PSOs). Each member of prison staff receives on average a total of six days of training per year. It could be argued that this is not enough to ensure that staff are confident and capable of performing their day-to-day duties. However, time away from operational duties is often difficult to achieve. Course attendance sometimes suffers as staff are 'pulled' from training courses in order to respond to operational demands. While it is important to have sufficient staff to ensure the safe and smooth running of a prison, it can also mean that staff access to training and development is sometimes more limited than would be considered ideal.

This chapter will consider recent trends in people management in the Prison Service, in particular the move from *personnel management* to *human resource management*. The chapter will also describe the initial training for prison officers, the largest occupational group in the Prison Service, before outlining some recent developments in training and development. The aim is to provide a description of the strategic approach to training and development in the Prison Service.

From personnel to human resource management

In the 1980s and 1990s, the public sector underwent a period of change based on the new right philosophy that the discipline of the marketplace was the most efficient means of improving performance. As a result, the public sector was opened up to competition and private sector practices were imported into the public sector, particularly the use of performance targets. This development, which has been termed New Public Management (NPM) (Hood 1991; Ferlie *et al.* 1996), also had an impact on elements of internal management, including finance and personnel (Hughes 1998).

Traditional approaches to personnel management have been described as administrative, process-based and employee-centred. As a result, these approaches have been characterised as having a welfare-orientated focus on non-managers, creating a separation between the work of line managers and specialist personnel work, and providing an environment where personnel is seen as a peripheral, organisational support function (Legge 1995). This contrasts with the development of human resource management (HRM), which has been described as resource-centred and directed at management. HRM focuses on aligning HR issues with organisational strategy, and making HR an integral part of the organisation and the practice of individual managers. The differences have been summarised as follows:

> HRM [is] a much more proactive function than personnel management. Whereas personnel management is about the maintenance of personnel and administrative systems, HRM is about the forecasting of organizational needs, the continual monitoring and adjustment of personnel systems to meet current and future requirements, and the management of change. (Miller 1993: 32)

This move from personnel to HRM was an integral part of the development of NPM, with a move from 'a predominantly "soft" welfare-centred, paternalist approach to personnel management to a "harder", market-orientated, rationalist one' (Farnham and Giles 1996: 112).

HRM encompasses a range of activities including: planning and employment; pay and reward systems; organisational design and work patterning; education, training and development; employee relations; and employee services, welfare, health and safety (Mullins 2002). The HR services in the Prison Service have developed extensively since the early 1990s, with increased delegation to a local level and increased professionalisation of services (Warren 2006). The latest phase of this, the People Strategy Programme, was launched in 2004, and saw the establishment and development of a shared service centre for transactional work with area-based specialist teams and establishment-based HR business partners providing advice, support and consultancy on HR issues (Warren 2006).

Training and development is an integral part of HR and has undergone a similar transition. An independent review of Prison Service training was carried out by Mouchel Consultants in 2000. This review highlighted significant shortfalls in the design, delivery and organisation of training. According to its findings, the Service lacked a robust training strategy to guide its activities, and there was a gap between national and local, prison-level training plans, with resources largely centred on top-down, prescribed mandatory training as determined by Prison Service Orders. The report also noted that line managers appeared to lack the ability to identify staff training needs and as a consequence attendance on training events was essentially 'CV' driven by individuals. The report also noted that the quality and skills of trainers were variable and that there was too much emphasis on 'chalk and talk' and traditional methods of classroom delivery. Other methods of training interventions, such as work-based learning and distance learning, were not in evidence. Finally, the report identified that the training venues were not readily accessible from some prison establishments across England and Wales. This was considered likely to discourage staff with 'carer' responsibilities from attendance. It was concluded overall that training was not aligned to the Prison Service business needs, was using outdated methods and was insensitive to the diverse needs of staff.

The consultants proposed a four-point plan to improve training and development, focusing on: the rationalisation of national training provision; the provision of more local, area-based training; the development of work-based learning and greater use of distance learning, computer-based learning and National Vocational Qualifications (NVQs); and the implementation of a new approach to leadership and management training.

The Prison Service Management Board approved the plan and the Service's first Training and Development Strategy was launched in November 2001. The Strategy began an ambitious programme of change aiming to deliver a stronger infrastructure that would support local training and local training management. The purpose was to improve efficiency, effectiveness and access to training by delivering less at the central staff college at Newbold Revel, Warwickshire, in favour of more training at or near the workplace, and to improve and assure the quality of training, encompassing not only the physical learning environment, but also the issue of whether the training received had made a difference in the workplace. Martin Narey, the then Director General of the Prison Service, endorsed the Strategy stating:

The impact of this ambitious programme will be felt throughout the Service. A more effective training function, clearly focused on the Service's business needs, will contribute to the delivery of our core objectives of protecting the public and reducing re-offending. (HM Prison Service 2001: 5)

In support of this Strategy, a new prospectus of courses was created with the aim of delivering fewer but more focused training days. Fundamental to the success of the Strategy was the decentralisation of training in favour of local delivery by area-based Training and Development Teams. The area teams work to strengthen local training management and delivery, help prisons to access training, support work-based learning, and work with area managers, governors and training managers to specify training needs and facilitate the provision of quality-assured, targeted training. As a result of this initiative, Local Learning Centres were also created to facilitate the local delivery of training and work-based learning away from the main Prison Service College. New Leadership and Management Development Programmes were established to facilitate career progression, supported by coaching and mentorship schemes.

The Strategy facilitated considerable improvement in the training and development of prison staff. By 2005, the decentralisation of the vast majority of training had been achieved, for example 43 per cent of Prison Officer Entry Level Training (formerly known as Prison Officer Initial Training) was delivered locally by nine establishments. A new Training Evaluation System (TES) was introduced, which considered the immediate impact of training, with further evaluation of its effectiveness in the workplace conducted at three- and six-months after delivery. The Certificate in Training and Development accredited by the Chartered Institute of Personnel and Development (CIPD) was introduced in 2003, providing the first accredited professional training qualification for trainers. Area Leadership Advisors were also recruited to support the leadership and management development programmes, involving first-line managers as well as middle and senior operational managers throughout the Service. In addition, a new Prison Service fast-track personalised development scheme (launched in 2003) open to individuals from within and outside the Service focused on developing a strong middle management tier within the Prison Service aimed at providing a pool of leaders for the future.

However, the National Vocational Qualification (NVQ) in Custodial Care failed to achieve its intended goal of facilitating learning in the workplace. The NVQ was offered to all new prison officers throughout the Service; however, enrolment was poor, and a lack of planning and resources meant that the infrastructure required to support the NVQ was deficient. Today, the majority of training that is delivered is still of a 'chalk and talk' nature. Attempts to introduce e-learning and other blended learning approaches have been severely restricted, in part because staff often have difficulty in accessing IT. In addition, security restrictions mean that many web-based learning programmes cannot be accessed via desktop PCs.

Despite such problems, these developments show that the Prison Service has made its first steps in transforming personnel into HRM, including the development of a training programme that was more responsive to both business and individual needs.

Prison officer training

As previously stated, the main focus of the TDG's portfolio concerns the preparation of newly recruited prison officers. It is worth exploring this further, as the training of new recruits to perform the prison officer role has changed considerably over recent years. The prison officer performs a unique, complex and challenging role:

> In any one day, an officer can be supervisor, custodian, disciplinarian, peacemaker, administrator, observer, manager, facilitator, mentor, provider, classifier and diplomat. Different situations require different blends ... Versatility and flexibility are key requirements. (Liebling and Price 2001: 43)

Apart from the generic description outlined above, today's prison officer will also perform a variety of additional roles including personal officer, family liaison officer, foreign nationals' officer, disability liaison officer, race relations officer, etc.

Over 2,000 new recruits are trained each year. Prison Officer Entry Level Training (POELT) has come a long way in recent years. In her book *Doing Prison Work*, Elaine Crawley (2004) describes in some detail the harrowing nature of officer training, based on fieldwork conducted between 1997 and 2000. At that stage, the basic training course took place over ten weeks, eight weeks of which was spent at the training college and two weeks spent at the establishment to which the individual had been recruited. While the course content aimed to sensitise new recruits to the need to be vigilant in security matters, Crawley found that the mandatory fitness training sessions were for some 'an exercise in humiliation' (p. 69). Many new recruits were shocked at the verbal and physical abuse that was given out by trainers, which was considered to be on a par with military-style training. Female recruits often fared worst. The positive aspects of training and the sense of embarking on a professional career were 'eclipsed' by the militaristic and paternal nature of the training programme (Crawley 2004: 70). These perceptions were compounded on return to the individual's establishment. The training did not appear to prepare recruits for work within a hostile and challenging environment, and many experienced a 'culture shock' (p. 75) and 'reality shock' (p. 78) during their first few weeks as officers.

The International Centre for Prison Studies and the Prison Service undertook a review of basic training between 1999 and 2001. The review found that the overall course content was too didactic and should be more experiential, that there was little specific-to-role training and that evaluation was not undertaken. As a result of the review, a new entry level training course was developed and implemented in 2001. POELT underwent a further review and was subsequently rewritten in 2003. The aim of POELT is to provide new prison officers with the core skills and knowledge they need to perform their day-to-day duties. It represents a platform upon which to build a professional career in the Prison Service, and attempts to instil in its students a life-long learning culture. It is now an eight-week course, providing essential foundation-level training for new entrant prison officers with the training shared between the home establishment and a training venue, which may be Prison Service College (PSC) Newbold Revel or one of nine local training centres.

The course aims and objectives are now aligned with the National Occupational Standards (NOS) for custodial care. Course materials cover important issues such as ethnicity and diversity, self-harm and suicide prevention, violence reduction, dynamic security and mental health awareness (Illingworth and Mabbett 2005). A number of authors have identified good interpersonal skills as essential for establishing rapport and helping with managing stress (Illingworth and Mabbett 2005; Crawley 2004; Liebling and Price 2001). As a consequence, interpersonal skills training is now firmly embedded within the POELT course. In order to prepare students for a career of life-long learning, students are now asked to complete a reflective journal. The journal helps the student to make cognitive links with different parts of the taught components of the course, as well as helping them to identify their strengths and weaknesses in particular areas. The journal also provides the student with invaluable reference material that they can refer to on return to their establishment (Illingworth and Mabbett 2005). The training has been well received, with positive course evaluations. However, establishments need to understand that this course is purely foundational and that opportunities and support for students to consolidate their learning and practise new skills is vital if they are to reduce anxieties that new recruits will inevitably face and help them gain confidence and competence in the workplace.

The new course is certainly a significant improvement on the previous version, utilising contemporary training practice, improving strategic alignment and taking account of individuals' domestic needs. However, the course is still relatively short, particularly when one compares it to other countries where initial prison officer training may run over two years (Tilt 1993; Coyle 2002). Such a lengthy period of training may have some benefit given that prison officers have themselves described that it can take 18 months or more to feel comfortable in the role (Crawley 2004). This is also particularly important if it is accepted that new recruits should be able to resist an organisational culture that is sometimes at odds with official intentions (Crawley 2004). This would also be beneficial given the strong cognitive, emotional and behavioural effects of becoming a prison officer (Arnold 2005). One step in this direction is the introduction from September 2007 of an NVQ as a compulsory element of the prison officer probationary period. This will require new prison officers to undergo a period of supported workplace learning, assessed against nationally recognised standards by assessors independent of the prison at which they work. This has the potential to produce a more objective professional benchmark for new recruits and to provide a counterweight to learning from more experienced colleagues, which can be of mixed quality.

Recent developments in Prison Service training and development

In 2004 the Prison Service embarked on the People Strategy Programme, which attempted to realise human resource management requirements that stem from the Service's five-year business strategy, *Securing the Future* (HM Prison Service 2005). The strategy outlines the plans for the next five years in relation to six priorities: reducing reoffending; public protection; decency; maintaining order and control; ethnicity and diversity; security; and prison health.

The measure of success for this strategy will in part be dependent upon how well staff feel they are prepared to meet the challenges that confront them. Investment in the training and development of staff will be essential if this strategy is to make a difference and meet its stated objectives. In response to the challenges ahead, TDG embarked upon a three-year initiative aimed at transforming learning and development across the Prison Service, entitled 'Professionalising the Prison Service'. This project forms part of the main People Strategy Programme.

As part of its plans to professionalise the Prison Service, TDG has created a Professional Development Framework (PDF), also known as 'The Skills Elevator'. This term captures the way that individuals may wish to enter and exit the 'elevator' at different points according to their personal abilities and aspirations. The concept of the PDF centres on the use of training and development programmes that are linked to the National Qualifications Framework (levels 1–7), with content embedded in National Occupational Standards as a principal benchmark (Qualifications and Curriculum Authority 2004). It seeks to establish a competence-based framework that will not simply work in isolation to inform training and development, but will be embedded in wider HR policies, including management succession.

The 'Professionalising the Prison Service' project consists of four work streams: curriculum development; National Vocational Qualifications (NVQ); training administration and delivery; and quality assurance. The first area, curriculum development, will review and update the existing curriculum, as well as design and create a new curriculum that will focus on meeting the future needs of the Service. Individual learning and development will, in future, be supported by a comprehensive mentorship framework. The second aspect is the reintroduction of the NVQ for probationary prison officers, as described above. The third area, training administration and delivery, aims to review the management of training in order to implement a more efficient model of delivery. The fourth issue is quality assurance, which seeks to develop an approach that meets the requirements of the Adult Learning Inspectorates' Common Inspection Framework (ALI and Ofsted 2005).

It is proposed that the creation and design of a PDF, underpinned by a new curriculum for the Service, will offer a number of benefits. First, it will help to create a body of staff with professional skills and aspirations. This will optimise the human resources potential of the organisation, as well as improve its reputation. Second, it will support national initiatives aimed at 'end-to-end' offender management, as introduced by the National Offender Management Service (Carter 2003; Blunkett 2004), providing both the technical training required and support for changes in attitude and culture. Third, the developments can improve the relevance and targeting of training and development to better support professional development, offender management, care and resettlement. Fourth, this will reshape existing arrangements to ensure that learning and development is directed at identified needs and linked to development. Fifth, it will develop the link between competency and contribution, providing staff with the skills to perform the tasks required of them and to respond to change, taking on the responsibility and accountability that the modernisation of working practices will demand. Sixth, it will support the modernisation and performance enhancements required by increasing contestability or market competition envisaged in the future (NOMS 2006), particularly by providing the skills to enable staff to operate more flexibly and drive up the quality of delivery. Finally, it provides a clearer alignment of training and development with organisational strategic priorities.

What will educating and training staff in line with National Occupational Standards achieve? National Occupational Standards (NOS) are statements of the skills, knowledge and understanding needed by individuals to perform competently in a particular job role or skill (see http://www.qca.org.uk/2677.html). NOS therefore provide a benchmark against which it is possible to measure an individual's performance in the workplace. Developing education and training interventions in line with NOS should equip individuals with the knowledge and skills they require to perform competently in the workplace. NOS can also provide an objective framework upon which to build methods of learning assessment, as well as evaluate the impact of the learning.

The development and creation of NOS is led by Skills for Justice, the dedicated Sector Skills Council and Standards Setting Body for the Justice sector (www.skillsforjustice.com). In England and Wales, the Justice sector members include the Prison Service, Police, Probation, Youth Justice, Crown Prosecution Service and voluntary sector organisations. Working in partnership with Justice sector organisations, Skills for Justice identifies the skills priorities and actions required for workforce development. The Sector Skills Agreement provides the framework upon which employers and employees within the Justice sector can determine the skill requirements, priorities and direction for the future, including the actions required to meet those needs, such as education and training initiatives. Skills for Justice have recently introduced an education and training quality mark for the Justice sector known as Skillsmark. This is a two-step accreditation process that recognises providers and endorses programmes and courses of learning. TDG is working towards achieving the Skillsmark accreditation for all its learning provision. The developments in the Prison Service are therefore linked to wider professionalisation in the criminal justice sector.

Professionalising the Prison Service is a challenging project and has attracted significant investment from the Prison Service to improve the future education, training and development of its staff. A return on investment will therefore need to be demonstrated. Efforts to establish the benefits of training have in the past been hampered by a weak research base. The lack of empirical, longitudinal information about the impact of learning has made it difficult for curriculum developers to design strategies and learning programmes to address the gaps in what students know, and the most effective methods of delivery. TDG proposes to become more research active. This will enable it to evaluate learning activities in more depth, develop learning materials and methods, and design appropriate teaching strategies for their delivery. In the future, TDG will look to establish networks and opportunities for collaborative research into the design and effectiveness of learning activities. By assessing the long-term benefits of educational provision, TDG will be better able to consider effectiveness and demonstrate the value of its contribution to the organisation.

Conclusion

Over the last 15 years, the Prison Service has undergone significant organisational change, particularly through the introduction of the techniques of New Public Management. Traditional bureaucratic personnel functions have been transformed and are now delivering strategically aligned human resource management. Training and development is a crucial part of this change. As Leopold (2002: 191) argues:

The integration of the practice of employee development is vital to achieve both internal coherence and to promote the interrelationship between human resourcing strategy and business strategy.

In the Prison Service, trends in training and development have included greater alignment with strategic priorities, the use of training and development as an aspect of change management, improving links with the wider criminal justice sector and linking training to external accredited standards. The first three of these trends illustrate the role of training and development as an integrated, strategic activity, while the fourth emphasises the issue of quality improvement. These changes have the potential to provide a more positive, effective and value-adding activity than has been possible in the past.

Seminar questions

1 How has training and development in prisons changed over the last 15 years?
2 What factors have influenced these changes?
3 What impact does organisational or occupational culture have on the effectiveness of training for prison officers?
4 What are the benefits and risks of linking development to the wider criminal justice sector?
5 How should the effectiveness of training for prison staff be measured?

Recommended reading

The transformation of training and development generally can be found in Leopold's (2002) *Human Resources in Organisations*, while the way that this has occurred in the public sector in particular is described in the chapter by Farnham and Giles (1996), 'People Management and Employment Relations'.

The best sociological descriptions of prison officer training are provided by Elaine Crawley (2004) in *Doing Prison Work* and Helen Arnold (2005) in her book chapter entitled 'The Effects of Prison Work'. Both of these are insightful and challenging and are strongly recommended to anyone interested in understanding training and development in prisons.

References

ALI and Ofsted (2005) *The Common Inspection Framework for Education and Training from 2005*. Coventry and London: ALI and Ofsted.

Arnold, H. (2005) 'The Effects of Prison Work', in A. Liebling and S. Maruna (eds), *The Effects of Imprisonment*. Cullompton: Willan.

Blunkett, D. (2004) *Reducing Crime – Changing Lives: The Government's Plans for Transforming the Management of Offenders*. London: Home Office.

Carter, P. (2003) *Managing Offenders, Reducing Crime: A New Approach*. London: Home Office Strategy Unit.

Coyle, A. (2002) *A Human Rights Approach to Prison Management: Handbook for Prison Staff*. London: International Centre for Prison Studies.

Crawley, E. (2004) *Doing Prison Work: The Public and Private Lives of Prison Officers*. Cullompton: Willan.

Farnham, D. and Giles, L. (1996) 'People Management and Employment Relations', in D. Farnham and S. Horton (eds), *Managing the New Public Services*, 2nd edn. Basingstoke: Macmillan, pp. 112–37.

Ferlie, E., Pettigrew, A., Ashburner, L. and Fitzgerald, L. (1996) *The New Public Management in Action*. Oxford: Oxford University Press.

HM Prison Service (2001) *Training and Development Strategy for HM Prison Service*. London: Home Office Communications Directorate.

HM Prison Service (2005) *Securing the Future: A Five-Year Strategy for the Public Sector Prison Service*. London: HMPS.

Hood, C. (1991) 'A Public Management for All Seasons', *Public Administration*, 69: 3–19.

Hughes, O. (1998) *Public Management and Administration: An Introduction*, 2nd edn. Basingstoke: Macmillan.

Illingworth, P. and Mabbett, A. (2005) 'Prison Officer Entry Level Training (POELT)', *Prison Service Journal*, 157: 11–13.

Legge, K. (1995) *Human Resource Management: Rhetorics and Realities*. Basingstoke: Macmillan.

Leopold, J. (2002) *Human Resources in Organisations*. Harlow: Pearson Education.

Liebling, A. and Price, D. (2001) *The Prison Officer*. Leyhill: Prison Service Journal.

Miller, S. (1993) 'The Nature of Strategic Management', in R. Harrison (ed.), *Human Resource Management: Issues and Strategies*. Wokingham: Addison-Wesley.

Mullins, L. (2002) *Management and Organisational* Behaviour, 6th edn. Harlow: Pearson Education.

NOMS (2006) *Improving Prison and Probation Services: Public Value Partnerships*. London: NOMS.

Qualifications and Curriculum Authority (2004) *The Statutory Regulation of External Qualifications in England, Wales and Northern Ireland*. London: QCA.

Tilt, R. (1993) 'Prison Staffing Issues in Europe', republished in J. Reynolds and U. Smartt (eds) (1996) *Prison Policy and Practice: Selected Papers from 35 Years of the Prison Service Journal*. Leyhill: Prison Service Journal.

Warren, C. (2006) 'Cell Block HR', *People Management*, 12 (20): 27–31.

Chapter 23

The experience of prison officer training

Helen Arnold

Custodian Counsellor Carer Coach Role Model Prison Officer
A Career as a Prison Officer More than a Jailer ... The job of a
prison officer is complex so we take your training very seriously.
(Prison Service Application Pack Brochure 2006)

... the process of 'becoming' a prison officer is a slow, difficult
and sometimes painful one, involving a significant degree of
culture shock and a complex process of acculturation. (Crawley
2004: xv)

Introduction

The aim of this chapter is to outline and illustrate some of the key
elements of the Prison Officer Entry Level Training (POELT) course,
and to describe the experience of undertaking the course both from
the perspective of a training cohort and from personal experience.[1]

The chapter focuses on the way in which the process of 'becoming'
a prison officer begins and the early stages of occupational
socialisation. Starting with a short overview of relevant literature,
there follows an outline of the structure and content of the prison
officer training course, as it was in 2002 when I completed it.[2]
Some general evaluations of the training and several interrelated
thematic findings regarding the process of being trained as an officer
during the initial residential training periods are then presented.
These findings are based on data obtained from: self-completion

questionnaires administered to trainee officers during the training course and follow-up interviews conducted six months after course completion; focus group discussions with trainee officers; informal discussions with the cohort during training; and the daily fieldwork research journal I maintained throughout the training period.

The exploration of the views, perceptions and experiences of new entrant officers, as well as my own, suggest that security, the role of Control and Restraint (C&R)[3] and concepts such as transition, liminality and institutionalisation are significant themes for further investigation. The chapter ends by offering some reflections and concluding comments about the nature of entry-level prison officer training and its impact on trainees.

Overview of literature

There are several recent publications in the UK concerning the work and role of prison officers that provide an insightful and comprehensive perspective into the working world of officers and the practical and emotional skills required to effectively perform the job (notably Liebling and Price 2001, and Crawley 2004, 2005). However, despite the obvious importance of training for prison officers, this issue has been relatively neglected, and academic and other literature regarding prison officer training is somewhat scarce. More specifically, there remains a lack of empirical research that focuses on the training of *new entrant* officers. The seminal work by Liebling and Price (2001) offers extensive research-based analysis and exploration of almost every aspect of prison officers and their role; however, references to, or depictions of, prison officer training are absent.

While the training course for new entrant prison officers has undergone many changes since its inception, both in terms of course content and structure (Vince 2006), published and accessible literature offering descriptive, interpretive or reflexive accounts of the training are almost non-existent. Much of the information concerning the training of new officers is in the form of internal Prison Service policy documentation (such as Prison Service Order (PSO) 4180) or commissioned evaluative review reports (highlighting recommendations for revision and resulting in the redesign and implementation of subsequent modified courses) that are not widely available in the public domain (such as that conducted by the International Centre for Prison Studies (ICPS) in 1999 (see Coyle 2002) and Crowley 2001). A short report of the re-evaluation of the

POINT course that took place in 1996 is provided by Needs (1997), a Prison Service employee, in the *Prison Service Journal*. Needs outlines changes to the structure and ethos of the course in a factual and informative way. However, despite the review process including 164 interviews with staff and 17 student officers in their final week of training, this data is not incorporated into the published article in any analytical or illustrative way and any experiential sense of what it is like to undergo the training is lacking. In a similar vein, Illingworth and Mabbett (2005) present a brief overview of further alterations to the POELT course that have taken place since I undertook the course in 2002.[4]

Crawley's research (2004) investigating the emotional nature of prison officer work offers a detailed and original account of how officers think, feel and act in their job. Based on observations and interviews, her study comes closest to providing a contextual framework for understanding the nature and role of the initial training course for those about to embark on a career as an officer in UK prisons. As part of her analysis, Crawley follows new recruits 'through both the formal and informal training processes and into their first, anxious days on the landing' (2004: 65). Reproducing numerous direct quotations, Crawley raises several key themes – such as reality shock, impression management, the pressure to conform and the use of humour as a survival strategy – and 'demonstrates that through an internalisation, over time, of prison rules (formal, craft and feeling rules), social practices ..., formal and informal routines and occupational norms, ordinary men and women "become" prison officers' (2004: xv). However, there are two notable limitations to Crawley's study: firstly, many of the officers' views she represents are retrospective accounts of the experiences of a training course that has changed significantly since she conducted her fieldwork; purely as a function of time, then, the findings may no longer be contemporarily accurate. Secondly, Crawley did not undergo any of the training procedure herself and was therefore unable to corroborate, or challenge and compare, the perspectives and experiences of others with first-hand knowledge.

Although there are a number of ethnographic and autobiographical accounts of prison officer work, the majority originate in the United States and most do not contain any in-depth discussion of the training experience (Marquart 1986; Kauffman 1988; Fleisher 1989; Dickenson 1999; Conover 2000; in the UK, Papworth 2000).[5] Participant observation lends a distinctive and unusual standpoint for reflection, interpretation and analysis and the level of access I was granted provided a unique insight into the experience of prison officer training in the UK.

In a thesis considering the role of the prison officer training course in preparing new staff for the emotional demands of the job, Vince (2006) explores the impact of training on the emotional skills argued by Crawley to be necessary for the effective performance of the prison officer role. New recruits were asked to complete a survey questionnaire consisting of four measures (anxiety, empathy, emotional intelligence and self-esteem) at three different time intervals (T1 = the first day of the course (after the observational induction week); T2 = the day prior to course graduation; and T3 = two months after becoming operational in the prison). Vince found that confidence levels rose considerably between T1 and T2 and thereafter remained static; that after two months' experience, 58 per cent felt they still had a lot to learn about the prison they worked in, despite the fact that new officers felt they acquired both emotional skills (such as how to deal with an upset/aggressive/suicidal/mentally ill prisoner) and technical skills (such as searching, use of C&R, handcuffs and radio) to a greater extent at the training college than in their first two months as an officer. Her study also reported significant differences in anxiety levels that decreased between T1 and T2, and increased between T2 and T3 to a level significantly higher than at both T1 and T2. In terms of emotional intelligence, Vince found that the new officers 'felt less able to regulate their own emotions after completing the training and less able still after working as an officer' and that their ability to regulate others' emotions decreased throughout the assessment period. She also found that 'the participants' skills at regulating others' emotions were not as good as skills at regulating their own', and that 'therefore it appeared that the training course had a negative impact'. Although anxiety did not impact on self-esteem, which remained relatively stable over time, it was found to be negatively correlated with emotional intelligence, suggesting that the greater the level of anxiety, the less the ability to regulate emotions. With regard to empathy, Vince discovered that scores were higher than for the normal population; that there was a small, but non-significant, increase in scores over time, suggesting that 'neither the training course nor working as an officer impacted on an individual's empathy skills'; and that there was a positive correlation between empathy and emotional intelligence. Vince concluded that the POELT course neither assessed nor taught emotional skills to trainee officers and that anxiety arising from a lack of 'jailcraft', insufficient knowledge of prison rules and procedures, and the unpredictability of prison life was the dominant impacting factor. The study pointed to significant deficiencies in officer training.

Outline of the Prison Officer Entry Level Training course

The revised training course for new entrant officers POELT (previously termed POINT – Prison Officer Initial Training) was introduced at the end of October 2001. The stated aim of the course was 'to produce officers who are trained in the core skills required of all prison officers, and who are sufficiently trained in a specific role to enable them to work efficiently within their own establishment' (PSO 4180, p. 4). The duration of the POELT course was eleven weeks. The first week constituted a familiarisation period spent at the 'parent' prison where candidates had applied to work. The fourth and fifth weeks and the eighth and ninth weeks were also spent in the prison. The other three two-week blocks were spent undergoing formal college-based training at one of the two Prison Service Training Colleges (Newbold Revel near Rugby, or Aberford Road in Wakefield).[6] In comparison to the (also eleven-week) POINT course, the main difference in the new course was an additional two weeks spent at the recruiting prison; six instead of eight weeks were spent at college.

The object of the familiarisation period was to allow student officers the opportunity to become familiar with their own establishment and its procedures, to learn the geographical layout of the prison, to become accustomed to the working environment of a prison and to visit all areas of the prison observing the day-to-day operations of the various departments (such as the chaplaincy, probation, the gym, visits, the gate, workshops, reception, healthcare and the segregation unit). The remaining designated four 'gap' weeks were to provide the opportunity for trainees to practise and contextualise the technical and interpersonal skills they had been taught during their in-college training. The individual recruiting prisons were responsible for preparing and implementing a suitable training timetable for each day the trainee was present. Throughout the periods in prison new recruits remained supernumerary and were not used operationally. They were closely supervised and allocated to a work system that permitted them to work alongside other staff in the residential areas of the prison and to accompany existing officers while carrying out their various duties (such as escorting prisoners around the prison, unlocking landings, searching prisoners, conducting roll checks, conducting cell fabric checks, searching cells, dealing with queries and applications, supervising prisoners on association and exercise, censoring mail, serving meals and monitoring the movement of prisoners on and off the residential wings). Most trainees were assigned to a particular residential wing where a significant amount of time was spent in order to build relationships with the wing staff, to get to know the prisoners and to become increasingly familiar with the regime and systems on that particular wing.

The two-week residential blocks at college were spent learning a wide variety of subjects categorised according to several central interrelated themes associated with a prison officer's role. These were: Security (dynamic security; wing security; rub-down, strip and cell searching; restraints and radio and escort procedures); Professional Working Relationships (peacekeeping; caring for prisoners at risk of suicide and self-harm; anti-bullying; mentally disordered offenders; managing people and visits); Sentence Planning (personal officer work; substance use; offending behaviour; report writing and interviewing; Incentives and Earned Privileges); Law (race relations, diversity and equal opportunities); Professional Conduct (authority and responsibility); Criminal Justice System (adjudications, standards and prison rules); and Statement of Purpose (vision and principles and key performance indicators). The course also included control and restraint (C&R) training and personal fitness sessions.

The training course employed a continuous assessment procedure and the entire programme was governed and supported by the use of reference workbooks covering all elements of the course. They included written and diagrammatic information pertaining to each of the modules taught at the college. The written material was required pre-reading for each of the corresponding college training periods at the outset of which students' knowledge was tested by means of a ten-question 'quiz'. The folders were also used to retain all assessment reports and the written work required of trainees, including a daily diary in which to record personal reactions to and feelings about the training process, and weekly accounts of 'self-perception and personal views of training'. 'Learning Outcomes' and 'Assessment Criteria', under the headings 'security' and 'care/resettlement' (when appropriate), were listed for each module. Based on evidence from both written responses from the trainee and practical demonstration of skills, the training managers at the prison then verified that the learning outcomes had been achieved and the assessment criteria satisfactorily completed.

One of the main reasons for the revision of the previous POINT programme was dissatisfaction with its didactic nature. One aim of the new course was to increase participation and recognise the existence of different individual learning styles. Thus the syllabus was taught using a range of methods and teaching aids such as videos, computer-aided presentations, group exercises, discussions and brainstorming, practical tasks and games, and role-play scenarios. Anecdotes, storytelling and relating real experiences, by both the tutors and the student officers, made a considerable contribution to the learning process.

At the college, student progress interviews with tutors were held at the end of each week. They were designed to address the new officers' performance during tutorials, such as attentiveness, punctuality, participation, enthusiasm and demonstration of knowledge and skills. Similar weekly assessment sheets regarding attitude and behaviour were completed by the training manager at the prison. A final report by the college tutor was provided commenting on character, personal performance, communications and relationships with others, knowledge base, decision-making and effectiveness. It concluded with an appraisal of the individual's level of competence. On successful completion of the training course, new officers remain on probation for a period of twelve months.[7] The purpose of the probationary stage was to give the newly recruited staff further opportunity to practise and contextualise the skills learnt during training and 'to show their suitability in terms of conduct, performance and attendance for confirmation in the grade or post to which they have been appointed' (PSO 4180, p. 4).

Research findings

General evaluations

> It builds character which is important and does give you the knowledge you need but I think the real training is in the first year or two doing the job.[8]

> The best thing about the course was the two weeks on, two weeks off so you get a real feel for your establishment, the environment there and its routine. The college is good for the basics and the teambuilding.

The experience of being trained as a prison officer was generally viewed by the course participants as satisfactory. The evaluative comments from within the questionnaires and interviews suggested that, overall, the new officers felt the training provided an adequate, informative and incisive overview of the job ('The training has been balanced and provided a good insight into a range of duties'). At the same time, they acknowledged the limitations of what could feasibly be taught within an artificial classroom setting ('Much of the job is not trainable'); applauded the periods spent in the prison gaining 'on-the-job experience' ('The gap weeks have been really beneficial'); and recognised that, although the course offered an important foundation, it would be during the forthcoming months that they would become better equipped for the realities of the job ('The real learning starts in post').

There were two key interrelated aspects of the training course that new recruits enjoyed the most: C&R and the shared teamwork experience (see below). There was evident enthusiasm for the social side of meeting, bonding and interacting with a variety of different people from diverse backgrounds; of helping each other through the often challenging parts of the course; and of learning from others ('I enjoyed meeting other people and socialising with them, listening to their experiences and realising you are not alone in how you feel'). In contrast, those elements of the course enjoyed least were the more academic components including the relative inactivity and length of 'heavy-going' or 'irrelevant' classroom (as opposed to practical) sessions: the 'very intense paperwork at the college', the 'volume of pre-reading', 'boring' and 'long-winded' lectures and 'written work' were all disparaged. Recruits wanted extra PE sessions (given the introduction of compulsory fitness levels), additional time at their prison, more interpersonal skills training and instruction 'on how to react to situations you might encounter on the landings' and 'dealing with confrontation'.

There were a multitude of responses to the question of what had been the most important thing the incoming officers had learnt, although most were connected to issues of security and safety (searching, vigilance, following procedures, supporting colleagues, being alert to conditioning from prisoners and C&R/self-defence) as well as the recognition that the job was complex, involved and entailed an unanticipated level of responsibility. They also acknowledged that their own 'attitude and approach to situations' and prisoners was imperative: being 'firm but fair', 'being yourself', having 'an open frame of mind' and recognising that 'inmates need to be looked after with humanity'.

When asked, six months into the job, to reflect on the usefulness and relevance of initial training, responses were mixed and somewhat less positive than at the end of the training course itself. With hindsight, from on-the-job experience and attempts to apply the learning from college, some scepticism had emerged as to the connection between the preparation provided by the training and the reality of the role. One new officer maintained that 'Most of it wasn't useful in the end. The training doesn't bear any relation to what we do in prison'. Others noted a similar incongruity and the critical, consolidating influence of the real circumstances of prison:

> There was nothing very important and nothing irrelevant. It's the prison environment you need to get used to. Most stuff I've not had to refer back to. You learn more when you're back here. Someone said to me 'At college you are taught; it's here you learn'. The most useful stuff was about professional working relationships and security.

> Most of it was useful, but not necessarily at the time. When you come back here, to your prison, then everything is put together – like a jigsaw. You come out of college and you still don't have a clue. You are given what you need to know at the college but when you get to your prison you're really left to sink or swim. It's a different world to what you're led to believe at college.

Although there was some perceived disparity between the learning at college and the practicalities of working within the prison environment, there was a striking correspondence between the features of the training course and the facets of the job that student officers found most constructive, useful and enjoyable. Given that the security aspects of the job (including C&R) represented the largest proportion of dedicated college-teaching time, it was unsurprising that it was again the procedural, security-related components of the training that received the most praise six months later. As asserted by Crawley (2004), '… the formal training programme sensitises new recruits to the need for vigilance in security matters' (p. 65). In addition, for many probationary officers, the social and relational elements of the job (working with and supporting colleagues, the 'sense of community' and 'teamwork', 'having a laugh and a joke' and 'interacting with prisoners') and the 'variety of routines', tasks and situations they were required to deal with provided job satisfaction. Responses indicated the existence of a 'continuity of experience' and adaptation that extended beyond the completion of training. New officers also spoke of how they felt they had developed and changed individually since they commenced their training; many felt they had become more assertive, self-assured and confident, more observant, alert, watchful and patient, but also more suspicious and mistrustful.[9]

The importance of C&R training: confidence and camaraderie

I messed up with the class commands. I felt I let the section down, I made a fool of myself and afterwards went back to my room to cry.

At the first introductory session concerning C&R and 'Use of Force', a video was shown demonstrating full C&R procedures. This was met with exclamations of incredulity and self-doubt – it appeared an unfeasible feat, and 'too complicated to ever be able to learn'. Throughout the training course it was the accomplishment of C&R techniques that dominated the fears and concerns of the group and was the source of most stress. Whether intentional or incidental, it was impressed upon trainees that C&R constituted the compulsory dimension of becoming a prison officer, and the C&R tutors presented its competent execution as a vital 'pass' module. Although, in theory, C&R was continually assessed throughout all 20 sessions (amounting to 30 hours), at the college, in practice, it was only after the end of the final practical assessments during the last week of the course that trainees were told whether they had passed or failed. The mastery of C&R was imprinted in the minds of the new officers as being the 'real' test of aptitude and the pressure to succeed was very evident. The context in which C&R was taught also meant that, although unequivocally a team pursuit, an individual's performance was clearly visible to others, and it was obvious that many felt self-conscious and physically inadequate. Officers were often singled out to partake in demonstrations with the tutors, which necessitated the infliction of controlled pain and regularly involved the use of sexual innuendo and sometimes direct deprecation (which was perhaps employed in a deliberate attempt to increase 'mental toughness' and resilience) by the tutors, which at times resulted in feelings of humiliation and degradation, particularly for female trainees.

Although C&R training sessions were underpinned by feelings of tension, anxiety and pressure to succeed, by the end of the course, and six months later, they were also described as being the most enjoyable (and certainly the most memorable) sessions by the majority of the training cohort. This was for several reasons. Firstly, trainees appreciated the physical nature of the task as a break from sitting behind a desk in a classroom: 'it felt good to be actually doing something'. Secondly, it was the process of learning C&R that bonded and united each section more than any other aspect of the training course. Teamwork, cooperation and communication with colleagues lay at the heart of effective C&R implementation and it was imperative for all section members to operate together efficiently. At the same time, the difficult and intricate C&R manoeuvres demanded determination, focus, perseverance and much rehearsal. Throughout the college training periods, many new officers organised and set aside numerous practice sessions themselves, outside the core timetable, and offered continual support, feedback and encouragement to each other. Thirdly, by the end of the course, having reached a recognised level of skill and passing the formal assessments (as all but one of the 48 course members did) the core collective experience of learning a complex system of techniques not only provided a sense of cohesion and solidarity but also an enormous sense of shared achievement, mutual pride and overwhelming relief and triumph. There was significant consensus among the cohort that both their own, and others', levels of self-confidence had noticeably increased and a true belief in their own ability to achieve had developed. However, as the period of the relative safety of training came to a close and the 'real world' of prison work approached new officers began to articulate their personal qualms and worries. For some, who had concerns about their own and others' safety, it was C&R that helped most in allaying their fears; as one officer said:

> Personally, I don't have any fears working as a prison officer as I am a lot more confident after doing the C&R course. If there was any problem with violence I feel I could look after myself and others to the best of my ability.

For others, confidence began to fade and, as Vince (2006) discovered, anxiety levels rose. The most discernible trepidations and misgivings included: 'making a mistake' or the wrong decision in the prison and being unable to remember what they had been taught; compromising security; 'not getting the routine right'; being too quiet, not assertive enough or 'too nice' to prisoners; not being able to deal effectively with confrontation or violence; being taken hostage; being 'conditioned' and manipulated by prisoners; being attacked or assaulted by prisoners; or discovering or seeing a prisoner who had seriously self-harmed, died, attempted or committed suicide.

Transition, 'liminality' and the college institution

> Every institution captures something of the time and interest
> of its members and provides something of a world for them.
> (Goffman 1961: 150)

At the outset of the POELT course there was an understandable and
discernable level of anxiety and apprehension among the cohort, as
well as a palpable degree of excited anticipation about the challenge
that lay ahead. The process of entering the arena of prison officer
training and the structured environment of the college could be to
some degree likened to that of prisoners entering prison to serve their
time, where there may be some degree of entry shock during the
early period of 'confinement'. Student officers embarking on a new
career and lifestyle undergo a period of adjustment and transition
characterised by 'a leaving off and a taking on' (what Goffman (1961:
27) calls 'role dispossession'): they are learning to 'become' something
previously unknown to them, leaving behind something of their 'old'
life, assuming a particular occupational identity and learning the
values, norms and practices of the prison officer world.

The process of integration, orientation and adaptation began on
arrival at the PSC on the first day when trainees were required to
'check in' at Reception, obtain a room key, unpack and immediately
change into uniform before lunch was served. All cohort members
then convened and were allocated to one of three sections, each
of which totalled 16 people, before filing into the lecture room for
a formal welcome by the senior college staff. The induction stage
continued with the showing of a video narrated by the then Director
General of the Prison Service and a 20-minute introductory talk by
the Head of POELT training. This was followed by a tour of the
premises, specifically the three sections of the gym, when PE and
C&R kits were issued. The remainder of the day was spent in the
dedicated section classroom where the majority of the training was
delivered and where trainees sat alphabetically in a semi-circle
around the room. A 'compact' was discussed, printed and signed
by all members of the section and a document detailing the college
rules and domestic arrangements was distributed. The expectations
of student officers were made very clear from the start; the emphasis
was on respect (addressing colleagues by their surnames and trainers
as 'sir'), support and professional standards of behaviour. A level of
competitiveness between the three sections was introduced by the
tutors who were keen to express their faith that 'their' section would
'be the best'.

It seemed evident that, as for prisoners, the admission phase for new officers was marked by feelings of uncertainty and a desire for emotional safety and predictability (which Gibbs 1982, argues is a fundamental need for psychological survival). A useful concept to consider in relation to the initial stages of socialisation is that of 'liminality'. This term refers to an ambiguous or indeterminate phase or period (limbo), where an 'individual passes through a cultural realm that has few or none of the attributes of the past or coming state' and is 'neither here nor there' but 'betwixt and between positions' moving from one stage of life to the next (Turner 1969: 94/95; see also Jewkes 2005: 374). In Harvey's (2005: 238) discussion of the transition into prison for prisoners, he states that: 'To be received into custody was to begin to leave one world and to enter another; individuals within their first few days were occupying a place on both sides of the threshold or boundary. They were between two worlds and entered a liminal phase.'

After less than a week at the PSC, it became clear that the context, regimentation and milieu of the college produced a close and somewhat conditioned community that was reminiscent of the prison environment.[10] There were several clear parallels between college life and life for prisoners, both in material terms and in terms of relationships with colleagues and management.

The core working day was from 8.00 a.m. to 5.00 p.m., during which time student officers were required to dress in uniform. At other times, and throughout residential training, a strict dress-code was to be adhered to. Whenever on college premises or in uniform it was compulsory for all students to carry identification and wear a name badge. Male and female students were segregated and assigned to different residential landings where each student was allocated a small, single study bedroom; toilets and showers were shared. Trainees were cautioned about the inappropriateness of visiting a landing of the opposite sex for reasons of decency and respect. If a visit was necessary, presence was to be loudly announced on arrival in warning to other residents. No alcoholic beverages were to be brought into the college; only alcohol purchased on site was permitted to be consumed. There were specific meal times and take-away food on the premises was forbidden. Every service for day-to-day living and training was provided and contained within the college grounds. Although there was no need to leave the campus, trainees were not prohibited from doing so after the core day had finished but were expected to return at a reasonable hour.[11] As a group, almost every waking moment was spent in each others' company, whether it be in the classroom, playing sport, eating in the canteen or drinking in the bar in the evenings. Each section was designated one or two tutors for the entirety of the course and every day there was an assigned section leader, identified by the adornment of a lanyard, accountable for a number of duties (such as leading some aspects of the C&R sessions; standing to report the (classroom) roll to any senior staff member who entered the room; taking responsibility for any relevant paperwork or administrative task for the section; ensuring the classroom was kept clean and tidy and completing a daily record maintained for each section including any significant events).

Life at the Prison Service College echoed Goffman's (1961) description of the characteristics of total institutions:

> The central feature of total institutions can be described as a breakdown of the barriers ordinarily separating [sleep, play and work]. First, all aspects of life are conducted in the same place and under the same single authority. Second, each phase of the member's daily activity is carried on in the immediate company of a large batch of others, all of whom are treated alike and required to do the same thing together. Third, all phases of the day's activities are tightly scheduled ... the whole sequence of activities being imposed from above by a system of explicit formal rulings and a body of officials. Finally, the various enforced activities are brought together into a single rational plan purportedly designed to fulfil the official aims of the institution. (p. 17)

The confined, secure and structured environment of the college and the collective experience of undergoing training resulted in a level of enforced intimacy, socially, domestically and emotionally. Some close and enduring bonds were established within the group very quickly. Course members had become integrated by their shared apprehensions as well as personal achievements and by the end of the course a genuine sense of *esprit de corps*, pride and camaraderie had formed. On a more negative note, the training course also began to shape new officers' views towards management. As the course progressed an anti-management attitude began to develop among the cohort which served to reinforce the solidarity of the group (see Kauffman 1988). This feeling of resentment towards senior personnel started, and was to some degree cultivated, by the hierarchy of rank between student and tutor. Although many new officers praised their classroom tutors for being friendly and professional, they felt that at times their treatment was demeaning and that the level of discipline and frequent collective reprimands for breaches of 'petty rules' resulted in a polarisation of officers and managers that is traditionally ascribed to relationships between staff and prisoners.

Reflections and concluding comments

Undergoing POELT was a challenging, emotional and character-building experience for trainee officers. Throughout the training, although the premise of maintaining a 'duty of care' was frequently alluded to and the concepts of respect and decency were regularly cited when discussing professional working relationships and ways of interacting with colleagues and prisoners, it was the security aspect of prison officer work that was emphasised above all else as the critical occupational value.

There were no formal training modules concerned with interpersonal skills and the delivery of care and support to prisoners. This was one of the major deficits of the course (which, as mentioned previously, has subsequently been addressed), together with the lack of discussion about the part imprisonment and officers may play in rehabilitation. The absence of guidance and instruction concerning these elements of a prison officer's role, combined with the dominance of security and control issues, contributed to new officers' attitudes towards prisoners. Although the course included frequent references to the need to treat prisoners with courtesy, dignity and empathy, this was almost always associated with occasions when officers were required to carry out practical, security-related tasks, such as searching, which constituted the majority of the residential training. Similarly, the importance of interacting with prisoners in an effective way, and utilising the requisite skills to enable constructive relationships and to establish trust (such as being friendly, calm, tolerant, self-controlled, assertive and professional), were not the focus of dedicated training sessions: relationships with prisoners were very much about security, both physical and dynamic, and maintaining order, discipline and control. In this respect, relationships with prisoners were denoted as procedural and instrumental and prisoners were, in a sense, objectified.

The needs and behaviour of prisoners were rarely normalised, and attitudes towards prisoners were developed through anticipation of 'extremes'. Much of the residential component of the POELT course suggested that prisoners could be difficult to manage, that they

413

were often dangerous, untrustworthy, violent, disingenuous, hostile, confrontational and potentially manipulative. New officers undergoing training, especially during the initial stages, were therefore generally mistrustful of prisoners, apprehensive about facing aggression and dealing with conflict and wary of conditioning, exploitation and intimidation. The received impression was that a degree of fear was necessary and adaptive, and that maintaining boundaries and emotional distance was imperative. These impressions resulted in over-caution, personal detachment and some aversion towards engaging with prisoners in more informal and proactive ways, or in ways that extended beyond meeting their basic needs and those of maintaining security, for fear of being compromised or manipulated. For these reasons, officers found a sense of 'security in security' and in learning the skills of C&R. Prisoners were people within their care, as opposed to people to care for or care about, and enacting a 'Duty of Care' was primarily about service and regime delivery: looking after prisoners by keeping them in custody and the preservation of life.

A review by the ICPS on behalf of the Prison Service of the induction training given to newly recruited prison officers concluded that there was a lack of clarity about what staff were being trained for (Coyle 2002: 82) and that 'the individual elements of the training course were very well delivered by the different groups of tutors but ... there was little overall concept of what the fundamental role of the prison officer was' (Coyle 2005: 95). The POELT course I attended was competently delivered and did cover in detail a comprehensive range of subjects (despite some omissions). However, it would appear that, while the emphasis on security did provide some clarity for trainees as to the nature of their role, this was very much about dealing with prisoners while in custody rather than about resettlement, preventing reoffending and helping prisoners lead a law-abiding life after release. The attitudes towards prisoners ingrained through the college training periods supported quite a clear notion that the job of a prison officer was to protect the public by preventing escapes. In this way, with security placed at the base of a 'hierarchy of role', the realisation of the Prison Service Statement of Purpose (and its values and principles) was only partially achieved. It was also questionable whether the POELT course was appropriate for those working in female, open or young offender institutions. The course was standardised, regardless of the type of prison in which trainees were to be working, and it was assumed that gap weeks in the parent prison would offset or complement the concentration on security, and provide the relevant context for additional and relevant skill development depending on the purpose and population of the establishment.

To conclude, in many ways, C&R training embodied the primary values of the training course and the apparent role of the prison officer. It encapsulated much of the experience of being trained and the process of 'becoming' an officer. It was portrayed as one of the core duties of a prison officer in maintaining a safe and secure environment for both staff and prisoners, was the most emotive component of the course, and was imbued with a meaningfulness not associated with other modules. The initial training course did impact on individuals in many positive ways, particularly in instilling self-confidence and efficacy, teamwork, loyalty to colleagues and a sense of unity, commitment and cohesion. Further evaluations of the impact of training may encourage more constructive elements to be incorporated into later training and development programmes in a manner that could contribute to a more affirmative and optimistic prison officer culture. Further training for officers, reflecting the inclusive and participative rather than purely instructive elements of initial training and emphasising skill recognition, the realisation of potential and shared achievement, may be designed in ways that inculcate positive professional attitudes and relationships between officers and prisoners, and officers and management, and are underpinned by a stonger sense of purpose and meaning and a stronger commitment to, and investment in, the goals and values of the organisation.

Seminar questions

1 The study by Vince (2006) found that new officers felt less able to regulate their emotions after completing the training course. For what reasons might this be the case?
2 How might the emphasis on C&R and security during initial training have a negative impact on trainee officers and the way that they conceptualise their job?
3 If you were given responsibility for redesigning POELT, how and why would you change the course structure and content? What would be the key elements of a prison officer's role that the training would focus on?
4 How would you go about conducting a study to evaluate the effectiveness of the prison officer training course and its impact on trainees? What would be your research design and what methods would you employ? Consider the issues, strengths and weaknesses of a participant observation study.

5. Is it possible to deliver a generic training course appropriate for officers working in different types of prisons (high security, local, open, female, young offenders), or should there be alternative tailored courses dependent on prison function, category and prisoner population?

Recommended reading

Liebling and Price's (2001) *The Prison Officer* constitutes a fundamental source of reference for anyone interested in the work of prison officers. It provides an appreciative and comprehensive discussion of their role (including peacekeeping, staff–prisoner relationships and the use of power and discretion). Elaine Crawley's (2005) book *Doing Prison Work: The Public and Private Lives of Prison Officers* offers a detailed sociological account of the social and occupational world of prison officers, and includes a chapter specifically concerned with recruitment, training and the process of becoming an officer. Ted Conover's (2000) *Newjack* is a gripping personal account of life for a new officer in an American prison which includes reflections on his seven-week preparatory academy training. Another American perspective is provided by Kauffman in *Prison Officers and Their World* who discusses both the values and attitudes of new recruits and the emotional, physical, moral and social effects of prison employment on officers.

Notes

1 This chapter is based primarily on findings from PhD research entitled 'Identifying the High Performing Prison Officer' carried out by the author at the Institute of Criminology, University of Cambridge. The study was funded jointly by the Economic and Social Research Council and the Prison Service as a CASE Studentship and was supervised by Dr Alison Liebling.

2 I began the course in February 2002 at the Prison Service College (PSC) Aberford Road and HMP Whitemoor and graduated on 3 May 2002 having successfully completed the course and passed each assessment.

3 Control and restraint techniques were developed throughout the 1980s as 'methods of dealing with violent incidents in a manner which reduced the possibility of injury to prisoners and which also provided maximum safety to staff' (Coyle 2005: 151).

4 The course is now termed the POELT Foundation Course and 'in response to the urgent need to recruit additional staff to supervise the increasing number of prisoners' it has been reduced 'from what might have been thought of already as a minimal period to eight weeks' (Coyle 2005: 94). After the initial induction week at prison, trainees spend two three-week blocks at a training centre interspersed with a 'gap' week back at

their establishment. At the end of the two teaching periods, students are formally assessed as to their competence and are required to complete a summative assessment exam; they are also required to maintain a 'reflective journal' throughout the course. The content of the new course includes specific modules on interpersonal skills (such as communication, assertiveness and relationship building) and highlights the importance of continuous personal and professional development. However, according to Coyle (2005: 94) '... in the short time available the main emphasis is on matters of security and discipline and on training in the techniques to control violent prisoners ...'.

5 Marquart (1986), as a participant observer, became a prison guard in Texas for 19 months between 1981 and 1983; Kauffman (1988) worked as a prison warder prior to her research; Fleisher (1989) took twelve months sabbatical as a professor and became a prison guard; Dickenson (1999) wrote an autobiographical depiction of prison life after 15 years as a correctional officer; as a piece of experiential journalism, Conover (2000) took the job of a prison officer at a prison in New York for almost a year; and Papworth (2000) wrote his autobiographical account after serving as a prison officer in the UK for 30 years.

6 There now exists only one PSC (Prison Service College) since Aberford Road was closed in November 2003. Although at the time this study was undertaken the majority of new officers were trained at one of the PSCs, as a result of the localised recruitment and training policy, some individual prisons were developing and running the training course for their own new recruits as well as those joining other prisons within the area.

7 The governing Governor of the parent prison was responsible for terminating the employment of trainee officers whose performance, attendance or conduct was deemed unsatisfactory. While at the college, grounds for termination of employment might include performance failings (such as handcuffing, C&R or inattention in class), attendance issues (such as sickness) and/or conduct issues (such as inappropriate behaviour or lateness). If failings were identified the college was required to notify the Governor who would then decide the course of action to be taken, such as whether the trainee should attend a subsequent course if improvement was attained and there was confidence that they were capable of achieving the necessary level of competence.

8 All quotes are from trainee officers unless otherwise stated.

9 See Arnold (2005) for a more detailed discussion of the initial, transitory and enduring psychological, emotional and behavioural effects of working in prison on prison officers.

10 Although it should be noted that there was a deliberate drive to demilitarise the POELT course with, for example, the abolition of marching and daily physical training.

11 On reflection, after the first week at the college, I was surprised to realise I had not even ventured outside the college building.

References

Arnold, H. (2005) 'The Effects of Prison Work', in A. Liebling and S. Maruna (eds) *The Effects of Imprisonment*. Cullompton: Willan, pp. 391–420.

Conover, T. (2000) *Newjack: Guarding Sing Sing*. New York: Vintage Books.

Coyle, A. (2002) *Managing Prisons in a Time of Change*. London: International Centre for Prison Studies.

Coyle, A. (2005) *Understanding Prisons: Key Issues in Policy and Practice*. Milton Keynes: Open University Press.

Crawley, E. (2004) *Doing Prison Work: The Public and Private Lives of Prison Officers*. Cullompton: Willan.

Crawley, E. (2005) 'Prison Officers and Prison Work', *Prison Service Journal*, 157: 3–10.

Crowley, S. (2001) *An Evaluation Report of a Pilot Training Programme for H.M. Prison Officers*. London: Learning Skills and Development Agency.

Dickenson, L. (1999) *The Keepers of the Keys*. Fort Bragg, CA: Lost Coast Press.

Fleisher, M.S. (1989) *Warehousing Violence*. London: Sage.

Gibbs, J. (1982) 'Disruption and Distress: Going from the Street to Jail', in N. Parisi (ed.), *Coping with Imprisonment*. London: Sage, pp. 29–44.

Goffman, E. (1961) *Asylums: Essays on the Social Situation of Mental Patients and Other Inmates*. London: Penguin.

Harvey, J. (2005) 'Crossing the Boundary: The Transition of Young Adults into Prison', in A. Liebling and S. Maruna (eds), *The Effects of Imprisonment*. Cullompton: Willan, pp. 232–54.

Illingworth, P. and Mabbet, A. (2005) 'Prison Officer Entry Level Training (POELT): The New Foundation Course', *Prison Service Journal*, 157: 11–13.

Jewkes, Y. (2005) 'Loss, Liminality and the Life Sentence: Managing Identity Through a Disrupted Lifecourse', in A. Liebling and S. Maruna (eds), *The Effects of Imprisonment*. Cullompton: Willan, pp. 366–88.

Kauffman, K. (1988) *Prison Officers and Their World*. Cambridge, MA: Harvard University.

Liebling, A. and Price, D. (2001) *The Prison Officer*. Leyhill: Prison Service Journal/Waterside Press.

Marquart, J.W. (1986) 'Doing Research in Prison: The Strengths and Weaknesses of Full Participation as a Guard', *Justice Quarterly*, 13 (1): 35–47.

Needs, A. (1997) 'Prison Officer Initial Training: The New Programme', *Prison Service Journal*, 113: 30–3.

Papworth, R. (2000) *Key Man*. Derbyshire: Richard Papworth.

Turner, V. (1969) *Ritual Process: Structure and Anti-Structure*. London: Routledge & Kegan Paul.

Vince, H. (2006) 'The Role of the Prison Officer Training Course in Preparing New Staff for Work as a Prison Officer'. Unpublished MSt thesis: Cambridge University.

Part 6

Conclusion

Chapter 24

Concluding comments on the social world of prison staff

Ben Crewe

This book has covered a great deal of terrain, and some summary comments and suggestions for further research are merited. One theme that features in a number of chapters in this volume is that of discretion and power. Sykes (1958) noted in his landmark study that, despite the huge power differential between staff and prisoners, the practical realities of prison life were such that the authority of officers was in fact highly deficient and the maintenance of institutional order was reliant on compromise or 'accommodation'. Conducting research forty years later, Liebling (2000) reiterated the centrality of discretion to officer work and argued that staff–prisoner relations could not be understood without an appreciation of how it was applied by front-line staff. Instead of constantly resorting to the rule book, officers routinely exercised localised judgment, based on the personal relationships that they built with prisoners, to reproduce everyday order and maintain the smooth flow of the regime.

As Liebling (2000) recognised though, discretion requires oversight and direction; it can be used 'for or against legitimacy'. Likewise, the role of discretion in ensuring order, the form in which it is employed and its consequences are all subject to change. Drake (this volume) argues that order in high-security prisons is now accomplished more through formal, procedural and situational means than through the nurturing of personal relationships. With such power at their disposal, uniformed staff are comfortable and confident. Yet with order less a matter of interpersonal negotiation and more a case of imposing rules and following routines, the officer role also appears to have been somewhat deskilled. Meanwhile, the reconstitution of prison management since the early 1990s means that officers now implement rather than embody penal power (Crewe 2007; Warr, this volume). Individual officers still have considerable discretionary power, but this power is limited to particular areas (for example, in relation to the IEP scheme), and the collective power of uniformed staff has been severely diminished. Power flows in new ways and through new techniques, but the consequences for those who hold it and those who are subjected to it are less understood. What cultures and behaviours do these changed circumstances promote?

Both Scott and Sim point to darker possibilities. Where discretion is unfettered or the prevailing culture of an establishment is punitive or indifferent, it is all too easy for staff to misuse their power, however localised or limited (and, of course, what feels limited or localised to staff can be of immense significance to prisoners). A key role of prison managers is thus to set the parameters of acceptable behaviour for front-line staff – to shape how discretion is applied. As Cheliotis notes, governors are not 'abstract, ghostly entities' and their capacity to exercise 'discreet discretion' should not be underestimated. Nor too should we jump to simplistic conclusions about managerial reforms, given that their aims have included the rooting out of what we might think of as 'bad discretion': the kind of extra-legal, discriminatory practices that characterised many regimes in the past. A system that ends the possibility of maverick leadership and unaccountable decision-making clearly has some advantages, particularly in an environment where the costs of unregulated sovereignty can be so high. In the eyes of many new-breed governors, managerialism is a means to moral ends, which places crucial ethical limits on what could otherwise be done in the name of public sensibilities and responsibilities.

Governors themselves exercise discretion within ever narrower parameters and are held increasingly accountable for the outcomes of their decisions. As Bryans (this volume) notes, it is responsibility rather than power that has been devolved to prison managers. It is striking that the same could be said of prisoners. By shifting power up the organisational hierarchy, and doing so in a way that enables control to be exerted 'at-a-distance', managerialism makes power feel more restrictive yet less tangible to all penal agents. In one recent study (Crewe, forthcoming), prisoners, uniformed staff and governors in one establishment expressed almost identical discourses of powerlessness, each group noting that, if the stratum beneath them remained compliant, they themselves had little leverage to achieve their ends. Without officer unrest, governors could not persuade their superiors that staffing levels were inadequate; without prisoner unrest, officers could not convince managers that staffing profiles were a danger to their safety. Prisoners were by no means entirely compliant, but they were certainly not defiant, and what resistance there was remained concealed and individualistic. Ironically then, those people who ostensibly held most power within the prison were reliant on those who held least to advance their concerns. These bureaucratic ironies have been noted before (see, for example, Mathiesen 1965); under managerialism, as power transcends the institution, their form requires further study.

The daily tasks of governance have also changed. Increasingly, the role of governor requires the kinds of generic management skills – resource management, entrepreneurial activity, contractual negotiations, and so on – that could be almost seamlessly transferred to and from sectors beyond criminal justice. This begs questions about the degree to which the prison is a special moral domain, with functions and characteristics that set it apart either from private enterprise or from other areas of the public sector. Bryans (this volume) notes a number of 'special features' that are distinct to prison governing: whether management applicants recognise these features or, indeed, whether they matter in terms of achieving decent, humane prisons are empirical questions that we cannot yet answer. When assessing their options, do graduates consider prison management schemes as any different from traineeships in the Health Service or in private corporations? As the public image of the prison and its recruitment activities have shifted (see McHugh et al. this volume), has there been a corresponding shift in the motives of new entrant governors? How are their values and ambitions reconstituted, cultivated or suppressed once in post, and with what consequences for prisoners? What does being a 'good governor' now mean in practice, and by what broader morals, standards and outcomes do we want to scrutinise these practical evaluations of quality? Are governors as confused as many outside observers are about what the system is now meant to be achieving?

Despite the increasing accountability that managerialism entails, and the recent focus on decency within the Prison Service, we should not be blind to the abuses of power that continue to blight an otherwise improving system. Where they occur, these abuses cannot be reduced to the personalities and pathologies of individual staff. If, as Scott suggests (this volume), notions of less eligibility and the inferior humanity of prisoners have become widespread in officer discourse, it is important to look for the structures and cultures that explain their presence. It seems plausible that the particular antipathy that many officers feel towards the human rights agenda relates to the widespread perception among staff that their own power and rights have been progressively diminished. It is also worth noting that staff are members of the wider public, and are as susceptible as anyone else to the messages that circulate within public discourse about the moral status of prisoners and the aims of imprisonment. Clearly too, to *some* degree, as its enduring nature suggests, some of the less desirable aspects of officer culture represent functional adaptations to the strains of the workplace, the demands of the job and the dangerous potential of power itself. At the same time, the existence in the UK of officer cultures that deviate considerably from the norm, most notably in HMP Grendon (Genders and Player 1995), indicates that much can be done to cultivate orientations that are more humane, trusting and empathic.

Many of the problems here relate to staff training and the early processes of workplace socialisation. One of Arnold's most striking findings (this volume) is that trainees undergo similar forms of role-stripping and resocialisation that Goffman (1961) charted in relation to inmates in his classic work *Asylums*. Like prisoners, then, although officers retain certain aspects of personality, the conditions of their training are such that they are also strongly conditioned into a range of assumptions about 'how things are done here', and are socialised from the start of their training into holding suspicious and cynical views about both prisoners and managers. These views are not promoted explicitly, but are an outcome both of the omissions in officer training and the tacit messages that trainees receive about what activities are valued. In some Scandinavian countries, prison officers undergo at least two years of social work-based training before they can work in prisons. In England and Wales, the course lasts only eight weeks, and it is made clear to trainees that control and restraint procedures are the 'real test of aptitude' and that relationships with prisoners should primarily serve the interests of institutional control and security. A hierarchy of skills and a set of normative assumptions are thus established. Perhaps it is unsurprising that there is little serious discussion during officer training of the appropriate aims of imprisonment or the causes of crime, but these are surely the kinds of issues that would help officers to reflect on their practices and recognise the inalienable rights and humanity of offenders. More striking is that little attention is given to the role of officers in aiding resettlement, despite this being one of the watchwords of the system in recent years.

The book contains a number of explicit and implicit recommendations, particularly in relation to staff training. But, as Andrew Coyle suggests (this volume), there seems little likelihood that significant investment will be made in these areas when the core concern of the Prison Service is to manage the rising population. The wider climate gives little comfort. Popular media and politicians stimulate public fears about crime and ignorance about prisons to which they claim to be responding, locking all parties into a punitive Mexican stand-off.[1] Meanwhile, the solutions to long-term, externally generated problems, such as poor race relations between prisoners and staff, will not be resolved through simple measures. Any assumption that improving these relations is merely a matter of increasing the number of ethnic minority staff should be punctured by findings (Bhui and Fossi, this volume) that, in a wider culture in which BME staff feel under particular scrutiny from their peers, they are often harsher on prisoners who share their ethnic backgrounds than those who do not. In any case, it is naive, not to say patronising, to assume that common roots or cultural reference points will trump stark differentials in institutional roles in shaping staff–prisoner interactions. These are highly complex relationships, which involve much closer and more intimate contact that many outsiders might imagine, while also being suffused with power. As several authors have noted (Drake 2006; Crewe 2005, 2006), staff and prisoners often exhibit apparently comfortable relationships, but these relationships are enforced on both sides, and are tainted by the inevitable presence of power and authority, particularly in notions of 'dynamic security'.

Despite the diversity of the prison workforce, the tendency remains for prison staff to be discussed as if they were a homogenous bloc. Yet, as all contributors have noted, staff cultures are complex and differentiated, and there are significant distinctions both within and between different staff groupings. As with prisoners, micro-cultures emerge among officers on single wings that are discernibly different from those elsewhere. Even in the most negative and brutal contexts, concern and humanity can be found among certain individuals and in certain locations, such as education classrooms and areas of worship. Cheliotis (this volume) reminds us that, just as bad acts occur and arise in banal forms and circumstances, so too do acts of kindness and compassion. Tait (this volume) directs us to the gendered dimensions of these subcultures, and shows the complex interaction of culture and gender in the provision of care. Both male and female officers are channelled into, or pushed out of, certain activities of custody

425

and care according to assumptions about appropriate forms of male and female behaviour (Sim 1994, this volume; Crawley 2004) but the precise transaction of (imported) gender and (institutional) culture varies greatly. As should also be noted, gender can 'empower' as well as constrain, giving cultural permission for at least some staff to exhibit care, even if this comes at costs both for the permitted and the excluded. How these gendered norms will determine the enthusiasm with which officers take up the new forms of work that NOMS will require is yet to be seen. Officers often come into their own when given 'ownership' of projects – and the chapter here by Bayliss and Hughes suggests that there is plenty of enthusiasm to be harnessed among uniformed staff – but some projects are clearly seen as more desirable than others.

Within the uniformed workforce, then, there are clear divisions and pecking orders. Work in segregation units, security teams and physical education is accorded more value than work with sex offenders or older prisoners, or involvement in therapeutic units or the delivery of offending behaviour programmes (Crawley and Crawley, this volume; Sim, this volume; Crawley 2004). As Sim notes in this volume (and see Crawley 2004), in some situations, staff members who undertake work that challenges prevailing norms meet 'burning antagonism' from their peers. The effects on prisoners are also significant. Scott (this volume) notes that prison officers often place their lives at risk to protect those in their charge (and such acts should not be dismissed) but the gendered occupational norms that characterise prison work are such that more value is attached to some forms of life-saving than others. Thus, in most establishments, to 'care' a prisoner away from death (e.g. suicide) carries less status than to 'save' a prisoner from a cell fire or a brutal attack on the wing. But, again, such generalisations have limited use, given the variations in prison officer work and culture between women's prisons, Young Offender Institutions, Close Supervision Centres and democratic therapeutic communities.

Several chapters note that many of the problems reported by staff – particularly in relation to racism, sexism and workplace bullying – are caused not by prisoners but by colleagues and managers. In some prisons, officers have reported trusting prisoners more than their own managers (Liebling 2004), a fact that says more about the chronically poor relationships between staff in many establishments than about good relationships on the landings. There are also major conflicts and professional distinctions between custodial and non-custodial staff. Staff working in education, health, probation, drug-work and other specialist areas hold allegiances to their professional codes and values and to the core operational imperatives of the prison that are often inconsistent. In applying their skills in the penal context, most specialist staff thus face some form of role strain, often experienced as ideological conflict with custodial staff. To suggest one example, prison drug workers must often be given information about the prison's drugs economy, or about an individual's temptation to resume his or her drug use, that would be of considerable interest to the prison's security team or to psychologists interested in issues of risk. Likewise, as Wheatley notes (this volume), to be effective, prison drug workers need to self-disclose and be emotionally responsive: behaviours that officers would be very reluctant to engage in, despite the key role of drug addiction in the offending behaviour of the majority of prisoners with whom they are working. For education staff, many constraints and frustrations relate to a performance agenda that is incapable of fully recognising the 'soft outcomes' (Bayliss and Hughes, this volume) of their role, including the feelings of humanity and individual care that Warr (this volume) describes as being key products of the teaching and learning environment in prison.

These inter-professional relationships and ideologies have significant implications for the reorganisations promised by NOMS (the National Offender Management Service). In turn, 'joined-up offender management' and the increasing involvement of both the voluntary and private sectors in criminal justice promise to reshape radically the nature of criminal justice work (although staff employed in prison education, vocational training and other areas are already 'bought in' from external contractors). The language of NOMS is of new 'partnerships', alliances and cooperation, but it would be astounding were there not also new rivalries, not only in terms of resources, but also in terms of professional norms and ideologies. Organisational priorities and working conditions will also change and, if pledges are realised, new skills in offender management will become core elements of custodial work.

The role of unions in this new world is unclear. Bennett and Wahidin (this volume) have described the current relationship between unions and public sector managers as an 'uneasy partnership', but this partnership is fragile. To some degree, it has been forged around a common enemy – the spectre of privatisation – which provides temporary unity without resolving most underlying conflicts between the POA and the Prison Service. Ironically too, the success of cooperation over the Isle of Sheppey market test might

427

ultimately help fracture the alliance. If the threat of privatisation is perceived as a weak or hollow one, there are only so many times that it will serve as a unifying force. Unions and managers already believe that private sector companies would be unwilling to bid for certain establishments, in which case the impetus for cooperation and improvement has to come from somewhere other than the threat of contracting out.

On the assumption that private sector involvement in prisons will, if anything, increase in coming years, the need to explore differences between public and private sector staff will also be paramount. In this area, there are a number of unresolved questions. The relative inexperience of private sector staff has some significant cultural benefits in terms of prisoner treatment, but also some dangers in terms of safety, order and intervention. Many prisoners prefer hands-off treatment by officers, but, for others, positive interventions matter as much as freedom from interference. We also know all too well that when 'laid-back' relationships go wrong, they can go very badly wrong indeed. Can good relationships – which are not the same as 'nice' relationships (Liebling 2004) – be achieved through means that do not involve lean-to-the-bone staffing, or be based on positive perceptions of prisoners rather than instrumental visions of control? Job instability for officers appears to have some beneficial outcomes for prisoners, in encouraging a weeding out of under-motivated and incompetent staff (McLean and Liebling, this volume). In the public sector, job comfort has, in the past, generated complacency, poor practice, over-confidence and waste. Where, then, is the optimum point between a staffing level that is dangerously and stressfully low, and one that is dangerously and needlessly high? Given their different value bases, priorities and tendencies in practice, how can each sector achieve this balance?

Private sector competition also has considerable implications for prison governors. On the one hand, privatisation has created a certain amount of ideological solidarity within the public sector Prison Service. At the same time, competition *within* the public sector (standardised measurements, league tables) has some clear downsides. With governors preoccupied by the performance of their establishment relative to other prisons, there may be less support from peers, less sharing of ideas and less inclination to shoulder corporate burdens (such as highly disturbed and demanding prisoners) that threaten budgets, targets or institutional order. The tensions caused by competition between public and private sector establishments are more significant. Information concerning best practice does not always flow freely between the sectors, each of which excludes the other from its annual conference, and there is widespread suspicion on each side about the data and individuals that are passed between them.

Given the lack of systematic evidence about differences in practices and outcomes in each sector, it is interesting in itself that the privatisation 'experiment' is set to continue. And just as, in the academic literature, much of the debate has remained rhetorical and ideological, among practitioners untested statements abound about the quality and competence of each sector. One public sector governor recently described the common view among his colleagues that managers who moved from the public to the private sector were simply 'the mediocre, the greedy and the pissed off' (personal communication). Yet many of those who have crossed over claim to have done so out of moral frustration or outrage. Often, they have become evangelical advocates of the private sector – its flatter management structures, the operational autonomy it hands to governors, and the speed and readiness with which it innovates – and harsh critics of what they consider to be a hide-bound and reactionary public sector. For such practitioners, there is no intrinsic conflict between public service values and private sector imperatives. The link between the two is undoubtedly complex, and the strengths and failings of each sector appear quite distinct (Liebling 2004). As yet though – and although direct outcomes are not the only ways we should measure the consequences of private sector competition, for there are broader issues of legitimacy and penal expansion to consider – we are in no position to gauge whether, and in what circumstances, privatisation 'works'. Not least, the private sector is itself differentiated, and there may be some private sector models of public service delivery that are more suited to the penal domain than others.

Another area in need of research relates to prison psychologists. In recent years, psychological expertise has become increasingly important in the prisons of England and Wales. This trend reflects a number of broader shifts, including a growing emphasis on 'public protection' and the emergence of a new, if somewhat limited, discourse of rehabilitation, often referred to as 'what works?' One outcome has been the expansion of structured offending behaviour programmes, widely introduced in 1996 and aimed at achieving the cognitive transformation of prisoners in the interests of public safety. Another has been the increasing role of psychologists in assessing and reducing the risk of prisoners with indeterminate sentences –

itself an expanding group. Psychologists are involved in other areas of prison work, in particular policies relating to suicide and self-harm and some areas of resettlement work.

Two chapters in this volume discuss prison psychologists in rather different ways. Towl and Crighton provide a comprehensive and dispassionate account of professional and organisational developments in prison psychology. Warr presents a more critical and emotional view of the role of psychologists in prisoners' lives, indicating the antipathy felt by many prisoners towards their authority and expertise. The distance between these accounts gives a clear indication of why independent studies are needed in this area. There is a great deal of official data about the demographics of prison psychology staff, their roles and aims, the assessment tools they use, and about many of the policies they have introduced and evaluated (see, for example, Towl 2003, 2006). Yet there is almost no systematic, sociological research on their views, practices and professional orientations. What social attitudes and cultural assumptions do they bring to their work, and how does their subjectivity bleed into their decision-making? How do they feel about the power that they wield, and how aware are they of the impact of their authority on their clients? As Warr's comments indicate, the power wielded by psychologists and the form of broad, pervasive power that they are taken to represent have turned them into the new enemies of the prisoner community (Crewe 2007, forthcoming). Anecdotal evidence indicates that many psychologists enter the profession with liberal-humanitarian motives, only to find that, in the current penal climate, their expertise is harnessed for more punitive ends. This is surely a highly discomfiting position for many psychologists, one with consequences for professional well-being and, as Warr suggests, for their capacity to obtain the forms of honesty to which they aspire.

Many of the same forces and discomforts are highly germane for probation officers, whose increasing role in 'breaching' prisoners is emblematic of the shift in their role from welfare to control. As Cheliotis asks in relation to all penal practitioners, how are these ideological shifts 'translated' into practice? Is there resistance? If psychologists have supplanted officers as the primary 'keyholders' of the sentence, then we should be asking the same questions of them that have traditionally been asked of uniformed staff: as representatives of state power, how have they been socialised, what is their culture, to whom are they accountable, and what is the relationship between the manner in which they exercise their power and the well-being and other outcomes of prisoners?

Perhaps a final area for thought is the link between practitioners and academics. The compilation of this book has been a fruitful exercise in academic–practitioner partnership, and has led to considerable reflection on the different expertise and knowledge that each group can provide in revealing a world that remains relatively invisible (or, perhaps, through its media representations, both hypervisible and yet barely understood) to the wider public. Academics underestimate the amount of robust internal research that the Prison Service undertakes on areas such as staff recruitment, development and other human resources issues. Naturally, this work is somewhat administrative in its focus, and often it is academics who then provide the conceptual torchlight that illuminates the wider meaning and significance of such data. Equally, practitioners hold much of the tacit knowledge that makes academic realisation possible and can provide all kinds of insights into the realities of the penal domain. In return, as academics who have taught practitioners at first hand can testify, theoretical reflection can give form to practical consciousness, reorganising and reshaping how the world that one takes for granted is perceived. We hope that this book will contribute to both worlds, and will shed some light on an environment with distinct and totalitarian features that creates unique problems and forms of socialisation for staff as well as prisoners.

Note

1 My thanks to David A. Green of Oxford University for allowing me to borrow this term.

References

Crawley, E. (2004) *Doing Prison Work: The Public and Private Lives of Prison Officers*. Cullompton: Willan.

Crewe, B. (2005) 'Codes and Conventions: The Terms and Conditions of Contemporary Inmate Values', in A. Liebling and S. Maruna (eds), *The Effects of Imprisonment*. Cullompton: Willan.

Crewe, B. (2006) 'The Orientations of Male Prisoners towards Female Officers in an English Prison', *Punishment and Society*, 8 (4): 395–421.

Crewe, B. (2007) 'Power, Adaptation and Resistance in a Late-Modern Men's Prison', *British Journal of Criminology*, 47 (2): 256–75.

Crewe, B. (forthcoming) *Wellingborough: Power, Adaptation and the Everyday Social World of an English Prison*.

Drake, D. (2006) 'A Comparison of Biographies, Practices, Cultures, and Orderliness of Two Maximum Security Prisons in England'. Unpublished PhD thesis, University of Cambridge.

Genders, E. and Player, E. (1995) *Grendon*. Oxford: Oxford University Press.

Goffman, E. (1961) *Asylums: Essays on the Social Situation of Mental Patients and Other Inmates*. Harmondsworth: Penguin.

Liebling, A. (2000) 'Prison Officers, Policing, and the Use of Discretion', *Theoretical Criminology*, 3 (2): 173–87.

Liebling, A., assisted by Arnold, H. (2004) *Prisons and Their Moral Performance: A Study of Values, Quality, and Prison Life*. Oxford: Clarendon Press.

Mathiesen, T. (1965) *The Defences of the Weak: A Sociological Study of a Norwegian Correctional Institution*. London: Tavistock.

Sim, J. (1994) 'Tougher than the Rest? Men in Prison', in T. Newburn and E. Stanko (eds), *Just Boys Doing Business*. London: Routledge.

Sykes, G. (1958) *The Society of Captives: A Study of a Maximum-Security Prison*. Princeton, NJ: Princeton University Press.

Towl, G. (ed.) (2003) *Psychology in Prisons*. Oxford: Blackwell.

Towl, G. (ed.) (2006) *Psychological Research in Prisons*. Oxford: Blackwell

Index

Integrated Behavioural Competency
Framework 381
intelligence gathering 158
intelligence information, use of 160
Intensive Development Scheme
(IDS) 374–6
inter-agency competition 250
inter-professional relations 426–7
interactions
legitimacy-building 163
workplace stress 145
International Centre for Prison
Studies 36, 392
interpersonal skills 143
interpretive denial 170
intimacy, prison work 140
intimidation, between staff 145
intra-agency competition 250
involvement in work 98t, 101–2,
106t, 109t, 110t

job analyses 379
job instability 428
job satisfaction 68, 74t, 75, 77, 90t,
360–1
job simulation assessment centres
(JSAC) 265, 377, 379–80
job stress 68, 81, 83, 90t
job vacancies 373
'joined-up' offender management
427
Joint Committee on Human Rights
report (2004) 352
Joint Industrial Relations Procedural
Agreement (JIRPA) 118–19, 126
jokes 55
judges 234

key performance targets 52, 59, 62n,
300
knowledge
denial of 170, 185n
prison drug workers 337–8

'laager' mindset 139

late-modern prisons, discretion in
247–58
leadership 223, 243, 266, 267, 272
Leadership and Management
Development Programmes 390
learning, prisoners' scepticism
towards 305
learning outcomes, prisoners'
education 303–4, 427
Learning and Skills Council (LSC)
299
Leeds prison 80
legitimacy 154–5, 156, 267, 421
legitimacy-building interactions 163
length of service
attitudes towards management
77–8, 110t
authority maintenance 104
commitment to Prison Service 89t
gender and peer relationships
76–7
involvement in work 102, 110t
job satisfaction 75, 77, 90t
perception of Prison Service 89t
public–private sector differences
96t, 97t
relationships with management
89t
stress of dealing with suicide and
self-harm 90t
length of time in current prison
Perception of Prison Service
99–100, 110t
public–private sector differences
96t, 97t
less eligibility, doctrine of 172, 176,
181, 183, 185–6n, 203
lesser breeds, prisoners perceived as
174, 183
liberal education 299, 300
life-saving work, value attached to
426
lifelong learning 392
liminal phase, prison officer training
411

organisations involved in 306–7
worth of education programmes
312
see also teachers; teaching
Prisoners' Education Advisory
Committee 299
Prisoners' Learning and Skills Unit
(PLSU) 301
prisons
adherence to expected standards
165
culture *see* occupational culture
discretion in late-modern 247–58
as distinct moral realm 173, 174,
182–3
education *see* prisoners' education
ethnic monitoring 62n
exercise of power and influence
223
healthcare and healthcare staff
349–63
increasing pressures on 232–4
management *see* prison
management
managerial complexity 223
as non-places 204
order in 153–65
organisational structure 236–8
privatisation 92
relations *see* relations
as a specific moral context 172–4
state of permanent crisis 238
see also female prisons;
imprisonment; *individual
prisons*; male prisons;
maximum-security prisons;
public and private sector;
working prison
Prisons and the Problem of Order
154
privacy rights, male prisoners 67
private prison sector 428
custodial services 220–1
delivery of offender services 293
pay and cost 94

protective race relations
structures 62n
staffing levels 94
see also public and private sector
private sector competition 125,
428–9
privatisation 92
implications 428–9
prison escort arrangements 283
relationship between unions and
managers 427–8
pro-rape attitudes 289
probation 279–93
discreet discretion 255
future role 291–3
historical context 279–83
managerialism 286–7
sentence planning, aftercare and
throughcare 285–6
staff employment 7
thematic report 291
probation officers
priorities and tasks 281–3
qualifications 394
relations
with prisoners 287–9
with specialist staff 291
with uniformed staff 289–90
sharing work between prison
officers and 283–4
Probation Service 255
problem-solving 270
procedural problems, order in
prisons 158
Professional Development
Framework (PDF) 394–5
professional distinctions, between
staff 426–7
professional orientation 102–5
Professional Psychology Advisory
Group (PPAG) 320
Professional Skills for Government
381
professional structure, prison
governors 219

11675025R00265

Printed in Great Britain
by Amazon.co.uk, Ltd.,
Marston Gate.